Technologies of the Novel

Based on a systematic sampling of nearly 2000 French and English novels from 1601 to 1830, this book's foremost aim is to ask precisely how the novel evolved. Instead of simply 'rising', as scholars have been saying for some sixty years, the novel is in fact a system in constant flux, made up of artifacts – formally distinct novel types – that themselves rise, only to inevitably fall. Nicholas D. Paige argues that these artifacts are technologies, each with traceable origins, each needing time for adoption (at the expense of already developed technologies) and also for abandonment. Like technological waves in more physical domains, the rises and falls of novelistic technologies don't happen automatically: writers invent and adopt literary artifacts for many diverse reasons. However, looking not at individual works but at the novel as a patterned system provides a startlingly persuasive new way of understanding the history and evolution of artforms.

NICHOLAS D. PAIGE, Professor of French at the University of California–Berkeley, is the author of *Before Fiction: The Ancien Régime of the Novel* (2011), awarded the 2013 ASECS Gottschalk prize, and *Being Interior: Autobiography and the Contradictions of Modernity* (2001). *Technologies of the Novel* was supported by a Guggenheim Fellowship.

Technologies of the Novel

Quantitative Data and the Evolution of Literary Systems

NICHOLAS D. PAIGE

University of California

Shaftesbury Road, Cambridge CB2 8EA, United Kingdom

One Liberty Plaza, 20th Floor, New York, NY 10006, USA

477 Williamstown Road, Port Melbourne, VIC 3207, Australia

314–321, 3rd Floor, Plot 3, Splendor Forum, Jasola District Centre, New Delhi – 110025, India

103 Penang Road, #05–06/07, Visioncrest Commercial, Singapore 238467

Cambridge University Press is part of Cambridge University Press & Assessment, a department of the University of Cambridge.

We share the University's mission to contribute to society through the pursuit of education, learning and research at the highest international levels of excellence.

www.cambridge.org
Information on this title: www.cambridge.org/9781108812849

DOI: 10.1017/9781108890861

© Nicholas Paige 2021

This publication is in copyright. Subject to statutory exception and to the provisions of relevant collective licensing agreements, no reproduction of any part may take place without the written permission of Cambridge University Press & Assessment.

First published 2021
First paperback edition 2022

A catalogue record for this publication is available from the British Library

Library of Congress Cataloging-in-Publication data
Names: Paige, Nicholas D., 1966- author.
Title: Technologies of the novel: quantitative data and the evolution of literary systems / Nicholas D. Paige.
Description: New York: Cambridge University Press, 2020. | Includes bibliographical references and index.
Identifiers: LCCN 2020024228 (print) | LCCN 2020024229 (ebook) | ISBN 9781108835503 (hardback) | ISBN 9781108812849 (paperback) | ISBN 9781108890861 (ebook)
Subjects: LCSH: Fiction–History and criticism–Data processing. | French fiction–Research–Data processing. | English fiction–Research–Data processing.
Classification: LCC PN3331 .P33 2020 (print) | LCC PN3331 (ebook) | DDC 808.3–dc23
LC record available at https://lccn.loc.gov/2020024228
LC ebook record available at https://lccn.loc.gov/2020024229

ISBN   978-1-108-83550-3   Hardback
ISBN   978-1-108-81284-9   Paperback

Cambridge University Press & Assessment has no responsibility for the persistence or accuracy of URLs for external or third-party internet websites referred to in this publication and does not guarantee that any content on such websites is, or will remain, accurate or appropriate.

*I dedicate this book to its most indefatigable supporters –
Becky Curry, for whom it may have seemed like a lifetime
coming; and Wyatt Paige, for whom it really has been.*

The segmentation of history is still an arbitrary and conventional matter, governed by no verifiable conception of historical entities and their durations. Now and in the past, most of the time the majority of people live by borrowed ideas and upon traditional accumulations, yet at every moment the fabric is being undone and a new one is woven to replace the old, while from time to time the whole pattern shakes and quivers, settling into new shapes and figures. These processes of change are all mysterious uncharted regions where the traveler soon loses direction and stumbles in darkness.

George Kubler, *The Shape of Time: Remarks on the History of Things* (1962)

Contents

List of Figures [*page* x]
Acknowledgments [xv]

Introduction [1]

PART I [15]

1 Truth Postures in the Novel of the Long Eighteenth Century [17]
2 The Rise and Fall of the Aristotelian Novel [41]

PART II [61]

3 Novel v. Romance I: Heliodorian Insetting [63]
4 Novel v. Romance II: The Fortunes of a Subtitle [79]
5 Novel v. Romance III: Measuring *Romans* and *Nouvelles* [91]
6 Documenticity I: Memoir Novels (and Other First Persons) [109]
7 Documenticity II: The Two Rises of the Epistolary Novel [125]
8 A "New" Third-Person Novel [138]
9 The Novel System in England, 1701–1810 [158]

PART III [175]

10 The Evolution of Narrative Technologies [177]

Annex: Premises and Protocols [203]
A Glossary of Novel Types [212]
Notes [215]
Bibliography [257]
Index [269]

Figures

1.1 Editorial pretense in Richardson and Rousseau [*page* 18]
1.2 Categories and subcategories of novels [22]
1.3 Novel types, 1681–1830 [26]
1.4 Nobody novels and somebody novels, 1681–1830 [27]
1.5 Truth status of nobody novels [28]
1.6 Truth status of real-world novels, 1681–1830 [29]
1.7 Temporal setting versus protagonist type [30]
1.8 Truth posture versus temporal setting in nobody novels (I) [31]
1.9 Truth posture versus temporal setting in nobody novels (II) [32]
1.10 Truth posture versus temporal setting in nobody novels (III) [32]
1.11 Nobody novels by narration type [33]
1.12 Pseudofactuality rates by narration type (I) [34]
1.13 Pseudofactuality rates by narration type (II) [35]
1.14 Invention rates by narration type (I) [36]
1.15 Invention rates by narration type (II) [36]
1.16 Pseudofactual variants [37]
2.1 Truth status of real-world novels, 1601–1750 [42]
2.2 Nobody novels and somebody novels, 1601–1750 [43]
2.3 Aristotelian novels by temporal setting (I) [44]
2.4 The temporality of Aristotelian historical novels [44]
2.5 Aristotelian novels by temporal setting (II) [45]
2.6 Aristotelian historical novels by protagonist type [46]
2.7 Historical novels [47]
2.8 The historicity of the French novel [48]
2.9 Truth postures of nobody novels (I) [49]
2.10 Temporal settings of nobody novels [50]
2.11 Truth claims in the nobody novel [51]
2.12 Truth postures of nobody novels (II) [52]
2.13 Temporal settings in the French novel [52]
2.14 Yearly novel production, 1601–1750 (estimates) [56]
3.1 Novels containing inset narratives [66]
3.2 Inset novel types [68]
3.3 Titled insets in Type 1 novels [71]

List of Figures

3.4 Inset novel types (breakdown I)   [71]
3.5 Inset novel types (breakdown II)   [72]
3.6 Inset novel types (breakdown III)   [73]
3.7 Length of real-world novels (I)   [76]
3.8 Length of real-world novels (II)   [77]
3.9 Length of real-world novels (III)   [78]
4.1 Novels subtitled *nouvelle*   [82]
4.2 Novels titled or subtitled *roman*   [83]
4.3 Novels subtitled *histoire*   [85]
4.4 Median lengths of novels by subtitle   [85]
4.5 Length of subtitled novels, standard deviation   [86]
4.6 Inset novels by subtitle   [87]
4.7 Variations of *nouvelle*   [89]
4.8 Subtitle uniformity   [89]
5.1 Distribution of novels by length, 1601–1750   [92]
5.2 *Romans* and *nouvelles* (I): criteria of length, insetting, and truth   [95]
5.3 *Romans* and *nouvelles* (II): insetting and truth criteria only   [96]
5.4 *Romans* and *nouvelles* (III): length and insetting criteria only   [97]
5.5 *Romans* and *nouvelles* (IV): length and truth criteria only   [98]
5.6 Counting *nouvelles* (I)   [99]
5.7 Subtitled *nouvelles* by inset type, 1651–1750   [100]
5.8 Counting *nouvelles* (II)   [101]
5.9 Subtitled *nouvelles* corresponding to formal criteria   [102]
5.10 *Romans* and *nouvelles*   [103]
5.11 US production of music albums, 1976–2000   [103]
6.1 Document novels (one calculation)   [110]
6.2 Forms of first-person novels   [111]
6.3 Varieties of document novels   [113]
6.4 *Nouvelles* and documents   [114]
6.5 Cumulative market share of *nouvelles* and document novels   [115]
6.6 Document novels and the production of all novels   [116]
6.7 Documenticity and the first-person novel   [118]
6.8 Documenticity of the memoir novel   [119]
6.9 Narrative person of inset narratives   [121]
6.10 Real-world inset novels by narrative person, Types 1 and 2 combined (subsamples)   [122]
6.11 First-person narration in the novel (estimates)   [123]
7.1 Epistolary novels, 1601–1750 (permissive count)   [126]
7.2 Epistolary novels, 1701–1830   [128]

7.3 Subject matter of pre-1751 epistolary novels (some permissive criteria) [129]
7.4 The rise and fall of the observational epistolary novel [130]
7.5 Epistolary novels of love [131]
7.6 Epistolary novels by subject matter [132]
7.7 Number of correspondents [133]
7.8 Epistolary novels by subject and correspondent type [134]
7.9 Documenticity of the epistolary novel [136]
7.10 Documenticity of memoir and epistolary novels [137]
8.1 Truth posture and narrative person [139]
8.2 Median length of nobody novels [140]
8.3 Median length of nobody novels by narrative type [140]
8.4 Major types of segmentation [142]
8.5 Chapterized novels by type [143]
8.6 Chapter title types [144]
8.7 Median length of third-person nobody novels [144]
8.8 Incipits of third-person novels [146]
8.9 Scene use in presentation of main action [148]
8.10 Third-person novels containing preliminaries [149]
8.11 Scene types (incipit position only) [149]
8.12 Three trends in third-person novels [150]
8.13 "Old" and "new" third-person novels (one scenario each) [151]
8.14 "Old" and "new" third-person novels (ten scenarios each) [152]
8.15 *Nouvelles* and "old" third-person novels [154]
8.16 Truth postures of third-person nobody novels by novel type, 1761–1800 [156]
8.17 Truth postures of third-person nobody novels by novel type, 1801–1830 [156]
9.1 Truth status of nobody novels (England) [159]
9.2 Major generic subtitles (England) [159]
9.3 Nonepistolary first-person forms (England) [161]
9.4 Epistolary novels (England and France) [162]
9.5 Truth postures of epistolary novels (England) [163]
9.6 Chapterized novels (England) [164]
9.7 Median length of real-world third-person novels (England and France) [165]
9.8 Scenes (incipit position only, England) [166]
9.9 "Old" and "new" third-person novels (England) [167]
9.10 "Old" and "new" third-person novels (averaged scenarios, England and France) [167]

9.11 Truth postures of third-person novels by novel type, 1751–1810 (England)   [169]
9.12 Yearly novel production (estimated, England and France)   [171]
9.13 Yearly novel production in words (estimated, logarithmic scale; England and France)   [172]
10.1 *Nouvelles*, Aristotelian versus nobody ("new loosest scenario")   [189]
10.2 Aristotelian novels by period of subject matter   [189]
10.3 Aristotelian novels by inset type   [190]
10.4 Truth status of "unspecified" novels   [192]
10.5 "Unspecified" and Aristotelian novels   [192]
10.6 The major novelistic artifacts   [193]
A.1 Items retained and reasons for exclusions (1601–1700 and 1751–1800)   [207]
A.2 Composition of sample (France)   [208]
A.3 Composition of sample (England)   [209]
A.4 Market penetration of French epistolary novels (two estimates)   [210]

Acknowledgments

The "monograph": theoretically it is a book on one subject, but to me the word always suggests the solitary toil of much humanities scholarship. While this was again the case here, I had a more-than-usual number (for me) of helpers. Many were undergraduates as well as graduates from my home institution (UC Berkeley), willing to learn the project's tagging protocols; having to subsequently verify their work didn't subtract a bit from the pleasure and profit of working with them. Many thanks, then, to the students of French 24 (Fall 2016) and French 245 (Fall 2015). An additional shout-out is due to a series of undergraduate research apprentices from 2012 and 2013 who were involved in an abortive attempt to tag for free indirect discourse; of these, Marisa Mito agreed to dedicate some of her time abroad after graduation to learning far more about the novels of 1828 than anyone should really have to. Additional tagging assistance was provided by Ty Blakeney, Lauren Dixon, Jonathan Haddad, David Rafoni, Trevor Sanders, and Travis Wilds. In Lausanne, Timothée Léchot expertly retrieved the necessary data from the one-of-a-kind works housed in the Bibliothèque du Château d'Oron. A number of interlocutors from Berkeley's D-Lab helped me convince myself that my project wasn't hopelessly misconceived from a "digital" and statistical point of view: thanks especially to Chris Hench, Scott McGinnis, Tom Piazza, and Claudia von Vacano. I also extend my deep gratitude to a number of scholars who have supported the project in different ways, often by making me sharpen my points. These include Oliver Arnold, David Bates, John Bender, Mathilde Bombart, the late Ross Chambers, Margaret Cohen, Melanie Conroy, Paul Dawson, Monika Fludernik, Elaine Freedgood, Alexandre Gefen, Benjamin Gittel, Marie-Hélène Huet, Vicky Kahn, Joshua Landy, Françoise Lavocat, Mairi McLaughlin, Franco Moretti, Brad Pasanek, Adrien Paschoud, Guillaume Peureux, Jonathan Sheehan, Rebecca Spang, Philip Stewart, James Grantham Turner, and Geoffrey Turnovsky. And Simon DeDeo provided a reference I don't know how I would have been able to do without. A fellowship from the John Simon Guggenheim foundation bought crucial time away from other professional responsibilities.

Introduction

This book is about the evolution of French and to a lesser degree English novels – by which I mean French- and English-language novels – from 1601 to 1830. And while *evolution* is very much at the center of my preoccupations, I do not offer a "story" about that evolution. There is no plot, as we might want if we thought of the novel moving forward, perhaps from birth, episode by episode, toward a resolution, some happy state of stability – as if, in other words, the novel's own history could be made into a kind of novel. Accordingly, there are no characters, either: no starring roles or cameo appearances for individual novels or novelists, lending a hand to the genre on its long journey. In fact, for reasons I will explain, I even doubt that there exists an entity, "the novel," that evolves. So when I say "the novel" or "the French (or English) novel," I do so not ontologically (as if this abstraction somehow had a kind of being) but pragmatically: the novel is a set of diverse practices grouped together based on shared traits, uses, and functions. So it's important to keep in mind that there is no one "thing" out there whose story we can (but really shouldn't) tell, because the novel is better thought of as a *system* of things: a system of literary artifacts.

In lieu of a story, *Technologies of the Novel* offers a quantitative account of the ceaseless yet patterned flux of the novel system over these twenty-three decades. But to give this brief description meaning, to explain why the whole project is not merely an inevitable consequence of enthusiasm for all things quantitative and digital, I need to give a brief account of my dissatisfaction – which is a methodological dissatisfaction – with previous histories of the novel. For the purposes of this introduction, I will for the most part keep accusations general: specific disagreements with scholars of the novel will become clear enough in the rest of the book. I propose, rather, a kind of caricature – hopefully recognizable – designed to highlight features of the historiography of the novel that I believe we have naturalized.[1]

The novel, we're often told, is the modern genre par excellence. Little wonder, then, that histories of the novel in England and France almost inevitably amount to modernity stories: they retrace not only the birth of a "new species of writing" (to use the language of more than one early observer) but also, and more crucially, the homologous process by which purportedly traditional worldviews – identities, subjectivities, epistemologies, governmentalities – were replaced by our own. The history of the novel is the history of how Then became Now, of Them becoming Us. Oft-told, the tale is also, therefore, two-poled – with, in between, a rich "period of transition," corresponding to the novel's proverbial rise over the course of the long eighteenth century.

Modernity narratives such as this do not and cannot recognize the manifest complexity of the cultural archive. Rather, they want to make it go away, to convert the diversity of practices – a diversity that is synchronic as well as diachronic – into epiphenomenal noise. That noise is said to mask the profound cohesion characterizing a given epoch, ruled by what Michel Foucault famously called an "episteme": a kind of template that organizes all knowledge production over a certain period of time. Whence the widespread idiom, also associated with Foucault, according to which such-and-such concretely observable discursive phenomenon is said to be *made possible* (or *thinkable*) by the invisible but all-powerful cause that is the episteme. Furthermore, and to more marvelous effect, this type of analysis reveals that discourses which to the untrained eye might appear unrelated or even at odds are in fact profoundly connected. And the more unexpected the connection, the more marvelous the effect.

Too often in histories of the novel, then, the cultural archive is not a disparate mass of stuff made by a variety of human actors operating under divergent and ever-changing constraints and motivations. Rather, it's a kind of text whose individual parts are all there for a reason – much like high schoolers are still taught, via trickle-down New Criticism, that no element of a poem or novel is insignificant. Everything fits together, provided you know how to read the signs. And indeed, rise-of-the-novel studies take individual cultural products like novels as signs. In this critical idiom, novels are now no longer autonomous signifying systems (like the New Critical poem was) but have become parts of the much larger signifying system that is Culture. (Thus, the implication of Stephen Greenblatt's preferred name for New Historicism, "Cultural Poetics": all discourse has in effect become a huge poem. New Historicism is a New Criticism writ very large.[2]) Culture can be grasped through the work, but not in the banal sense that the work might be said to be a particularly fine example of a period's or place's preoccupations. Instead of being the visible part of a visible whole – shorthand or synecdoche – the work functions much more mysteriously as a clue to an *invisible* wholeness (a wholeness traversed, like that of the New Critical poem, by tensions and paradox).

Modernity is the common name for the invisible wholeness. In rise-of-the-novel studies, individual novels clue us in on a process of change: the slow revolution, not necessarily grasped consciously by the writer, that turns the foreign wholeness of the premodern into the familiar wholeness of now. The fact that modernity is often viewed critically – things were better before! – makes no difference: busters and boosters share the same methodological premises. And canonicity itself isn't my beef: unless we change our premises, it won't help to study more novels, or novels by the Others of literary history. The reason so many historians of the rise of the novel are content with just a few texts isn't merely habit and convenience. Rather, a few texts are all you need if those texts just happen to be *magical* – magical, because they are privileged links with the world of true causes. The job of such critics is to follow the wormholes threading between the objects of the phenomenal world and the world beyond. That's amazing: who wouldn't want to be part of such a critical journey? And it's comforting: we can rest again, no longer in the hands of God but now in the bosom of Culture, which, even if we hate it, at least makes sense.

Of course, all histories of the novel don't operate *precisely* like this, even when they are indeed modernity stories: sometimes, after all, it's held that people – great writers and thinkers – are actively responsible for bringing modernity into existence. It's a particularly common view of cultural evolution, of course. Great individuals drive things forward with their great works. They break the mold, disrupt the status quo, change the paradigm: with X, the novel is born; with Y, the novel becomes truly modern; after Z, the novel will never be the same again. The individual creates, and other individuals, now all drones or epigones, imitate. Until by some miracle someone again emerges from the crowd to shake us out of our collective torpor, our enslavement to genre or tradition. This position appears staider than the idea that literary works are surface effects of an invisible cause, and in a way the conceptions are incompatible. Yet in practice the two get along just fine, because the greatness of individual writers is simply rewritten as their uncanny sensitivity to the subterranean cultural transformations of the moment. Hence, we manage to have our cake and eat it too, making deep Culture our subject while staying within the comfort zone delimited by a few fetishized, often taught figures.

Technologies of the Novel is designed to break completely with the assumptions I've just caricatured. It is not a modernity tale: as I said at the outset, this book offers no characters, no plot leading to Now. Nor is it an antimodernity tale, claiming, as some have, that we supposed moderns are just going through the archetypal motions.[3] *Technologies of the Novel* is, instead, an a-modern study: a study of the novel that simply puts aside the category of the modern. Not of *novelty*: novelty exists. But unlike modernity, it does not arrive just once. It is constantly being generated by our innovative species. We are always creating new artifacts, among which are novels. The novel, I will ultimately argue, can be profitably compared to the engine, the telephone, or the toilet: it's not one "thing" that is constantly changing, it's actually an array of discrete artifacts made into a family not because they share DNA but by dint of a shared function within a given culture.

Novels, then, are artifacts created by human beings. The proposition's banality stands in stark contrast to the rhetoric adopted by typical histories of the genre, where the novel invariably does a lot of heavy, world-historical lifting. I'm not, of course, denying the global impact of certain successful artifacts: the gun, the shipping container, the noodle, among the hundreds we can choose from – including, arguably, the novel itself. But acknowledging this is quite different from claiming that novels – or guns, noodles, and shipping containers – are of a piece with a more massive and all-pervasive transformation that is the advent of modernity. In common parlance, or maybe just the idiom popularized by Fredric Jameson, we speak of the "logic" of cultural phenomena, that is, of the way that they are profoundly imbricated with one another and with the realm of true causes (usually, Capitalism).[4] But looking for the hidden "logic" comes down to noting patterns and resemblances, which sometimes mean something, but more often don't. Don Quixote, according to the Foucault of *The Order of Things*, was the last representative of the Renaissance episteme, still stuck in a world of analogy and resemblance – "a diligent pilgrim," Foucault describes him, "breaking his journey before all the marks of similitude."[5] But how can Quixote's adventures put an end to "the old interplay between resemblance and signs" when we still have literary historians? Rise-of-the-novel studies sees giants – Modernity, Capitalism, the Individual – where by a more sober reckoning there are just windmills: technological artifacts.

This is a taunt, but it's also a proposition about how we could start to think about the novel. What would a technological understanding of literary evolution look like? For starters, and as I've hinted, it would speak of "the novel" only as shorthand for a system of objects serving roughly the same purpose. Those objects themselves would be seen as formal artifacts that are not historically stable. First, because they need to be invented: they cannot simply arise in sympathy with the "logic" of their historical moment. And invention is in fact a process, since successful artifacts cannot emerge fully formed from the head of their inventor. Just as the internal combustion engine, say, is still going through considerable refinements, various novelistic artifacts – say, the epistolary novel – actually need to be "worked on" by their users: tinkered with, adapted, sometimes repurposed. And just as the windmill, once abandoned by the industrialized West, can stage a comeback as a "green" electricity generator, novelistic artifacts can also be exhumed and made to do new things. When I speak of the evolution of "the novel," then, I really mean the evolution of all these types of novels – a systemic evolution. Thus, we really have two different sorts of evolution, which, as I will eventually argue, may be evolutionary in a different way: one occurs at the level of the artifact (the windmill), another at the level of the system of artifacts (power production).

If the comparison between novels and windmills is useful – I'll raise much later the question of whether it is merely an analogy – then "the novel" is indeed a system of discrete and evolving artifacts. The epistolary novel, the memoir novel, the third-person "omniscient" novel we associate with the realist nineteenth century: these are some of the novel's many technologies that compete with and relay one another over the course of its history. Technologies, not genres. Whereas genres are usually thought of in terms of their contents, technologies are formal arrangements. "Genre" suggests a segmentation of a logical whole, or distinct pieces of the puzzle that is literature; technologies can be adapted for many various and sometimes contradictory purposes – moral uplift, but also pornography. Genres may be something close to Northrop Frye's archetypal modes or else the mere generational blips described by Franco Moretti;[6] technologies need time to develop and spread, as well as to fall into disuse, which they almost always do.

Like any technology, the technologies of the novel do not develop on their own, either naturally or in accordance with the internal imperative of "working better" than previous artifactual iterations. "The 'working' and 'nonworking' of an artifact," writes one Science and Technology Studies scholar, "are socially constructed assessments, rather than intrinsic properties of the artifact."[7] Indeed, modern Science and Technology Studies, with its strongly constructivist bent, has been formulated to counter an earlier history of technology, one that insisted on the implacable necessity of innovation – human inventiveness as driven by the fulfillment of fundamental biological needs, and driving toward the advancement of humanity. But "progress" is a term with only relative meaning: it must be understood, writes George Basalla, "within very restricted technological, temporal, and cultural boundaries and according to a narrowly specified goal."[8] Thinking along these lines rids us of the temptation to map formal change in the novel onto deep "shifting paradigms." Partly, there's just way too much formal change for that: if each of the successive formal waves

I will be talking about needed a paradigm for a cause, "paradigm" would be stripped of the momentous importance that makes it a popular term to begin with. No, novelistic artifacts are just things invented by humans in accordance with their values – values that themselves are always changing, so that the form that works in 1780 may not work as well in 1820.

Though I'm going to postpone until the last chapter a more detailed exploration of how Science and Technology Studies may relate to literary history, one further "technological" point needs to be made. People ceaselessly produce novel artifacts, but they can't produce any artifact at any time. That is, the artifacts they produce – in accordance with their perceived needs or possibly just because their culture prizes innovation for its own sake – have to come from somewhere. One novelistic artifact that will figure in this book is third-person, "omniscient" novels about protagonists whose literal existence is a matter of indifference: this is more or less the type of novel one thinks of as "the classic nineteenth-century novel." One obvious reason people don't write such novels in the seventeenth century is because their values are different. That is only one reason, however. Another is that third-person omniscient novels with fictional protagonists need to be invented: they evolve from something else that isn't present in the seventeenth century. Our practices, therefore, are *materially* as well as axiologically constrained. "Whenever we encounter an artifact, no matter what its age or provenance, we can be certain that it was modeled on one or more preexisting artifacts," writes Basalla, who dubs this change-within-continuity "the stream of made things."[9] This, of course, is why it makes sense to speak in terms of evolution and not just plain "change": evolution is *constrained* change.[10]

Material constraints, axiological constraints, but not, I think, epistemological constraints: it's really to confuse the matter to say that a nineteenth-century artifact is – to return again to the vocabulary popularized by Foucault – "unthinkable" two centuries earlier. People don't invent this or that form of the novel because the episteme has shifted, or because some new notion of personhood is ascendant or because that novel synchs with the logic of capitalism. Their new practices derive from a ceaseless interaction between their values (conscious and unconscious) and the material constraints placed on them by the old artifacts they have at their disposal; the new artifacts then help to create new values and desires; and so on and so forth. That some of those values involve personhood or capitalism or what counts as knowledge – obviously. But they are just values, not worldviews, Zeitgeists, or conceptual orders.

Technologies of the Novel has some broad claims to make about shifts in values over the nearly two hundred and fifty years studied here, along with lots of little claims about the rises and falls of individual artifacts. And as I've just suggested, it also makes the more general proposal that the evolution of these artifacts is best understood as properly technological. It avoids, however, causal claims: it is a dangerous business, I think, to try to pin specific formal swerves to whatever sociopolitical events happen to occur within their vicinity (the absolutist court, the Revolution), or to link a form to a given socioeconomic group (the military aristocracy in steady eclipse, the ever-rising bourgeoisie), or to explain it as the material symptom of an emerging ideology (the exchange economy, the liberal subject). On the one hand, the sheer historical elasticity of most of these purported "causes" makes for a situation in which they can be wheeled in to explain whatever is in need of explanation. On the other, there is the standard danger of taking correlation for causation. Correlations are everywhere, especially for humans trained as hermeneuts, that is, trained to make meaning out of patterns in artworks. All correlations are not necessarily red herrings, of course. For instance, it may well be true that certain forms of the novel are practiced more in the provinces or abroad than in the capital, or that others are practiced more by male aristocrats than by bourgeois women. Unfortunately, to conscientiously weigh the merits of such associations would require data I have not attempted to gather. This book is by design a largely descriptive account of a cultural system's behavior. Customary histories of the novel have made for a situation in which we really don't know some very basic facts about that history: if novels lengthen or shorten over time, how many of them in the eighteenth century take the form of first-person memoirs, what proportion, in the 1670s, have historical settings – that sort of thing. So just because I don't talk about reasons for formal change doesn't mean that I hold that literature evolves on its own or that writers are writers only and not also social animals turning around and around in the cage that is historical context. Such a position would be ludicrous. I assume that values both literary and extraliterary are behind what people read and write, that those values are ever-changing, and that all people at any given moment don't share the same ones. To the extent that I do ask "why," I focus the question on the patterns discernable in the record of the artifactual evolution of the novel.

The urge to study literature as a large system is very much associated with certain branches of Digital Humanities: Moretti calls it distant reading; Matthew Jockers, macro-analysis.[11] While the scale, in *Technologies of the Novel*, is very much macro and distant, in other respects this study has not been produced with the typical Digital Humanities toolkit – word searches, collocation studies, and the like. Instead, I analyze "metadata" that I myself have created through the hands-on, passably old-world manner of consulting novels (physically or digitally) that I categorize and measure according to a number of formal features. The many graphs in this book come from these "tags" and measurements: basically, I'm counting, and counting relatively small numbers. The properly *digital* nature of this process can be debated. Arguably, no one thing that I do here couldn't have been done by analogue means a hundred years ago. On the other hand, digitization of primary sources and above all the invention of the ubiquitous yet still magical spreadsheet have enabled me to undertake a project that otherwise would have required considerably more travel and untold hours of calculation and graphing. Even if the only algorithms I've used are the ones most computer-users have gotten used to – the ones running silently in the background of our garden-variety applications – they are just as indispensable and every bit as "digital" as the more exotic tools now also available: Latent Dirichlet Allocation, a topic modeling algorithm; measurements of Kullback–Leibler divergence; the text analysis environments of DocuScope and WordHoard; and the Google Ngram Viewer.[12]

Technologies of the Novel is, then, digital and distant; but it is most certainly not antianalogue or anticlose. All literary interpretation isn't "magical"; all meaning is not on the surface; individual works can indeed be shown to be representative of wider practices and ideologies; the canon may in many cases be a good proxy for the archive. And quantitative methods are not intrinsically more "scientific" than those of close reading: I want more data about the history of the novel, but how different is this from a scholar directing attention to understudied aspects of *Middlemarch* in the hopes of arriving at a better understanding of George Eliot's art? Those previously invisible passages are data too. And we want rich data not because at a longed-for level of richness it will reveal the truth to us, or make the humanities truly scientific. More modestly, the richer our data, the more our explanations are *constrained* – thus reducing the risk of critical whimsy – and the more probable and convincing they become. In my opinion, rise-of-the-novel criticism has been data-poor and thus largely unconstrained: it is a relatively simple matter to come up with explanations – even ingenious explanations – when one has only to correlate a few carefully chosen elements.

Most researchers want rich data, but of course there are always practical limits, digital tools or no. *Technologies of the Novel* traces decade-to-decade changes over nearly two and a half centuries of the novel's so-called rise. Yet while we have excellent or at least serviceable bibliographies covering this considerable span, I have not tagged *all* novels produced during this period. Rather, I've tagged a sample of each decade's production, according to a procedure I discuss in detail in the Annex. Very briefly, the figures given for a decade are estimates derived from a consultation of all available novels published for the first time in given years of that decade – for example, years 7, 8, and 9. ("Available" means slightly different things for the English novel than for the French; this too is explained in the Annex.) The number of given years varies according to the production since low populations need heavier sampling than larger populations. For most of the span, I have examined more than half of all novels published, sometimes eighty percent or more. The total corpus, English and French, contains approximately two thousand novels. In our era of Big Data, researchers' aspirations often gravitate immediately to huge data sets; yet as a practical matter, sampling can provide nearly as much information as a census.

More important than the sampling procedure itself, however, is the population sampled. In this matter, too, the Annex provides more detailed justifications, but some basic orientation is necessary up front. After all, what is a novel in the first place? How do novels differ from biographies, histories, travel narratives, and so on? It's an unavoidable question, to which I give both a pragmatic answer and an age-old philosophical (more precisely, Aristotelian) answer: a novel is a work classified by previous bibliographers as a novel, and a novel is a plotted narrative. (I use the latter criterion to weed out disparate works included by bibliographers who deliberately sought to cast a very wide net.) More important, perhaps, is a second question: what constitutes the *system* of novels? Those being published for the first time only, thus giving a series in which each point has equal value? Or should we attempt to assay the "footprint" of individual novels – by paying more attention (but how much?) to those being reedited, translated, exported, anthologized, mentioned by other writers, featured in circulating libraries, or published in the cultural center – Paris and London – as opposed to, say, in Nantes and Edinburgh?[13] And shouldn't foreign novels being translated into French or English be part of the system? Obviously, many choices are possible; equally obviously, some of them are trickier than others to implement. And some are potentially deforming: studying only republished works – works with a history of success – is tantamount to doing a history of innovation using "winners" alone. By contrast, I am interested in losers as well, being mindful that many winners were for a time losers, in the sense that the commercial successes of given forms – say, the memoir novel – were preceded by a lot of mostly anonymous failure. For a form to "work," a series of people need to work on that form. In this account, what loses or wins – or wins and then loses, since formal dominance doesn't last forever – is measured by counting the number of individual new products (novels) that incorporate a given formal trait. *Technologies of the Novel* is not, therefore, a study of consumption; but the one-sided nature of my focus is more apparent than real, assuming that over the long term the choices of producers can never be independent of the choices of consumers. The premise, then, is that there must be some sort of (probably imperfect) feedback loop, whereby the reception of artifacts (partially) determines subsequent production. In this study, the population of novels for any decade – which I refer to as "novel production" or "the novel market" – is made up of first-time publications of works originally written in French (or English, in the chapter dealing with cross-Channel developments). This choice, which is pragmatic in addition to being motivated by the intellectual considerations I've just laid out, should not be taken to imply that there are not other ways to measure the novel's production and the success and failure of its forms (and I heartily encourage others to pursue them).

But why should we think that a formal analysis of the novel market would be interesting in the first place? The systemic and quantitative focus of this book derives not from my perception of an abstract "need" for a history of the novel commensurate with our digital moment, but because I had a question that I could not answer otherwise. Scholars started to raise the question about a hundred years ago: why did many novelists in the eighteenth century pretend their novels were literally true? In the last few decades, a number of influential solutions have been put forth (mostly for England), all arguing in one way or another that the modern (English) fictional novel resulted from a conceptual change whose history leads back to eighteenth-century truth pretense. In my last book, I set out to follow in their path and give an account that extended to France the argument about what Catherine Gallagher has famously called "the rise of fictionality."[14] The writing of that book, however, undid my confidence in the method, which involved the type of magical reading I've just critiqued (no doubt with the zeal of the convert). And while I was able, in an eleventh-hour recalibration, to avoid reading my carefully selected base texts as windows onto an invisible conceptual change, the result was that I knew I hadn't answered the question. For to even approach the question of *why*, we need to know *what* happened (which we didn't): how far back did the truth pretense go? How were novels written before it? When popular, how many novelists used it and how many didn't? Did it fade away quickly or was it stubbornly persistent? The only way of answering such first-order questions is by looking at a lot more novels, yes, but more crucially, by looking at them *systematically*, in roughly the manner I have described. Examples and counterexamples, no matter how doggedly we multiply them, can never prove a trend. The whole point of cherry picking is to get pleasing cherries, not to know just how rare those cherries are. If you want to know what else is in the bin, you have to empty it out.

The ten chapters of this study are split into three parts.

Part I tackles head-on the problem of the truth pretense to which I have just referred. Chapter 1 covers that pretense over the period in which previous scholarship has repeatedly (albeit vaguely) located its heyday and its eventual decline – the years 1681–1830. And while previous scholarship did at least get the "decline" part right – truth claims more or less disappear over those years – it turns out that a systematic study of the archive reveals crucial complications. On the one hand, the replacement of truth claims with the acknowledgement of what some might label "fiction" simply doesn't occur on a timetable that would support any of the explanations traditionally offered. On the other, it becomes easy to see that truth claims themselves have a history, and that that history does not at all correspond to the hazy assertion (also made by previous scholars) that the "true story" novel was some sort of dialectical reaction against an earlier fanciful novel, one that frequently goes by the name of romance. Chapter 2 therefore backtracks to 1601, examining the rise of the truth pretense (which will later fall) as well as an earlier rise (and fall), that of novels with various sorts of historical subject matter. Taken together, the chapters of this section describe, then, a succession of three dominant truth strategies or postures: the Aristotelian novel (which takes known individuals as it subject matter), the pseudofactual novel (which asserts the literal existence of protagonists of whom no one has heard), and the invented – possibly "fictional" – novel (which is indifferent as to the literal existence of its protagonists).

Three truth postures over nearly 250 years: that is relatively slow change, and indeed, the two postures I am able to track completely (the Aristotelian and the pseudofactual) take over one hundred years each to come and go. However distinct I believe these postures to be from one another, that distinction comes from their subject matter rather than their form. An understanding of the evolution at work needs to take in more artifactual dimensions. To give an example: Aristotelian novels can take the form of long third-person novels featuring interlocking first-person inset narratives; or – essentially at a different moment – they can be much shorter third-person narratives with little to no insetting. Such artifactual forms, however, are not chained to a given truth posture: short third-person narratives with little to no insetting are also found with pseudofactual postures. The microchapters of Part II describe these artifacts and their cycling, a cycling that only imperfectly overlaps with the truth postures examined in Part I. Five major artifacts retain my attention. Two I've just mentioned – the short, minimally inset form known as the *nouvelle*, and the long, inset novel usually called a *roman* (but that for reasons I will explain might better go by the name of the Heliodorian novel). Two additional artifacts are associated with the pseudofactual posture: these are the first-person forms of memoir and epistolary novels. The fifth artifact is a particular type of third-person novel that expands rapidly at the turn of the nineteenth century – a longer third-person novel with specific structural and narrative traits. It is this artifact, indeed rarely advanced as true, that may strike some as distinctively fictional. Part II is rounded out by an additional chapter that provides a comparative look at the situation in England over the years 1701–1810.

Parts I and II are thus largely descriptive; in Part III, which contains just one chapter, I step back and develop the technological model to which I've repeatedly alluded, and that I believe makes the best sense of the observed data. My most basic position is that the literary forms I've isolated are evolving technological artifacts competing with others in the accomplishment of tasks that producers and consumers feel are important at any one moment. More specifically, and leaning heavily on W. Brian Arthur's theory of technological evolution, I argue that the novel over this period underwent three successive morphings, one of which can better be described as what Arthur calls a *redomaining* – a moment when artifacts were drawn from a discursive domain previously outside that of the novel and introduced into the novel system.[15] But these morphings mustn't be confused with paradigms or epistemes or even with "periods" plain and simple: on one level there are moments of rupture, but at the same time change is slow and constant; the artifacts associated with a given domain themselves evolve; and most important, the artifacts don't have to evolve in the way they do. The changes I describe happened, but they could have happened earlier, later, or maybe not at all. Indeed, in the English system, though broadly similar to the French, various changes did happen earlier, later, and not at all. No necessity – historical, ideological, artistic, nor even technological – explains the record, which is what it is because of a lot of different people made a lot of decisions for a variety of reasons and that's how it turned out.

The chapters of this book are designed to be read sequentially, in that I unfold the various classifications I use (e.g., the alternate-world novel, the document novel, the *nouvelle*) bit by bit. Many of these "tags" are my own confection: I've come up with them in a back-and-forth between my initial hunches and the archive. The advantage is that they correspond very well to period practice, and the disadvantage is that they don't necessarily correspond to common literary-historical categories and genres (e.g., the baroque novel, the sentimental novel, the Bildungsroman, the Gothic novel). As such, they will be mostly unfamiliar to readers, and I spend more time toward the beginning of the book in an expository mode; once the main categories are in place, I am able to move more quickly. Readers needing clarification on terminology may consult the Glossary of Novel Types.

While the graphs on which my argument is based figure directly within the text, a smaller set of graphs containing auxiliary information – and designated here by an "E" (e.g., Figure E3.3) – are available from an online repository, as are the data used to compose all the graphs.[16]

Unless otherwise indicated, all translations are my own.

PART I

1 Truth Postures in the Novel of the Long Eighteenth Century

There it is, smack in the middle of the title pages of two of the most popular, most canonical novels of the European eighteenth century: *Clarissa* (1748), "published by the Editor of PAMELA" and *Julie, ou la nouvelle Héloïse* (1761): "Letters [...] collected and published by J. J. Rousseau" (Figure 1.1). It's a familiar yet puzzling feature of the period's textual landscape: why would Richardson, Rousseau, and many of their contemporaries bother to make claims of literal truth? Given that we now see right through the pretense and can call a novel a novel, wouldn't readers at the time have done the same?

Realism and *fiction* are the answers that scholars in turn have proposed. They are basically the same answer, with the second nuancing the first. The older answer says that the editorial posture of Rousseau and Richardson is an effect of the novel's slow turn toward empirical reality and away from the idealized world of the genre often called romance. At first, what novels lack in terms of realist contents – plots still being extravagant and representation of the everyday material world rudimentary – novelists make up for with hyperbolic claims of literal truth. But once novelists have a practice to match the novel's new vocation, the pretense of literal truth can fall away, leaving the perfect mirror of nineteenth-century realism. The title pages of *Clarissa* and *Julie*, then, are just what early realism looks like.[1]

The more recent answer clarifies matters by positing that realism's essence is better described not as transparent mimesis but rather a uniquely supple form of reference. By this reckoning, claims of literal truth are a way of coming to grips with the *tertium quid* that lies between truth and falsehood – fiction, whose slippery power comes from being *like* the real but not identical to it. Richardson and Rousseau's postures are part of the collective work of bringing this new concept into collective focus. Their title pages are just what early fiction looks like.[2]

On the one hand, then, the claim of literal truth is more about imperfect technique; on the other it is more about an imperfect concept – or rather, a great concept imperfectly intuited.

Such are the main answers to a question that surely must be central to understanding the European novel's history. Given that the title pages of

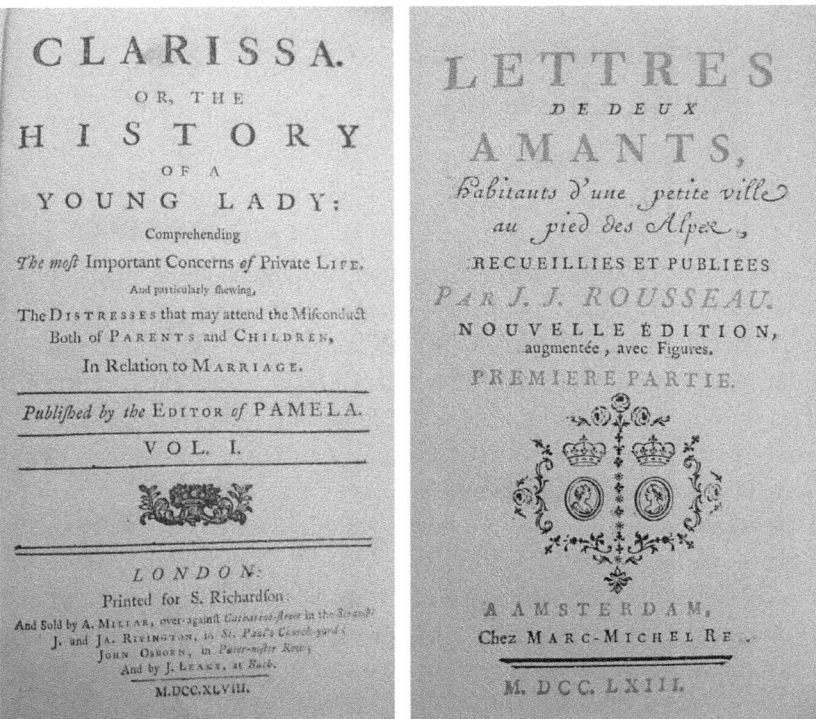

Figure 1.1 Editorial pretense in Richardson and Rousseau (Collection of the Bancroft Library, University of California, Berkeley).

Julie and *Clarissa* seem so superfluous to us now, how can they not constitute a historical puzzle? Doesn't it appear at least impressionistically true that Rousseau and Richardson are worrying about something that Balzac and Dickens and Eliot don't? Yet if the question is real, there are nonetheless some fairly obvious obstacles to mapping such particulars onto a narrative of rising *realism* or *fiction*. Both narratives are patently chauvinistic and teleological; and the argument about *fiction* in particular seems unacceptably treacherous. Surely humans are fiction-making animals;[3] Aristotle distinguished the historian from the poet on the issue of adherence to the facts;[4] Cicero classified three forms of literary narrative, one of which, *argumentum*, "recounts imaginary events, which yet could have occurred";[5] one of the demonstrable origins of modern novelistic practice, the Greek novel, made no more claims of truth than did the nineteenth-century realist novel.[6] And so on.[7] Yet the puzzle remains. Those title pages are a strange artifact we can't wish away.

Does the novel really "become" fictional? If it does, when did it do so? Such are the questions of this chapter and the next, and that I will take up again in my final chapter.[8] But what do we mean by fictional? After all, since it doesn't appear that Richardson and Rousseau were perpetrating hoaxes, couldn't we claim that their novels were already understood as fictional?[9] And then there's the worry, already expressed, that literature has long been seen as something different from history, and that it's just human nature to play with – maybe to better test or reinforce – the boundary between fiction and fact. Skeptical deconstructionists, meanwhile, might even start from the premise that *everything* is always already fictional anyway. These are hefty issues, both cognitive (how do humans experience the real world and the worlds of dream, play, representation?) and philosophical (Is there a real world? Can we know it? Is all narrative a kind of fiction-making?).[10] It's safe to say that if we have to resolve or even seriously confront them before we take on the matter of Richardson and Rousseau's pretense, we will never get started.

Happily, however, there's no need to know what fiction "really is," and in fact for the bulk of this chapter and the next I am simply going to put the term aside. (It will be recalled in Chapter 10.) Instead of talking about how novels at one moment or another are or aren't fictional, I will proceed by establishing categories capable of accommodating all the "truth postures" of the period's novels. So, to give the prime example, novels accompanied by a truth pretense such as that of *Clarissa* or *Julie* will be in one category. There are, however, many more categories, and I ask the reader's patience for the time required to lay out, up front, the most basic of them. This time is all the more necessary because my categories are, for better or for worse, mine alone: they don't correspond to period nomenclature, and they only partially echo classifications used by previous scholars. Crucially, however, my categories do correspond to distinctions in period *practice*: writers and readers of the time didn't call their novels by the names I will be using, but they did overwhelmingly recognize the distinctions I'm making – distinctions which I make only because it's their practice that has led me to make them. And after having evaluated some two thousand novels of the period, the classifications seem to me the only ones that will help us to get at Richardson and Rousseau's pretense historically – to understand its origins, diffusion, and eventual disappearance.

At the center of the historical puzzle lies the pretense to truth. But from the very beginning of scholarly interest in the subject, this pretense has been difficult to pin down. Are we talking about "editors" like Rousseau and Richardson, presenting texts purportedly by other people? About authors claiming to relate true stories – gossip or "human interest" narratives about unknown contemporaries? About writers who trumpet their use of source material for narratives about well-known figures from history? What, in the end, do we mean by "true"?

Let's start with a distinction between *somebody* novels and *nobody* novels.[11]

The characters of the former are somebodies in the sense of being important people – people known to readers who pick up the novel, indeed people whose renown is such that writers can expect readers to *want* to pick up their novel. In some cases, these somebodies are simply famous (or infamous) contemporaries, but in the main they are from the past: they have survived the winnowing of time and forgetfulness by dint of having their memorable actions set down in previous books. So somebody novels build their plots around contemporary celebrities and known historical or legendary figures.[12] For this reason, I will also call them by the more resonant name of *Aristotelian* novels – "Aristotelian," because they correspond to a widespread understanding of the *Poetics* and poetic invention, according to which the best literary characters were people of renown who had done important things – heroes, in other words. (Indeed, the venerable rhetorical term *inventio* referred not to the invention of a storyworld out of whole cloth, but rather to the poet's finding or choosing of his or her materials.[13]) The job of the Aristotelian novelist was to choose among the coordinates furnished by tradition while fabricating *ex nihilo* other elements – including supporting characters – that would add up to a compelling plot. The point was not that Achilles or Cyrus "really" existed or that the novel was empirically "accurate," but that such well-known, sanctioned subjects were, by definition, superior to plots about people no readers had ever heard of before picking up the book. Thus, the Aristotelianism of a novel depends on subject matter alone, not on the level of historical faithfulness brought to bear on it. Certain authors of Aristotelian novels may well want to stress that they are using all the best sources on Elizabeth I or Julius Caesar. But for my classifications, these truth affirmations are superfluous: a novelist whose subject has extratextual sanction is writing an Aristotelian novel; I stop well short of trying to gauge the historical bona fides of the finished work.

Nobody novels, by contrast, concern run-of-the-mill private individuals of whatever social rank unknown to readers before they open the book. The presence or absence of truth pretense makes sense only regarding these: authors of Aristotelian novels do not attempt to convince readers that their protagonists exist for the simple reason that readers already know who those protagonists are. When nobody novels are affirmed as true, we have the *pseudofactual* novel.[14] The classic case is the editorial posture of Richardson and Rousseau. *Clarissa* and *Julie* are *document* novels – accounts purportedly composed by someone other than the person publishing them, and typically taking the first-person form of letters and memoirs. Not all pseudofactual novels take the form of documents, however – far from it. The second type of pseudofactual novel is the *true story*, in which author-narrators narrate an event they have heard of or witnessed. These are usually third-person works – or, if one prefers, works with heterodiegetic narrators.[15]

Other nobody novels are freely advanced as the creations of the author. Such works may be advertised as "true" in the sense that they help readers grasp moral truths, or in the sense that they tell us how society really works and how people really behave, or even in the sense that their characters are based on observation of an ethnographic or sociological nature. Nonetheless, when it comes to the historical existence of the characters, the authors of this type of nobody novel admit invention. As such, I will call these works *invented* novels, with the proviso that I'm referring specifically to the explicit invention of protagonists as opposed to the crafting of plot (which according to one premise of my study is a defining feature of all novels [see the Annex]). This nomenclature is designed to skirt – but only for the time being – the question of whether such novels are "fictional" in a way that Aristotelian or pseudofactual novels are not.

Some nobody novels affirm truth, others affirm invention – but others still offer no information whatsoever on the literal existence of their characters. Are these not labeled because the truth claim is implicit? Or because, on the contrary, it is assumed that the author made everything up? Such questions – good ones which will be taken up presently – need to be distinguished from another, which is: are these novels really pseudofactual or really invented? This latter question has no answer, because the investigation concerns postures alone. A novel that says nothing about its truth status can only be an *indeterminate* novel, and not an unmarked pseudofactual or invented novel. The latter do not exist, because these tags only refer to markings in the first place.

Thus far I have isolated four main categories of novels: Aristotelian, pseudofactual (including both documents and true stories), invented, and indeterminate, with the last three categories united by their subject matter – the doings of nobodies, as opposed to the deeds of somebodies. But all four are united on a deeper level still: they concern what I will unapologetically call the "real world," that is, a world which has a basic if variable contiguity with respect to the world of the reader. Compare these with alternate-world novels – in the main novels whose contents would have been qualified at the time as "marvelous." These include narratives in which nonhuman actors speak, imaginary voyages, and above all the full Enlightenment panoply of "tales" – fairy, oriental, and philosophical. I also include in the category of alternate-world novels allegories in which characters personify abstract qualities, though these are rare. With such subject matter, concerns about historical truth and invention are misplaced. Those concerns are relevant only to real-world novels.

It is thus my assertion that all novels in the period under study can be apportioned to one of five main categories, which can be laid out schematically as in Figure 1.2. (*In the period under study*, I repeat: many of these distinctions would be treacherous or irrelevant in much literature from 1850 forward, as well as for literature from before 1600.)

Many further discriminations are possible and indeed vital, but they will be made within these major (sub)categories. The classification procedure just outlined inevitably raises a series of questions.

The first involves the believability of pseudofactual truth assertions. As I noted at the outset, it seems odd that people bothered with a pretense that we now dismiss with a smile or a wink. Were Rousseau and Richardson simply catering to a reading public that was more gullible and literal-minded than our own sophisticated age – maybe subtly nudging them toward critical thought, toward the "willing suspension of disbelief"?[16] In fact, though we have reception information for only a small fraction of novels of the period, the information we do have suggests that assertions were not taken at face value.[17] The prefix "pseudo," then, is intended to stress that writers did not intend for their assertions to be believed. Such propositions can best be understood not as semantic but as rhetorical or pragmatic: they ask to be taken not as statements that can be judged true or false, but as statements that perform a function with respect to the values of speaker and audience. A rough analogy might be public speakers who kick things off by remarking how happy they are to be there: under normal circumstances, the utterance is semantically empty but performatively meaningful. Granted, in both the case of pseudofactual novels and that of public speakers, there are contexts in which the affirmations may well

	Real-world			
Somebody (or Aristotelian)	Nobody			Alternate-world
	Pseudofactual	Indeterminate	Invented	

Figure 1.2 Categories and subcategories of novels.

trigger a semantic evaluation – is this *really* true? – but they don't need to and usually don't.

The data presented in this book will support this understanding of the pretense better than competing ones – such as those that stress evolving epistemological mindsets. But for the moment, it's enough to underline that my classifications in no way involve guessing how novels were processed by real readers. Similarly, classifying a novel as pseudofactual entails no judgment about how realistic or believable it is. By extension, one must not think that pseudofactual novels are any more or less realistic than Aristotelian novels or invented novels. The only thing that is being evaluated here is the nature of the subject matter, and in the case of nobody novels, the presence or absence of the pretense. I freely admit that some truth assertions strike me as intrinsically more plausible than others: people, even novelists, do sometimes tell bona fide true stories; and I'm sure that some real correspondences, for example, figure in my samples. Nonetheless, my counting treats them equally.[18] Any other protocol would be madness: assessing the believability of truth postures is as much a fool's errand as trying to rank Aristotelian novels according to their historical accuracy.

Second, many specialists of the Enlightenment novel especially will point out that alternate-world novels *are* occasionally prefaced with claims to truth. This does not, however, make necessary their inclusion under the pseudofactual banner. Such claims are parodic, generating humor through the misapplication of a convention. I've just said that I consider the truth pretense in general to be a kind of pragmatic or rhetorical utterance. And when it is applied to works that cannot be literally true, the reader is jolted back to the semantic thrust, which is usually bracketed. It's this jolt that produces humor. In my opinion, parodic uses of this sort – roughly comparable to, say, spoofs of the generic conventions of spy or horror movies – do not "attack" the conventions parodied, as if trying to disabuse readers who take them literally. As such, it will not do to view such parodies as signs that some canny readers are getting wise to the absurdity of the herd's behavior and beliefs – signs, in other words, of progress. Moreover, parodic affirmations by definition can only occur in alternate-world novels, which as we'll see are a strong presence precisely when pseudofactual affirmations are still prevalent as well. The conventions and the parodies thereof exist alongside one another, symbiotically; the latter are not a stage in the disintegration of the former.

Third, I've mentioned that my categorization of real-world novels revolves around the referential status of their human characters, specifically their protagonists. Many novels, of course, mix invented and publicly known characters, and indeed the intermingling of the real and the invented within literature is a perennial irritant in theories of fiction: Baker Street existed in Doyle's London, but not 221B Baker Street; Napoleon has a walk-in part in *War and Peace*. Here too I will dodge the philosophical issue. Admittedly, somebodies and nobodies (as well as somethings and nothings) often cohabit the same novels, but instead of trying to smooth this ontological scandal, we can simply describe the forms the cohabitation takes. For my purposes, when nobodies are major characters, we have a nobody novel, whether or not there are a few somebodies haunting the wings. If a somebody character is a protagonist, the novel is Aristotelian, no matter how many nobodies are fabricated to make things interesting. And though we can certainly imagine the possibility of a novel that would blur the distinction between protagonist and minor characters, in practice, in this period, the distinction is not a problematic one.

Fourth, the division of novels into alternate-world and real-world prompts the perfectly reasonable rejoinder: What is the real world? Surely the sense of what is plausible varies according to time and place; and the "laws of physics," certainly, are discovered and understood over time. Pointedly, one project of the early modern period was to separate mere superstitions from perplexing but real physical phenomena – to separate ghosts from hot air balloons, magnetism from electricity. (The gothic novel can obviously be seen in such a context.) For me, any text that poses the question of what is possible is a real-world text, no matter if the question is given answers that are scientifically or experientially dubious. Alternate-world novels do not function this way.[19] As one might expect, a few texts do lead to hairpulling on the part of the classifier, though it is important to remember that now-familiar literary artifacts that might greatly complicate the distinction – the counterfactual novel, science fiction – did not exist in the period studied. To say that *in this period* a clear line separated real-world novels and alternate-world novels is to describe the way the vast majority of people wrote, not to stipulate that they had to write that way or to set limits as to what literature can do.

Are distinctions I make – between somebody novels and nobody novels, between real worlds and alternate worlds – always crystal clear? Of course not, and in some cases, we'll discover families of artifacts we haven't anticipated, or differences between artifacts that at first appear identical. Such challenges are a normal part of the enterprise. Intimacy with the novelistic archive helps us to refine the categories we use to explore it. At a certain point, however, the refinement becomes unproductive. To be sure, there are always problem cases – books that appear to present features of two different categories, books that blur boundaries, books that are *sui generis*. These are the kind of books that much literary and narrative theory fetishizes, and depending on your interests, rightly so: sometimes they may be where the interesting conceptual, aesthetic, and ideological issues lie. (More often, though, they are just odd – and forgotten.) Still, once you start counting, problem cases fade into insignificance. They may be interesting, but they are rare. The fact is that most writers behave more or less like their contemporaries. In novel writing as in other human behavior, there are norms: while nothing forces people to do what other people are doing – certainly not a force such as an episteme! – most actors nevertheless end up choosing from a limited number of everchanging possibilities. And the quirky outliers, the ones that neither fit into our existing categories nor push us to establish a new category? They are apportioned to the category that is the least bad match.[20]

Finally, in this chapter and throughout this book, all novels are tagged for formal features "by hand," that is, by examination. The tagging process for the categories used in this chapter is the following. Some categories are assigned based on evaluation of the subject matter: are the protagonists people whose names come from legend or history? Is the subject matter real-world or alternate-world? Truth pretense is located for the most part in the novel's paratexual apparatus: on title pages, and in prefaces, postfaces, and dedications.[21] A broad range of factors determine factual or fictional presentation (pseudofactual or invented, according to my tags), and it is certainly not always made with the same explicitness. In the easiest cases, authors or "editors" discuss the provenance of their factual narrative, or on the contrary speak of what went into devising their fictional creation. In other cases, the cues are more subtle and contextual. (This is also to say that some novels are more vigorously pseudofactual – or invented – than others.) Sometimes titular indications are all we have to go on: *histoire de ce temps*, *nouvelle*, and *roman* are some generic tags with truth connotations – but connotations that are in fact context-dependent. (In certain periods, *nouvelle* clearly announces "news" [i.e., gossip], whereas in others, it doesn't; before about 1700, referring to your novel as a *roman* does not necessarily imply that you are renouncing claims on the literal existence of your characters.) In all cases, "indeterminate" is the default categorization, meaning that there must be a concrete justification for pushing a novel's presentation in the pseudofactual or the invented direction. (We will see that some novels are characterized by hesitancy or contradiction in their truth posture; these are a given separate tag.) I repeat that *in no case is my estimation whether I think the novel "was" an authorial invention or received as such*: these propositions are meaningless in the context of the present study, where I weigh presentations alone.[22]

Let's start with the most basic of distinctions I've just detailed – between real- and alternate-world novels. For the period 1681–1830, samples of the novelistic archive indicate the proportions shown in Figure 1.3. (Sampling procedure is detailed in the Annex.) Alternate-world novels are a small component of the overall production – less than 10 percent, on average. Some decades show much stronger representation: notably, the totals for the 1740s and 1750s reflect the popularity of philosophical tales in Enlightenment discourse.[23] In this chapter and this book more generally, alternate-world novels will not retain much of my attention. This doesn't mean that I think they are a poor cousin of the "novel proper." The fact that real-world forms interest me more than alternate-world forms may well be a form of mimetic bias; however, this is a bias that, as Figure 1.3 shows, is inscribed in the history (and not just historiography) of the novel itself. It's not that modern scholars such as myself obsessively focus on one type of novel when contemporaries made much more capacious use of the art form. In fact, our focus reproduces theirs: massively, novels were real-world.[24] In this respect, we have, really, the same interests as our forebears.

More to the point, my choice to play down the importance of alternate-world novels is motivated by a number of factors. First, their popularity is brief: only for a few decades do they make up a significant portion of the production. Second, it is really only in those decades that something like a "typical" alternate-world novel exists – essentially, the philosophical tale.[25] Most of the production for other years is made up of a hodge-podge of different items that don't constitute anything like a tradition or genre,

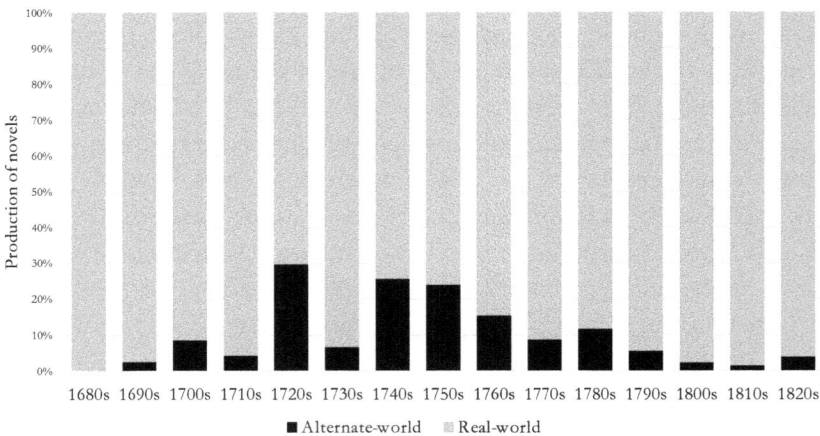

Figure 1.3 Novel types, 1681–1830.

simply because there are too few of each. Third, the formal arrangements of alternate-world novels do not mirror those of their real-world counterparts. Of notable importance to this chapter are two interrelated facts – that marvelous and allegorical novels are very rarely first-person "documents," and that by definition, the truth pretense they on occasion carry can only be, as I've noted, parodic. This is why most subsequent graphs will tabulate real-world novels alone, novels whose evolutions – especially in the crucial years in the heart of the Enlightenment – would be muted by the inclusion of alternate-world novels. However, returning the latter to the calculations would not fundamentally alter any of my findings. It would simply muddy their presentation.

Within the category of real-world novels, we can observe a clear trend in subject matter (Figure 1.4). We witness here the "nobodification" of the novel. At the beginning of this period, most novels take as their subjects known people – from history, legend, or current events. The dominance of this Aristotelian mode – and in the following chapter we will look at just how far back it extends – erodes over about half a century: by the 1730s, they represent at best 20 percent of the production and appear to retreat still further in the 1760s and after. Given this, it should be obvious that the enduring scholarly impression that early novelists were quite concerned with the literal truth of their works has an empirical basis: it derives not only from pseudofactual affirmations ("These are real letters," and so on) but also from the frequency with which writers before a certain point took known people as their subjects.

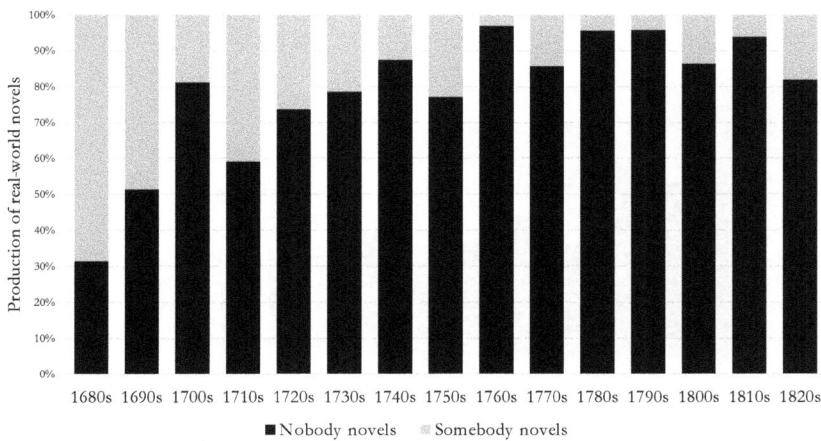

Figure 1.4 Nobody novels and somebody novels, 1681–1830.

And those pseudofactual affirmations were also frequent – though there doesn't appear to be any specific moment in the eighteenth century after which they are not, according to Figure 1.5. This graph does register an obvious change, if perhaps a surprisingly slow one: only with the turn of the eighteenth century does pseudofactuality register a clear hit. Nobody novels that advertise their invention are uncommon before the 1740s, when, rather suddenly, they come to represent roughly a third of the overall category. Levels of invented novels then subside – though we may wonder if this is significant – before registering a more even and sustained advance over the balance of the century. There is, however, an upper limit to the proportion of novels classified as invented: they never get much beyond 40 percent, and indeed plateau a little under that figure during the opening decades of the eighteenth century. What takes up the slack is the category of indeterminate nobody novels. This may not be surprising, since it stands to reason that by these years the assumption of invention on the part of writers and readers makes its overt declaration less important. Similarly, one might suppose that in the earlier part of this period, indeterminate novels were left without truth markers because of the converse assumption that nobody novels were supposed to be true. For the bulk of the span, however, no clear "horizon of expectations" can be deduced: though pseudofactual novels outnumber invented ones, they don't enjoy a clear hegemony. We can't, then, know why authors leave them unmarked (and it's a good bet they have various reasons for doing so).

Taking Aristotelianism and pseudofactuality together, it is clear from Figure 1.6 that eighteenth-century novelists were indeed very concerned about presenting their works as true – either true because they took known people as their subjects, or true because they were telling true stories about

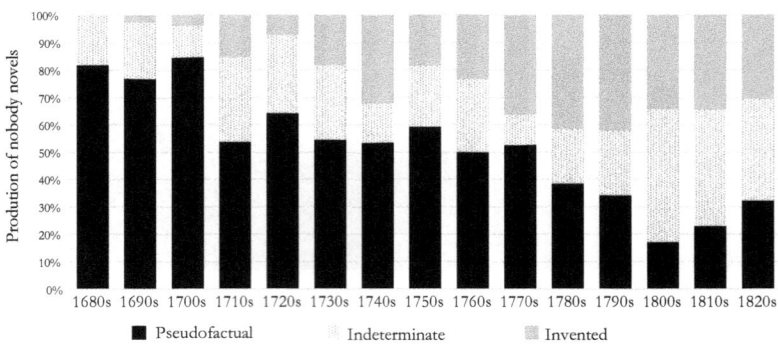

Figure 1.5 Truth status of nobody novels.

1 Truth Postures in the Novel of the Long Eighteenth Century

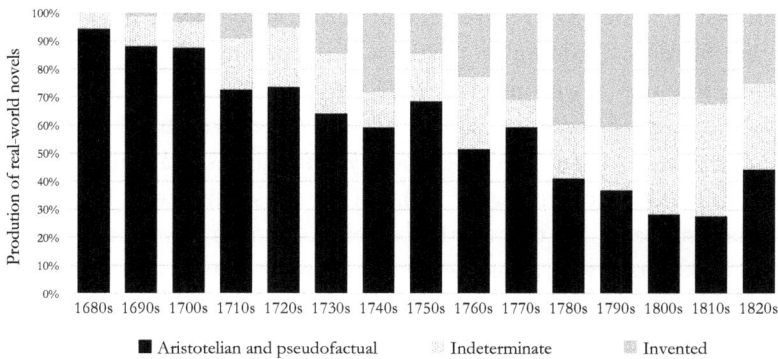

Figure 1.6 Truth status of real-world novels, 1681–1830.

unknown people. Literal truth of one sort or another is a near inevitable feature of the novel over the first three decades of the span. Nonetheless, this new measure makes it clear that novels remain in the truth camp for seven decades more: though the Aristotelian novel retreats over the course of the eighteenth century, its residual production is nonetheless enough to enhance and extend the dominance of what we might want to broadly call the "referential" or even "nonfictional" mode. Even at the opening of the eighteenth century, novelists appear much more concerned with truth than many accounts have suggested. Thus, we have so far both a confirmation and an undermining of most accounts of the arrival of "fictionality": yes, novels at one point were massively indexed to literal truth; but no, this predilection does not appear to have disappeared, only receded to minority status – and quite slowly at that.[26]

One difficulty with these graphs is that their bars are made up of items that are not necessarily identical; that is, a graph measures one particular attribute, but any novel has manifold attributes (only some of which, obviously, I have tracked). As a result, one can easily come away from Figure 1.6 with the impression of a steady erosion of truth claims, whereas Figures 1.4 and 1.5 help us to see that this apparently steady erosion is only the end result of two different changes. The pseudofactual posture of nobody novels remains essentially plateaued for seven decades (1711–1780); Figure 1.6's suggestion of a steady downward trend is an effect of the addition of the totals for Aristotelian novels. And by the same token, that plateau itself may not be what it appears: it may hide changes going on within pseudofactual novels and nobody novels more generally.

Nobody novels, it turns out, are by and large novels with contemporary settings; Aristotelian protagonists, by contrast, are most often plucked from history. The result is that the nobodification of the novel is also a presentification. Tracking proportions of nobody novels and proportions of contemporary novels in Figure 1.7 shows the correlation between the two. The upward trend of both features as we move into the middle of the century is obscured somewhat by anomalous readings from the 1700s (already visible in Figure 1.4), but the most important lesson is the correlation itself.[27] Of course, the correlation does not mean that novels with contemporary settings are *invariably* nobody novels. Some nobody novels do have historical settings, especially from around the turn of the nineteenth century (this is the "historical novel" associated with Scott, and it explains the increasing divergence from the 1800s on); and some Aristotelian novels take as their subject contemporary somebodies (i.e., celebrities of the day), especially before 1701. On the whole, however, these variants cancel themselves out. In practice, the nobody novel is also a contemporary novel, while the Aristotelian novel is historical.

Since this observation holds over the entire period, it doesn't directly help us understand what nonetheless appears to be changing within nobody novels – that is, both the growth of invented novels, which becomes very obvious by the 1740s, and the plateaued level of pseudofactual ones. Factoring in the nobody novel's truth claims, however, reveals a specific moment of change. Figure 1.8 demonstrates that pseudofactual nobody novels are also contemporary novels, and vice versa – for a time. Pseudofactuality is tightly correlated with contemporaneity for the first half-century of this span (as it is before 1681 as well, though it obviously does not figure on this graph).

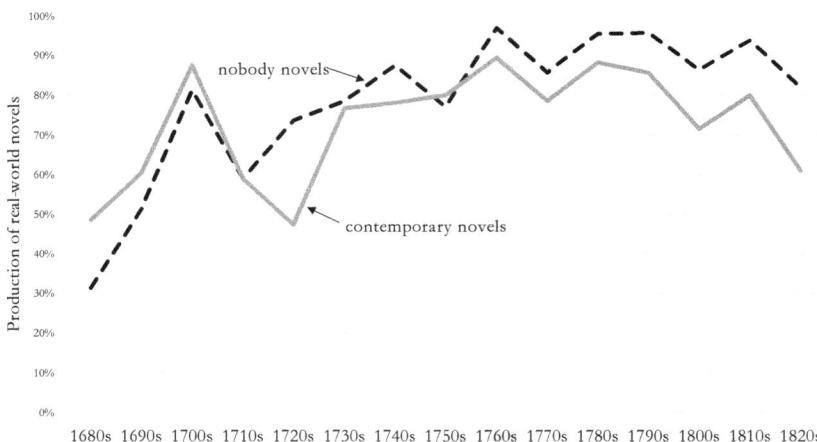

Figure 1.7 Temporal setting versus protagonist type.

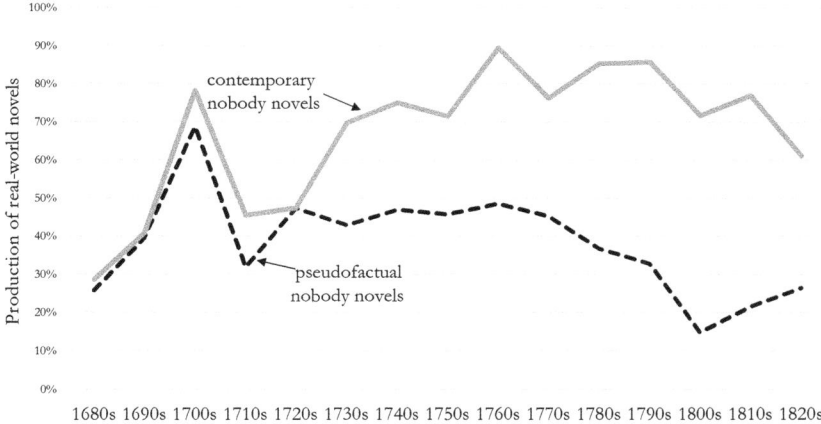

Figure 1.8 Truth posture versus temporal setting in nobody novels (I).

This correlation breaks down in the 1730s, after which contemporaneity and pseudofactuality pursue very different destinies. Conversely, indeterminacy and invention correlate with noncontemporary settings – in the main, historical settings, but also unspecified settings whose temporality is impossible to pin down. And that correlation, while not as sharp as the previous one, breaks down at the same moment (Figure 1.9).

Without this being apparent in overall tabulations of truth posture (Figures 1.5 and 1.6), the 1730s jumps out as a moment of change. At this point, truth posture and temporal setting operate independently. The change is confirmed if we plot the percentage of the three nobody novel truth postures that have contemporary settings. Since the numbers of indeterminate and especially invented nobody novels is small prior to the 1730s, and since small populations lead to dramatic chance variations, it helps to group the span by five-decade intervals. And again the production of the five decades prior to 1731 stands out. At the turn of the nineteenth century, we see in Figure 1.10, truth postures are completely independent of temporal setting: pseudofactual, indeterminate, and invented novels have contemporary settings the same amount of the time (84 percent of the time, roughly). But that independence, which holds nearly as well for the middle half-century of the span, was not there prior to the 1730s. Before then, while pseudofactual novels almost always had contemporary settings, invented novels had them only 20 percent of the time; indeterminate novels were in the middle, at around 50 percent.

Thus, pseudofactuality steadily declines over 150 years, and the thing that is declining is, from the beginning to the end, roughly the same

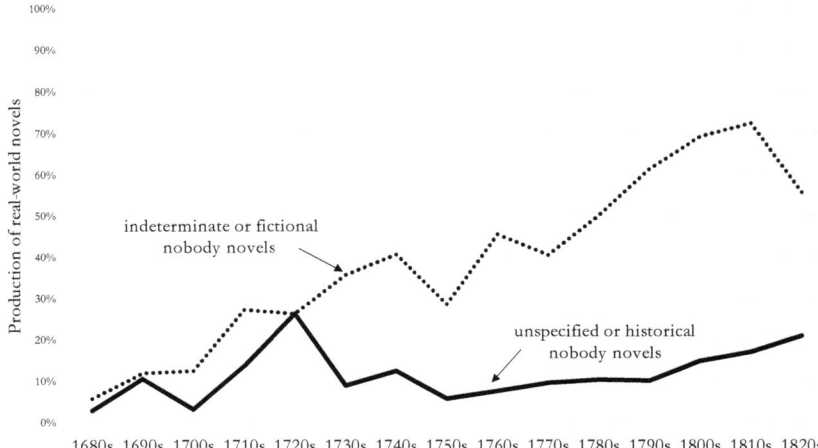

Figure 1.9 Truth posture versus temporal setting in nobody novels (II).

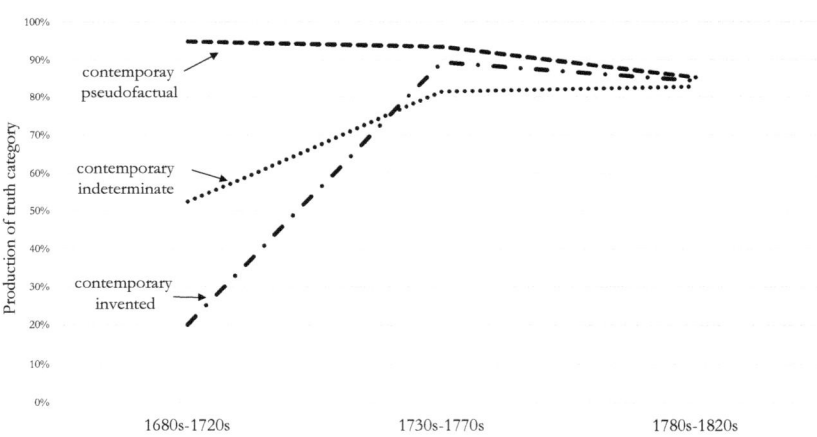

Figure 1.10 Truth posture versus temporal setting in nobody novels (III).

thing, at least by the criterion of temporality. But this is not the case with indeterminacy and invention: the change in the 1730s suggests that novels tagged invented and indeterminate before this date do not look quite like similarly tagged novels from later. In other words, even if Figure 1.5 gives the impression of a steady growth of invented nobody novels from the 1680s (first zero, then a few, then a few more, and so on), some sort of a break is in fact hidden – until temporal setting is taken into account. This implies that pre-1731 invented novels are not simply pseudofactual novels with a different preface, because the former rarely have the contemporary settings that the latter almost always do. Early invented novels, we have cause to suspect, don't look like the later ones.

And temporal setting is not the only variable to consider. Narration type – meaning first- and third-person forms – is also changing. In Figure 1.11, we see the proportion of third-person novels, along with two kinds of first-person novels. One – the major player – is what I call the document novel: these works take the form of a memoirs and letter collections. The other category of first-person novels is a grab-bag of minor variants – frame narratives, travel narratives, observational narratives, and narratives that focus not on a life (as does the memoir) but on a single episode. While the presence of the latter category is a kind of background noise, the first-person document novel rises and falls with symmetry; it also has an intriguing double peak, first in the 1740s and then again in the 1770s.[28] The third-person novel is more or less a mirror image of the document novel, falling away before returning at the end of the span. And the first meeting point of the two major categories is the 1730s. Thus, the tight correlation between truth posture and temporal setting (Figures 1.8–1.10) ends at about the same moment that the first-person document novel is ascending to hegemony.

These other measures suggest that the first fifty years of the span are relatively homogenous, despite what appears in Figure 1.5 to be an initial retreat of pseudofactuality in the 1710s. In fact, looking at Figures 1.5 and 1.11 in tandem, we might discern in the span three broad periods. The first, lasting from 1681 to 1730, is characterized by third-person novels set in the present said to be true stories; the second, from 1731 to 1780, is dominated by first-person document novels, still set in the present but with much more varied

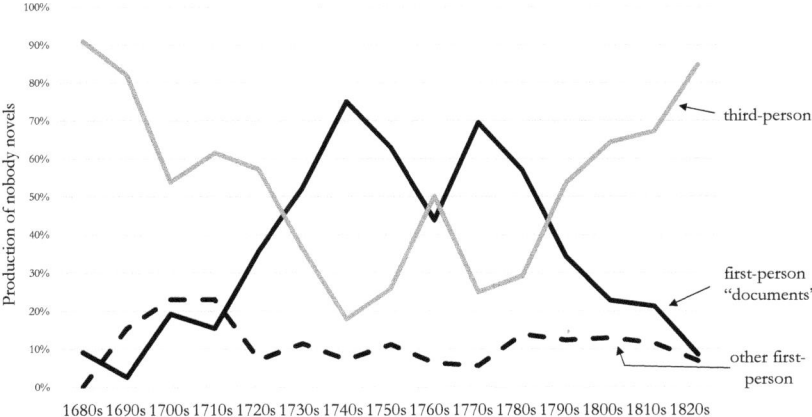

Figure 1.11 Nobody novels by narration type.

truth postures; the third, from 1781 on, sees an erosion of pseudofactuality along with first-person forms, while indeterminacy expands markedly. Breaks between these spans are not radical: the document novel, for example, starts its rise in the 1720s and falls off noticeably only in the 1790s; pseudofactuality is already less dominant from the 1710s, and falls off gradually after the 1770s. Nonetheless, and again despite the general impression from Figure 1.5 of "more and more" invention and "less and less" pseudofactuality, the heart of the eighteenth century would seem to be something of a plateau – a stalemate between pseudofactuality (dominant at around 50 percent of the production) and invention (a minority choice, at an average of around 25 percent).

The stalemate endures precisely as long as first-person document novels prosper. This is no accident, since first-person novels are considerably more likely to be claimed true than third-person novels – at least over the middle half-century of the span. The calculations in Figure 1.12 are subject to more decade-to-decade volatility than others due to the smaller sizes of the sample subsets; notably, the number of third-person nobody novels in the samples from the 1740s and 1770s is low, and therefore the appearance of sudden rises and falls in those years should be treated with special caution. Indeed, the figures for any one decade are of minimal interest: we should instead be looking for trends. And there do seem to be some. We can see, first, that the nobody novel's seven-decade plateau of pseudofactuality (first displayed in Figure 1.5 and reproduced in Figure 1.12 as a light gray dotted line) looks at least a little different if we break the novels out by narration type. During those decades, first-person works are more likely than third-person works to carry affirmations of truth – just over one-and-a-half times more likely. The rate differential, however, is not a permanent characteristic of narration

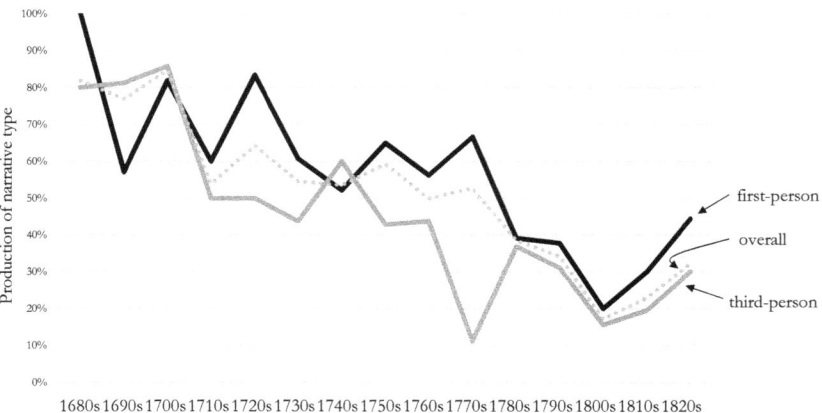

Figure 1.12 Pseudofactuality rates by narration type (I).

type, and based on the trends visible in Figure 1.12, we can cluster the decades to compose Figure 1.13. Book-ending the plateaued period we see situations that are approximately mirror images of one another. Upstream, both first- and third-person works are usually advanced as true, with a slight, nine-percentage-point edge for the latter. Downstream, relatively few of either form are advanced as true, with first-person works holding, now, a slight edge. The middle decades stand out as years with a more noticeable differential of 20 percent.

This is not to say, however, that the third-person novel was more hospitable to admissions of invention: fewer assertions of truth do not translate directly into more admissions of invention on account of the presence of novels with no mentions of truth status. In fact, as a rule, third-person novels were simultaneously less likely to be affirmed as true and less likely to be admitted as inventions (Figure 1.14). With the exception of a notable divergence starting in the 1780s, invention rates for the two narration types are more closely aligned than pseudofactuality rates. Again to minimize decade-to-decade variation, and respecting the trends suggested by Figure 1.14, we can group the decades, this time into fifty-year clusters. Figure 1.15 shows that if first-person works more consistently display pseudofactual postures, this does not mean that third-person works are more easily "fictionalized" (in the sense of incorporating invented protagonists). In fact, given that the differential in the middle five decades of the century is relatively small, admissions of truth do not appear to have much to do with narration type at all. This becomes still clearer when we discover the source of the striking divergence after 1780. It turns out that the increased likelihood of claims

Figure 1.13 Pseudofactuality rates by narration type (II).

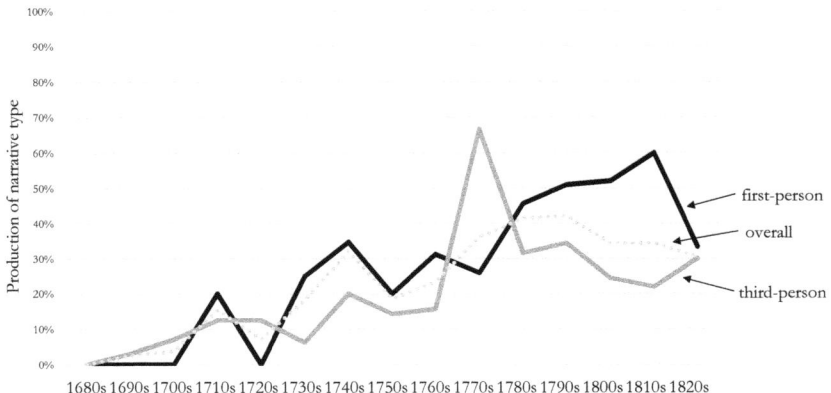

Figure 1.14 Invention rates by narration type (I).

of invention in first-person works comes from the asymmetricality of my tagging protocol itself: though *all* novels accompanied by an explicit admission of invention are classified as such, *first-person* novels can also be so classified when the name (or gender) of the author named on the title page does not match the name (or gender) of the protagonists; when these "mismatches" are removed and categorized as indeterminate, narration type has no effect on invention rates. It turns out, then, that third-person novels acquire admittedly invented protagonists no more easily or quickly than first-person works, and vice versa. The only salient impact of narrative type is on pseudofactuality, where the vogue for first-person novels with truth affirmations helps to create – but is hardly solely responsible for – the posture's long plateau.

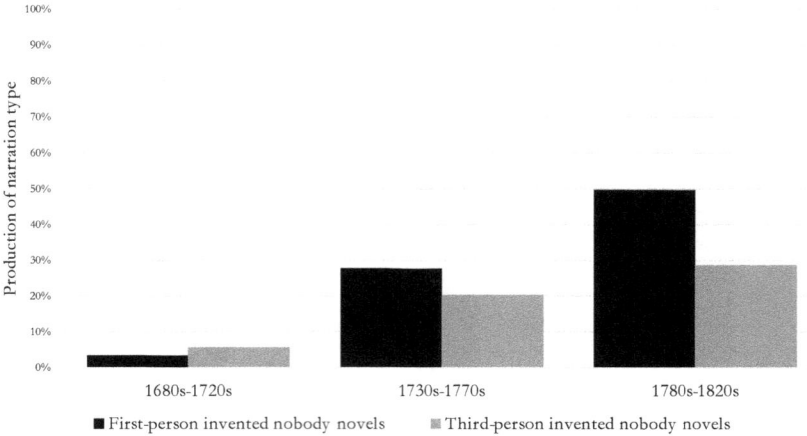

Figure 1.15 Invention rates by narration type (II).

Thus far, I have measured the presence or absence of truth claims; but it might be objected that the *quality* of those claims could potentially vary quite a bit. An obvious supposition would be that truth affirmations become increasingly ironic.[29] Along these lines, I have isolated a number of pseudofactual variants: irony, but also equivocation ("this may or may not be true") and a mixed type of affirmation characterizing some first-person document novels, admitted as fabrications while simultaneously claimed as being "based on" real events.[30] Is there any evidence that these types of affirmations multiply as the period advances?

Figure 1.16 reveals that although all these variants are present from fairly early on in the span, pseudofactuality's waning decades see a multiplication of some of them. From the 1780s onwards, ironic affirmations, which had been rare, become a permanent feature of the pseudofactual landscape. And from the 1760s, claims of basing first-person novels on real events witness a noticeable expansion. Both of these variants are associated with certain types of narration. "Based on" affirmations by my definition can only occur with first-person texts; but irony, which can show up anywhere, turns out to be a more pronounced feature of third-person texts, with epistolary novels proving especially resistant to it.[31] At any rate, both expansions – in "based on" and ironic affirmations – do correlate well with the overall decline of pseudofactuality, which as we've seen can be detected by the 1780s. Thus, not only are fewer novels overall declared to be true, the declarations themselves weaken. This information does not change the "calendar" for the abandonment of pseudofactuality, but it does suggest that the mode's retreat, starting in the 1780s, is more precipitous than indicated by Figure 1.5.

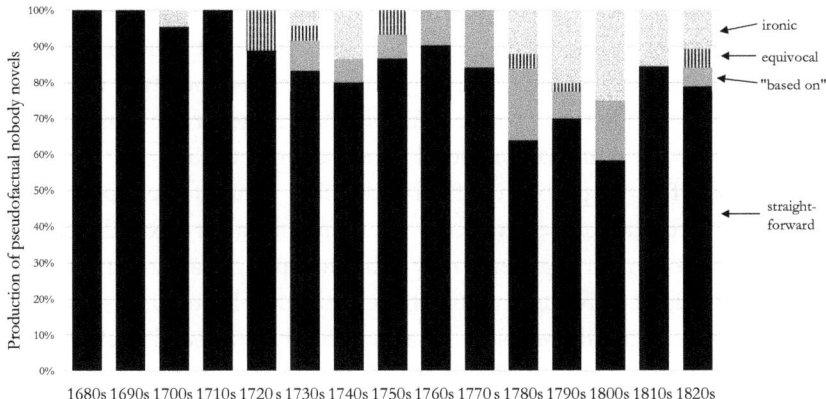

Figure 1.16 Pseudofactual variants.

Over the long haul, the truth pretense (more or less) disappears. Of course, we already suspected that much – even if pseudofactuality's resilience in the 1810s and 1820s comes as something of a surprise. (Without data from later decades, it is obviously impossible to know whether the 1820s sample is a fluke or the start of a trend.) But the point of amassing detail on the change is that better data constrains the explanations one can plausibly offer for it. The fundamental explanation I will be proposing for the evolution of literary forms – that they are best understood as behaving like technological artifacts – will be advanced only much later in this study. For now, it is enough to assess the general "shape" of the pseudofactual posture's disappearance. For that shape should immediately cause us to discount the plausibility of certain explanations already offered by scholars.

"Historians of the novel have shown that, as the [eighteenth] century advanced and readers learned to accept the norms of literary realism, novelists tended to drop claims to reality or factuality," writes Dorrit Cohn, summarizing the scholarly consensus on the disappearance of pseudofactual claims.[32] There are two interrelated assertions here: first, that the nature of the change is gradual ("tended to drop"); second, that this gradualism can be explained as the result of a learning process ("learned to accept"). Often, that learning process is expressed as fatigue: people tire of a device – the found manuscript – that is used too often, becoming less and less its dupe and deploying it with increasing irony.[33] But is the disappearance of pseudofactual claims truly gradual? Figure 1.5 indicates seventy years of relative comfort with the truth pretense – seventy years during which over 50 percent of novels contain it and during which the percentage of avowedly invented novels fluctuates without gaining steam. This is a strange learning curve indeed, since not much learning gets done for a considerable span of time. And by the same token, where is the fatigue? We've seen also that it's simply not accurate to say that ironic uses push out serious ones; the former do start to multiply, but only when the pseudofactual novel has already retreated. Seventy years: multiple literary generations must have had relatively the same comfort level with pseudofactuality.

There is a further problem with the idea that pseudofactual pretense is "dropped" over the course of the century: more than a paratextual assertion that writers stop making, pretense may be bound up with narrative form itself. In other words, the invented nobody novel – the novel composed according to the "norms of literary realism" – may not simply be a pseudofactual novel that has lost its fussy prefatory remarks by editors and eyewitnesses. After all, it is important to recognize that the eclipse of pseudofactuality correlates with the late-century expansion of the third-person novel. This is the third-person novel that for the time being we've only glimpsed – a novel modeled neither on the Aristotelian poet's third person, informing us of the deeds of heroes of renown, nor on the third-person report of contemporary "news." It is only this novel – the subject of Chapter 8 – that is largely free of truth claims.

By contrast, the document novel – at least in France – seems to have had truth claims "baked in." Yes, document novels were demonstrably separable from those claims: they could be given different prefaces, and indeed starting in the 1730s – in other words, around the time the form started to grab a significant share of the market – they were, with authors freely signing their names to a nobody's memoirs or letters. Yet the proportion of authors who did so – already about 30 percent by the 1740s, and more detailed figures will be offered in Chapters 6 and 7 – changes little until the 1790s. This, of course, is the moment the new third-person novel starts its expansion. It is only then that first-person forms – now residual – become less pseudofactual. What if it is more the takeover of a new artifact, rather than a change in an old one, that explains the retreat of pseudofactuality? This is the hypothesis that will be explored in Chapter 8.

The deference to literal truth will pass. But not quickly, and not because some brave souls will have shown the way. The fact is that at any one moment, people see matters differently. This is why pseudofactual preference was hardly universal: for some six or seven decades, a considerable number of nobody novels were admitted as fabrications. From a practical point of view, pseudofactuality must have had its drawbacks. The first was the awkwardness of insisting on truth without actually demanding readers' belief, well captured in a famous letter in which Richardson explains to William Warburton that he wished to keep up the "air of genuineness" about Clarissa's letters without actually having his readers think them genuine.[34] Second, the pseudofactual first-person document novel had the built-in disadvantage of conflicting with recognition of authorship: it reduced people who might aspire to the role of professional author to playing, unconvincingly, the role of editor. Thus, one can sympathize with the frustration of the author of a number of first-person document novels, the marquis d'Argens, who in 1739 complained about the obligation of asserting that novels were about real individuals: "The author of a romance or a novel [*un roman ou une nouvelle*] has had enough genius to imagine a plot [*un sujet*], to decorate it with the circumstances that captivate and move the soul of the reader. So why can't he invent names? What prevents him?"[35] It's a perfectly commonsensical observation, to which one can only respond "nothing." Nothing prevented people from writing novels with admittedly invented protagonists, and they did from the 1730s on. But not nearly as many people as chose to write novels with protagonists advanced as real. That is, until roughly the 1790s. The marquis d'Argens didn't "understand" anything about fiction, he just had an opinion about a better way to write novels – and it didn't sway most people, who had other investments.

A last problem with the "gradualist" model is not so much the idea of gradual change itself, but rather the assumption of a *passage* from one steady state to another. In this view, the eighteenth century becomes – to its credit – a rich "period of transition," that brings us from some former state of archaism to the familiar shores of modernity. In this respect, eighteenth-centuryists are probably no more chauvinistic than specialists of other periods, convinced that something momentous is afoot precisely in their bailiwick. Surely such conviction is not unjustified, for something is always afoot, and change is always happening. At the same time, we often misrecognize the changes happening in our period of study as the only decisive ones, assuming that others are merely small modifications in an otherwise coherent way of doing things. Along these lines, one impression easily derived from Figure 1.5 is that the strong percentage of somebody novels and pseudofactual nobody novels in the 1680s and 1690s is the end of a long dominance: those imposing bars make for a good "before." Yet what looks like a before is just a moment like any another, with its own history. The following chapter picks apart that 1680s baseline, which is not, it turns out, the edge of some cold, hard glacier of tradition melting in the heat of the Enlightenment sun.

2 The Rise and Fall of the Aristotelian Novel

Beginning around the 1730s, as we've seen, French novelists start to admit the invention of their protagonists in ways they hadn't in the previous half-century. There had been admittedly invented novels before, of course; but prior to 1731, these books displayed characteristics – crucially, setting – that discourage us from viewing them as harbingers of what happens later. Nonetheless, it is difficult to avoid coming away from Figures 1.5 (page 28) and 1.6 (page 29) without the impression that something is *already* changing starting in the 1690s: small quantities of invented novels appear; indeterminate novels expand a bit; and pseudofactuality starts a slow retreat from its nearly complete dominance in the 1680s. Of course, things in those years *are* changing – that is in the nature of things – but they are not necessarily *beginning* to change. The 1680s, in other words, are not the solid rock that will slowly erode over the course of the following century. Rather, the situation in the 1680s – a decade chosen as a starting point for Chapter 1's inquiry into truth postures because of the orientation provided by previous scholarship – should itself be historicized. After all, if you are writing in 1681, you may be at the point of departure for a new trend, but you also may be at the middle or end of some earlier trend.

Indeed, it's the latter possibility that would seem to be the case. Extending Figure 1.6 back in time easily undermines the tempting assumption that the dominance of pseudofactual and Aristotelian novels was representative of some sort of premodern, "literalist" mindset, stretching back into the mists of time (Figure 2.1).[1] The 1680s (and more generally the period running from the 1680s to the 1700s or possibly the 1720s) turn out to be part of a trend whose beginning is debatable – the 1660s? or the 1640s, discounting a potentially anomalous reading from the 1650s? – but that is nonetheless indisputably a trend. Over roughly the first half of the seventeenth century, the percentage of novels featuring either truth claims or subject matter of renown is not substantially different from what it will be during the heart of the Enlightenment; the rates of the years 1661–1730 are effectively an anomaly. But this is only a jumping-off point for further inquiry. How much do the novels that make up the black bars from before the 1660s resemble

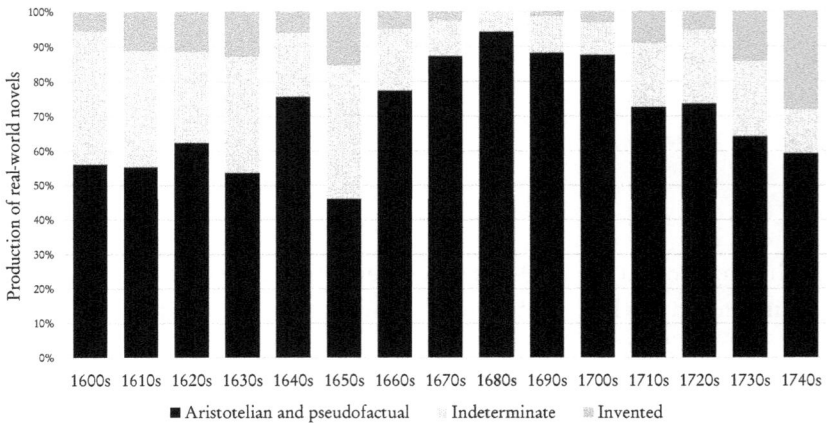

Figure 2.1 Truth status of real-world novels, 1601–1750.

those after in terms other than simply the existence (attested or purported) of their protagonists? How important are the comparatively large numbers of indeterminate novels in the years before the long "truth bump"? Do the few invented novels of the seventeenth century look like those from 1701 to 1730, like those from 1731 and after – or neither?

Roughly similar questions attended the analysis of Figures 1.5 and 1.6, but answering these new ones requires much additional information. Figure 2.1 attempts to hold constant the four categories that produced the earlier graphs (Aristotelian [somebody] novels, plus the three kinds of nobody novels). But this consistency is somewhat artificial. After all, my categories have no transhistorical value: they were developed through interaction with the archive of the long eighteenth century, in order to make certain traits measurable. Other periods, however, have novels with other traits. To cite a key difference, pseudofactual document novels, which comprise a very large segment of the eighteenth-century production, are very nearly a null category before 1680; conversely, Aristotelian novels, more prominent than they will be after 1681, use known heroes and historical settings in a manner that necessitates much finer discriminations than the ones that have proved adequate until now.

Indeed, for most of the previous chapter, it was enough to focus on nobody novels – the novels that to varying degrees sported those intriguing pseudofactual prefaces and that by the turn of the eighteenth century already make up the majority of new novels published. But Figure 2.2 shows that in the seventeenth century, it is the somebody (Aristotelian) novel that has an impressive rise (as well as fall).

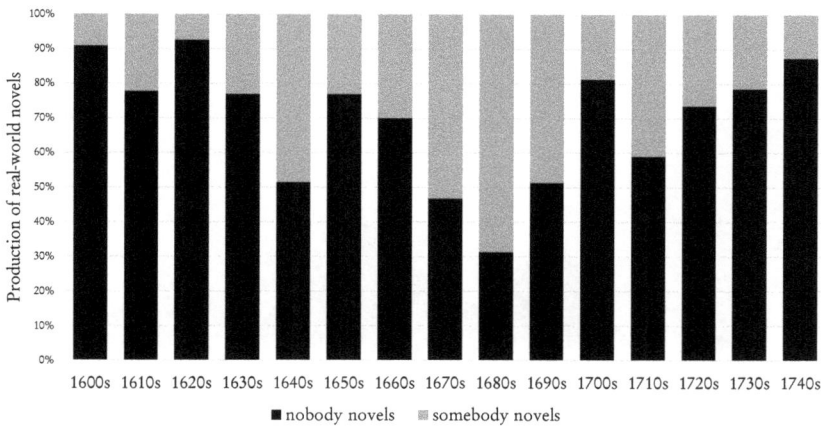

Figure 2.2 Nobody novels and somebody novels, 1601–1750.

The type of novel that in the opening decades of the eighteenth century steadily loses out *to* the nobody novel had actually wrested its dominance *from* the nobody novel much earlier on. For reasons we will see, the seventeenth-century rise of somebody novels is not as smooth as that of eighteenth-century nobody novels: the 1640s to the 1660s present some odd figures. On the other hand, Figure 2.2 does reveal that the three- or four-decade heyday of the "true novel" toward the end of the seventeenth century also corresponds rather well to the ascendancy of the Aristotelian novel. Above all, we may again wonder if the earlier nobody novel that loses out to the somebody novel is the "same" nobody novel that later returns with a vengeance.

We can wonder about that later. I want to focus first on the Aristotelian novel, whose history is more complicated than it first appears. Until now, I've remained schematic about what actually constitutes an Aristotelian novel since by the eighteenth century, the form was in eclipse. It was enough to say that Aristotelian novels – I repeat that the category is my own and nowhere figures in the terminology of the period – draw their protagonists from history, legend, or current events. But the latter terms obviously cover a good deal of disparate ground, and in fact, the rise of the Aristotelian novel needs to be mapped with a more finely grained classification of its subject matter.

How many Aristotelian novels are contemporary? For a while, hardly any, according to Figure 2.3. Then the 1660s see the beginnings of a trend – a substantial number of novels taking as their subjects not heroes of the past but rather contemporary celebrities.[2] Over the half-century stretching from the 1670s to the 1710s, an average of 35 percent of Aristotelian novels have these contemporary settings. One way of putting this development would be to say that Aristotelian novels register the effects of a "presentification" – the

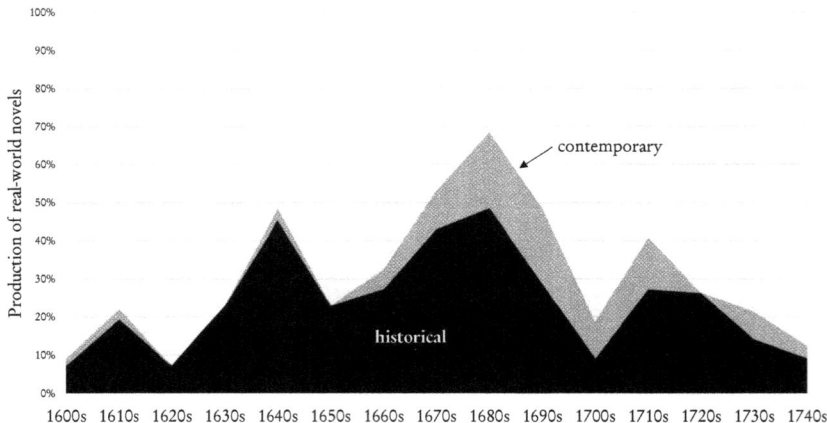

Figure 2.3 Aristotelian novels by temporal setting (I).

tendency of novelistic subject matter to become increasingly proximate, temporally speaking. (We will see that presentification affects nobody novels as well.)

But even Aristotelian novels with historical settings – the dominant variety – might be said to presentify as well, in a slightly different sense. After all, the past offers a lot of different history to choose from, ranging from the remote to the closer at hand. Figure 2.4, which divides the 150-year span into three-decade intervals because of small sample subsets, shows a clear evolution. Aristotelian novels start out the century by taking aim very far away from contemporary France, at a mythical or biblical reservoir of material.[3] Thus, the Aristotelian novel of the first three decades of the century bears little

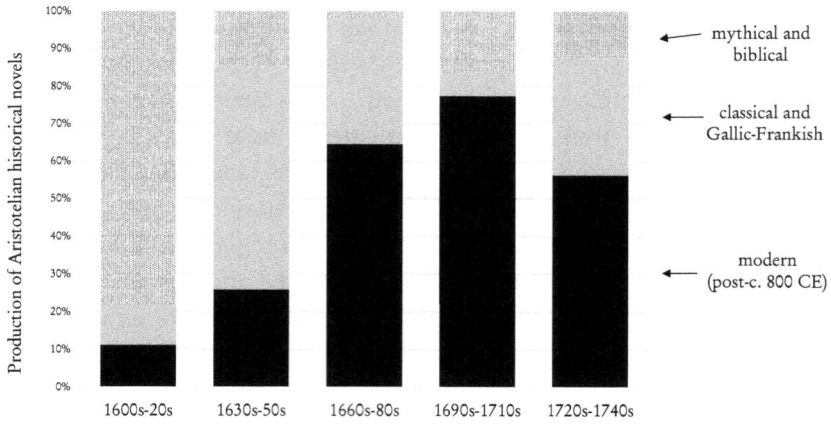

Figure 2.4 The temporality of Aristotelian historical novels.

resemblance, from this perspective, to its "descendants." These subjects are then abandoned in favor of subjects of classical antiquity, which in turn are largely supplanted by modern ones – "modern" in a very loose sense, meaning anything from after the time of Charlemagne. With the caveat that the situation seems to rediversify modestly at the tail end of this span, as the number of such novels is dwindling, Aristotelian historical novels increasingly center on more recent periods, and the cusp of the takeover of "modern" subject matter – roughly, the 1660s and 1670s – corresponds as well to the expansion of Aristotelian contemporary novels visible in Figure 2.3. Redoing the latter by breaking out Aristotelian novels with modern subjects, as in Figure 2.5, makes that expansion even more obvious. Figure 2.5 also raises the possibility that the apparent "double rise" of Aristotelianism – it peaks first in the 1640s and then again in the 1680s – may be due not only to the vagaries of sampling but also to the fact that we are measuring two related but different objects. (We will see that the twin peaks have another explanation as well.)

Of course, one might also phrase the presentification of the Aristotelian novel as a new preoccupation with historicity – by which I mean the idea that the novelist should focus on heroes for whom there is better-quality source material. This is a generalization, since some classical subjects are more extensively documented than some that are, chronologically, closer to home: if you are writing a novel about the twelfth-century Byzantine princess Irene Angelina, "modern" though she may be, you will need a lot of imagination (as did Des Barres, in *Irène, princesse de Constantinople, histoire turque* [1678]). And I haven't attempted to track the frequency with which Aristotelian

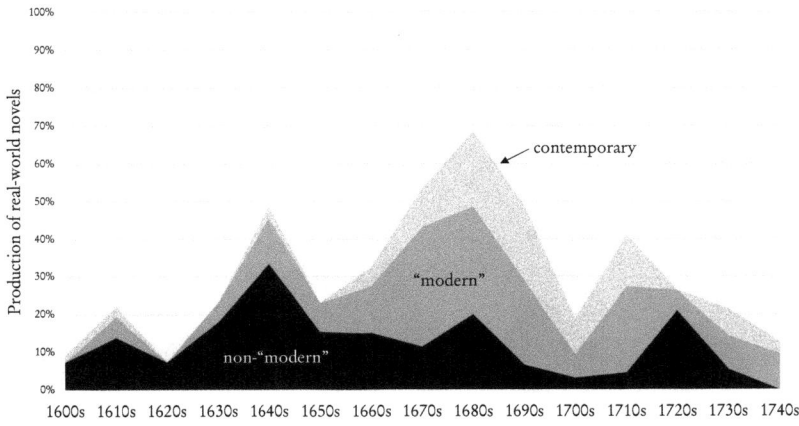

Figure 2.5 Aristotelian novels by temporal setting (II).

novelists allude to their sources.[4] But the hypothesis that the issue is really a change in what counts as historical – or what counts as a suitable historical protagonist – finds corroboration in some other measurements.

Indeed, one such measurement reveals an Aristotelian variant I haven't mentioned until now. The category of the Aristotelian historical novel encompasses in fact two distinct practices that can be termed "weak" and "strong" Aristotelianism. I have noted that Aristotelianism in no way forecloses all invention of characters: the poet's (or the novelist's) plotting may well benefit from the creation of minor characters, revolving in the ambit of the known heroes.[5] My sense at the outset of my research was that invented *protagonists* were another matter: I was well aware that such examples existed, foremost among them the eponymous heroine of *La Princesse de Clèves*;[6] but they were, I felt, outliers or extreme cases. More familiarity with the archive of novels published before 1660, however, revealed many *titular* protagonists with no historical or legendary sanction, nevertheless plunged into a plot involving well-known figures. These were not the kind of historical novels we associate with Walter Scott, and that foregrounded nobodies against a background of somebodies. Rather, this variant revolved around something more like *invented somebodies*: unknown princes or very often princesses in close interaction with heroes of renown.[7]

Breaking Aristotelian novels into these two categories, then, gives Figure 2.6, which reveals a second way that the form is becoming more historically oriented. Weak Aristotelianism appears to correspond well to the decades that favored classical subject matter (see Figure 2.4). And indeed, the three temporal settings have distinct tolerances for the admixture of invented and

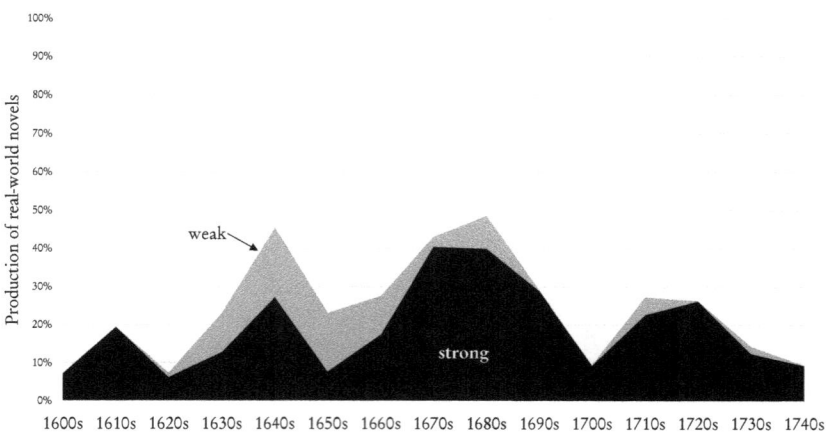

Figure 2.6 Aristotelian historical novels by protagonist type.

historical protagonists. Classical subjects are the most promiscuous, being strong 78 percent of the time; mythical and biblical subjects are entirely resistant to invented protagonists since all examples are strong; and modern subjects, strong 88 percent of the time, are in between. These figures are for the entire 230-year span. Aristotelianism is considerably weaker for both modern and classical subjects over the years 1621–1660.

We can capture the increasing interest in a more "historical" use of history in one further way.[8] In the previous chapter, I alluded to the fact that Aristotelianism was strongly correlated with historical settings: not only were most Aristotelian novels historical, as shown in Figure 2.3, but in addition, most historical novels were Aristotelian. The correlation holds until the 1780s: after that point, which is the context for the novels of Scott, most historical novels are in fact nobody novels. As a point of comparison, in the ten decades running from the 1680s to the 1770s, Aristotelian historical novels outnumber their nobody counterparts by about three-and-a-half to one. But here too, the situation looks different if we extend the inquiry back in time. In fact, the dominance of the somebody historical novel over the nobody historical novel dates only to the decade I've repeatedly cited as a kind of turning point – the 1660s. Before then, historical novels are somebody novels only about half the time.

We can attempt to represent these many changes in historicity by giving more visual "weight" to some historical novels than to others. Adding nobody historical novels to the Aristotelian totals of Figure 2.6, and (for the record) extending the range all the way to the 1820s, gives Figure 2.7. Already, this helps us see that the double peak of interest in specifically Aristotelian historical novels is at least slightly misleading: with

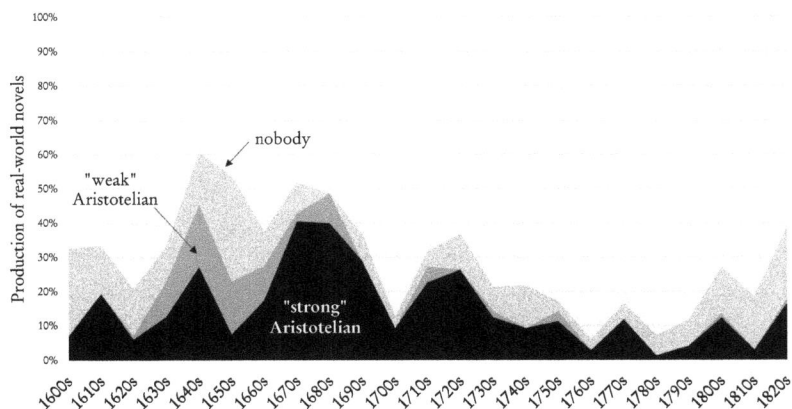

Figure 2.7 Historical novels.

the exception of a brief dip in the 1660s, historical novels more generally make up about half the French production for a half-century. We also have a better sense of the change occurring in the 1660s, as stronger forms of historicity displace weaker ones. This displacement can be still better captured with a finer gradation of the various types of historicity found within the Aristotelian historical novels. One solution would be to deem strong Aristotelian novels with modern settings "more" historical than strong Aristotelian novels with classical settings and to proceed down from there, through the weak varieties, followed by novels that are mythical and biblical. This gives five different categories, plus nobody historical novels, to which one might attribute, for the sake of argument, the weakest historicity of them all. In Figure 2.8, the darker the area, the greater the historicity of the novels represented. For sure, this type of gradation is artificial and relies on debatable weightings (Is a novel with a biblical subject really "less historical" than a weak Aristotelian novel taking place in ancient Persia?). Nonetheless, the heuristic does help underline two distinct developments, the first covering the years 1631–1660 and the second from 1661 and tailing slowly off over the following century.[9]

Two developments, but nonetheless developments presenting a certain measure of continuity: again, a half-century enthusiasm for historical novels straddles the moment of change situated in the 1650s and 1660s. This continuity falls apart, however, if we put aside Aristotelian (somebody) novels and look instead at their nobody counterparts. Although Figure 2.2 indicates that the preponderance of nobody novels in the early part of the

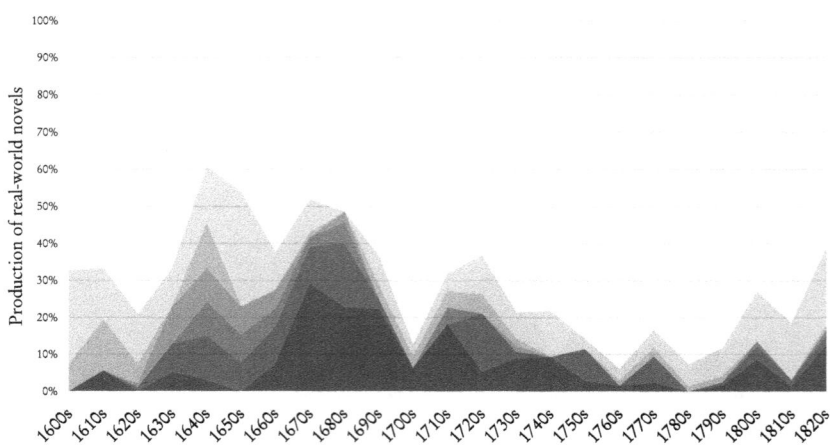

Figure 2.8 The historicity of the French novel.

seventeenth century is comparable to that of the novel of the mid-eighteenth century – in other words, on either side of the Aristotelian novel's rise and fall – the truth postures of the early nobody novel are markedly different from those of the later version. Figure 2.9 is Figure 2.1 without Aristotelian (somebody) novels, and the effect of the subtraction is notable. Figure 2.1's inclusion of Aristotelian novels, whose popularity straddles the 1650s and 1660s, contributes to the appearance of continuity: we might hazard, for example, that truth claims are simply "on the increase" as we move from the 1630s to the 1680s. But Figure 2.9 starts to undermine this interpretation by suggesting an alternate possibility – that we have in fact two periods of relatively stability, a six-decade one (1601–1660) followed by a five-decade one (1661–1710).

So, continuity or rupture? The latter possibility is bolstered by a consideration of temporal setting. Most real-world novels are set in the past or the present, of course. Most – but not all, especially before 1661, when a considerable number of novels feature settings without temporal markers. Such is the case, notably, with a genre such as pastoral: notwithstanding *L'Astrée* (d'Urfé, 1607–27), a western European sensation that has a specific historical setting, most pastorals do not. Likewise, chivalric novels tend to come with no temporal markers.[10] If we classify the production according to this feature, as in Figure 2.10, we again spot a clear trend. In the previous chapter, I was able to skirt the issue of "unspecified" settings for the simple reason that after 1680 (or, as it turns out, 1650), there are relatively few of them. But the situation before the 1650s is dramatically different. There, unspecified settings are nearly as common as contemporary settings.

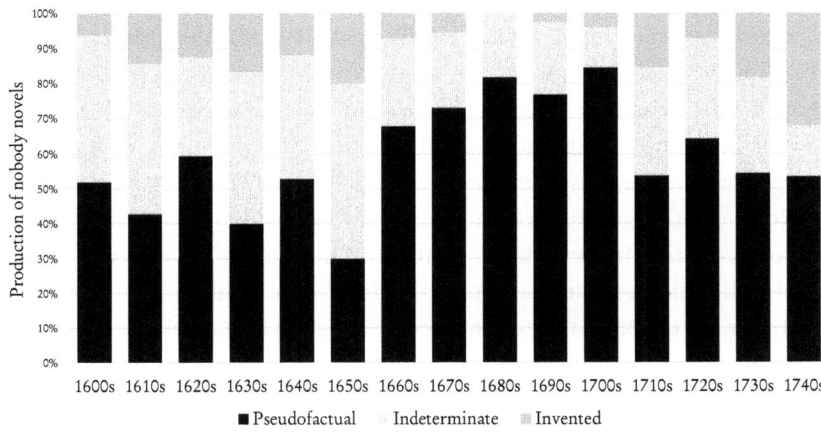

Figure 2.9 Truth postures of nobody novels (I).

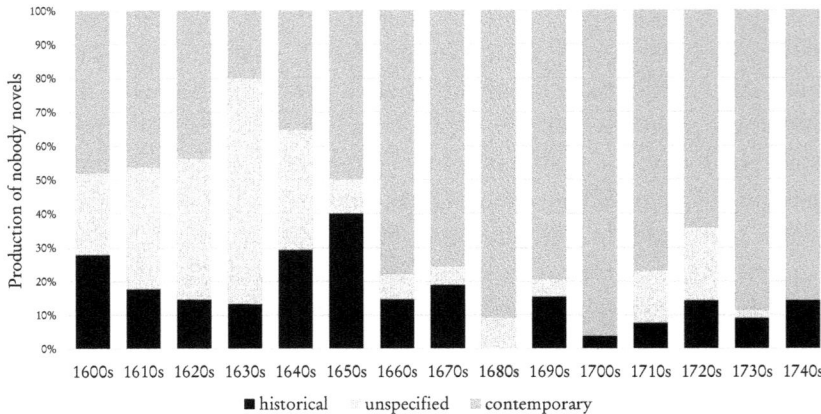

Figure 2.10 Temporal settings of nobody novels.

The likelihood of a midcentury upheaval is also enhanced by making a distinction within truth claims. In Chapter 1, I separated standard pseudofactual postures from ironic or equivocal variants. Making this particular distinction in the seventeenth century leads nowhere: ironic and equivocal truth claims are virtually nonexistent during the period. Another set of distinctions, however, is much more telling. These relate to telling "true stories" under some sort of a veil. I am not referring to the familiar warning that in the interest of innocence or modesty, authors have changed the names of the protagonists (and occasionally of the city or country where the story takes place): this commonplace is so common over the entire period covered by the present study that it is not worth tagging. The veils to which I am referring are different. The first involves a specific spin on widespread assertions of "changed names." In these novels, which I call works of "transposed" truth, novelists say they are transposing a current event into a noncontemporary setting so as to make it unrecognizable. In the second variety, authors state that names and sometimes settings have been changed but imply that readers should be able to supply the real names of recognizable contemporaries. I call these "keyed" novels, as in *roman à clef*.

No doubt the *roman à clef* is a historically broad phenomenon. It has, however, distinct instantiations. In the Enlightenment, for example, it was used politically, as antimonarchical satire.[11] Such subversive works are relatively uncommon: they are a trace presence in the novelistic landscape of the eighteenth century (and in fact none appear in my samples). The keyed novel of the seventeenth century is another matter entirely: it is usually laudatory rather than satirical, and for a number of decades, it makes up a considerable proportion of all published novels. And it differs from the more conventional true story and from novels of transposed truth by the peculiar quality of its truth claim – the latter being not so much a *pledge* that the events had really transpired but rather as an *invitation* to read apparently fanciful narratives as concerning people who could be identified by readers in the know.[12] Accordingly, the titles of these keyed novels often act as teasers, promising real stories of celebrities "under" a novelistic veneer – say, *Histoire celtique, où sous les noms d'Amindorix et de Clélanire sont comprises les principales actions de nos rois* (Hotman, 1634).[13]

These two variants on the standard pseudofactual truth affirmation are for the most part a pre-1661 phenomenon, as seen in Figure 2.11.[14] The peak of interest in these alternate truth claims comes in the 1640s, and their retreat is rapid: again, the 1660s appears to be some sort of threshold. With this information, we can nuance our understanding of truth postures in the nobody novel, confirming that their midcentury change is indeed more radical than Figure 2.9 suggested. As Figure 2.12 shows, what before looked like considerable pseudofactuality in novels before 1661 in fact hides a change: transposed and keyed novels dwindle and disappear after that date.

Yet some tendencies *do not* change from one side of this divide to the other. True, if we take "pseudofactual" in the narrower sense as shown in Figure 2.11 – that is, excluding keyed novels and novels of transposed truth – the production history of such novels from one half of the century to the other now looks quite different. But these more tightly pseudofactual novels look broadly similar, at least when it comes to temporal setting. 89 percent of seventeenth-century pseudofactual novels are contemporary

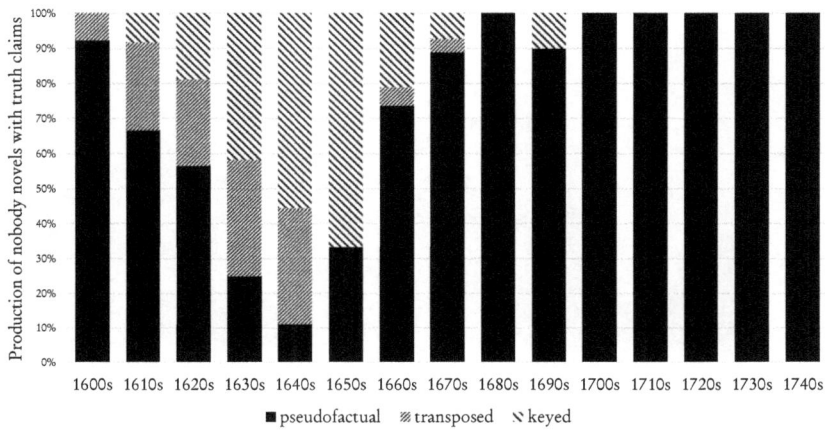

Figure 2.11 Truth claims in the nobody novel.

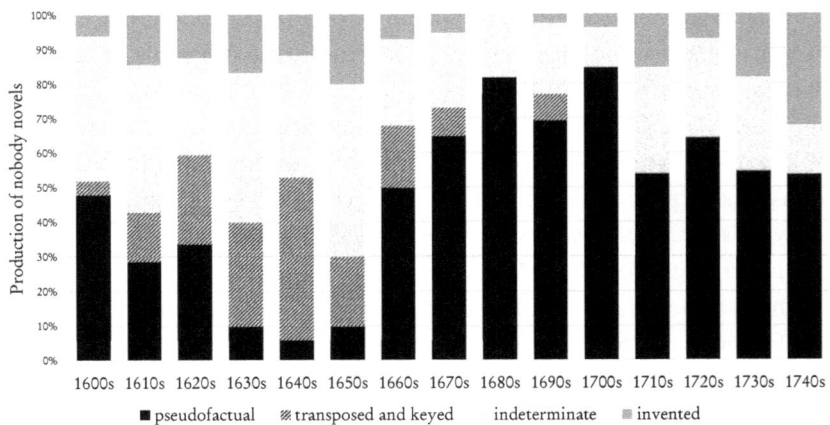

Figure 2.12 Truth postures of nobody novels (II).

novels, and that percentage remains roughly the same from the beginning to the end. The converse holds as well, since 75 percent of the period's contemporary novels are pseudofactual. As we saw in Chapter 1 (Figure 1.8, page 31), the correlation between these two characteristics breaks down after the 1720s. Before then, however, the correlation is strong, and if we were to extend Figure 1.8 back to 1601, we would see that nothing radical separates the years 1681–1730 from the years 1601–1680.[15]

Nothing, save of course the sheer increase in nobody novels set in the present. Looking back at Figure 2.11, one is tempted to speak of a new interest in truth claims. But Figure 2.13 shows that we could also phrase this as a new interest in novels set in the present since the two phenomena

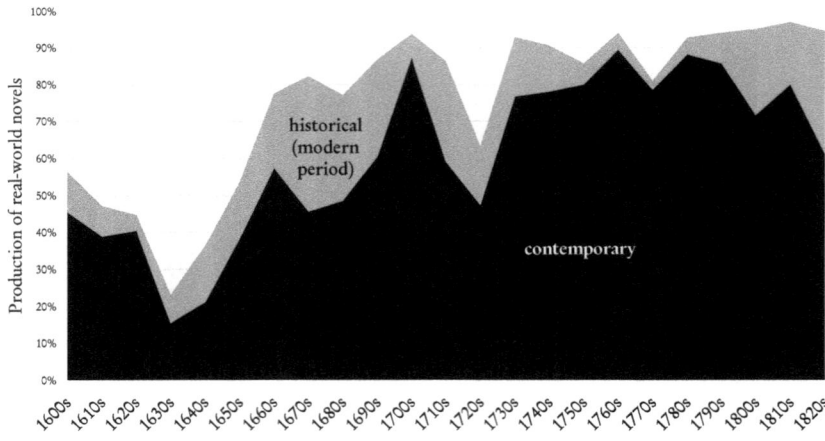

Figure 2.13 Temporal settings in the French novel.

go together. I've already spoken of a presentification within the Aristotelian novel, which becomes increasingly oriented toward modern subject matter ("modern" very broadly defined as post-Charlemagne). And now we see that the nobody novel presentifies as well. These two "presents" are not quite the same thing, since one designates in fact a type of interest in a relatively recent past. Yet whether or not we choose to call these two developments by the same name, they are largely concurrent developments. Historical novels with modern settings start their increase in the 1630s and 1640s and expand markedly in the 1670s; the rise of contemporary novels is a bit delayed but much more sudden, with market percentage soaring between the 1640s and 1660s. The cumulative effect of these roughly simultaneous movements is that by the 1660s, the temporal settings of French novels look nothing like those of the first half of the century. From Figure 2.13, it is easy to see the rapid (and more or less permanent) loss of tolerance for the type vague and far-off settings that were common in the first half of the century. (It is also obvious that such tolerance was itself variable since the novel at the beginning of the seventeenth century had modern-historical or contemporary settings half the time.)

If the French novel was ever "traditionally" something – that is, in possession of a stable truth posture passed down from generation to generation – that tradition would have to be sought out before 1601. For after that, everything seems continually up for grabs. Stability is certainly not to be found in the high rates of pseudofactuality and Aristotelianism that characterize the last third or so of the seventeenth century and that erode (in the irregular fashion described in the previous chapter) over the course of the eighteenth. I've been calling those exceptional decades a "truth bump" relative to what happens both after and before. But the bump metaphor has the disadvantage of implying a norm or mean – as if affairs in the mid-eighteenth century merely return to where they were one hundred years earlier. This is not, however, the case, since the truth postures of the novel before the 1660s look little like those in the 1730s. What can we say about the novel before the truth bump, and does the data confirm, undermine, or revise the customary way of understanding literary history?

Ordinarily, we are told that the novel replaces "romance" – or alternately that the modern novel, or the novel proper, replaces an archaic form of the novel that goes by the name of romance. People mean a lot of things when they say romance. For example, romance, peopled with heroes, is supposed to be idealist, whereas the novel, realist by definition, focuses on imperfect, everyday protagonists. Romances are also supposed to be interminably long, featuring not one or two protagonists but a gallery of characters whose full chronicling delays narrative resolution as long as possible. I will take up the romance–novel chestnut at more length in the following three chapters, which will ask whether this venerable distinction can be measured. But one salient characteristic of romance as commonly understood is of course tightly related to the problem of truth postures. This is its unbelievability, its lack of common verisimilitude, its never-never land dreaminess. Should the data in this chapter, data which show an apparent break in novelistic truth postures around the 1660s, be taken as confirmation of romance's existence?

The question can be made more precise still, for in the French context, the 1660s have long been singled out as a moment of rupture, at once literary and political — the 1660s, but more exactly 1661, the year Louis XIV decides to govern alone. As part of his quest to build a centralized, administrative, "absolutist" state, the king quickly assembles a stable of artists associated with a movement retroactively baptized (neo)classicism: the writers Racine, Molière, Boileau, and Perrault; the painter Le Brun; and the landscape architect Le Nôtre. At an additional degree of separation from the king is the novelist whose name has become synonymous with the "modern French novel"'s inception – Lafayette, author of two works of comparable contemporary fame, *La Princesse de Clèves* (1678) and *La Princesse de Montpensier* (1662). Because of its date, the latter occupies a particularly symbolic role in French literary history: it is difficult not to see this short novel, tightly focused on the documented history of the French wars of religion a century before, as a symptom of an age breaking definitively from the aesthetic and political past. Just as Louis XIII's empowered ministers and peripatetic court make him the antithesis of his son's absolutist Versailles, an older French novel – romance, or in French the *roman* – is the natural foil for Lafayette's two historically rooted princesses and the form they are said to launch – the lapidary *nouvelle*.[16]

The famed *roman–nouvelle* distinction (as well as the supposed rupture that the novel is said to represent with respect to romance) lies at the heart of the most common understandings of the novel's history and as such figures high on the list of this book's areas of inquiry. Indeed, it will be particularly important in the context of the technological explanation I develop later. Already, however, the data on truth postures is not wholly friendly to the idea of a turning point of 1661. It is of course true that the novel of the 1660s, statistically, doesn't look anything like the novel of the 1630s. However, only one measurement shows a break in the 1660s precisely: this is the percentage of pseudofactual novels (Figure 2.12). The rest suggest something at least slightly less sudden and more difficult to attribute to the "absolutist moment." Unspecified temporal settings start shrinking in the

1640s and already in the 1650s are as scarce as they are in the 1660s (Figure 2.10); meanwhile, contemporary settings show continuous gains beginning in the 1640s. Though strong "modern" Aristotelianism does make an initial push in the 1660s, its weaker variants had prepared the way starting in the 1630s and 1640s (Figure 2.6). Transposed and keyed novels recede to minority status in the 1660s; but this movement was already clear by the decade before (Figure 2.11). And so on.[17] The result is that while something clearly happens to the French novel, that something is in fact the sum result of a number of microchanges that don't all align. The safest thing to say is that the composite change that becomes obvious in the 1660s was already underway in the 1650s: the two most salient tendencies of the previous decades – toward a weakly historical novel and the growth of claims of transposed or keyed truth – peak in the 1640s. As such, even if it's possible to cling to the idea that absolutism provides rich soil for a new type of novel, the seed itself – to continue the metaphor – would seem to sprout in the chaotic, preabsolutist 1650s.

To be sure, abandoning 1661 and the idea of political–aesthetic homology does not entail renouncing the idea of romance's displacement by the novel: all the graphs really show, it could be argued, is that the displacement starts a bit earlier. However, it is important to remember that the story of romance's replacement by the novel is yet another before/after, then/now advent narrative; as such, we would expect the situation before the 1650s to exhibit broad uniformity. But if something happens in the 1650s, other things happen still earlier, so that the novel of the 1630s and 1640s actually represents a change from the 1600s and 1610s. Thus, Figure 2.7 records an early vogue for historical novels between the 1630s and the 1660s; and Figure 2.11 shows that novels prior to the 1660s had an affinity for a pair of special truth claims but also that the affinity was itself a historical development of the first half of the century. If we want to call the novel of the 1630s and 1640s "romance," we can; but thus shorn of its *longue durée*, the term can hardly do the heavy literary–historical lifting it was devised to do.

And is there really a break in the 1650s? On one level, obviously, but on another, maybe not.

The first thing to note is that the suddenness of the change traceable to the 1650s is odd. As a rule, quantitative literary history tends to work against the critical impulse to locate moments of rupture, and indeed most of the changes described in this book are relatively gradual.[18] But here, the bulk of the data seem to point to one specific decade. Why the 1650s? There is an obvious external explanation called the Fronde – the revolt against the young Louis XIV's regent and mother, Anne d'Autriche. This explanation,

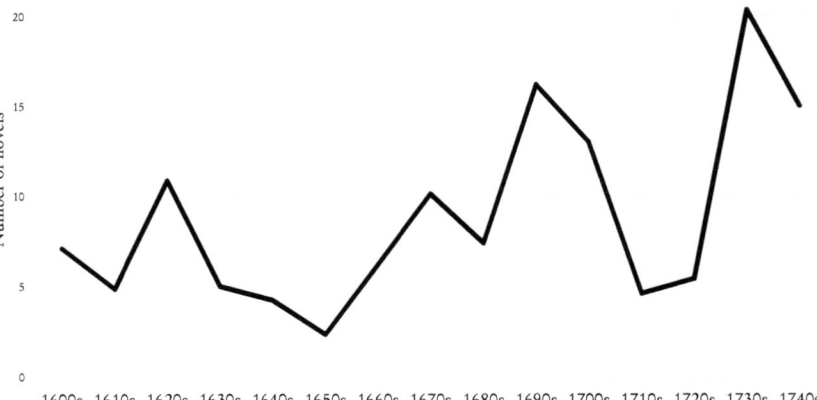

Figure 2.14 Yearly novel production, 1601–1750 (estimates).

however, is qualitatively different from explanations that would seek some sort of formal homology between absolutism and a new kind of novel. The Fronde, which lasts from 1648 to 1652, is important simply because it drastically curtails the production of novels in French, as the estimates in Figure 2.14 show.[19] One might speak, here, of a virtual extinction – a moment when people stop writing novels, surely because of the political situation. (The average of just over two novels per year in the 1650s is actually pushed up by the recovering production of the second half of the decade: no new novels at all were published in 1652 and 1653.) And the novel that emerges from the ruins is simply no longer the same novel. This is one logical explanation, then, for the fact that the growth cycle that is observable in the 1620s, 1630s, and 1640s – the growth of weak Aristotelianism and the truth postures of keys and transposed settings – is so much shorter than any other major formal trend I have found in the course of my research. This production crash also helps explain the general lack of "overlap" between the dominant novel of the 1620s, 1630s, and 1640s and the dominant novel of the 1660s, 1670s, and 1680s: here, instead of a situation where someone's rise is simultaneously someone else's fall, we have something more like a repopulation of a deserted terrain.[20] (Compare, for instance, to Figures 1.4 [page 27] and 1.11 [page 33], which show the gradual displacement of somebody novels and the alternate destinies of first-person and third-person novels.)

At the same time, this break mustn't be exaggerated, for the two key truth trends may well bridge the divide of the 1650s. The first is the pseudofactuality of the nobody novel. Figure 2.9 shows pseudofactuality increasing markedly between the 1650s and the 1660s; we might also note the stark discrepancy between the average pseudofactuality rate for 1601–1660 (46 percent) and that for 1661–1710 (77 percent). But I've already pointed out that the production of novels in the 1650s is small, and, by the same token, so is the sample – only 10 nobody novels, as compared to 17 the decade before (already not a very robust figure) and 28 the decade after. In other words, sheer chance, which always plays a role both in sampling and in the measurement of small populations, may well explain why the figure for the 1650s is not 50 or 60 percent – and had it been, we would of course be tempted to see a steady increase in pseudofactuality from the 1630s on into the 1660s and beyond. The safest thing to say is that while late-century writers were especially insistent on their novels' pseudofactuality, writers from the first half of the century were *already* fairly insistent on it. Pseudofactuality in the nobody novel increases, but there is no sea change.

Somebody novels don't change so much either. Figure 2.5 shows the impact of the Fronde on the Aristotelian historical novel: it retreats, but it then returns. Figures 2.3 and 2.5 do confirm that the Aristotelian novel that returns is no longer quite the same as the one that retreated: it prefers modern history to classical history and strongly Aristotelian protagonists to weak ones. Not quite the same, but despite the change in details and the unusual double peak, caused by the Fronde, we have here a sort of novel that rises and falls over a century or so – from the 1630s to the 1730s or 1740s. Indeed, if we want to locate a "before," here, the 1620s would seem to be the place: it is then that Aristotelian novels – save for those taking biblical or mythical subjects – were virtually unheard of.

Over the bulk of the period covered by this study, the relationship between the novel and the reality of its subject matter fluctuates a little but remains broadly consistent. Most novels are said to be true or concern known individuals; a good number contain no specific references to literal truth; and a few carry explicit admissions of invention. This last category expands notably in the 1730s and advances still more in the 1780s and 1790s; indeterminates balloon in the 1800s. Nothing in the record – not the 1790s, not the 1730s, not the 1650s – registers any tectonic "shift" of the collective cognitive paradigm. And so if we are looking for the causes behind the consistency with which nearly two centuries of novelists approached the problem of truth, let's start at the most humdrum level possible: surely literal truth was important to them. They valued it – or, rather, most people in most contexts valued it. And the prefaces of novels are littered with information on why this was so: after all, we are very frequently at pains to justify and explain our values – precisely because they are neither universal nor hardwired.

I will talk at more length about values, as well as their intersection with more artifactual constraints, in Chapter 10. But as an immediate illustration, let's consider the rise of the Aristotelian novel, whose popularity is partially responsible for the late seventeenth-century truth bump. That rise, which we've seen starting in earnest in the 1630s, was not an effect of a change in historical worldviews but rather of the application of commonplace Renaissance poetological thought to the composition of novels. Tracing that application – which surely has a rich sociological context – would of course lead us far afield. But I can offer a quick discussion of a well-known text that explicitly aligns the novel with ancient (and modern) epic. This is the preface to *Ibrahim, ou l'illustre Bassa*, usually attributed to Georges de Scudéry and published in 1641 – in other words, the moment that witnessed the explosion of interest in the Aristotelian novel at the expense of other uses of historical settings.[21] Here, Scudéry insists on *vraisemblance* as the touchstone of poetic excellence: without it, a work can have no aesthetic effect, it cannot "touch" or "please."[22] That *vraisemblance* has a number of dimensions, of which a crucial one is subject matter. Faithful to Aristotle, who stated that things that had really happened were necessarily more conducive to "conviction" than those that hadn't,[23] Scudéry says that to increase *Ibrahim*'s verisimilitude, "I wanted the foundation of my work to be historical, my main characters to be attested in true History as illustrious personages, and the wars to be real ones." This historical grounding was crucial, he reasoned, to the emotional appeal of the novel. "How can I be touched by the misfortunes of the Queen of Guindaye or of the King of Astrobatia since I know their kingdoms are nowhere on the universal map, or more precisely, in the realm of things?" Such fabricated royalty will not do, and accordingly, Scudéry's eponymous hero is Pargali Ibrahim Pasha (1493–1536), the first Grand Vizier of the Ottoman Empire.

Thus, we have here a claim for the importance of what I'm calling Aristotelianism, an importance attributable not to the abstract allegiance to "doctrine" often associated with French classicism but rather to the pragmatic need to interest audiences in characters and action. And being an affair of pragmatism, Aristotelianism – like the descriptive and pragmatic *Poetics* itself – was quite elastic. Here too, *Ibrahim* is instructive. Scudéry says that his choice of major historical actors will *donner plus de vraisemblance aux choses* [give more verisimilitude to things], with the *plus*, here, indicating that Aristotelianism is not an all or nothing proposition: unknown actors can have verisimilitude too – they'll just have less of it. Variable verisimilitude is a good thing for Scudéry because despite his insistence upon the attested illustriousness of his main characters, the heart of the novel is in fact a fabrication: the two young lovers in whose story the historical Ibrahim himself is but a player are historical nobodies. Scudéry takes pains to point out the illustrious birth he attributes to them; but he discreetly passes over the matter of their not being "attested in true History."[24] Yet, the fact is that such contradictions were never fatal for Aristotelian reasoning: the assumption was that nonroyal characters did not need to have historical referents because such individuals – from aristocrats to commoners – could plausibly be said to have escaped the attention of any chronicler.[25] History's silence is therefore an invitation for the poet to invent. Attested subjects are the best, yes; but all sorts of grafts onto the trunk of history can be made to bear productive poetic fruit.

So behind the Aristotelian novel is argument – reasoned, though obviously not unanswerable; also variable, since Scudéry is but one voice among many; and surely motivated, socially speaking, with Scudéry's point being that some people's novels are more prestigious than others'. But the relation between arguments and practices is notoriously ambiguous. We don't always do what we say we want to do; and we often reverse-engineer explanations for what we have already done (prefaces being a great place for this). Our practices are thus linked to our values and rationales but not reducible to them. *Ibrahim* is a prime example: Scudéry doesn't really practice what he preaches.[26] And indeed, over the course of its career, the Aristotelian novel evolves. It does not merely become more popular, it *homogenizes* as it becomes more popular. Figure 2.8 makes this quite obvious. In the 1640s, 1650s, and 1660s, the Aristotelian novel is a cluster of related practices: temporal setting varies as does the "strength" of the protagonists' Aristotelianism. But the form's second and higher peak corresponds to a much more uniform practice: novelists strongly prefer strong Aristotelian novels, especially those set in nearer periods. (Numerous examples of this apparent "isomorphism" – the sociological term for the tendency of competing organizations to come to resemble one another – will be found throughout Part II.) In other words, the Aristotelian rationale is voiced early on, but it does not dictate a single practice. Although people do write the novels that correspond to their beliefs about what novels should do, their writing also appears to have an *artifactual* dimension. Writers need to invent forms, with invention understood as a negotiated process happening over time and between many different actors.

The history of truth postures cannot be the history of how people have variously conceived "fictionality." In fact, until the tail end of the eighteenth century, I don't think there is in France any dramatic variation in the general (but not universal) valuation of literal truth, which is really just to say the belief that the best object of literature – the most prestigious object, the most morally and emotionally affecting object – is real people. What does vary a lot are the artifacts invented with that valuation in mind. In other words, until now, I have been studying something on the order of content – not content in a generic sense (gothic ghosts, sentimental tears, romance heroics) or in the sense of topoi (love at first sight, abduction by pirates, the doppelganger) but on the much more abstracted level of somebodies and nobodies. This allows us to compare the truth postures of novels written at vastly different moments and that in fact look little like one another on a formal level (and indeed on many other levels of content besides the renown of their protagonists). Yet we've already observed that under the fluctuations of Aristotelianism, pseudofactuality, and so on, are formal artifacts that arise, have their day, and then more or less die out: the Aristotelian novel, the document novel, the specific third-person novel that spreads in the late eighteenth century. (The die-off of this last artifact cannot register in my data, since it postdates the 1820s.) These – and a few others – are the subject of the next group of chapters.

PART II

3   Novel v. Romance I

Heliodorian Insetting

Around 1660, it is often claimed, a mass literary extinction occurs in France. The *roman héroïque*, characterized by its multivolume heft and larger-than-life protagonists, suddenly falls from fashion; then, the landscape of fiction is colonized by a shorter and more realistic form, the mammalian *nouvelle*. For scholars of the French novel, this is a dramatic moment – "a complete reconfiguration of the generic system of prose fiction," according to one commentator.[1] Moreover, it's a threshold whose crossing was commented on at the time. As a result, our retrospective impression of a break is confirmed by local informants, already celebrating the victory of modern taste – their collective awakening to the fundamental and now embarrassing immaturity of a previously dominant and prestigious cultural form.

The *roman–nouvelle* distinction, which will be the subject of this and the following two chapters, is a vital one for literary history: it is the French face of the familiar English opposition between *romance* and *novel*, and like the latter, it is asked to do a lot of literary–historical work. It should go without saying that my task here will be to see if we can measure the distinction. And indeed, we can. But as with the measurement of pseudofactuality's decline, having actual decade-by-decade numbers is going to put a lot of pressure on the traditional scholarly narratives surrounding this change: the change exists but not really as usually understood. Already we can see some basic empirical reasons to question the idea of a watershed around 1660. Recalling what we've seen in Chapter 2, much unites novelistic practice across the 1660 threshold. And more generally, little if any of the data we've examined up to now has documented a sudden extinction; on the contrary, decline is typically slow, as if dominant forms possessed a kind of cultural inertia. And on the growth side, we've seen how long it takes the document novel – to give just one example – to gain a foothold. Can it really be that one dominant form was replaced, essentially overnight, by another? To anticipate a conclusion that only the technological hypothesis developed in Chapter 10 will bring fully into focus, there are indeed *romans* and *nouvelles*, but the relation between these two literary artifacts is in fact a *contiguous* one.

The traits long associated with the novels on one side or another of the purported 1660 divide are varied. Du Plaisir, the most quoted of the local informants I've referred to, provides a good guide to the main issues. In his 1683 *Sentiments sur les lettres*, he adumbrates the various sources of the new and for him entirely justified French aversion for the kind of novels that not very long before had been a mark of French prestige. Here is his list of problems with *romans*: "their prodigious length, their mixing of so many disparate stories, their overly numerous characters, subject matter that is too historically remote, their confusing architecture, their dearth of verisimilitude, [and] the extravagance of their plots."[2] The last two issues are related and have to do with the kind of moral believability typically associated with classical *vraisemblance*; I'm going to set aside these traits, which are obviously challenging to measure. The other issues, however, are much more traceable, and many of them are in fact ways of describing the same fundamental formal property. For aside from the issue of subject matter – its historical remove, which we've already had occasion to examine in Chapter 2 – everything relates to narrative economy. Excessive length, first; plus too many different narratives concerning too many characters; and then what Du Plaisir calls the *la construction* of the works, which I translate as architecture. Indeed, if the *roman* was long – I'll quantify this presently – it wasn't so just because it had more characters and sprawling "baroque" plots. More important, it had the structural peculiarity of being largely composed of inset narratives – not digressions pursued by the main narrator but rather backstory supplied by the characters themselves. These insets could be hundreds of pages long – often so long that tellers needed to break them off and, after nourishment and rest, resume them the next day. Characters could relate their own story or someone – a confidant, a servant, a relative – could do it for them. The insets could be absolutely vital to the comprehension of the main plot; others related to the main plot only thematically, as echo or counterpoint; many were purely tangential, a kind of narrative "bonus track."[3]

Du Plaisir singled out insets for chiding. "No one recites stories in novels anymore," he wrote, with a relief bordering on the cognitive: in the old *roman*, keeping track of who was speaking drained a reader's energy. Besides, reasoned Du Plaisir, for the creation of suspense, the best policy was to get us interested in following the hero's fate straight to the end. The old *roman*'s "confusing architecture" of multiplied inset narratives was in fact also geared toward generating suspense, but the tactic, thought Du Plaisir, was a bad one. "The tiresome beauty of starting a work by its end," he continues, "has fallen from fashion."[4] To be precise, however, the works he skewers didn't start from the end, they started from the middle – *in medias res*. The *in medias res* beginning went hand in hand with inset narratives; indeed, they made the insets necessary. In such novels, the reader encountered at the outset a sort of enigma – usually revolving around the identity of the protagonists – which was then elucidated through the characters' exchange of narrative.

Du Plaisir's use in this context of the word "beauty," however qualified, is important: the inset structure was, from the beginning, what gave the French novel its aesthetic bona fides. And that beginning we can locate with unusual precision. In 1547, Amyot published his French translation of Heliodorus' *Aethiopica*, a third- or fourth-century Greek work that had been saved – with all the improbability of a romance heroine's rescue – from the sack of Buda in 1526. Humanists took great interest in classical artifacts, obviously, and a series of Greek novels were published and translated in these decades. But the volume Amyot translated in 1547 had a fortune unequalled by any of these others, even Amyot's other translation coup, Longus' pastoral *Daphnis and Chloe*. And what set it apart for Amyot and subsequent generations was precisely the narrative architecture that Du Plaisir was later to chide. France's native production of "poorly sewn" novels – and here Amyot was clearly taking aim at chivalric works – struck the humanist as akin to "the delirium of some madman's feverish dream."[5] (The filiation between this remark and the spirit of *Don Quixote* has been noted by at least one critic.[6]) Heliodorus, by contrast, gave us masterly Aristotelian plotting: a beginning, a middle, and an end, only – and this was, for a novelist, the stroke of genius – not in that order. His novel's *in media res* gambit excited in readers a desire to know both the backstory and the conclusion, maintaining what Amyot called the "suspension of the mind" and what we might call simply suspense. As such, the *Aethiopica* partook of the prestige of the *Odyssey* and the *Aeneid* (which had likely been Heliodorus's model in the first place). This – unlike infinitely extendable chivalric works of the late Middle Ages such as *Amadis of Gaul* (attrib. Montalvo, pub. 1508)– was truly a novel a humanist could love.[7]

Such is, then, the obvious origin of the narrative architecture that by the 1680s was but a cumbersome relic. But how, exactly, was the Heliodorian form adopted (and adapted) in France? How dominant did it really become? Was Du Plaisir right in saying that no one in the 1680s used insets anymore? And are modern critics, piggybacking on him, right to situate its abandonment in the 1660s – precisely the moment (and could this really be an accident?) of the triumph of Louis XIV's absolutism?[8]

For maximum context, Figure 3.1 records inset novels – by which I mean novels that feature insets and not novels that are themselves set into larger texts – as a percentage of the entire production of real-world novels over the

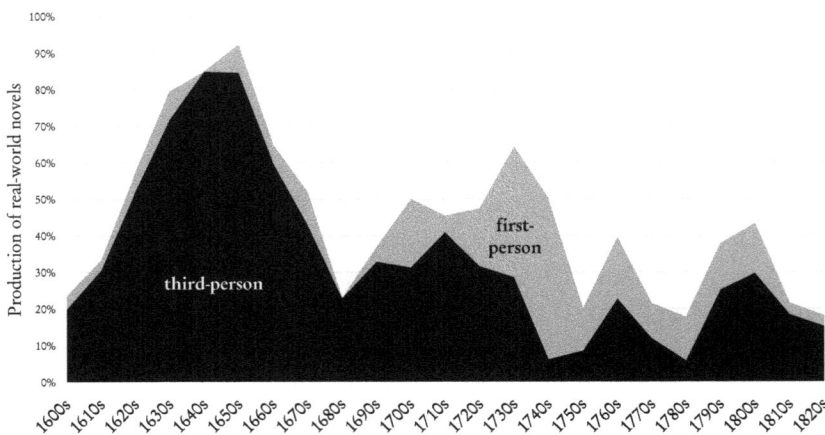

Figure 3.1 Novels containing inset narratives.

period covered by this study. It includes not only novels patently modeled on Heliodorus but also those with other types of insets, which I will itemize presently.[9] Novels are broken out by the narration type of the frame narrative. The shifting proportions of third- and first-person inset novels is expected: they follow the popularity of third- and first-person novels more generally. Indeed, if one averages the data for the entire period, narrative person has no influence whatsoever on insetting: first- and third-person novels are each inset precisely 45 percent of the time. Interestingly, this comparability holds well over different periods within the overall span: for example, in the seventeenth century, first-person novels are inset 50 percent of the time and third-person novels 51 percent; from the 1780s on, insetting rates drop for both narrative types, to 34 and 33 percent, respectively.

Figure 3.1 does appear to give us a good idea of where Du Plaisir was coming from: he was writing in 1683, and sure enough, the 1680s is a low point for the practice.[10] But the graph also seems to contradict what literary history has done with his insider's report. The 1660s, after all, don't seem especially special (they are merely the start of a decline, after a peak in the 1650s). And upon inspection, we should notice that Du Plaisir himself never exactly singled out that decade as pivotal: "Little histories [*histoires*] have entirely replaced the big romances [*romans*]," he declares, but the replacement need not be interpreted as the result of sudden and transfiguring revulsion for the outgoing form, much less situated precisely in the 1660s. It's as if modern critics, entranced by the near simultaneous appearance of the last volume of Scudéry's long, inset *Clélie* (1660) and Lafayette's short and noninset *La Princesse de Montpensier* (1662), and by the fact that the decision of Louis XIV to govern alone (1661) separates them both, can only read Du Plaisir's text as confirming a rupture they have other reasons to believe in. Those reasons, however, are not empirical. They are based instead on the conviction that literary artifacts must be homologous with respect to the socioeconomic structures of their time – that ideology is form. In this particular case, the idea is that the abandonment of the supposedly unruly, inset *roman* is of a piece with the interrelated arrival of classicism (Boileau: "*Ce qui se conçoit bien s'énonce clairement*," or, "When we properly conceive of something, we express it clearly"[11]) and absolutism (the panoptic sight lines of Versailles and Louis's centralized administration more generally). Leaving behind the narrative profusion of the *roman* for the linearity of the *nouvelle* is thus part of "the march toward monarchical centralization [...] and the triumph of so-called classical aesthetics."[12] Yet, in the 1670s, over 50 percent of novels are inset novels; and this insetting, though it will flag (precisely around the year [1682] that sees Louis XIV installed definitively at Versailles!), reprises its popularity over the first half of the thoroughly postclassical eighteenth century.

One thing that the sheer regularity of the inset novel's trajectory over the period from the 1600s to the 1680s should suggest is that something specific is happening there, as opposed to later, when the ups and downs become more haphazard. In other words, the kind of insets that return following the trough of the 1680s may well not be the kind that left. More specifically, all the novels in Figure 3.1, inset though they may be, are not necessarily *Heliodorian* novels of the type Du Plaisir criticizes. Let us call the latter works Type 1 inset novels: the narratives contributed by multiple characters serve to flesh out a plot which otherwise would be incomplete.

The first thing we learn from Figure 3.2 is that the vogue for inset novels in the seventeenth century is more properly a vogue for a specific type of inset novel. Without the "Heliodorian," or Type 1, novel, the proportion of inset novels wouldn't change much over the course of the seventeenth century; on the other hand, the second rise of the inset novel – the one that starts in the 1690s – would still be perceptible. Another thing visible from Figure 3.2 is that the Heliodorian novel has a very different baseline than inset novels more generally, which at the start of our period already make up over 20 percent of the production. Type 1 insets, however, are barely present in the 1600s: 2 percent of the production, which, it turns out, is just one novel. This would suggest that the story of the French Heliodorian novel is essentially a seventeenth-century one.

This rather belated development – a full half-century after Amyot's translation of the *Aethiopica* – deserves scrutiny. As my samples stop at

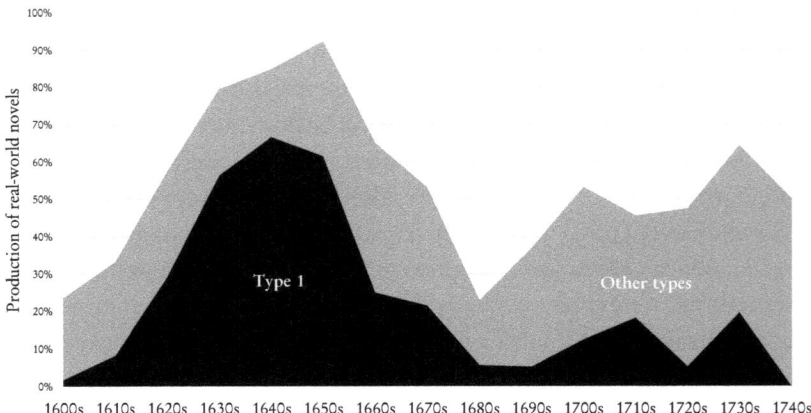

Figure 3.2 Inset novel types.

1601, the following remarks are based on more traditional literary history, which has long documented the influence of Heliodorus on European literature. In France, the uptake was not long in coming. In 1555, Colet titles his translation of the chivalric *Florando de Inglaterra* (1545; Anonymous) *L'Histoire palladienne*, a fairly obvious reference to the title used by Amyot in his translation – *L'Histoire éthiopique*, which in any case is evoked explicitly in the work's preface. Colet, however, was just trying to dress up his *Amadis* imitation in fashionable Heliodorian garb: it has none of the structural peculiarities of the Greek novel, and another five years go by before the appearance of an original French novel actually composed with the Heliodorian pattern in mind. This is Aneau's *Alector, ou le coq* (1560), which patently displays its difference from the chivalric tradition with an *in medias res* beginning and an abundance of inset narratives. Despite this promising beginning, however, there is no follow-up: neither *Alector* nor the numerous critical reflections on the graces of the *ordo artificialis* tempt any imitators until the tail end of the century.[13] *Alector* is a dead-end.

It is only on its second introduction that Heliodorian insetting takes root in French soil and does so through two distinct paths. The first consists of explicit imitations of the Greek novel. The inaugural text of the second French uptake of Heliodorus was in fact something more than an imitation: it was a hoax. In a variety of authenticating paratexts, Fumée informs the reader of *Du vrai et parfait amour* (1598) that the novel is a translation of a Greek original – a pre-Christian original that antedates all the known Greek novels.[14] And unsurprisingly, Fumée composes the work according to the insetting I've been calling Type 1. But Fumée stands out from the authors who, in his wake, will offer imitations: even in works that clearly reference the Greek novel in general and Heliodorus in particular, the inset pattern is not observed with such care. Hérembert's 1599 *Les Aventureuses et Fortunées Amours de Pandion et d'Yonice*, for example, is essentially a calque of Achilles Tatius's second-century *Leucippe and Clitophon*, in which a first-person narrator contemplating a painting is drawn into conversation by a nearby young man, who proceeds to recount his life. Yet, Herembert's version completely eliminates the inset structure of the original.[15] Similarly, in 1600 appears *Les Parfaites Affections*, whose Greek filiation is indicated by its title (which echoes the title of the work "translated" by Fumée); its *in medias res* opening, however, gives way not to the multiple flashbacks that prolong the enigma but rather to one long inset that apprises the reader of the protagonist's back story in one fell swoop.[16] And if the title of Du Lisdam's *Histoire ionique* (1602) is an obvious homage to the *Histoire éthiopique*, the book's insetting is weak in comparison to its model: while a final short inset narrative does clear up all identities, most of the first-person tales told by characters met by the protagonists have no direct link to the main plot. These are the most obvious imitations of the Greek novel in the years before 1611.

Yet Heliodorian insetting also traveled a different, less obvious path.[17] This path led through the forests of pastoral, straight to the one third-person Type 1 inset novel in my sample from the 1600s. Europe's top-shelf writers didn't, it turns out, write imitations of Greek novels but instead integrated the latter's narrative inventions into the fashionable pastoral genre, whose foundational text is Sannazaro's *Arcadia* (1504). The *Arcadia* contained no insetting whatsoever, but many of the major pastorals from the second half of the century do: Montemayor's *Diana* (1559), Cervantes's *Galatea* (1585), and Sidney's *Arcadia*. The last is a particularly telling example. The first version of the text, written in the 1570s, contained some minor insets, as well a scene evidently modeled on the *Aethiopica*; the work's overall structure, however, mirrored drama's five acts. By contrast, the much-expanded *New Arcadia*, posthumously published in 1590, is fully structured by insets, of which there are eleven.[18] Although not every pastoral of the period displays this formal trait – and some use different, non-Heliodorian insetting techniques[19] – there's little question that a pastoralist of ambition would be familiar with and tempted by the technique.

One such ambitious pastoralist is d'Urfé, whose monumental *L'Astrée* is the single novel from the 1600s sample classified as a Type 1 inset novel. (*L'Astrée*'s first volume appears in 1607.) D'Urfé's use of inset narratives one-ups even Heliodorus: their function isn't only to resolve the central enigma involving the eponymous shepherdess and her lover Céladon but in addition to weave into that main plot a huge array of characters. The latter tell their own stories, which in some cases directly cross paths with those of the main lovers and which often serve as a kind of thematic counterpoint: *L'Astrée* thus becomes a kind of encyclopedia of different ways of loving – and acquires in the process its encyclopedic dimensions.

Though the success of *L'Astrée* was of course enormous, it is no doubt impossible to isolate its precise responsibility for the practice that would come to dominate novel production in France. After all, exposure of later audiences to the structure came not only through d'Urfé, but also, for example, through *The Trials of Persiles and Sigismunda* (1617), Cervantes's masterfully Heliodorian "other" novel, whose long popularity we now tend to forget.[20] And of course, the *Aethiopica* itself was continually being read and translated. It would therefore be dangerous to argue that because the popular *L'Astrée* was the only Type 1 inset novel of the 1600s, it should therefore be considered the "trunk" of the tree whose arborescence is seen in Figure 3.2. In fact, pastoral novels did not have a terribly bright future, and in the main, the Heliodorian inset novels that prosper in from the 1620s to the 1650s are Mediterranean in scope: they tend to feature substantial, usually maritime, displacements, taking protagonists from Gibraltar to the Near East. I have not attempted to quantify the two paths (the "Greek" [or Mediterranean] and the pastoral). Nevertheless, it seems safe to conclude that although the device *could* be uncoupled from such settings – occasionally with *L'Astrée*'s spectacular success – there was for whatever reason a strong pull back to the Heliodorian original. In other words, what was influential about *L'Astrée* – in the sense of reproducible – was its insetting, not its "pastorality."

One clue to this influence can be gleaned from a typographic innovation, present in *L'Astrée* but otherwise virtually unused in other inset novels of the decade or, to my knowledge, before: the titled inset. That is, the stories told in *L'Astrée* have individual titles, centered and offset from the main text: *Histoire de Ligdamon*, *Histoire de Célion et de Bellinde*, and so on.[21] And this innovation, apparently introduced by d'Urfé, eventually becomes a nearly inevitable trait of the inset novel, especially the Type 1 inset novel. Figure 3.3 shows its spread.[22] The bar for the 1600s is of course made up of *L'Astrée* alone – the only Type 1 inset novel, which has titled insets. From there, however, we can see titled insets spread at a pace similar to that of Type 1 insets in general: the proportion of titled insets to untitled insets in this class of novels roughly mirrors the proportion of the class to all third-person novels, with steady increases until the 1640s. As Type 1 inset novels become more popular, titling the insets also becomes more popular; and once established, this practice becomes a standard feature of Type 1 novels.

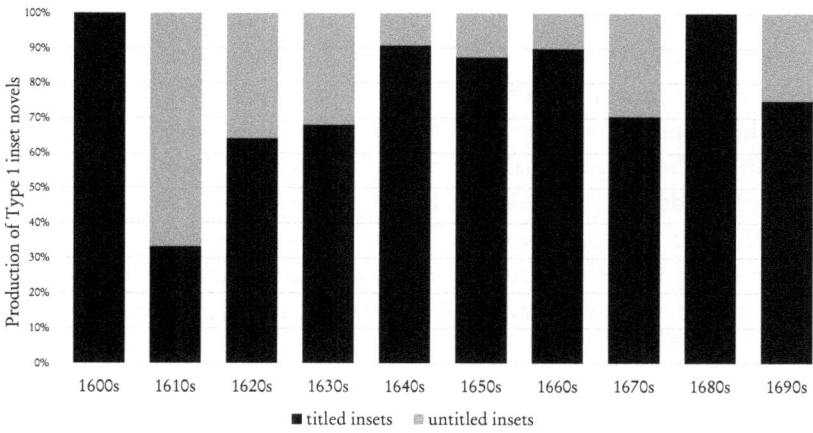

Figure 3.3 Titled insets in Type 1 novels.

Let's take a closer look at other types of inset novels, the ones that compete with Type 1 novels. I have identified five, and to make them visible – many of them are fairly minor variants – I am now going to plot inset novels alone, allowing us to better see the types that are gaining and losing popularity. In Figure 3.4, we see again Type 1 novels, along with two other variants that can plausibly be related to the Greek novel. The dominance of Type 1 novels is of course reflected here, along with the generally later success of two other types, both of which present a simpler architecture. Type 2 novels are similar to Type 1 novels in that they use insetting to furnish information that is absolutely crucial to the reader's understanding of the overall plot.

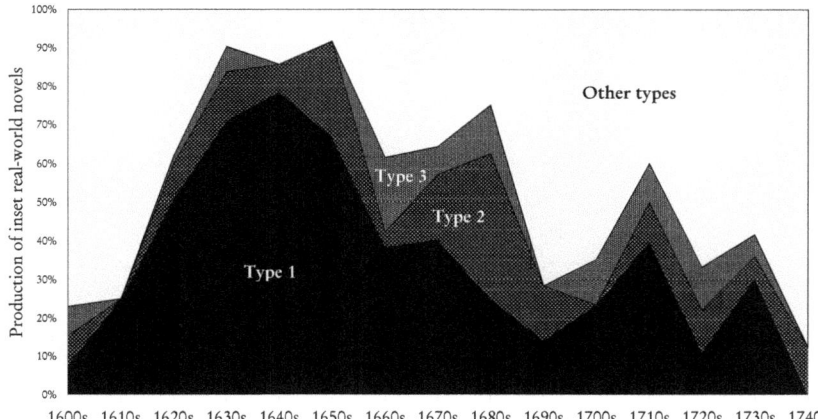

Figure 3.4 Inset novel types (breakdown I).

In contrast with Type 1 novels, however, Type 2 novels contain only one (or in rare cases two) major inset narratives: as such, they do not give the same impression of a narrative web. Type 3 novels are simpler still. They feature an actionless frame narrative in which one character recounts his or her personal story to another. (Occasionally, that other character then reciprocates.) Not exactly Heliodorian, such insetting does nonetheless have a Greek antecedent: Achilles Tatius's *Clitophon and Leucippe*, mentioned above, in which a first-person frame narrator meets a young man who proceeds to tell the story of his amorous misfortunes.[23] And both Type 2 and Type 3 novels increase their share of the inset novel "market" only after the Heliodorian novel is well established. It's as if the latter, as it declines, breaks down into these less complicated, stripped-down variants.

If insetting is *concentrated* in Type 2 and Type 3 novels, Type 4 novels can be thought of as *diluted*. Type 4 novels resemble the first three types in that they feature characters who tell either their own stories or those of people to whom they are close (homodiegetic narratives, in narratological parlance). By contrast, these insets are not vital to the comprehension of the novel's plot: while they extend the storyworld outward in new directions, the center of that storyworld is not to be found in the insets but instead on the main narrative level. Prune away the insets of a Type 1, 2 or 3 novel and you have a mangled narrative; a Type 4 novel, so pruned, simply becomes more focused.

Judging by the historical distribution of this variant visible in Figure 3.5, it appears to be easier to "master" than the marquetry of Type 1: its presence is felt quickly. Of course, one possibility is that such insetting might have been,

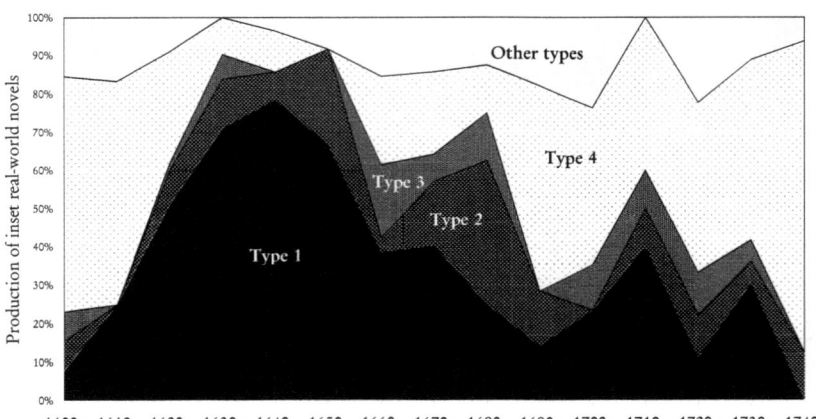

Figure 3.5 Inset novel types (breakdown II).

before 1601, a constant, if low-level, presence in French novels, one whose use has nothing to do with the influence of Heliodorus. But a qualitative survey of the works appearing in the very thorough descriptive bibliography of Frank Greiner suggests that this is not the case.[24] The most probable scenario is that the first decade of our sample does indeed represent an increase in insetting, and the first way most writers use insets is by making them an addition to the main narrative, not an integral part of it. The subsequent runaway success of Types 1 to 3 would seem to come mostly at the expense of Type 4 insetting, which is nearly squeezed out during the peak years of 1631 to 1660. A bit later, as people start to abandon the Heliodorian novel, Type 4 inset novels make a comeback, and indeed their healthy market percentage in the 1690s – the strongest in 70 years – is indicative of a bright future: a "loser" for most of the seventeenth century, Type 4 insetting proves supple and useful and survives long after its more spectacularly successful relative is dead and buried.

The remaining two inset types comprise little of the total production, and in addition would seem to come from more indigenous narrative stock. Type 5 novels have a *Decameron*-like structure, where the main narrative level contains little to no action and serves as a frame in which characters exchange stories (sometimes related but more typically unrelated to the characters themselves).[25] Type 6 novels, probably the least interesting and at any rate rarest of all the variants, do have action on the main narrative level; insets are limited to pauses, during which characters tell stories unrelated to them (heterodiegetic narratives).[26]

According to Figure 3.6, Types 5 and 6 are a residual presence over practically the entire span, but they are, like Type 4 novels, squeezed by the

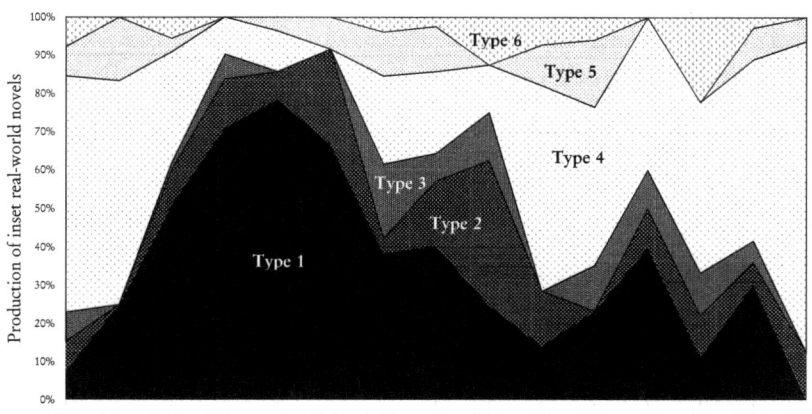

Figure 3.6 Inset novel types (breakdown III).

success of Greek insetting. Indeed, we remark in this series of graphs a clear phenomenon of homogenization: as a form becomes hegemonic, it becomes more uniform. Better, a "form" – here, the inset novel – should be understood as a nebula of related but not identical artifacts. The peak popularity of the form corresponds to a kind of homogenization of practice: within the nebula, one particular artifact effectively marginalizes the others. But that marginalization is only temporary. After the wave of popularity, the nebula rediversifies. Heterogeneity, homogeneity, followed by heterogeneity again – at least until Type 4 inset novels take over, much further down the road.

Six types, then: and I could have tried to be more precise still, in ways that might well confirm the correlation of homogenization. Notably, within Type 1 novels, we might have been able to discriminate between those that start with a narrative enigma along the lines of the *Aethiopica* and those that do not. (This is to say that in many narratives, the "puzzle" whose pieces are ultimately assembled isn't given up front, to the reader, but emerges in the course of the characters' interaction. Alternately put, the reader doesn't know at first that the narrative does in fact begin *in medias res*.) Also, within Type 1 novels, we could count those that take place against the pan-Mediterranean backdrop featured in the *Aethiopica* – one that allows for trademark scenes of abduction by pirates – and thus distinguish them from those with much more domestic scenery. My suspicion is that this additional precision would simply point again to the decades 1630s–1650s as particularly Heliodorian: if you are still practicing Heliodorian insetting in the 1690s, the chances are that you're doing so in a much looser manner.[27] (An example: Bédacier's *La Comtesse de Mortane* [1699], in which two Parisian aristocrats, having decided to avoid the king's festivities in Fontainebleau, go off to the countryside and tell each other their troubles, which will eventually be sorted out through the intervention – and inset narratives – of other characters.) Which is also to say that some narrative devices are detachable with respect to their model and that it is precisely such adaptability that explains why some devices prosper longer than others.

"No one recites stories in novels anymore," wrote Du Plaisir in 1683. Strictly speaking, he was wrong about his present moment: even in the 1680s, the lowest point for inset novels since the first decade of the century, nearly a quarter of all novels contained insets of one sort or another. And he was wrong about the future: inset novels in the 1690s comprise over a third of the production of novels and regain considerable ground from there. But from another point of view, Du Plaisir *was* right: a certain type of inset novel was, for all practical purposes, dead, and it stayed dead. This was the traditional Heliodorian novel – the Type 1 inset novel that wove multiple

3 Heliodorian Insetting

"flashbacks" together in order to produce a narrative. Death, however, may not be the best metaphor: the hegemony of Heliodorian insetting simply weakens, or breaks apart, allowing the proliferation of a variety of models, none of which will ever achieve the popularity of the first but all of which, collectively, will remain an important part of the novelistic landscape for well over a century to come. Around the Heliodorian shipwreck bobs a lot of narrative debris that will be gathered up and put to use by later creators.

Insets were at the heart of Du Plaisir's objection to the old *roman*, for they were creators of narrative dispersion and confusion: so many characters told tangential stories that the novel became unwieldy and the reader lost track of who was speaking and what was happening in the main plot. But insets didn't *have* to have such an effect: indeed, for promoters such as Amyot, they gave a text like the *Aethiopica* a properly Aristotelian form, in contrast to the purely accumulative logic of the chivalric novel and its episodes. Arguably, more than two different historical reactions to one single artifact, or the simple cycle of enthusiasm followed by lassitude, we may well have to consider the possibility that Type 1 novels, however clearly derived from Heliodorus, had become, through a process of amplification, something a least partially different.

In truth, it's not hard to find confirmation that at the peak of its popularity, Heliodorian insetting was, depending on your perspective, either not what it once was or else much, much more. After all, the *Aethiopica* featured six characters narrating stories; by the novel's midpoint, these insets had elucidated the obscured identity of the heroine Chariclea, whose story then proceeded to unfold linearly. But Gerzan's *Histoire africaine* (1627) has 17 narrators; La Calprenède's *Cléopâtre* (1646), 22; and each will use insets not simply to flesh out one single, narratively crucial enigma but instead to intercalate a variety of subplots, while postponing resolution of the main plot until the very end. One could therefore say that the Heliodorian novel, which initially seemed the remedy for the infinite extensibility of the native chivalric novel, had itself been reengineered to be extensible as well. From this viewpoint, the diversification of inset types after the 1640s may have resulted from attempts to prune this overgrowth. The ones that gain the most ground are, as a rule, quite focused: Type 2 novels have one speaker (occasionally two) telling a tale vital to the understanding of the central hero (or two central heroes); Type 3 novels are equally focused, with their single-subject plot entirely contained in the inset; even Type 4 novels, which do try to preserve the old value of narrative "diversity," carefully hierarchize insets lest they overwhelm the main plot.

Something no doubt happens *within* Type 1 novels over the course of their triumph in France, something to which Du Plaisir and others react. I have not kept close enough track of insets to follow this evolution: it would help to know how many insets each Type 1 novel contains and the ratio of pages narrated by characters to pages narrated by the third-person narrator; it would be equally interesting to know the ratio of insets directly related to the resolution of the main plot to those devoted to purely tangential back stories.[28] In lieu of these statistics, however, I have kept track of length, a feature which looms large in Du Plaisir's critique. Du Plaisir suggests that insetting and prolixity are inseparable; and the new novel he trumpets is not only linear, it is short: "Little histories [*histoires*] have entirely destroyed big romances [*romans*]," to recall his opening salvo.[29] Does the spread of Heliodorian insetting actually correlate with length? Are other types of insetting compatible with shorter forms? Could Type 1 novels be in fact "shrunk" back to something like the economic form Amyot appreciated? The case of Lafayette, author of the *Princesse de Clèves*, provides a semicanonical hint that this might be possible: her *Zayde* (1670–71) is a self-consciously Helidorian novel that is not particularly long.

Graphing the length of all real-world novels for the period presents us with a familiar curve.[30] The congruence of Figure 3.7 with respect to earlier graphs of inset novels is manifest. Insets and length both peak in the 1640s; by the 1680s, both are at a low ebb. We can also see a substantial discrepancy between median and average length in the 1640s, 1650s, and 1660s: length is more strongly variable in these decades. A calculation of standard deviation from the mean reveals that in fact four decades stand out – the three mentioned above and the 1600s. These are years in which a few novels are very, very long.[31] There is some discrepancy, then,

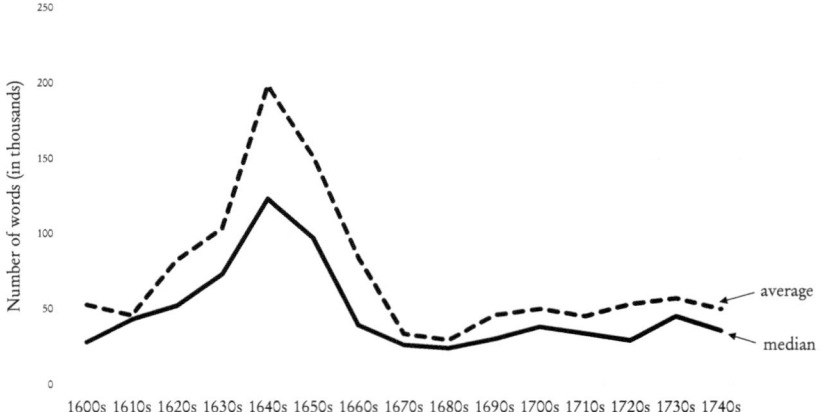

Figure 3.7 Length of real-world novels (I).

between general behavior and outlier behavior. Notably, very long novels are more present in the 1660s than one would expect, given the median for the decade.

Unsurprisingly, the similar shape of the length graph and the inset graph is no accident. The novels that really push up the length figures are also novels that contain insets, as Figure 3.8 demonstrates. Noninset novels show surprisingly minimal variation. Some shortening occurs, but it starts already in the 1640s, after a peak which is hardly vertiginous; the closing decades of the century, meanwhile, do not look much different from the opening decades. And the homogeneity with respect to length is remarkable: this sort of novel has no major outliers. The situation for inset novels is completely different: they are the ones responsible for the huge diachronic and synchronic swings of Figure 3.7.

And yet if insets correlate well with length, they do so only for part of the span: insetting regains substantial ground after the low point of the 1680s (Figure 3.1), while the length of novels increases very modestly. In other words, the heft of the inset novel is not predestined: for the first two decades of the century, inset and noninset novels correspond very closely in length, a situation that is reestablished in the last three decades of the century. Of course, we might suspect that the lack of correspondence in the post-1700 developments visible in Figures 3.1 and 3.7 is caused by the retreat of Type 1 novels specifically: that is, the inset novels that caused the swelling of length from the 1620s to the 1660s are simply very rare in the years after 1681. But while it's true that they become much rarer, even late Type 1 novels follow the pattern, according to Figure 3.9.[32]

Figure 3.8 Length of real-world novels (II).

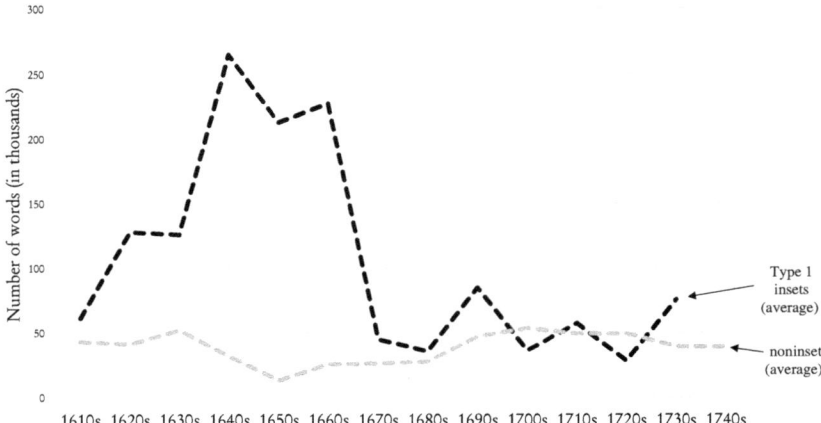

Figure 3.9 Length of real-world novels (III).

Inset novels – even Heliodorian inset novels – can be short, provided people want them to be so.

But talking more precisely about what short novels look like requires a second investigation, one that puts aside the rubric of the "Heliodorian" for the more familiar opposition – sanctioned by centuries of use – between *romans* and *nouvelles*.

4 | Novel v. Romance II

The Fortunes of a Subtitle

Recalling again Du Plaisir's 1683 pronouncement, novels become linear, short, and – to skirt the potentially anachronistic term *realistic* – verisimilar. The critic conceptualizes the shift via a lexical opposition. The old form is the *roman*; the new form is the *nouvelle*. English readers rightly see in these terms *romance* and *novel*, whose first clear use as a dichotomy dates roughly to the same moment. In his famous preface to *Incognita* (1692) – but famous only for the use of the dichotomy – Congreve declares that:

Romances are generally composed of the Constant Loves and invincible Courages of Heroes, Heroines, Kings and Queens, Mortals of the first Rank, and so forth; where lofty Language, miraculous Contingencies and impossible Performances, elevate and surprise the Reader into a giddy Delight.... Novels are of a more familiar nature; Come near us, and represent to us Intrigues in practice, delight us with Accidents and odd Events, but not such as are wholly unusual or unprecedented, such which not being so distant from our Belief bring also the pleasure nearer us.[1]

It has been pointed out that the neatness of the opposition – which in Congreve turns exclusively on subject matter and comparative believability, without the additional historical and formal distinctions found in Du Plaisir – is belied by contemporary use, very much fluid, and even contradictory.[2] (The original 1679 English translation of Lafayette's *La Princesse de Clèves* [1678] – along with *Don Quixote* and *Robinson Crusoe,* no doubt the most paradigmatic "first modern novel" – sports in fact the subtitle "the most famed romance.") Fluid as it may for a time be, in English, the opposition eventually hardens.[3] In French, however, it does not: Du Plaisir's terminology, though part of a wider contemporary enthusiasm for the word *nouvelle*, was just a hiccup, and in French, to this day, novels are called *romans*.[4]

Compared to the embrace of the category of *romance* in histories of the English novel, the eventual terminological failure of *nouvelle* has somewhat dampened French literary historians' invocation of *roman* as a foil. But *somewhat* dampened, only: the proliferation of *nouvelles* in the decades around Du Plaisir is nevertheless widely seen as a watershed. Sometimes that watershed is local – linked to the specifics of Louis XIV's absolutism and the "classical" regime – but more often it is, by implication or explicitly, of much wider import. In a word – that well-worn word again – it's the watershed of Modernity. The *nouvelle* ushers in – along with the increased verisimilitude and concentration trumpeted by Du Plaisir and others – a new kind of reading (based on, among others, identification and absorptive illusion), a new kind of subjectivity (founded on interiority and emotion), and ultimately a new ethos (in which heroic exemplarity is replaced by imperfect individuality).[5]

But is it possible to isolate the *roman* and the *nouvelle* – that is, treat them not as "abstractions" (as McKeon has famously called romance) but as actual things, as paper artifacts? Putting *certain* works in one category or another isn't much of a problem. Thus, Henri Coulet, a major French historian of the French novel, writes, "Nothing gives a better feel for the difference between [*roman*] and [*nouvelle*] than reading Saint-Réal's *Dom Carlos* [1672] right after La Calprenède's *Faramond* [1661–1670]."[6] True: the pessimism and historical precision of the former seem worlds away from La Calprenède's dreamy celebration of France's remote past – a novel so verbose that he didn't live to complete its twelve volumes. But Coulet himself quickly concedes that Saint-Réal was not representative, and of course, the broader problem is that although extremes are useful for drawing schematic distinctions, most novels aren't extreme. A literary historian hoping to go through a list of published novels tagging each as *roman* or *nouvelle* would be quickly brought back down to earth. A short novel might well be idealistic or distressingly unbelievable; it might start *in medias res* and feature flashbacks. Longer novels can be linear, finish badly for all concerned, and show care in the use of historical sources. And what is short, what is long? Coulet chose an obvious target, but very, very few novels in seventeenth-century France – less than 1 percent – possess the easily flaggable heft of *Faramond*'s million-odd words.

I'm certainly not the first to point out the slipperiness of the *nouvelle* – and of course, it's hard to see how any such definition could be otherwise.[7] But even if we can't simply assign *all* works to one of the two categories, it would be surprising if there was, in fact, no way to measure a change that by all accounts is so momentous, so formative of our shared literary landscape. In the previous chapter, we've already seen that novels do in fact get shorter and that a certain type of inset novel gets rarer. This is a start, though it leaves us far from knowing a number of things. What proportion of novels in any given decade actually possesses the formal characteristics that critics since Du Plaisir have associated with *romans* and *nouvelles*? Does their rise and fall confirm to accepted periodization? Does it increase or decrease the plausibility of the customary explanations for the change? All this may seem at first like nitpicking: surely the disappearance of the Heliodorian novel traced in the previous chapter tells us enough. Nonetheless, given the immense and centuries-old critical investment in the opposition between *nouvelle* and *roman* – and in the similar novel–romance dichotomy – the stakes would seem high enough to warrant further effort.

This and the following chapter examine the opposition by taking two different and complementary tacks. One major source of our conviction in the *nouvelle*'s novelty is the temporary though dramatic success of the term itself – in critical discourse but especially as a generic subtitle. That is, contemporaries actually did the modern literary historian the favor of labeling some novels *nouvelles*. Tracking this practice will be the subject of the present chapter. But this strategy, though essential, is incomplete. One problem is that the labeling was haphazard: some novels widely considered *nouvelles* didn't come with the subtitle, while others may well have had it only because the author or bookseller thought the buzzword would help move the merchandise. Worse, *roman* was almost never a generic subtitle, meaning that a symmetrical study of the two forms becomes impossible: we may be able to get a handle on the *nouvelle*'s rise but not the *roman*'s fall – never mind the latter's *own* rise, which is never studied because of the (unwarranted) assumption that the form had always been there. Thus, the following chapter will turn to tracking the two artifacts using formal criteria other than the presence of subtitles.

The full story of the French use of the word *nouvelle* is a long one and does not completely overlap, for example, with that of *novela* in Italian.[8] To be sure, the use of *nouvelle* was bound up with the influence of Italian and Spanish forms: the anonymous *Cent Nouvelles Nouvelles* (c. 1462), as well as Marguerite de Navarre's *Heptaméron* (1558), were modeled on Boccaccio; later compendia, such as Sorel's *Nouvelles françaises* (1623) and Scarron's *Nouvelles tragi-comiques* (1655), were more proximately linked to Spanish updatings of Boccaccio by Cervantes and de Zayas. In French, however, the word referred not only to a literary genre but also to a posture of truth: already in the *Chanson de Roland*, a *nouvelle* was an oral report of a recent event.[9] Thus Sorel, writing in the 1660s, still expected that texts designated as such "be about things recently transpired, otherwise there would be no reason to call them *nouvelles* at all."[10] The French case was also distinctive in that it was precisely around the time Sorel wrote these words that *nouvelle* started to be used generically in the singular – that is, to designate not the elements of a collection, typically exchanged within a frame narrative, but rather freestanding works divorced from any simulated oral exchange. A *nouvelle* was now a *written* narrative report.

"Calling" books *nouvelles* is, then, a matter of semantics and categorizing, as when people now say (or people at the time said), "*La Princesse de Clèves* is a famous *nouvelle*." The same goes, obviously, for *roman*. But it is also a matter of book history: the term figures on the title pages of numerous novels as a kind of generic marker, roughly in the manner that by the early nineteenth century, in France and especially England, novelists (or booksellers) will routinely add the subtitle "*roman*" or "A Novel" to titles. It's this use as a generic subtitle – distinct, then, from earlier plural uses within titles (*Cent Nouvelles Nouvelles*) – that hints at something legitimately new occurring just after the midpoint of the seventeenth century. Figure 4.1 records all variations of *nouvelle* as a generic subtitle, expressed as a percentage of real-world novels.[11]

The generic tag *nouvelle* has a circumscribed life, first appearing in the 1650s, maintaining significant popularity for a half century, and then tailing off. The shape of the curve is not surprising in the context of the present study: the gradual rise to a peak and the time scale of the rise and fall (roughly a century) are things we've seen before and will see again. That shape, however, doesn't conform entirely to the common wisdom about the *nouvelle*. Literary historians tend to speak of the *nouvelle* as a sudden enthusiasm, whereas here we see steady growth. Moreover, given that the *nouvelle* phenomenon is habitually treated as the domain of *dix-septiémistes*, the sheer length and symmetry of the curve is potentially surprising: though its rise corresponds well to ideas received about "classicism," a good portion of the form's career takes place in the postclassical, proto-Enlightenment years of 1691 and onward.[12] (In this, the curve looks much like that of the

Figure 4.1 Novels subtitled *nouvelle*.

strong Aristotelian novel examined in the previous chapter, and I will return to this resemblance, which is not accidental.)

If this measure seems to confirm the accepted view that there were no *nouvelles* before the 1650s, we need to keep in mind that all it really tells us is that novels before that date did not carry the subtitle, and at this point, things get complicated. One obvious complication is that many novels may have been considered *nouvelles* without being so labeled. Writing in the 1660s, Sorel noted that "the little stories [*petites histoires*] now being published can be described as *nouvelles*, although they don't bear that title."[13] They were, in fact, starting to bear it – to the tune of about 25 percent, according to Figure 4.1. But the remark suggests that at least some of the remaining 75 percent of novels may simply have been unmarked "little stories." Indeed, it is ironic that the only *nouvelle* remembered by nonspecialist literary history – *La Princesse de Clèves* – carries no subtitle. In other words, many texts we – and people of the time – like to call *nouvelles* were not explicitly advertised as such. But if some of the texts appearing alongside of labeled *nouvelles* were simply unmarked *nouvelles*, does this mean all unmarked texts were *nouvelles*? Couldn't there be some *romans* among them? Or some other novels that simply fit neither designation? We can extend this worry further upstream: it may be premature to conclude that the appearance of labeled *nouvelles* marks the arrival of a new sort of novel. Had the fashion never been for a new thing but simply for a new term?[14] Were some unmarked novels before the 1650s actually already *nouvelles*? The possibility is worth entertaining.

As briefly noted earlier, *roman* was used so infrequently in title and subtitles that its study is of limited help. Despite the scarcity of use, the distribution visible in Figure 4.2 does at least tell us that novels titled *roman*

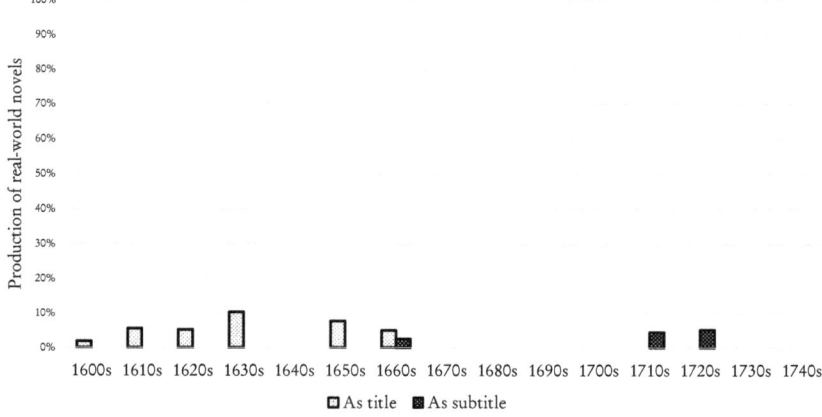

Figure 4.2 Novels titled or subtitled *roman*.

and novels subtitled *nouvelle* don't show much chronological overlap: the former date from the 1660s and before, whereas the latter date from the 1650s and after. Curiously, the same can be said of *roman* as a title and *roman* as a subtitle: historically speaking, their uses are distinct, with the subtitle *roman* making its (weak) appearance alongside that of *nouvelle*, after novels titled *roman* have disappeared. A closer, qualitative look may help clarify the situation. For example, from the 1650s on, the term *roman* is often attached to comic novels – to novels that self-consciously reprise ("mock" is too strong a word) tropes associated with *romans*: *Le Roman comique* (Scarron, 1651), *L'Heure du berger, demi-roman comique ou roman demi-comique* (Le Petit, 1662), *La Vie de Pedro del Campo, roman comique dans le goût espagnol* (Thibaut, 1718). Of interest is also the last novel of the period to feature the term, *Rhamiste et Ozalie, roman héroïque* (Anon, 1729), a reprise of the *romans* of the previous century, but in a nostalgic key. We can thus say that after the 1650s, uses of the term are distancing – they reference a practice implied to be of the past – thus confirming the idea that the *roman* is in fact associated with the first half of the seventeenth century. On the other hand, inspection of the few books titled *romans* in that earlier period reveals that they do not always conform to our idea of what a *roman* is supposed to be. They do not as a rule feature Heliodorian insetting (Type 1 and 2 insets of Chapter 3), and though one is fairly long – the aptly named *Roman héroïque* (Logeas, 1632), at well over 300,000 words, is longer than Rousseau's notoriously lengthy *Julie* – another from the same decade comes in at a very *nouvelle*-ish 20,000 words (*Le Roman de l'inconnu* [Humbert, 1634]). So although analysis of titles does suggest that before 1660s is the place to look for *romans*, it cannot take us much further.

As if the absence of *roman* as a subtitle weren't bothersome enough, we also have to contend with the presence of another subtitle besides *nouvelle* – *histoire*. Though the latter was never as popular as *nouvelle*, its historical distribution is much different – and disturbingly unaffected by the supposed upheaval in the novelistic landscape sometime around 1660. Figure 4.3 does not reveal an obvious surge of *histoires* in the 1650s or 1660s; in fact, no real patterns emerge at all. Are these *histoires* similar to *nouvelles*, or does the subtitle come with its own associations? To this synchronic question, we can add a diachronic one: are *histoires* from one end of the period to the other even the same artifacts?

Let's approach these questions by returning to the matter of length, examined briefly in the previous chapter in the context of the Heliodorian novel – those (generally) long novels with lots of a particular kind of insetting that became popular from the 1620s to 1640s. Figure 4.4 shows

Figure 4.3 Novels subtitled *histoire*.

median novel lengths by subtitle: variants on *nouvelle*, *histoire*, and finally books with no generic subtitle at all. To compensate for the fact that many of the decades simply don't have enough *histoires* to nullify the effects of outliers, the graph in Figure 4.4 takes the median of two-decade segments (or three, for the final segment).[15]

The first thing obvious is the brute fact that the supposedly radical shortening of the novel in the 1660s is much more like a return to a mean of between 30,000 and 40,000 words.[16] It is also true, however, that subtitling a novel *histoire* or *nouvelle* does seem to have carried associations with brevity and that those associations – at least from 1661 on – are virtually indistinguishable since both terms track together. From 1661 to 1680,

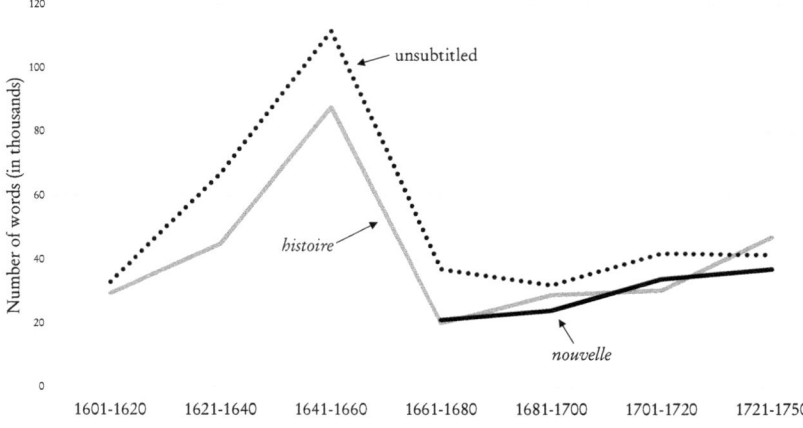

Figure 4.4 Median lengths of novels by subtitle.

subtitled novels are considerably shorter than their unsubtitled kin. But the association is not a permanent feature: by the end of the period, it is gone; and at the beginning of the period, it appears to have not yet formed. During the opening decades of the seventeenth century, *histoires* are the same length as unsubtitled novels: 29,500 words versus 33,000, or close to a tie. For the next set of decades, although *histoires* are notably shorter than others, Figure 4.4 reminds us that they lengthen along with the novel in general: *histoire* does not yet designate a "short novel." That association comes only in the 1660s, following the appearance of *nouvelle*. At that point both subtitles advertise particular brevity. At that point, but not forever: the effect disappears as subtitles themselves disappear, starting in the 1720s, when median novel length is around 40,000 words irrespective of subtitling.

Yet median lengths alone don't tell the whole story: they don't tell us if there is wide variation in the length of *histoires* or *nouvelles*. And indeed, from this perspective, the two subtitles are not exactly indistinguishable. From the 1660s on, the median length of both *histoires* and *nouvelles* may well be about the same, but the standard deviation from the mean, visible in Figure 4.5, indicates that their averages are not: *nouvelles* are much more tightly bunched around that mean. Another way of putting this is to say that longish *nouvelles* are rarer than longish *histoires*. We also see that although *histoires* in the opening two decades of the century were uniformly short, the next two segments show very high volatility: during these decades, even if *histoires* are somewhat shorter than unsubtitled novels, there are a lot of long *histoires*. Indeed, in order even to make the graph readable, I needed to suppress one figure from the 1641–1660 segment: Scudéry's *Clélie, histoire*

Figure 4.5 Length of subtitled novels, standard deviation.

romaine, whose million words would have made the scale such that the later differences between *histoires* and *nouvelles* would have effectively disappeared. But even eliminating this outlier, we see that in these decades, other novelists beside Scudéry used *histoire* in reference to longer works. The safest thing to conclude is that *histoire* appears to have acquired associations with shortness only when the term *nouvelle* is introduced; and even then, *nouvelle* advertised brevity more consistently than the older subtitle. By the time of the *nouvelle*'s senescence, however – after 1721 – the term's connotations are weakening as it is applied to novels of historically unusual length.

Of course, brevity is only one of the formal characteristics often (since Du Plaisir) associated with *nouvelles*, the other major one being linearity, that is, the abandonment of the inset structure. But the correlation between the inset structure and subtitles is less clear than the previous one (Figure 4.6).[17] Before 1661, *histoires* are less frequently inset than unsubtitled novels; but the vogue for insetting affects them much like the vogue for length – that is, they follow the general trend. Of course, this is unsurprising, since Figure 3.8 (page 77) tells us that long novels are also inset novels. Less clear are the figures from 1661 on: subtitles don't appear to carry any reliable connotation of linearity. Whatever modest association there may be during the 1661–1680 period is quickly reversed, as first *histoires* and then *nouvelles* become, in fact, even more reliably inset than nonsubtitled works.

That said, maybe there were *nouvelles* and *nouvelles*. Indeed, novels were called not only *nouvelles* and *histoires* but also *nouvelles historiques*, *nouvelles galantes*, *histoires espagnoles*, and so on: in producing the above graphs, I have funneled this diverse nomenclature into two categories. Might this

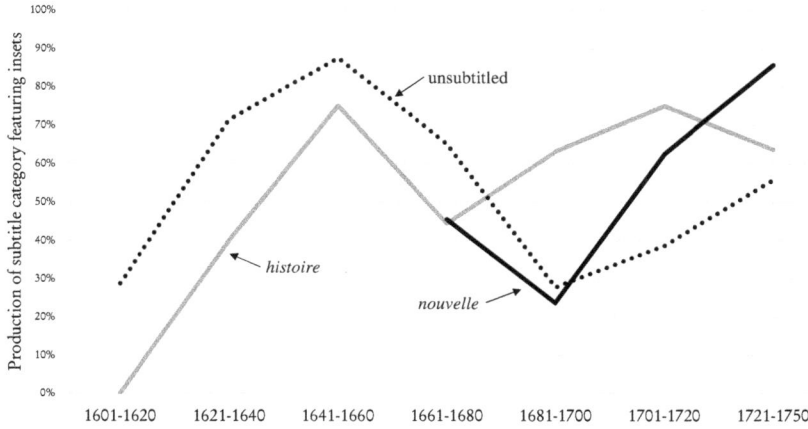

Figure 4.6 Inset novels by subtitle.

choice mask other correlations? Between specific subtitles and insetting, for example, perhaps *histoires véritables* retain insetting while *nouvelles galantes* do not. As it turns out, the only noteworthy connotation with respect to linearity appears to be the adjective *galant*: both *nouvelles galantes* and *histoires galantes* incorporate fewer inset narratives than other *nouvelles* and *histoires*, which on balance do not differ much from unsubtitled novels over the period 1651–1750. But the difference is not dramatic: *nouvelles galantes*, the most linear of all subtitle declinations, still feature insets 32 percent of the time, as opposed to 53 percent of unsubtitled novels.[18] Overall, we must conclude that despite Du Plaisir's testimony, *nouvelles* (and *histoires*) were not particularly associated with linearity.

Correlations between certain subtitles and temporal settings, however, are stronger. As a broad category, *nouvelles* are just barely more likely to have contemporary settings than not. Yet this indifference masks two clearer associations: *nouvelles historiques* and *nouvelles galantes* are something of opposites because the one tag is applied mostly to historical novels (66 percent of the time), the other to contemporary ones (80 percent). And while the temporal settings of *histoires* as a group are not drastically different from those of nonsubtitled works – mirroring, therefore, *nouvelles* as a group – this too is misleading since specific *histoires* do carry strong correlations. The formula *histoire*-plus-place almost exclusively applies to works set in the past (94 percent), while someone picking up a *histoire galante* or *véritable* can expect a contemporary setting (86 percent of the time). Yet, it seems notable that the formal connotations of most subtitles are far from automatic: *nouvelles historiques* usually have historical settings but don't a full third of the time; and geographical provenance, so important in *histoires*, comes with no temporal associations in *nouvelles*. The fact is that leaving aside a few specific combinations, most don't seem to connote anything special at all.[19]

Yet, if these various subtitles are not (usually) predictive of setting or linearity, this is not to say that their use is merely arbitrary. They pattern historically. While the terms *nouvelle* and *histoire* in subtitles are present in over 40 percent of the production for seventy years, this longevity masks a quicker cycling at the level of specific subtitles. Figure 4.7 tracks the careers of a few popular variants of *nouvelle*.

At first, *nouvelle* suffices, without modifiers, and for two decades it has no serious competition. But its popularity steadily erodes with the invention, in the 1670s, of the appellations *nouvelle historique* and *nouvelle galante*. *Nouvelle historique* bursts onto the scene in this decade, and this in fact is its peak, though it remains in relatively wide use for another three decades. The spread of the *nouvelle galante*, by contrast, is more gradual, not peaking until the 1700s.

Figure 4.7 Variations of *nouvelle*.

All this variation means that while the practice of giving novels generic subtitles takes the better part of a century to play itself out, the subtitles themselves come and go more rapidly, potentially peaking immediately (as with *nouvelle historique*) and remaining in use over more like forty years. Moreover, the end of the "macro" cycle (of all subtitles) does not quite correspond to the end of the last "micro" cycle (a specific subtitle). As the practice ages and declines, it becomes more haphazard; variation in the use of specific formal features increases as interest in the larger formal category tapers off. Figure 4.8 plots the occurrence of the popular designations *histoire galante*, *nouvelle*, *nouvelle galante*, and *nouvelle historique* against all other subtitles. Although the figure

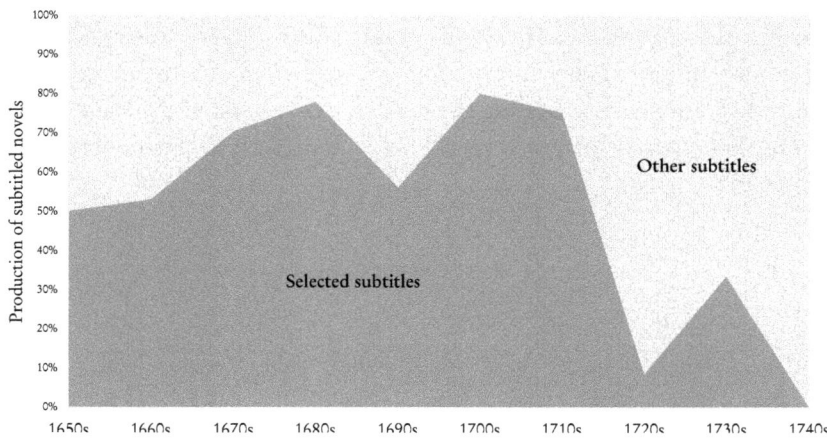

Figure 4.8 Subtitle uniformity.

for the 1690s is somewhat anomalous, the period of maximum popularity is mostly made up of a few subtitles used intensively. By contrast, as the practice of subtitling declines, diversity of subtitling increases – thus explaining, for example, the relatively strong representation of forms of *histoire* as subtitling as a whole is petering out (see Figure 4.3).

So, starting in the 1650s – the decade marking the appearance of the subtitle *nouvelle* and the alignment of the older term *histoire* with it – are subtitled novels different from nonsubtitled novels? Overall, that answer has to be: not really. They *are* shorter – though only for a time. But otherwise, clear formal differences are limited to a few specific subtitles: *histoire*-plus-place indicates books almost always set in the past and more likely to contain insets, and *nouvelles galantes* are less likely to contain insets than other works. As a result, the presence of subtitles is easily quantified; but those subtitles don't appear to characterize books vastly different from those without subtitles. It's therefore difficult not to recall Sorel, affirming that many *nouvelles* simply weren't labeled as such; difficult not to confirm the nagging feeling – there from the beginning – that subtitling is a largely arbitrary paratextual fashion rather than an index of textual changes; and difficult, lastly, to square the supposed importance of the subtitle with the vexing and unavoidable *Princesse de Clèves*. Indeed, the latter is everyone's favorite *nouvelle*, and yet it doesn't have the subtitle, is much longer than novels that do (56,000 words versus 21,000 words for *nouvelles* of that decade), and has insets to boot (Type 4 insets, according to the categorization of the previous chapter). If *La Princesse de Clèves* is not a *nouvelle*, then what is it? And the same question can be asked of all the other unsubtitled works from after 1660. Are they *romans*? Some kind of third entity? Or are there they also *nouvelles*, only somewhat less *nouvelle*-ish than those sporting the subtitle? And given that the seventeenth century opens with rather short, rather linear novels, we are also confronted with the uncomfortable possibility that post-1660 novels may not be much different, formally, from novels predating the explosion of interest in the Heliodorian model. The *nouvelle* may well be old news: not a turn to the modern but a return to the mean.

5 Novel v. Romance III

Measuring *Romans* and *Nouvelles*

The growth of novels subtitled *nouvelle* (or *histoire*) is, then, a significant feature of the landscape of the French novel. Yet it is still far from certain that subtitled *nouvelles* and *histoires* are really different from other novels at the time without these subtitles or even from at least some novels before that time; and as I've noted, subtitles are useless when it comes to figuring out what a *roman* might be. This chapter adopts a different approach to mapping the suspected replacement of *romans* by *nouvelles*. The approach consists of picking a family of formal characteristics besides subtitles that long-received critical opinion has associated with each of the categories and then seeing how they behave over time. Thus, to invoke Wittgenstein's famous point about family resemblances, these novels – and the third-person novels they replace – would form a family not because each and every one shares a common feature but because of a pattern of overlapping similarities.[1] (From this point on, then, my use of the word *nouvelle* mirrors that of *roman*: the terms refer to a category of works sharing certain formal traits but no longer, as in the previous chapter, to works bearing that subtitle.)

Following commonplaces about the *roman*, let us suppose that it is long, features insets, and – this is important – seems unconcerned with its relation to history. The *nouvelle*, by contrast, is short, linear, and turned toward history – the history of this or that period but also the history of the present, as it were. All these characteristics, however, are in need of further discussion.

(1) Length. Terms like long and short have meaning only relationally, so we need to define the terms with respect to the length of novels generally. The average length of novels over the century and a half is 66,400 words. "Short" might mean simply "below average," but quickly it becomes obvious that this criterion would commit us to considering as short some 73 percent of all novels. This is because a few very long works inflate the average. (All by itself, Scudéry's *Artamène, ou le Grand Cyrus* [1648–1653] – by far the all-time heavyweight at nearly 2 million words – pulls up the average by 3,000 words!) Using the mean length rectifies this: if we proceed this way, anything under 37,000 words – that is, below the 50th percentile – is

short. Unfortunately, this has the effect of excluding the paradigmatic *nouvelle*, Lafayette's *La Princesse de Clèves* (1678), whose 56,000 words, we now realize, do not make it particularly short.

Whatever our decision regarding "short," the distribution of data conspires against the desire to set the bounds for "long" novels symmetrically. Obviously, if we just took the 50th percentile as our over/under mark, we would be saying that there would be no middling novels, neither short nor long. But if we were to take, say, the top third percentile as our long novels and the bottom third as the short ones, we would commit ourselves to numbers that intuitively seem wrong: only novels under 27,000 words would be short, whereas anything over 54,000 (not even the length of the *Princesse de Clèves*!) would be long. The real problem, here, comes from the fact that lengths are not distributed in a nicely shaped bell curve: very long novels are rare, but very short novels are quite common; in fact, the shortest novels are the most common of all.[2] In setting our boundaries, we will need to take the shape of Figure 5.1 into account. The good news is that we can set multiple boundaries: in one calculation, a *nouvelle* might be anything under the mean, while in another – why not? – it might be anything at or under the length of the *Princesse de Clèves*.

(2) Linearity. In the previous chapter, my efforts to correlate insetting with subtitle use ignored the inset types itemized in Chapter 3. Thus, I didn't ask if the works in question fit inset narratives into a Heliodorian puzzle, recalled the *Decameron*'s storytelling exchange,

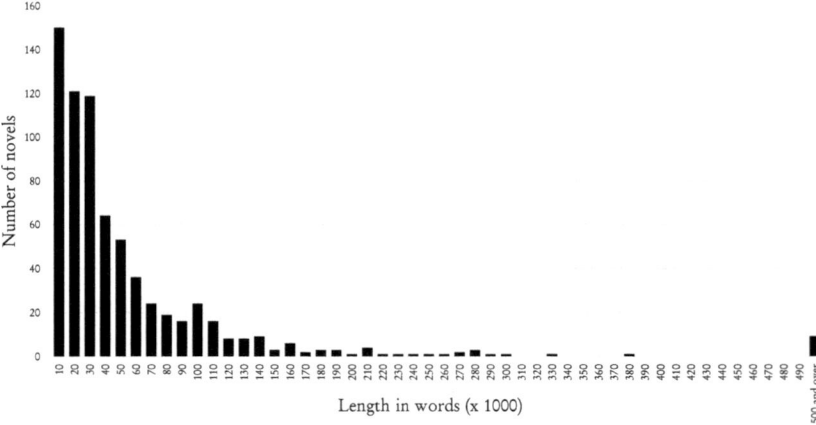

Figure 5.1 Distribution of novels by length, 1601–1750.

or merely featured a character's homodiegetic narration as a kind of bonus to or outgrowth of an otherwise cohesive plot. But of course, the *roman* is associated with the Heliodorian inset structure specifically, in which flashbacks are integral to the plot's development (Types 1 and 2 in the classification developed in Chapter 3). So we can consider the presence of either of these inset structures as we count up *romans*. The *nouvelle*, on the other hand, is trickier. We have already seen in Chapter 3 that although Heliodorian insetting becomes rarer during the years associated with the *nouvelle*'s triumph, other forms of insetting are still very frequent. Thus, although we may want to count as *nouvelles* only those works that have no insets, we may also consider expanding the category to include some forms of non-Heliodorian insetting. Likely candidates are Type 4 inset novels (novels like *La Princesse de Clèves*, in which characters tell stories tangentially related to the main narrative) and Type 6 novels (in which characters pause to tell stories unrelated to the otherwise cohesive narrative of which they are part).

(3) Truth. *Romans*, it has long been said, are fanciful, *nouvelles* more verisimilar.[3] Though the idea of trying to measure verisimilitude should immediately give us pause, in fact many of the distinctions regarding subject matter and truth posture developed in Chapter 2 can be used to define, heuristically, the families of *romans* and *nouvelles*. Part of the *nouvelle*'s supposedly superior verisimilitude, for instance, derives from its relation to history, be it past or contemporary. *Nouvelles* set in the present are almost uniformly said to concern true events: indeed, we've seen that the term very much connotes "news" (of a gossipy variety). So one characteristic we can look for in novels classified as *nouvelles* will be present-day settings accompanied by the assertion of truth. However, many books considered at the time as *nouvelles* (and indeed regularly labeled as such) contained historical subject matter – as did some novels considered *romans*. Which historical subjects belong to the *roman* and which to the *nouvelle*? We've noted that over the course of the seventeenth century, historical settings shift from a biblical or classical past to modern Europe, so that might be one possible distinction: given that Du Plaisir reproached the *roman* for its "excessive antiquity,"[4] we can put novels on European history in the category of *nouvelles* and those on classical subjects in the category of *romans*. Similarly, the observed replacement of novels set in the past and peopled by nobodies with novels featuring known historical personages as characters can also furnish a criterion.

(4) Narrative person. There is one final characteristic of both *romans* and *nouvelles* that is rarely made explicit: both are associated with the third person. The exclusion of first-person works makes no difference to our tabulation of *romans* simply because so few novels from the period of the *roman*'s popularity are in the first person anyway. But for *nouvelles*, the stipulation is crucial. In its absence, there would be no way to separate *nouvelles* – short(ish), more or less linear, "true" – from the wave of pseudofactual document novels that came after and that are the subject of Chapters 6 and 7.[5]

With these criteria in mind, let's imagine sixteen scenarios for *romans* and sixteen for *nouvelles*, each reflecting permutations of the three variables of length, linearity, and truth, and then perform sixteen counts each. Proceeding in such a manner acknowledges that there is no way of establishing which novels "are" *romans* and which "are" *nouvelles*. Their characteristics are too fluid (What is short? What is linear?) and, fatally, many books combine characteristics from both categories. Our goal is simply to count heuristically – that is, with the hope that our counts tell us something useful about a historical change that has, until now, been described only impressionistically – and thus, quite possibly, misunderstood.

(For the detail-oriented, permutations are as follows. For each kind of novel, *roman* or *nouvelle*, let us suppose three different length limits, two different definitions of linearity, and three of truth. For the *roman*, "long" will mean novels in the 80th, 90th, or 95th percentile [which translates as those over 79,000, 118,000, or 173,000 words]; for *nouvelles*, shortness will be defined as being in the 33rd or 50th percentile for the period [under 27,000 or 37,000 words], or simply – and this is obviously a whimsical limit – no longer than the *Princesse de Clèves* [under 57,000 words]. In addition, *romans* will need to contain, in one scenario, Type 1 insetting [i.e., standard Heliodorian insetting]; in another, Type 2 insetting [simplified Heliodorian insetting] will also qualify. *Nouvelles* can be interpreted strictly as those works with no insetting at all; or the category may be taken to include as well Type 4 and Type 6 insetting, in which characters tell stories that are not integral to the book's narrative architecture. Finally, concerning truth posture – readers will need to refer to the categories used in Chapter 2 – *nouvelles* will be defined as works set in the past containing nobodies asserted as having really existed, "strong" Aristotelian historical works with modern European subject matter, and novels with contemporary settings that are affirmed as being true stories. *Romans* are nearly anything else: "weak" Aristotelian novels, "strong" Aristotelian novels with biblical or mythological subject matter, historical novels about nobodies not said to have existed, novels with contemporary or unspecified settings of indeterminate or invented status, and finally novels claimed as "keyed." Here, keeping in mind Du Plaisir's remark about the *roman* being historically removed from the modern reader's frame of reference, a first possible permutation involves "strong" Aristotelian novels with classical subject matter. In one scenario, these are put into the *nouvelle* category [given their relatively tight bond with history], while in a second, they are considered to show the characteristics of *romans* [because they are historically remote]. A second permutation removes "weak" Aristotelian works having a modern historical setting from the *roman* category and tabulates them instead with *nouvelles*.)

And it turns out that how one counts matters to the *quantity* of *romans* and *nouvelles* that one locates – restrictive scenarios produce lower counts – but *not* to their distribution. In Figure 5.2, I've reduced the eighteen scenarios for each artifact to six because it turns out that many are redundant or nearly so. At least within the limits set for the variables, the basic fact of the rise and fall of *romans* and *nouvelles* should not be a matter of debate. *Romans* are a five-decade phenomenon, and they come and go with impressive symmetry. The life span of *nouvelles* is more like eight decades; and while they reach their peak in three decades, just like *romans* had done before them, they have a longer senescence. The elongated tail end of the *nouvelle*'s popularity may explain why literary history has so stubbornly viewed the early eighteenth century as a period in which the novel was "in search of itself": for whatever reason – I will offer a hypothesis in Chapter 10 – document novels simply do not replace the *nouvelle* as decisively as the *nouvelle* replaced the *roman*.

Figure 5.2 *Romans* and *nouvelles* (I): criteria of length, insetting, and truth.

Before talking about what Figure 5.2 does to accepted accounts of the novel's rise – in some senses it appears to confirm them, while in others, it shows a lot that is new – more time needs to be spent on what it is and isn't measuring. Again, none of these lines is more "accurate" than another because our sense of what a *roman* or *nouvelle* derives from a modulable cluster of characteristics. This is also to say that what we have to measure is something like how *intensely* a given book is a *roman* or *nouvelle*. The books that are most intensely *romans* or *nouvelles* are found in the lower curves of the graph: they are rarer. As we move up, we start including more books – the ones whose length becomes increasingly moderate, ones that include more types of insetting, and so on. And so it is that many (but not all) books that do not fit into any of the scenarios may well be considered *romans* or *nouvelles* – just less so than the ones captured in Figure 5.2. (Not all books, because some of them, notably "documents" like the memoir or epistolary novel, are so formally distinct that even with a particularly elastic scenario they wouldn't fit into either category and because others incongruously combine traits associated with the two types – short works featuring Heliodorian insetting, for example.) Obviously, then, more scenarios are possible, especially because the length factor can be (almost) endlessly varied. At a certain point, however, they start returning information that suggest we've gone too far.

We could, for example, disregard length entirely, which would reduce the number of scenarios down to two per artifact. And perhaps, surprisingly, in many respects, the results are not terribly different from Figure 4.4 (page 85). In Figure 5.3, peak figures for the *nouvelle* have hardly budged:

Figure 5.3 *Romans* and *nouvelles* (II): insetting and truth criteria only.

very few *nouvelles* with the requisite linearity and truth posture contain 57,000 or more words. (And since that limit had been set with *La Princesse de Clèves* in mind, this means that Lafayette's paradigmatic *nouvelle* is in all probability one of the bulkiest *nouvelles* ever published.) But figures for the *nouvelle*'s predecessor have changed: a significant number of novels of 79,000 words or less nonetheless contain features associated with the *roman*. And not only are the numbers higher. *Romans* now peak not in the 1640s but 1650s: length becomes unfashionable (marginally) more quickly than insetting or "lax" truth postures. This shape makes this graph more supportive of the traditional dating of the *roman*'s extinction to 1660. On the other hand, disallowing length as a criterion has the inconvenient effect of implying that the *roman* actually never goes extinct: *romans*, according to these calculations, continue to show a stubborn presence through the 1730s. What this alternate calculation giveth (to comfort our habitual narratives), it also taketh away.

We can also imagine retaining length as a factor and eliminating either of the remaining two criteria. Figure 5.4 retains length and insetting, eliminating stipulations as to truth. *Romans* remain nearly untouched: novels that are long and feature Heliodorian insetting already have "lax" truth postures, and so filtering for the latter does next to nothing. But a "tight" bond with truth is much more essential to the definition of the *nouvelle*, for without the criterion, the number of *nouvelles* swells across the *entire* time span, including the years 1631–1650. Thus, discounting truth posture has little effect on *romans* but a bothersome one on *nouvelles*, which, in such a telling, aren't really new in the 1650s.

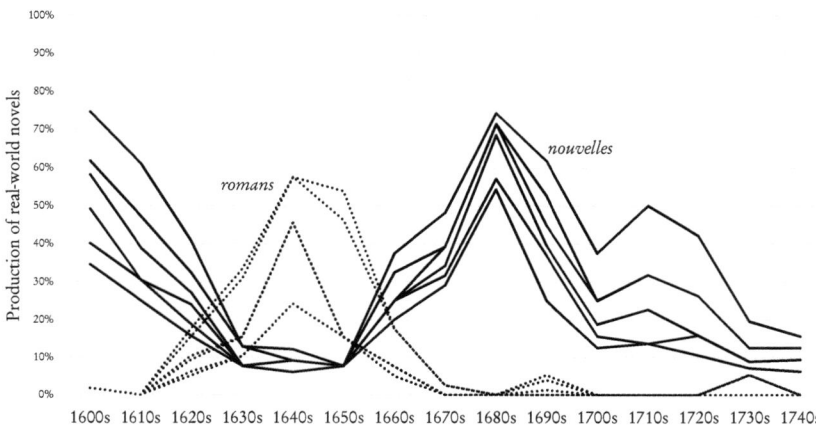

Figure 5.4 *Romans* and *nouvelles* (III): length and insetting criteria only.

The impact of insetting criteria may first appear weaker. Of all the two-variable calculations, Figure 5.5 resembles the most the three-variable Figure 5.2: both kinds of novels have the same peaks and neither surprises us by always being present (even *nouvelles* zero out in the 1640s). Generally the numbers are more robust and the curves plumper: the rise and fall of the *nouvelle* in particular has become less staggered. And now there are *nouvelles* in the 1650s.

All in all, between Figures 5.2 and 5.5, there doesn't seem to be too much to choose from. But this is intriguing. Following Du Plaisir, literary historians had always considered linearity as a key feature of the *nouvelle* – all the more so to modern critics because the homology between linearity on the one hand and Cartesian rationality and Ludovican centralism on the other is so inviting. (Conversely, the *roman*'s insetting has always appeared self-evidently "baroque.") Yet, we've already seen in Chapter 4 that subtitling suggests that contemporaries did not seem to associate *nouvelles* with noninset novels, and this new information bears this out. Not only does the insetting criterion not do much, its absence may be in fact preferable. If the superior regularity of Figure 5.5's curves is not in itself decisive – regularity is reassuring, but some trends do hiccup – the fact that it shows *nouvelles* in the 1650s does seem a distinct advantage: after all, it is precisely in this decade that the subtitle *nouvelle* is first used (see Figure 4.1 [page 82]). From this fact alone, one can conclude that the graph in Figure 5.2 is not registering (some) novels that contemporaries themselves called *nouvelles*. These are novels that contain insetting of a type that we've judged incompatible with linearity – either Types 3 and 5 (novels constructed of thin frame narratives

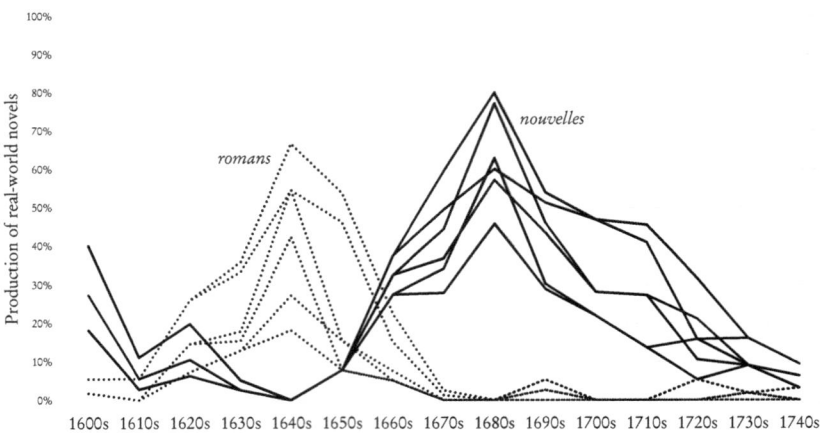

Figure 5.5 *Romans* and *nouvelles* (IV): length and truth criteria only.

plus insets, usually multiple) or insetting (wrongly?) associated with the *roman* (Types 1 and 2).

Indeed, comparing the two methods of counting *nouvelles* is instructive. It was clear from the outset that relying on nomenclature – the presence of a subtitle – produced undercounts: Sorel said as much, the example of the *Princesse de Clèves* was impossible to ignore, and, on a more general level, Figure 4.1 (page 82) told the story of a success that was ultimately middling (only in a couple decades did *nouvelles* make up more than a third of percent of the production). Counting by form is an opportunity to rectify these problems (Figure 5.6). Whether counting by subtitle produces lower counts than counting by form depends on how permissive the formal criteria are. The results from applying the strictest scenario tell us that there were fewer *nouvelles* than there were books actually called *nouvelles* by contemporaries – a discrepancy that strongly suggests that the strictest scenario is simply too strict. It is only the most permissive scenario that shows significant numbers of *nouvelles* that aren't captured by the subtitle counts, especially in the peak decades of the 1680s and 1690s. This is intuitively satisfying, though of course the intuition that books like the *Princesse de Clèves* are common – books taken then and since as *nouvelles* but without the subtitle to prove it – may be erroneous.

Because of the discrepancy in figures for the 1650s, we know that at least some novels called *nouvelles* at the time do not fit the three-variable formal criteria. What we don't know is whether this is common: it may be that formal criteria miss a few subtitled *nouvelles* but – in the case of permissive scenarios – add more than they miss; or it may be that there is

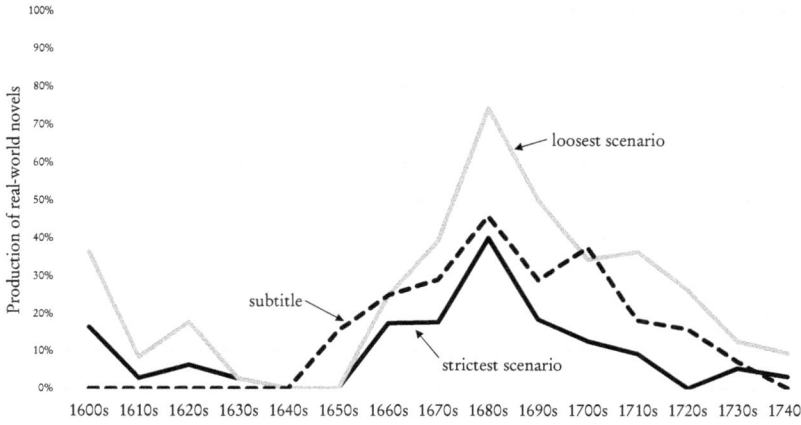

Figure 5.6 Counting *nouvelles* (I).

actually little overlap between the counting methods and that they routinely count different novels as *nouvelles*. It turns out that there is overlap but perhaps less than one would want. In the 1660s, for example, the permissive scenario returns ten titles, which is the same figure obtained by counting by subtitle; yet, only four of these are returned by both. This is to say that only 40 percent (four out of ten) of the subtitled novels correspond to the loosest formal criteria for defining *nouvelles*. Over the entire period of the subtitle's use, the formal criteria do better, but they still miss large numbers of books that contemporaries labeled *nouvelles* – about 43 percent of them. The inability of formal criteria to capture *all* of subtitled *nouvelles* is not worrying: as noted previously, authors may have applied it not because their novels looked like anyone's conception of a *nouvelle* at the time but simply because the term was popular. Nonetheless, the numbers for even the permissive scenario seem low. Are there any specific formal characteristics that contemporaries associated with the *nouvelle* that even the permissive scenario has been leaving out?

By showing some *nouvelles* in the 1650s, Figure 5.5 provides the hint: novels that have insets that look like they belong in *romans* were nonetheless often labeled *nouvelles*. Indeed, *pace* Du Plaisir, contemporaries simply did not see the *nouvelle* as a fundamentally "linear" form, as Figure 5.7 shows. Only by a small majority are subtitled *nouvelles* linear. The permissive scenario counts novels with inset Types 4 and 6 – insets that are related but not integral to the narrative. But it leaves out the still more important group of *nouvelles* possessing the Heliodorian architecture, here in patterned fill: this seemingly "baroque" technique represents nearly a third of the "classical" novels advertised as *nouvelles*.[6] Letting these types back in

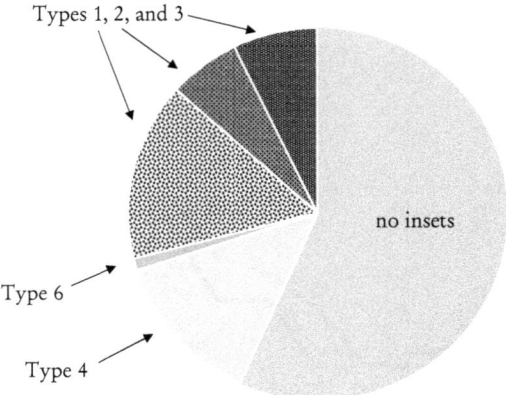

Figure 5.7 Subtitled *nouvelles* by inset type, 1651–1750.

improves our ability to capture subtitled *nouvelles* with formal criteria: a new scenario, composed of all the criteria in the loosest scenario plus these inset categories, returns 70 percent of the books that contemporaries called *nouvelles*. The gain is visible in Figure 5.8.

Is it possible to do better? Only with progressively diminishing returns. The other 30 percent of subtitled *nouvelles* are made up of works excluded by range of different formal criteria that would have to be tweaked one by one. Some don't fit the length category (with most relatively long subtitled *nouvelles* – longer that the *Princesse de Clèves* – hailing from the eighteenth century). Others have first-person narrators – usually frame narrators or observers recounting a purportedly true story – and we may want to devise a scenario that lets those in, while continuing to filter for memoir and epistolary novels. But such modification would be overly fastidious. One thing worth noting, however, is that the capture rates of all the scenarios are better in decades clustered around the peak of the *nouvelle*'s popularity. Figure 5.9 is another confirmation of a phenomenon I've noted repeatedly: as forms become popular, they become more homogenous. Thus, the first decades of *nouvelles* are marked by diversity, as people apply the term to a variety of different items. After a time, *nouvelle* acquires a more limited set of connotations – basically, the ones literary historians still think of today. But as the fashion for *nouvelles* fades, the term again loses its specificity.

Because of this inevitable heterogeneity, contemporaries' use of *nouvelle* can only be a guide: it tells us when our scenarios are way off and when they are closer to the mark. But that mark is a moving target, in that there are better and worse scenarios but no perfect scenario. And *roman* is

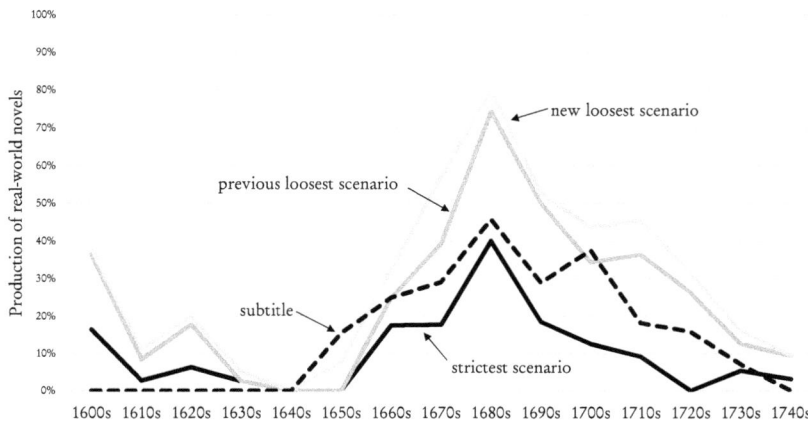

Figure 5.8 Counting *nouvelles* (II).

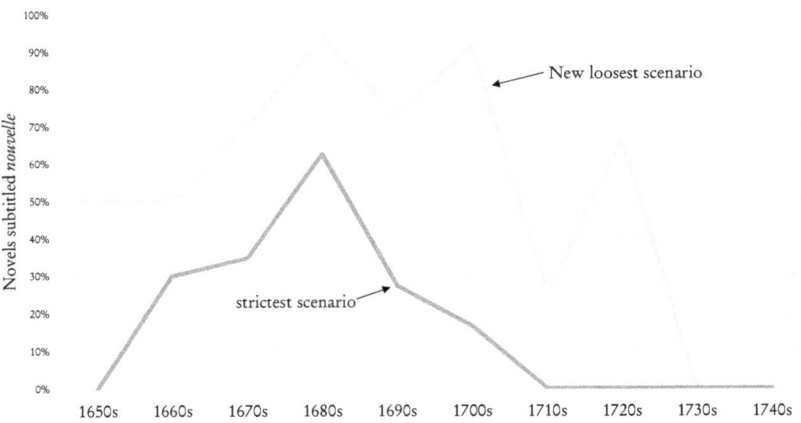

Figure 5.9 Subtitled *nouvelles* corresponding to formal criteria.

trickier still: since the word was not used as a generic tag, contemporary use cannot control our scenarios. Nonetheless, the above explorations will help recompose the graph in Figure 5.2.

We can do a couple of different things. The first is simply to include some still more permissive scenarios: the scenario, just explored, that recognizes that *nouvelles* were less associated with linearity than we thought; an additional scenario allowing in as well any work subtitled *nouvelle* regardless of its length, insetting, or truth posture; and scenarios that are less Procrustian in consideration of length, in which a *roman* need only be over the seventy-fifth percentile (68,000 words) and the *nouvelle* under. Better still, however, is a representation that stresses, visually, that all *romans* and *nouvelles* aren't equal: some *romans* are longer than others, some *nouvelles* more linear, and so on. Figure 5.10 includes the range of familiar scenarios incorporated in Figure 5.2 plus the more permissive scenarios I've just mentioned. (*Romans*'s market penetration is represented on an inverse scale so as to allow for simultaneous display of the artifacts.) And here, the darker the shading, the more "intensely" the novels fit the criteria we have associated with *romans* or *nouvelles*. Interestingly, with *nouvelles* at least, the looser scenarios add more to the rise and fall than to the peak – another sign that peaks are more formally homogenous than periods of growth and decline.

Skeptics might say that this series of graphs merely puts some numbers to what we knew all along – that around 1660, the *nouvelle* replaces the *roman*. But this would be plain wrong. In fact, the graphs make it very difficult for literary historians of France to tell the same old narrative of the *nouvelle*'s triumph. And they perturb reflexive Anglophone literary history

5 *Measuring* Romans *and* Nouvelles

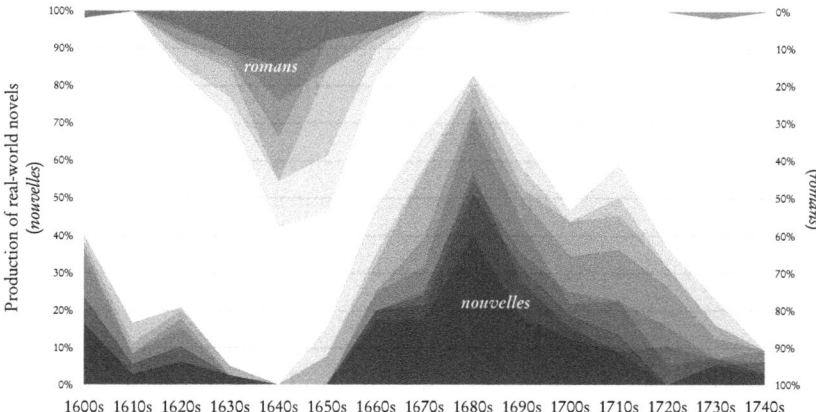

Figure 5.10 *Romans* and *nouvelles*.

as well: despite the fact that my data comes from France alone, it nonetheless suggests that the well-worn opposition between romance and novel is not simply "oversimplified" but so fatally misleading that it must be scrapped.

For starters, what does it actually mean to say that the *nouvelle* "replaces" the *roman*? Is it like saying that the CD replaces the vinyl record and the cassette because it provided a technology so superior (in terms of consumers' desires) that it simply took the market away from its competitors? Maybe not quite. Figure 5.11 shows the subsequent triumphs of the cassette and the CD.[7] The market for recorded music is split up into just a few technologies: these are always changing, but there are only a limited number of formats available at a given moment, and dominant formats are very dominant.

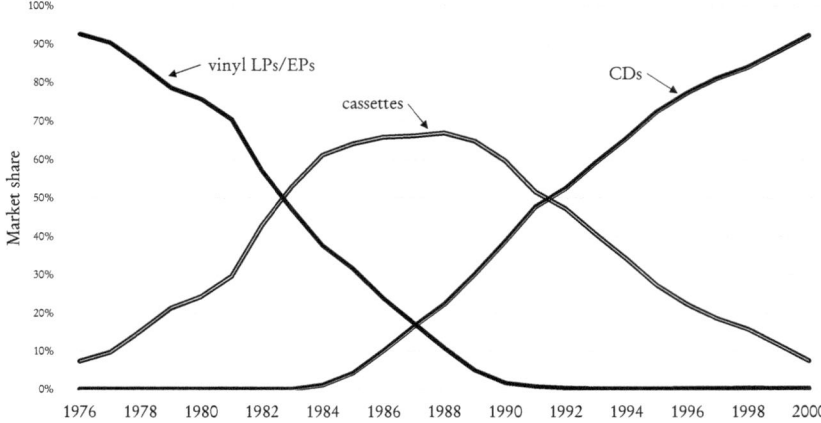

Figure 5.11 US production of music albums, 1976–2000.

This means that one more CD translates as one less record or cassette.[8] The market for novels, by contrast, is more diverse: every step of the way, there are always considerable numbers of novels that were neither *romans* nor *nouvelles* and that cannot be slotted into any other neat category either. A *nouvelle* might be the book that a given novelist wrote instead of a *roman*; but the novelist might also have written a *nouvelle* instead of some *other* kind of novel. Similarly, a writer may have stopped writing *romans*, only to switch to novels that weren't *nouvelles* either – maybe, say, to novels that had certain characteristics of both. Hence, the *nouvelle*'s gain was not necessarily the *roman*'s loss.

Though Figure 5.11 is complicated by the presence of three artifacts, its lesson is still clear enough: one form steadily gains the market share of rival forms. But Figure 5.10 doesn't really look like this because there is very little chronological overlap between *romans* and *nouvelles*. It's an apparently small point but one that has the effect of undermining the idea that the *nouvelle* drove the *roman* to extinction. *Romans* are going strong in the 1640s and 1650s, after which their production plummets. At the same time, the *nouvelle* starts to take off. The two phenomena obviously appear linked, but how, precisely? On the one hand, there is the intuitively satisfying possibility that the *nouvelle* caused the *roman*'s decline. But on the other, we should wonder if migration toward the *nouvelle* didn't merely accelerate a decline in *romans* that would have occurred anyway. First, consider the information that Figure 5.10 provides on the 1650s. All scenarios for counting *romans* except for the most permissive one indicate the 1640s as the form's high point; the stricter our definition of the *roman*, the more obvious that high point is. The decline of the *roman* is thus already visible in the 1650s. Meanwhile, all scenarios for *nouvelles* except the new ones showed none in the 1650s: in other words, in order to find *nouvelles* in that decade, we need to count items that aren't particularly *nouvelle*-ish. If this reasoning is correct, then we must conclude that the *roman* is already weakening even before the *nouvelle* is a clear option. Second, though the *roman* then quickly loses market share, falling to between 10 and 18 percent from half or more, books characterizable as *nouvelles* do not pick up all of the loss: books *not* characterizable as *nouvelles* also increase. The *roman* is abandoned; but the *nouvelle* doesn't immediately pick up the slack. Indeed, even in the 1670s, when literally there are no more *romans*, the new form is far from its 1680s peak: it continues to grab a market share that wasn't the *roman*'s to begin with. It is probably right to say that in the absence of an attractive competitor form, the decline of the *roman* would have been more protracted. Still, in the course of the present study, it has become obvious that literary forms peak and fall away. While the speed of the fall varies, peaks simply do not last: maximum popularity is never a plateau. In other words, like all literary forms, the *roman* was doomed, *nouvelle* or no.

A further problem with the CDs versus vinyl analogy lies in the crucial fact that these literary forms are not perfectly discrete artifacts. (Whence the need, obviously, for a representation like the one in Figure 5.10.) Between, say, the 1670s and the 1680s, *nouvelles* do increase their market share; but it's not accurate to say that they do so at the expense of identifiable alternate forms. Such forms do, I think, exist: notably, first-person document novels, which are the subject of the two following chapters. Document novels, though, are rare birds over the period of the *nouvelle*'s dominance. Almost all of what is left are not non-*nouvelles* or non-*romans* but rather novels that could be counted as *nouvelles* or *romans,* were our criteria still looser. Is a short, linear novel that makes no claims to truth more a *nouvelle* (on account of its length and insetting) or a *roman* (on account of its truth posture)? Probably more like a *nouvelle*, but this hasn't been captured by any of our scenarios. One could generate still more scenarios to account for such titles, and they would have the effect of filling up Figure 5.10 with still lighter shades of gray. The only areas remaining white would represent books such as document novels – books whose characteristics we had judged as fundamentally incompatible with *roman*- or *nouvelle*-hood. Thus, both artifacts grow as a result of formal homogenization, as more and more novels look more and more like *romans* or *nouvelles*.

(I will postpone until Chapter 10 broaching a final and crucial conclusion suggested by the analogy with recorded music: *romans* and *nouvelles* are much more like eight-track tapes and cassettes, respectively, than they are like vinyl and CDs. Despite the gap that this chapter has been devoted to establishing – and that is real – *romans* and *nouvelles* are two technologically kindred artifacts.)

The second commonplace that these graphs should help us to put to rest is more far-reaching. This is the wizened literary–historical association between the *nouvelle* and modernity. The implication of such arguments seems to be that somehow the form *is* the modern novel – which is strange, given that it's common knowledge that eighteenth-century first-person forms replace it. (Of course, eighteenth-century specialists see *those* forms as the modern novel, and so on and so forth: happily there is and there will always be some new form in which scholars of whatever period can discern the coming of the modern, which means people like them.) But if we've always known that the *nouvelle* (or the realist novel or the modernist novel) doesn't last, the fact is that we manage to look away so that we can go on telling the important story of how Then becomes Now. Beyond giving us an approximate idea of how many novels of whatever category there were in such-and-such a decade, this chapter's graphs counter our scholarly denial with a certain brute visual effect: it becomes impossible not to see *cycles*, and difficult, therefore, to ascribe to one up-and-down a modernity that is denied to another.[9] Doubtless it remains possible to argue that all novel forms from the *nouvelle* forward are modern, united by something the *roman* didn't have. There may be such a sine qua non condition of the "real" novel, but I would wager that when pressed defenders would offer nothing more than a vague evocation of some spirit of modernity.[10] How could anything else unite the array of practices running from the *nouvelle* to the postmodernist novel and beyond? *Romans* were doomed, I've said; and doomed, in turn, was the form that replaced them. And the one after that, and the one after that.

Furthermore, if *nouvelles* aren't modern, *romans* can't be archaic. Literary historians of France have long focused on the 1660s because it was pretty obvious even to a casual observer that a new form was at hand and because the 1660s were associated with French literary modernity more generally (classicism) and with a kind political modernity as well (absolutism). But no one cared to look for the beginning of *romans*, for the simple reason that they weren't supposed to have a beginning. They were supposed, rather, to recede back into the "mists of time," supposed to represent stasis, tradition, and idealism so that the *nouvelle* could be all about contingency, adaptability, and realism. But here we see clearly that those mists of time last precisely five decades and that writing a *roman* in the 1630s or 1640s is no more and no less modern a gesture than writing a *nouvelle* fifty years later.

Indeed, it is high time to dissipate the confusion resulting from our own historical position to wit the relation between *romans* and "romance." Weighing the merits of the many meanings given by modern critics to the term "romance," comparing those meanings to the ones circulating in the sixteenth, seventeenth, or eighteenth centuries – this could well be the matter of an entire book.[11] We can, however, easily invalidate one meaning in particular. This is the one that sees French *romans* as a (late) manifestation of romance – romance, meaning the kind of old books that Cervantes so memorably pilloried in *Don Quixote*, thereby (it is said) bringing into existence the novel.[12] Keeping in mind the famous text of Congreve's, cited at the outset of the previous chapter, there may well be a certain axiological similarity between the chivalric *Amadis of Gaul* (attrib. Montalvo, pub. 1508) and the heroic *Artamène* (Scudéry, 1649–1653): both do indeed feature the "invincible courages … of mortals of the first rank." But in the seventeenth century, lumping the two together would have been ludicrous for the simple reason that, as detailed in the previous chapter, the Heliodorian novel was designed as the Humanist *antidote* to the chivalric novel. There is no need to puzzle over why the French were still writing romances when, clear-eyed, Cervantes had already run them through with his *Quixote*. Cervantes and the French writers of *romans* were on exactly the same page: all sought to modernize the novel, which involved – among other things – moving it away from what we can roughly describe as chivalric "episodism" through recourse to the Heliodorian form.

Thus, the vogue for the *roman* – which with some complication is basically the period name for what I've also dubbed the Heliodorian novel – sits perfectly well with Cervantes' project. The peak visible in Figure 5.10 is not belated but right on time: it follows the cutting edge represented by some of the novels mentioned in the previous chapter – Sidney's *New Arcadia* (1590), Fumée's *Du vrai et du parfait amour* (1598), d'Urfé's *L'Astrée* (1607–1627), and Cervantes' *The Trials of Persiles and Sigismunda* (1617). (*L'Astrée*, by the way, is the only novel of the 1600s that answers any of the scenarios for *romans* in the above graphs; though often advanced as the last great pastoral novel, its status as a formal precursor is unquestionable.) Only time would make this type of novel look like the type of novel satirized by *Don Quixote*; only time would make it appear puzzling that Cervantes could be the author both of this take-down of "romance" and of the "romance" *Persiles*. How much time? One indication might be the popularity of *Persiles* itself, which rivaled that of the *Quixote* well into the eighteenth century but then flagged. By the 1780s, for someone like Clara Reeve, the chivalric and the Helidorian had become an indistinguishable, unreadable, archaic mass. And thus her *The Progress of Romance* – "progress" consisting of romance's metamorphosis into the novel – asks, "What shall we say of a man who had produced *Don Quixote* and could afterwards write a book of the same kind he had satirized?"[13] Readers in the seventeenth century would never have asked such a question, based as it is on a false premise generated by a historical remove.[14]

The final question raised by all these graphs is whether the *nouvelle* was really new to the 1660s. It certainly looks new compared to the 1640s, when there appear to be none. But all scenarios for counting *nouvelles* – once the subtitle itself is not an issue – show substantial quantities of such artifacts before the rise of the *roman*. What is suggested, of course, is that the *nouvelle* marks a reversion to a previously common practice, one that had been pushed aside by the very temporary vogue for the *roman*. Caution, however, is warranted, and not only because the 1601 cut-off keeps us from seeing what happens before. For one, judging from the data we have examined until this point, revivals of once-popular forms would appear to be rare. Figure 2.7 (page 47) indicates that Aristotelian and (especially) non-Aristotelian novels have a vigorous second life in the late eighteenth century after their previous peaks a century or more before. But this case is actually instructive. That is, it is only in terms of very limited formal criteria that the crop of historical novels at the turn of the nineteenth century resembles those of the seventeenth: the determining factor in Figure 2.7 is the type of historical protagonist featured. In other respects, however, no reader could possibly mistake the two artifacts. For example, if we tagged for descriptive passages of "local color" – the French Romantics' term for textual information that distinguishes one (peripheral) time or place from that of the (urban) Here and Now – and added this second criterion into our calculations, the apparent revival would no doubt disappear, leaving us with incommensurable groups of historical novels. Similarly, a closer reading of "*nouvelles*" from the 1600s or 1610s would probably turn up additional variables enabling us to distinguish these texts from the ones that flourished much later in the century.

I suspect, then, that the *nouvelle* is actually new to 1660s France. Newness, however, is nothing special: it is a permanent feature of the literary landscape.

6 Documenticity I

Memoir Novels (and Other First Persons)

Chrétien de Troyes begins his *Cligès* (c. 1176) with a nod to a written source: "This story, which I intend to relate to you, we find written in one of the books of the library of my lord Saint Peter at Beauvais."[1] One surmises that the hero Cligès didn't possess customary epic renown and that the allusion to a written source was intended to reassure readers of the value of the subject matter, lest they imagine that it was simply made up. (Chrétien continues: "The book is very old in which the story is told, and this adds to its authority.") Such allusions to source documents in literature must have a long, interesting history, no doubt tangled up in the transition from oral to written poetic forms.[2]

But documents *as* literature: that's a quite different phenomenon. Only as we approach the eighteenth century are readers informed that they have before them not books composed by a writer using bona fide and credible source texts but rather the actual documents – perhaps pruned or groomed – written by protagonists. The documents, which are almost uniformly first-person documents, eliminate the role of the poet–historian, creating in its stead the liminal position of the "editor," vouching for the authenticity of the material he or she presents. Radical novelty in literature is not easy to find, but the document novel may just be such a black swan: the form seems without earlier analogues. More astonishing than its brute novelty is the success of its "market takeover": nonexistent before 1660, the document novel comes to represent up to two-thirds of all new novels published in France over the heart of the eighteenth century.[3]

The takeover looks something like the curve in Figure 6.1. I say something like, for this is just one possible calculation, derived from a specific take on what should "count" as a document novel – a subject that will take up this and the following chapter. Still, we can make a few preliminary observations. First, document novels clearly rise and then fall and in a roughly symmetrical manner given the temporal bounds of the sampling. Second, this transformation of the novelistic landscape takes a lot of time to play out – roughly the same amount of time, for instance, as the *nouvelle*'s career lasts. Thus, the triumph of the document novel, temporary as it is, does not map on to a literary generation or school and cannot be dismissed

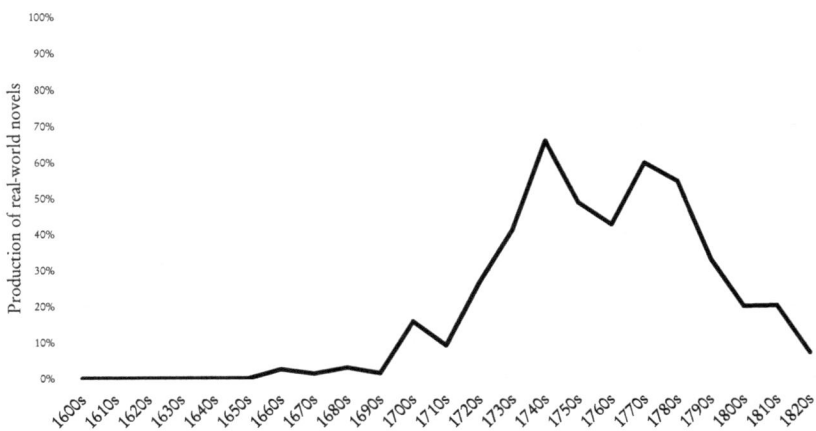

Figure 6.1 Document novels (one calculation).

as a *courte durée* "fashion" or "craze." Finally – and here we see a shape we haven't seen before – the document novel's success has two clear peaks coming three decades apart, in the 1740s and then in the 1770s.

But what, exactly, is a document novel? An epistolary collection, advertised as being a real correspondence; a memoir found at the bottom of a drawer; an ancient third-person text, discovered in some medieval castle: all these would seem to qualify in obvious ways as "documents," that is, texts originally written for private purposes and then subsequently ushered into print.[4] Yet, a little reflection – and perusal of the library – brings other examples into view whose case may not be so clear-cut. What of a memoir – real or fictional – that is written for publication? For example, the anonymously published *Roman sans titre* (1788) begins: "Everyone in this world has his mania; mine is to write my story. May all of France have a mania for reading it!"[5] Is such a first-person text, published by its putative author, still a document at all? What about an epistolary novel presented, quite frankly, as a novel? These are serious complications to the idea of the document novel; but they are also helpful questions, in that they point to a hypothesis: maybe first-person novels – which certainly aren't new to the seventeenth century – acquire at that time a kind of "documenticity" that they then proceed to lose. Think of the Western tradition of first-person texts – taking the term to refer to texts with first-person narrators active within the storyworld.[6] Petronius gave us the *Satyricon* long ago, and at least one Greek novel (Achilles Tatius's second-century *Leucippe and Clitophon*) features a first-person (frame) narration; then come the Renaissance examples, such as Francesco Colonna's beautifully strange *Hypnerotomachia Poliphili* (1499) and of course the Spanish picaresque tradition. All these and others are undoubtedly in

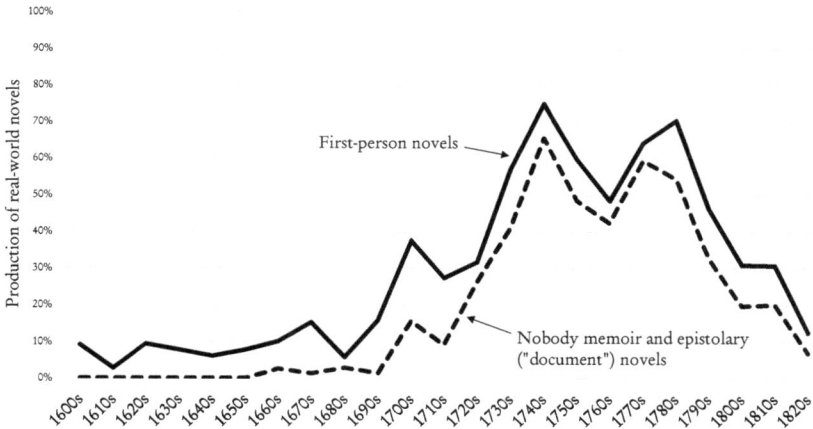

Figure 6.2 Forms of first-person novels.

the first person, and – as long as we don't take too parochial a view of the term – probably novels as well. They are lacking, however, documenticity, meaning the suggestion that they were written privately and then – without their hero–author's knowledge – taken public.

What we need to understand, then, is the relationship between document novels and other first-person novels – of which there are obviously more than the ones tracked in Figure 6.1. That graph showed only memoirs and epistolary novels taking as their subject characters I've called nobodies (see Chapter 1); moreover, the calculation ignored the complication, just mentioned, that all such novels may not possess the same degree of documenticity. Yet in fact there are not *many* more first-person novels than these, as Figure 6.2 shows.

The "rise" of the first person starting in the late seventeenth century is entirely imputable to two specific narrative artifacts, memoir and epistolary novels. Other first persons preexisted these forms, but they never made up a significant part of the real-world novel production: just under 7 percent prior to the 1660s and just under 8 percent for the entire seventeenth century. And over the 230 years of this study, memoir and epistolary novels represent 67 percent of all French first-person novels published.

So how did the document novel develop? Did it emerge as a transformation of previous first-person novels? What did first-person novels look like before they acquired "documenticity"? And are there types of document novels that do not take the form of memoirs or letters? To answer these questions, we need more precise categorization. I have divided first-person novels into a number of categories. *Epistolary novels* take, obviously, the form of letters. (The many varieties of epistolary exchange will be examined in the following chapter.) The narrative backbone of *memoirs* is the narrator's life; their organizational principle is biographical. *Episode narrator novels*, by contrast, are more tightly plotted and properly dramatic: they recount a single episode or experience.[7] *Travel novels* are organized as the unfolding of a trip. In *observer narrator novels*, the first-person narrator is not the protagonist. *Frame narrator novels* have first-person narrators who introduce inset narratives. Finally, *lyric* novels are so named because of their resemblance to the stance of the Petrarchan poet: in these (rare) texts, a male lover narrates in a general or a symbolic manner the unfeeling behavior of his female love object.

Because of the small number of all of these types before the end of the seventeenth century, a decade-by-decade plot of their frequency presents no useful information. But we can compare the distribution of first-person novel types from before the apparent emergence of the document novel around 1670 to the types that prosper during the ascent of documenticity, from 1671 to 1740. In the latter period, memoirs make up 54 percent of all first-person novels; and epistolary, travel, episode, observer, and frame narratives share the remainder, roughly equally. But prior to 1671, the situation is radically different. Then, lyric, frame, episode, and observer novels make up 92 percent of all first-person novels, again in roughly equal proportions; a few memoirs and epistolary works split the rest. Thus, prior to the memoir novel's rise, first-person forms are a heterogeneous group; and it is a small group at that, containing roughly thirty works over seven decades. The result is that the most frequent of the types (observer narratives) numbers only in the single digits.[8] In other words, though there are unquestionably first-person novels before 1670, no one artifact possesses anything like popularity, and the link between examples of each artifact may well be tenuous (an author of an observer novel can probably not be imagined to be following a "model"). All this changes over the next seven decades, with a huge advancement for memoirs; the small uptick in absolute numbers for most of the other forms doesn't even keep up relative to the expanding production. Among other changes, travel novels appear, whereas lyric narratives – whose filiation with Renaissance poetic custom is obvious – disappear. And though epistolary narratives show gains, they are essentially an also-ran for this entire period.

The ascendency of the document novel isn't quite represented by Figure 6.1: memoir and epistolary novels taking as their subject nobodies are the most important kinds of document novels but not the only kinds. Again, these are barely present for the first forty years of their existence, make some strides in the 1700s, and then commence their meteoric rise in the 1720s. This expansion, however, is in fact the result of a process – a refinement of the more inchoate but also more robust interest in documents. Part of that interest is visible in what one might call report novels – novels reproducing the text of a "letter" written to an acquaintance. And another part consists of *apocryphal* memoirs and letter collections – that is, documents attributed to somebodies of the day. None of these variants is particularly important over the long haul, but they do distribute historically in significant ways, as we can see in Figure 6.3, which displays these other document novels alongside the ones that are destined to a better future.

What is obvious – besides the origin of the double peak in document novels, a result of the asynchronous popularity of its major artifacts – is that consistent but modest use of documents prepares the break out of the memoir novel in the 1720s. Prior to that decade, only one-third of document novels take the form of nobody memoir novels or – and there are few during these years – epistolary novels. Novelists experimenting with document forms prefer two other options – the weaker first-person of the report novel and then somebody memoir novels. Yet, starting in the 1720s, everything changes: one form of documenticity has marginalized all the others. Between 1721 and 1750, 77 percent of all document novels are nobody memoir novels. This artifact is therefore the result of a now-familiar process of homogenization within the broader class of document novels.

So, while something does begin in the 1660s, that something isn't really the invention and subsequent spread of one specific artifact. Instead, the 1660s inaugurate an incubation period during which a number of strategies

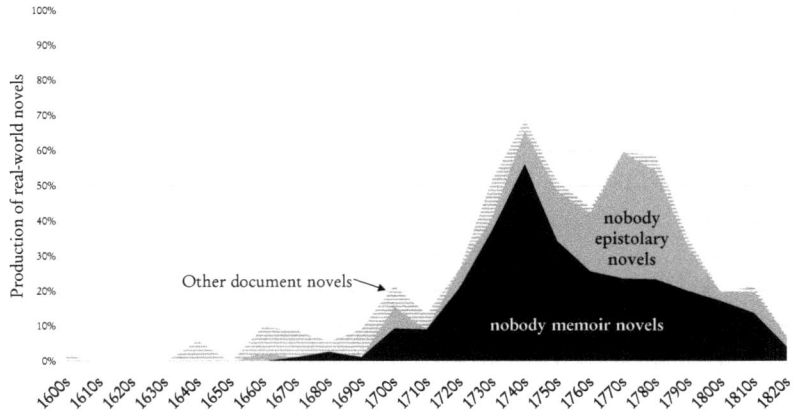

Figure 6.3 Varieties of document novels.

for integrating first-person documents are tried out. In its early decades, the memoir novel is closely associated with contemporary somebodies – much more so than the third-person novel of those years, which registers only modest interest in such protagonists. (The somebody novel over the seventeenth century as a whole is overwhelmingly historical.) During the half-century running from 1660s to the 1710s, memoir novels featuring somebodies significantly outnumber those with nobodies. The numbers of each are relatively small, but statistically speaking, the early memoir novel is an apocryphal memoir novel: seven out of ten concern known personalities of the day. Third-person novels register historically high interest in contemporary somebodies over the same period as well but the high is less significant: only 23 percent. For whatever reason – I will speculate presently – the memoir novel is at the outset rarely a nobody novel.

At whose expense do document novels finally prosper? An answer is close at hand from the previous chapter: the *nouvelle*. Using what I called in Figure 5.8 (page 101) the "new loosest scenario" – comprising works under 57,000 words with strong truth postures but many insetting possibilities – we can see in Figure 6.4 the document's novel takeover quite clearly. The first-person document novel's (slowish) rise correlates very nicely with the *nouvelle*'s (slowish) fall. Indeed, it's the memoir novel's ascent in the 1720s and 1730s that appears directly responsible for the *nouvelle*'s sharp decline in those same years, after hovering at about 50 percent of the production for the previous three decades.

And here – in contrast to what we saw with the "replacement" of the *roman* by the *nouvelle* in the century before – the one's gain is close to

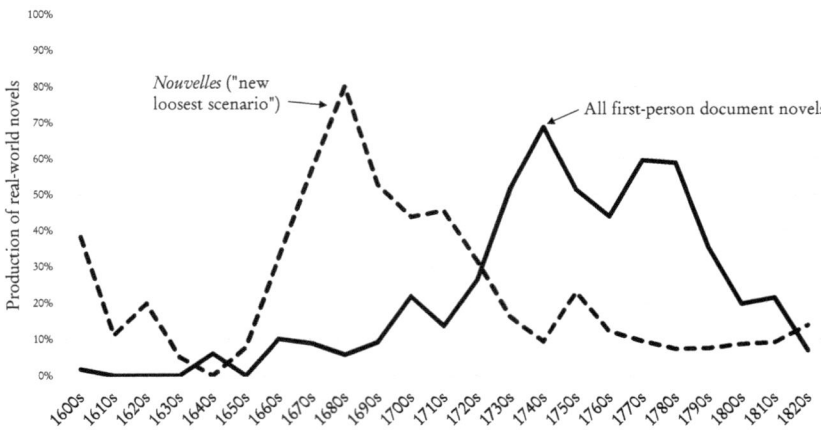

Figure 6.4 *Nouvelles* and documents.

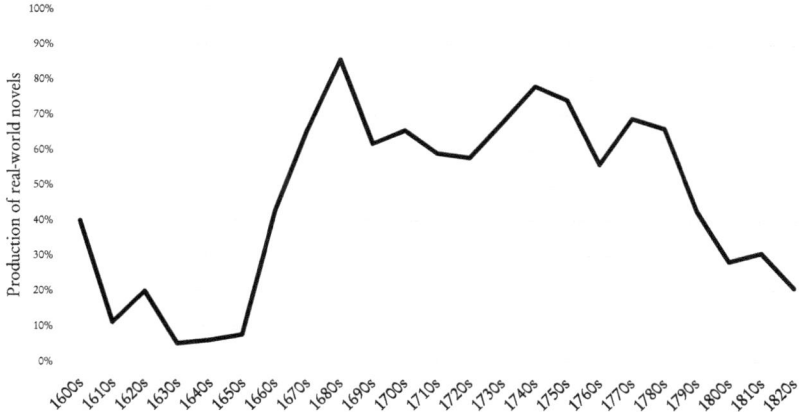

Figure 6.5 Cumulative market share of *nouvelles* and document novels.

the other's loss. Figure 6.5 adds the figures for both types of novels, and it indicates only a slight trough between the peak of the earlier form and the peak of the later one. From the 1690s to the 1720s, there is indeed some "slack" – more novels than usual that are neither *nouvelles* nor document novels. For these four decades, 63 percent of novels fit these two categories. Of the rest, 18 percent would count as *nouvelles* but for their failure to fit the new loose scenario in terms of either length (they are over 56,000 words), or their specific insetting (they feature *Decameron*-style frames), or their specific truth posture (they are "indeterminate"). A further 10 percent are nondocument first-person narratives. The rest – about 9 percent – are something else: books that miss being *nouvelles* for other reasons still (e.g., works over the word limit *and* featuring "*Decameron*" insetting; Aristotelian works on mythological subjects; and so on). All these books are the formal flotsam and jetsam of the novel. They aren't worlds apart from the forms used by the majority of writers; those forms themselves vary a good deal, but the ones that aren't counted with them simply vary more. This trough does confirm to some extent the idea, commonplace among historians of the early French novel, that the turn of the eighteenth century represents a fallow period during which novelists were searching for a way forward. Only to some extent, however: the majority of novels published nevertheless corresponded to either the waning or the waxing form, and in this the transition from *nouvelle* to document novel looks much more like what happened in the recorded music market (Figure 5.11, page 103) than did the handoff from *roman* to *nouvelle*.[9]

(If Figure 6.4 indicates a rather straightforward takeover, it also presents a curiosity, which I will note parenthetically while postponing explanation for the final chapter. *Nouvelles* and document novels come in at roughly the same time – the 1650s for the former, the 1660s for the latter. Yet their success is strikingly asynchronous: the *nouvelle* reaches its peak in just three decades, while the document novel takes upward of a century. This remarkable discrepancy may not be so strange. In Chapter 2, we saw that Aristotelianism of one sort or another characterized the novels across the "divide" of the 1650s; in Chapter 3, we saw that the practice of insetting, though evolving, did not respect that break either. Thus, there is much more continuity between the *roman* and *nouvelle* than between the *nouvelle* and the document novel. Technologically, it proved easier for writers to adopt.)

One further observation about the takeoff of the document novel is in order, for that takeoff does not correspond only to the decline of *nouvelles*. It also accompanies a notable expansion in the production of novels (Figure 6.6). Novel production varies a good deal, but for forty years, from 1671 to 1710, something of the order of ten new novels a year were published. The 1710s and 1720s saw production sputter to half of that: the *nouvelle* was hanging on in terms of market share, but it was a weak market. In the 1730s, however, some twenty new novels a year hit the market, and though production continued to vary, this was more or less the new normal – not a wholesale revolution, as is sometimes said, but certainly a sustained uptick.[10] The success of the nobody memoir novel in this decade was not only in proportional terms. It was also a success in sheer numbers. The *nouvelle*, one might note, didn't falter in this decade because fewer were published: in fact, the sample for the 1730s suggests that some 3.3 *nouvelles* appeared each year, compared to

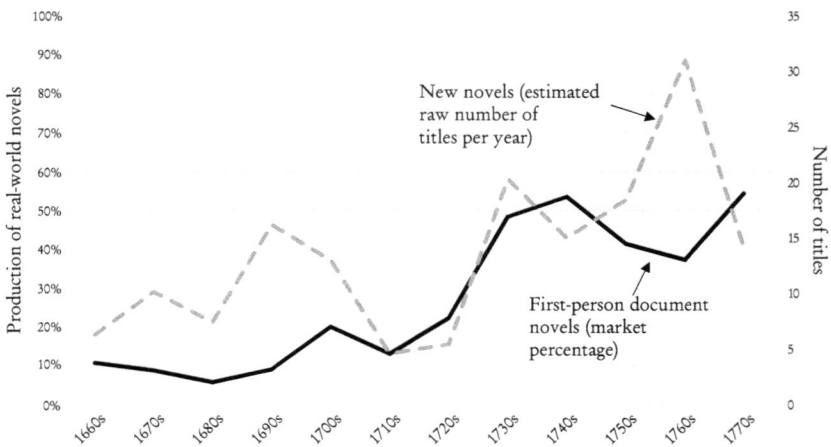

Figure 6.6 Document novels and the production of all novels.

1.2 the decade before. But it profited unequally from the expanded market, since document novels went from one a year in the 1720s to 9.2 in the 1730s. Although the correlation between the rise of the document novel and a rising production of novels may of course be a coincidence, it does appear that this particular rising tide lifted some boats more than others.

One explanation for the substantial growth in the production of novels in the 1730s might be found precisely in the popularity of one new novelistic form. That is, it's a given (from the data) that the device of the memoir was successful relative to other devices: it got a bigger piece of the pie. But maybe the pie itself was getting bigger precisely because of that popularity – because, in other words, of the expressive possibilities opened up by the new form, possibilities that encouraged more writers and readers to produce and consume novels. This is merely a hypothesis, one that would need more data to strengthen; on the face of things, it may be more probable for relatively small markets (such as the one for novels in the first half of the eighteenth century) than for large ones. Suffice it to say that in addition to the type of external motivating factors traditional literary history reaches for to explain the expansion of novels in the 1730s – a concomitant expansion of the bourgeois reading public (always a convenient explanation one can situate wherever one pleases[11]) or (more convincingly) the cultural rebirth following the turbulent Regency years[12] – we might do well to consider this more artifactual factor: the memoir novel made it clear to people that the novel could do things they hadn't realized they wanted to do. It effectively changed behaviors. Of course, my figures cannot prove that this is the case, and it would certainly help to know how well the production of new novels in these years tracks with, say, the production of new plays, or indeed with the printing of old novels or translations: if the production of new novels outpaced the production of these other sorts of works, we would have at least some evidence that the novel was a special case.

Let's return now to a problem I raised at the outset of the chapter, which was to know if the first-person novel "de-documentifies" after its documentation. That is, if we consider a document novel to be one that presents for public, print consumption a document created for a private purpose, would a memoir novel admitted as an author's invention have documenticity? What about a purportedly authentic memoir written expressly for publication – self-published, as it were, and perhaps preceded by a preface not by an editor but by the memorialist himself or herself? Figure 6.7 separates out these arguably "less" documentary first persons from the more documentary first persons of memoirs and report novels and includes as well first-person forms possessing

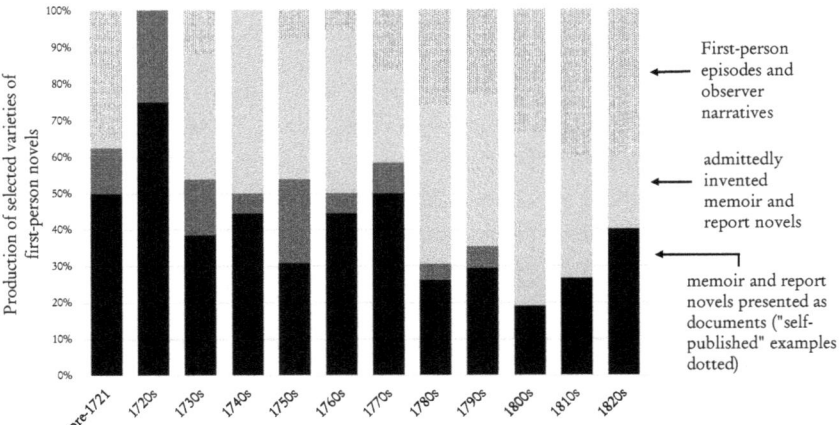

Figure 6.7 Documenticity and the first-person novel.

no documenticity – episode and observer novels. (Missing, then, are epistolary novels – to be examined in the following chapter – as well as the minor first-person forms of travel, frame, and lyric narratives.) Prior to the 1660s, we've seen, document novels were virtually nonexistent. Starting in the 1660s, they appear with more regularity, staging a "takeover" of the first-person novel, accomplished by the 1720s. This would mark the documentification of the first-person novel, a process whose regularity is of course undermined by the small size of the first-person novel population itself during these years. But nondocument first-person forms then stage a steady return, at the same time that memoirs are increasingly presented as inventions and that the form's "self-published" variant disappears. If this "de-documentification" starts quickly, however, it is nonetheless slow: already in the 1730s, many memoirs are presented as inventions, but the share of the latter changes little until the 1780s, at which point there is a slight additional retreat. Memoirs prove difficult to dissociate from their origins as a real-world form of discourse pressed into service as a novel. By the end of the period covered here, it is more likely for a first-person novel to take nondocumentary forms – episode and observer narrations – than of a de-documentified memoir. In a market now nearly taken over by the third person, these nondocumentary forms grab more of a shrinking pie.[13]

An additional way of measuring an erosion in documenticity simply involves the word "memoirs" itself, along with the word "life" – a standard designation for biographies. We might hypothesize that novels with these words in the title (or subtitle) have more documenticity than those that don't: as the memoir novel becomes ensconced as a familiar narrative mode, the real-world discursive origin of the mode becomes effaced. There is evidence of this in Figure 6.8. At the start of the period, the terms *mémoire* and *vie* are prevalent in titles. (The figures from the 1720s do not follow this pattern, but the subsample here – four memoir novels – is very small.) During the heart of the century, the terms are present in the titles of a little over half of memoir novels, but a clear erosion characterizes the last third of the century. (The small number of memoir novels in the last two decades of the sample makes those particular measurements unhelpful.)

But there is one more major first-person artifact I have not yet discussed. It is invisible in Figure 6.2, for it is not in any accepted sense a "first-person novel." It is also *rendered* invisible by scholarly preconceptions. Certainly, it's true that there are few first-person novels in the seventeenth century and that there are a lot in the eighteenth. It is also true that this brute fact – long obvious even without reliable quantitative measures – comforts the "objectivity" and "subjectivity" commonly associated with these respective centuries. The remark Blaise Pascal flung against Montaigne – *le moi est haïssable* (the self is hateful)[14] – has come to define an age obsessed with idealism, rationality, aristocratic decorum, and indeed with the third person. "The idealist novel [of the seventeenth century]," writes Thomas Pavel, "is usually told impersonally (i.e., in the third person), as if to communicate to the reader the objective force of the fundamental ideal."[15] In such a light, "the passage from the omniscience of the seventeenth-century novelist to the necessarily reduced perspective of personal point of view was deeply linked

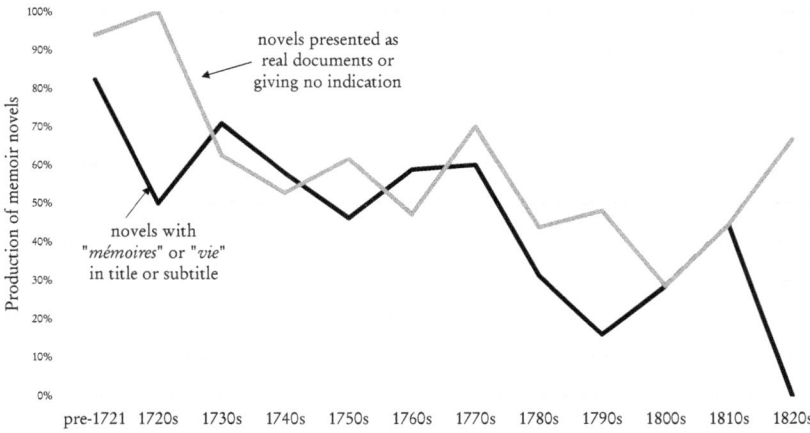

Figure 6.8 Documenticity of the memoir novel.

to a wider mutation" – a mutation that now organizes culture around the individual.[16] To be sure, standard literary history acknowledges occasional uses of the first person but points out that they were the work of writers fundamentally opposed to the reigning classical ethos and thus marginalized for their free thinking – the irreverent Sorel, in his picaresque *Francion* (1623); the persecuted Théophile de Viau, in the tantalizing fragment known as *Première Journée* (1623); and the visionary Cyrano and his *Etats et empires de la lune* (1657).[17]

All this ignores, however, a massive chunk of first-person narration occurring not as free-standing texts (that would then be called "first-person novels") but *within* third-person texts – to wit, within the inset novels examined in Chapter 3. To recap, these novels provide the backstory of various characters via those characters' own oral narrations of their lives or a part thereof to other characters. Perhaps the only commentator to pay attention to inset narratives in the context of first-person discourse is Jean Rousset, who insists that reasons of classical propriety dictated the erasure of the first person that Heliodorus's example introduced into the long *roman*: "most novelists do their best to skirt the very *I* that the system of insets [*insertions*] they practice would actually seem to prescribe.... This eviction is not total, but it intensifies as the century wears on."[18] The purge of the first person is achieved, according to Rousset, by having squires and ladies-in-waiting tell the stories that protagonists used to tell themselves. The difficulty with Rousset's hypothesis is that empirical evidence does not confirm it. While it's true that certain novels conspicuously avoid first-person insets – even theorizing the impropriety of telling one's own adventures (notably the well-known *Clélie* [Scudéry, 1653–1661], to which Rousset refers) – the vast majority make use of them at all points covered by this study. Figure 6.9 shows that Rousset is correct to the extent that more mid-seventeenth century writers opt for third-person insets than at any other time; but the effect is short-lived. At any rate, his contention was probably underwritten less by empirical observation and more by the commonplaces about the seventeenth and eighteenth centuries I've just referred to. One can't very well have the first person rise when literary history has long wanted it to, if in fact it has been there all along.

But Figure 6.9 is a blunt instrument: it amalgamates all inset types, and more important, it classifies novels as having first-person insets even if only one of its usually multiple insets is actually in the first person. It also gives us no sense of how quantitatively important first-person narration is within the third-person novels that feature it. After all, it might be that the total percent of the novel given over to this kind of narration is

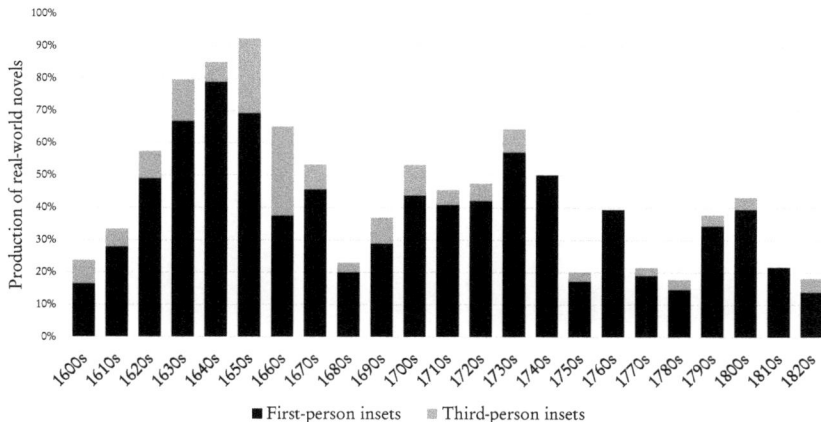

Figure 6.9 Narrative person of inset narratives.

minimal. Unfortunately, the scrutiny required to quantify all the insets in the sample would require more labor than I was able to devote to the problem. I can nonetheless offer some sense of the amplitude of first-person narration within the seventeenth century novel specifically, at least the variety most closely associated with Heliodorus. This information comes from a subsample. For eight of the ten decades of the century (the 1620s through the 1690s) and the years 7, 8, and 9 of each decade, I have isolated all insets within "Heliodorian" works (Types 1 and 2) and tagged them for length and narrative person. This enables us to see how much of these novels is taken up by which kind of narration. And it turns out that while Type 1 novels devote a greater percentage of their pages to first-person narration (37 percent) than Type 2 novels (30 percent) – and less to the main third-person narration – the composition of both types is broadly similar (see Figure E6.1). Overall, 35 percent of the pages of Types 1 and 2 inset novels is given over to first-person narration. Historically, there is some movement, visible in Figure 6.10. Again, bearing out one of Rousset's contentions, we see that first-person narration does retreat to some extent in the midcentury: the expansion of insets in those decades is mostly an expansion of the third-person variety. Yet, first-person narration never represents less than 25 percent of the total pages of this kind of novel, and those percentages appear to rise substantially after the midcentury mark.

Overall, how important are these numbers? If we were to tabulate narration in the first person generally, rather than simply "first-person novels," what would the picture of the century be like? The data presented above is limited – subject to caution, not only because of the smaller samples involved but also because it relates to Types 1 and 2 inset novels only. Nonetheless, it can be used

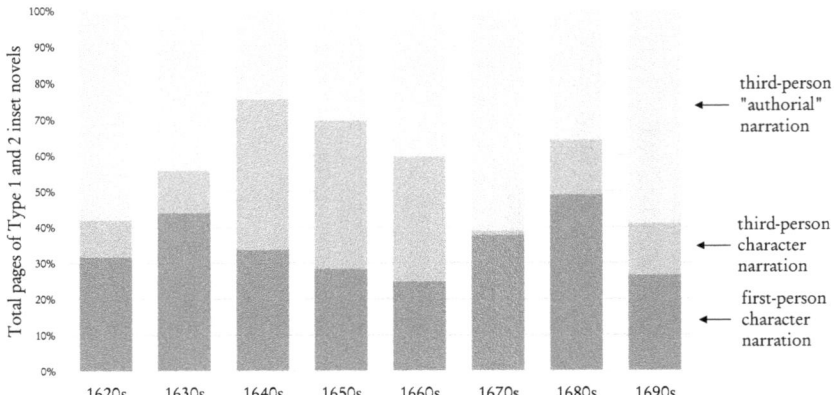

Figure 6.10 Real-world inset novels by narrative person, Types 1 and 2 combined (subsamples).

to produce heurisitic estimates of first-person narration over the century by divvying up novels according to how much of it they contain. In other words, a novel that is made up of 50 percent of first-person insets and 50 percent of third-person narration (either in the main narrative or in other inset narratives) will be counted as half a first-person novel and half a third-person novel. To start, let's recalculate the average first-person percentage of Heliodorian novels by considering only Types 1 and 2 novels that contain first-person narration in the first place. (That way, we will not impute such narration to novels that can't have any of it.) Both types average 38 percent. Further, let us assume that Type 3 novels – novels in which (usually) two characters meet and one precedes to tell his or her story (which is sometimes reciprocated) – consist of 90 percent first-person narration – but again, only if their insets are in the first person. (The figure of 90 percent strikes me as reasonable since the frame narratives are flimsy and take up little space – a trait that sets the type apart from Type 2 novels.) As an estimate for Type 4 novels (which contain backstories not integral to the plot) with first-person narration, I will use a figure of 15 percent. Type 5 novels (*Decameron*-style exchanges) usually feature third-person insets, but for the ones that do contain first-person narration, I will estimate 20 percent. Only two Type 6 novels contain first-person narration, and I will simply leave these out of the calculation.

These estimates, combined with true "first-person" novels, can give us a better idea of the importance of the first person during the century.[19] Making the graph in Figure 6.11 requires recourse to a fiction, of course, but one that enables us to "recover" about 72 novels-worth of first-person narration. (For simplicity, I have not broken out the contribution of each

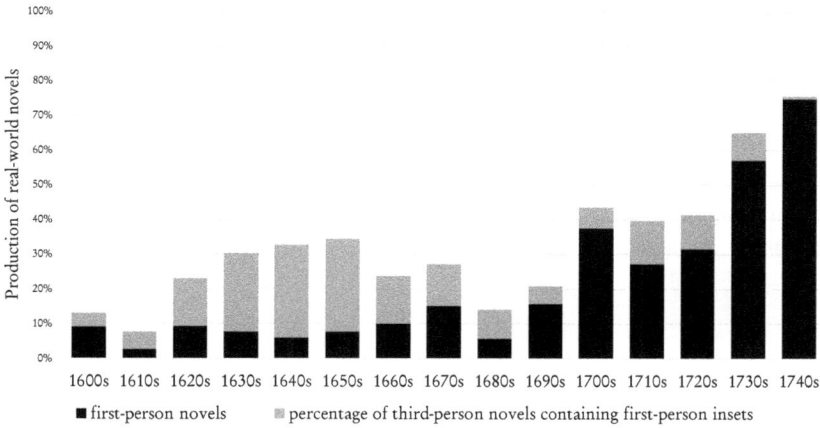

Figure 6.11 First-person narration in the novel (estimates).

inset type, but the Heliodorian varieties are responsible for 78 percent of this material.) As such, it provides a valuable corrective. Although the use of the first person in the seventeenth century does not rival what happens after the adoption of the memoir novel, it is clearly a "mainstream" practice and greatly exceeds what one would expect from measuring properly first-person texts alone. And against the claims of Rousset, the heart of the seventeenth century is prime ground for the *I*: though texts in the middle decades contain somewhat less first-person narration proportionally, the preponderance of Types 1 and 2 novels makes up for it. First-person narration tracks, then, with the fortunes of the Heliodorian novel. The 1680s and 1690s represent the point of historic scarcity of the first person; this moment, dominated by the relatively linear *nouvelle*, also sits between the decline of the Heliodorian form and the rise of the first-person document novel. (See Figure E6.2.) Because of the abandonment of the Heliodorian form, the novel loses its central first-person technology. It gains a new and improved one with the memoir.

Thus, to measure the importance of seventeenth-century first-person narration is not simply to contest clichéd views of the classical ethos. It is also to begin to recognize the properly *technological* character of these literary forms and more precisely the discontinuity between them. The embedded first-person narration typical of Heliodorian novels in no way "became" or "evolved into" the memoir novel: one died out – or rather was reduced to a marginal role – and the other was developed, but only after a lag of decades. In all likelihood, both served the same general purpose, summed up by a French master of the memoir novel, Prévost: "The best novelists have not dreamed up any more powerful way of pleasing and involving the reader than to put their narrative in the mouth of the hero himself."[20] But just as in aviation the combustion engine and the jet engine serve the same purpose – gaining and maintaining the altitude and speed of the aircraft – the latter in no way comes from the former. And so while the jet engine obviously offers improved *performance* with respect to the combustion engine, it is not an improved *version* of its predecessor. The memoir novel was such a technological leap: it moved first-person narration from the hero's *mouth* to the hero's *pen*. I will explore further the nature of this leap in Chapter 10.

7 Documenticity II

The Two Rises of the Epistolary Novel

The invention and triumph of the epistolary novel makes for a nice story in France. A nice anthology, even: one was put together in 1983 by Bernard Bray and Isabelle Landy-Houillon. It included five short novels, foremost among them the *Lettres portugaises* (1669, attrib. Guilleragues) and especially Graffigny's proto-feminist hit *Lettres d'une Péruvienne* (1647), which had never been available in modern pocket book format; a few other curiosities rounded out the volume. Bray and Landy-Houillon's goal was to offer "a truly complete panorama" of the genre's origins – a panorama that excluded, of course, Montesquieu's *Lettres persanes* (1721), presumably on everyone's bookshelf already.[1] In the *Lettres portugaises* and two additional novels from the late seventeenth century, it was easy to spot the early gestation that preceded the triumphs of Montesquieu and Graffigny, which in turn were built on by Rousseau (*Julie, ou la Nouvelle Héloïse*, 1761) and Laclos (*Les Liaisons dangereuses*, 1782). Such a string of masterpieces confirmed that the epistolary novel was a major narrative form in France for well over a hundred years. One could also add – the editors of the anthology didn't – that France's best writers apparently recognized the form's literary potential long before the English, who had to wait for Richardson's novels of the 1740s.[2]

It's a coherent story, but Figure 7.1 offers one possible count of epistolary novels published before 1751. I will call it the "permissive" count, for reasons I will explain.[3] Things start off with a bang in the 1660s – or more precisely in 1668 and 1669, where the first examples are clustered – only to stagnate (at best) over the next sixty years. In the 1730s and 1740s, we finally see a substantial increase in titles, but even this belated rise must be put in perspective – the perspective of an expansion in the overall number of novels published.

In this view, the moment of progress, if such a term is justified, is pushed firmly into the 1740s, when the form's market percentage doubles previous highs, hitting 14 percent. On their appearance, the *Lettres portugaises* and the *Lettres persanes* were culturally important novels, and indeed they still are. It's much less clear, however, that they were part of a more general

Figure 7.1 Epistolary novels, 1601–1750 (permissive count).

discovery or invention of the epistolary form. Judging from Figure 7.1, only the much later *Lettres d'une Péruvienne* can plausibly lay claim to that.

For fans of the "gestation" argument, matters get worse. After all, everything hinges on what we agree to call an epistolary novel, and to arrive at the above figures I put up a big tent. Not, granted, the biggest tent possible: any book made up of letters, most would agree, isn't necessarily an epistolary novel. Hence, the above numbers do not include collections of letters designed as manuals in the tradition of the medieval *ars dictaminis* – say, *Essais de lettres familières sur toutes sortes de sujets, avec un discours sur l'art épistolaire et quelques remarques sur la langue française* (Furetière, 1684).[4] Excluded as well are collections on miscellaneous subjects: *Commerce de lettres curieuses et savantes* (Grimarest, 1700), for example, which offers an assortment of letters – really essays – on subjects ranging from gladiators to Furetière's ground-breaking dictionary, published not long before. Collections of correspondence by noted personalities were also set aside – *Lettres de messire Roger de Rabutin, comte de Bussy* (1697).[5]

The dividing line between exclusions like these – presumably uncontroversial – and others is hazy. For one, many early epistolary novels are built on the conceit of observation: characters exchange letters commenting on the society around them, relaying disparate pieces of gossip, telling stories. Such works tend to be discontinuous and minimally if at all plotted: imagine the *Lettres persanes*, minus its famous harem plot. So where, precisely, is the border between an observational epistolary novel and a mere letter miscellany of the type mentioned earlier? As for excluding real correspondences, the problem is obviously that in an age of pseudofactual pretense, many, if not most, letter novels were advertised precisely as real correspondences. Furthermore, some correspondences apocryphally attributed to celebrities cohere narratively: such is the case, for instance, with *Lettres de Ninon de Lenclos au marquis de Sévigné* (1750), in which the famous courtesan offers the young marquis pointers on how to seduce a certain countess. And finally, a number of early published epistolary exchanges did not in fact appear as stand-alone works: sometimes such exchanges were set within larger letter collections (e.g., *Lettres nouvelles de M. Boursault … avec sept lettres amoureuses d'une dame à un cavalier* [Boursault, 1697]) or else appended as an epistolary "annex" to third-person narratives (*La Religieuse pénitente, nouvelle d'Artois, avec quelques lettres que l'on croit être de l'auteur de cette histoire* [An, 1699]), a bit in the manner of the bonuses on DVDs.

Counting epistolary novels obviously involves, then, discriminations; these are undoubtedly subjective, but criteria can nevertheless be made explicit. The figures presented in Figure 7.1 include works structured as a series of discontinuous observations, provided that the actual exchange of letters is thematized enough to give readers the impression that they are reading a single "work." They include as well correspondences of celebrities when those correspondences cohere around the subject that was the *sine qua non* of novels at the time – love. They include works featuring epistolary annexes. They even include works that did not meet the 10,000-word minimum length I've used in the rest of this study. The bad news for those who think that the epistolary novel is gathering steam over these nine decades is that even with a very liberal definition of the form, the numbers are paltry, as we've just seen. And if we harmonize our view of the epistolary novel with general criteria of "novelness" used both elsewhere in this study and in the bibliographies on which its sampling is based, the figures are still less impressive. Figure 7.1 shows five works featuring epistolary annexes, seventeen observational epistolary works in which the interaction of the letter writers is undeveloped and plot essentially nonexistent,[6] and seven works under 10,000 words. Excluding them cuts the raw numbers of epistolary novels by about half, which has the effect of nullifying the market take-off that Figure 7.1 suggested we locate in the 1740s. (See Figure E7.1.)

I have been saying "the epistolary novel": the items retained can surely be so called. But it's important to recognize that from another point of view – the view of people writing and reading, say, in the 1690s or the 1730s – the category probably didn't exist. After all, "epistolary novels" are a startlingly negligible feature of the novelistic landscape of the period: the tokens are so few that we can well wonder if the type was recognizable for contemporaries. Undeniably, the *Lettres portugaises* and the *Lettres persanes* are both composed of letters. But the idea that they might belong to a single formal class of novels is something that may well occur only to someone who has seen a lot of such creatures – notably, to someone who knows what will happen later, after 1750. In other words, there are obvious "family resemblances" between those two canonical works, but the resemblances become obvious only once we know there's a family. And before 1750, most of what we seem to have is a number of isolated artifacts that may very well not share the same DNA.[7]

But of course, the epistolary novel does eventually become a collectively recognized practice, acquiring a kind of typical shape. When, exactly? Figure 7.2 shows the market penetration of epistolary novels from 1701 on, now expressed as a share of real-world novels.[8]

Once it finally starts rising, the curve is predictable: a peak, falling away evenly on either side. The figures are no doubt more modest than many literary historians would expect: in the 1770s, the high-water mark for the form, one-third of French novels are epistolary novels; the following decade shows just under a quarter, and figures fall away considerably from there. Not much, given how strongly we associate the eighteenth-century novel with its epistolary variant and not much, given the preponderance of epistolary novels in the canon: *Julie* and *Les Liaisons dangereuses*, obviously, but also the successful novels of Riccoboni, Charrière, and Cottin that have, in the wake of feminist studies, appeared on syllabi (among others, and respectively: *Lettres de mistriss Fanni Butlerd*, 1757; *Lettres de mistriss Henley*, 1774; and *Claire d'Albe*, 1799). Undoubtedly, there was a fashion for the form, but it's not as if it ever became truly hegemonic. As we saw in the last chapter, the memoir novel had much more significant dominance.

Figure 7.2 Epistolary novels, 1701–1830.

But the real mystery is surely the long gestation – if it is really a gestation. And to get at this, we need to return to the early years and to the permissive definition I alluded to. For, as with the memoir novel, "the" early epistolary novel was really a nebula of obviously related but heterogeneous practices – including, for example, the relatively rare practice of epistolary documents as an annex to a third-person novel. Most letter novels of the period can be divided into observational plots and love plots. As suggested earlier, observational works can be further divided into two separate categories. Type 1 observation works contain sufficient characterization of the letter-writers (they have backstories, things happen to them in between the letters) and sufficient thematization of letter-writing (they reply to previous missives) to give the work novelistic coherence. Type 2 observational works, lacking such coherence, are the ones that I don't consider novels and that are included earlier under the permissive scenario. Still, their inclusion helps give a sense of early epistolary practice, as we see in Figure 7.3.[9] Prior to 1721, epistolary works are divided about equally between novels treating love and works of observation. Over the following two decades, observation takes over the epistolary form. In all these years, unplotted observational nonnovels outnumber their plotted novelistic cousins.

Another way of putting these inchoate beginnings is to say that to the extent the epistolary novel does start to rise from the 1720s, it does so because it is perceived as being good for a certain specific type of novel. Indeed, the long upward slope in Figure 7.2 is actually hiding another rise – and fall – now visible in Figure 7.4.

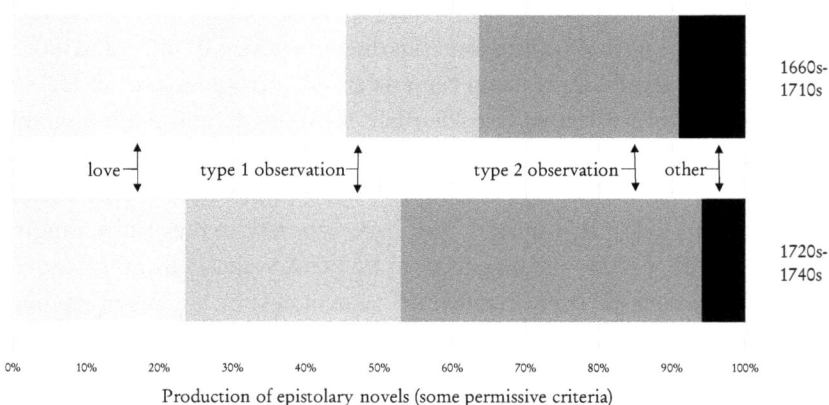

Figure 7.3 Subject matter of pre-1751 epistolary novels (some permissive criteria).

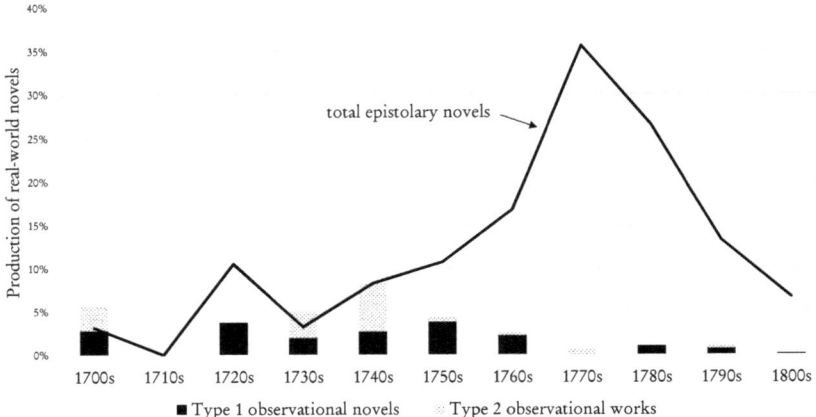

Figure 7.4 The rise and fall of the observational epistolary novel.

The rise is feeble, to say the least: never do Type 1 observational novels make up more than 5 percent of the total production of novels, though the inclusion of Type 2 works helps see the use as a peaking and falling away.[10] Two canonical novels belong to the rise and fall – the *Lettres persanes* and the *Lettres d'une Péruvienne*. But by the time epistolary novels start to achieve their maximum penetration – the 1760s – this variety is on its way out. Montesquieu and Graffigny made good use of the epistolary form, we might say. But it's closer to the mark to say that they helped develop *one* epistolary novel, a novel that would soon be all but abandoned in favor of a different one.

And in fact there is one additional hidden rise: epistolary novels of love must also be divided into two – thematically divided, though we will see that the division is also a formal and historical one. The first variant was already visible "from the start," as it were, in the *Lettres portugaises*. Just as it's not hard to see why the epistolary format was particularly suited to novels of social observation, the format's use for amorous discourse seems intuitive and indeed was probably familiar, say, from the celebrated correspondence of Heloise and Abelard: lovers writing to each other, testifying to and philosophizing about their passion, reproaching one another their slights, and so on.[11] But there is a second distinct type of love plot – the sentimental love plot. Besides its derogatory one, "sentimental" can have a variety of meanings, ranging from the fairly precise definitions used by literary and cultural historians to much more elastic uses in which the term simply becomes synonymous with "affective" or "emotional." My use here is close to the understanding of scholars such as David J. Denby and Margaret Cohen, who've isolated typical features of eighteenth-century sentimental plots – the way, for example, they pit love (aligned with virtue) against social convention (seen as unexamined prejudice). In short, the sentimental novel is of a piece with Enlightenment critique, in which "nature" is leveraged to break down existing social order – in other words, to unmask what has passed for natural as arbitrary cultural convention. In this type of epistolary novel, then, love is less a passionate but a solipsistic bond between two individuals than the promise of a new order in which loving individuals can realize a happiness that is never separate from virtue and that ultimately radiates out from the couple to society as a whole.[12]

Let's divide, then, epistolary novels with love plots into two categories, one for the sentimental epistolary novel and a second, catch-all category for all other letter novels whose primary subject is love (pining or quarreling lovers, couples separated by adventurous circumstances, and worldly seductions).[13] For ninety years starting in the 1660s, the few letter novels concerning love that we have are all of the latter sort. Then, there is an abrupt change (Figure 7.5). Viewed in this manner, saying the epistolary novel takes a long time to rise may not be quite right. In fact, for novels of one kind of love, it never becomes particularly useful, whereas novelists writing about a slightly different subject matter adopt the epistolary form very quickly. Unfortunately, I tagged epistolary novels alone for subject matter, so we cannot compare the prospering of the sentimental novel generally to that of the sentimental epistolary novel specifically. (Sentimentality is usually associated with the second half of the eighteenth century, at any rate.) Figure 7.6, however, adds back in observational novels so as to get a fuller picture of the changes. (Epistolary novels not figuring here have didactic, educational, erotic, and other miscellaneous subjects; they amount to about 12 percent of the entire production.) The epistolary novel that refuses to rise has subject matter different from the one that rises spectacularly.

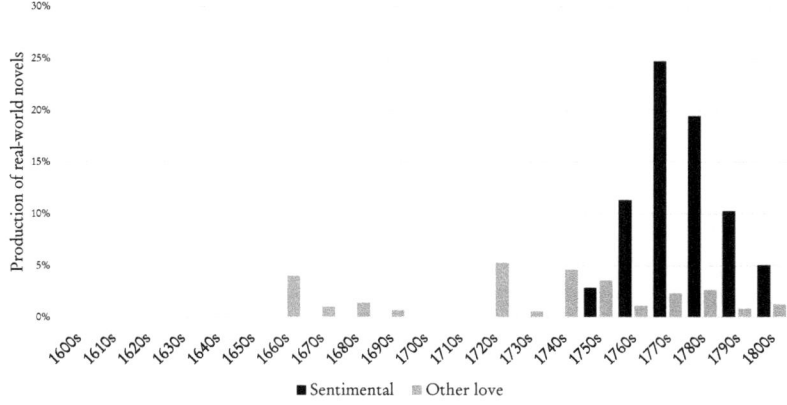

Figure 7.5 Epistolary novels of love.

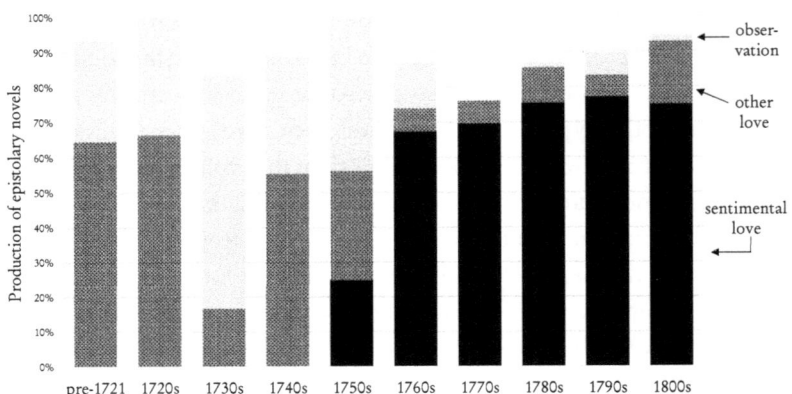

Figure 7.6 Epistolary novels by subject matter.

But it is not just that new subject matter has been as if "poured into" the selfsame form. In fact, the new subject matter correlates with formal change. Perry Anderson has written about the "technical innovation" that Montesquieu introduces to the epistolary novel: a structure, qualified as "polyphonic," in which multiple correspondents write to multiple recipients. Before then, other geometries had been exploited: the *Lettres portugaises* followed the model of one correspondent writing to a single recipient; the much earlier *Processo de cartas de amores* (Segura, 1548), customarily cited as the very first epistolary novel in Europe, featured two correspondents exchanging letters; and the much translated observational novel *L'esploratore turco* (Marana, 1684) had one correspondent sending dispatches to multiple recipients. (The fifth permutation possible – multiple correspondents writing to one recipient – Anderson reckons to be a "null category.") Montesquieu's innovation, for Anderson, is key: it explains why the epistolary format here is no longer "a flimsy vehicle for philosophical disquisitions." Montesquieu takes the letter conceit well beyond the "unstable mixtures" proposed over the 150-odd years since the *Processo de cartas*, arriving at the "synthesis" they had lacked. "The ingenious design of Montesquieu's novel permitted for the first time a kind of fusion."[14]

Anyone familiar with the novel, and especially with Montesquieu's careful work distributing dated letters in nonchronological sequences, would probably agree with Anderson's declaration of ingenuity. But was Montesquieu the origin of later canonical polyphonic novels such as *Clarissa* and *Julie*? To tag epistolary novels for the geometry of their correspondence, I've simplified Anderson's categories, reducing them to three: those featuring one, two, or multiple correspondents.[15] As a percentage of the total production of epistolary novels, the types break down as in Figure 7.7.

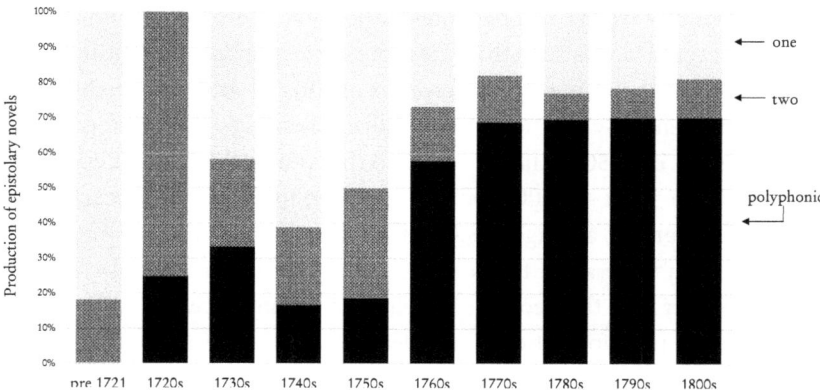

Figure 7.7 Number of correspondents.

It may well be that the *Lettres persanes* represents the world's first polyphonic epistolary novel: in France, at least, none existed before; almost all consisted of the letters of just one correspondent. But it's also true that this "technical innovation," seemingly so superior in the formal "synthesis" it enables, spends some four decades looking for users. In fact, it's only with the sentimental epistolary novel in the 1760s that this formal variant meets substantial success. At that point, quite suddenly, polyphonic novels become the majority choice and represent a stable 70 percent of the production over the last 40 years of the time span.

The closer we look, the more Montesquieu's novel looks like a historical anomaly. Indeed, before it finally and definitively "takes" in the 1760s, the polyphonic form actually retreats following some initial success. Equally striking is the failure especially of epistolary novels with love plots to experiment with the feature: before 1751, only one out of thirteen such novels employs the format (it is from 1742). The figures for observational epistolary novels are higher, at 20 percent – a figure that nonetheless strikes me as low, given that these are the books most temporally and thematically proximate to Montesquieu.[16] It's probably safest, then, to say that Montesquieu's success has nothing to do with the much later dominance of polyphony, which correlates with the arrival of a kind of subject matter that did not even exist when Montesquieu wrote.

Statistically and historically, it would seem that there are three distinct types of epistolary novels. First, the observational variant that we've seen "rise" – the word is a little misleading – from the 1720s to the 1760s. This novel does not change much over time, not even around the 1750 point that marks a pivot for the epistolary form in general. Before 1751, the observational novel is on average 61,000 words long and, as I've said, uses a polyphonic structure 20 percent of the time. From 1751 on, it still averages 61,000 words and becomes only a shade more polyphonic – 24 percent of these works have three or more correspondents. Looking at this type of novel, then, one would have no inkling of any sort of change in epistolarity generally. But novels with subjects relating to love change hugely from one side of 1750 to the other. Up to that point, this kind of epistolary novel is quite short – 29,000 words – and monophonic 60 percent of the time. Afterward, it averages 78,000 words and is polyphonic 69 percent of the time. If we bracket the complication of length and simply focus on subject matter and the geometry of the correspondence, as in Figure 7.8, the wholesale transformation is still clear. (This graph ignores the relatively small number of epistolary novels [12 percent] that concern subjects other than observation or love.) Novels with a simple correspondent structure (i.e., one or two) are represented with horizontal lines. Certainly, a percentage of sentimental novels adopt that older, previously dominant structure, but the real expansion occurs in the polyphonic type, represented with dotted fill.

These figures suggest that novels like the *Lettres portugaises* and the *Lettres persanes* never really "evolved into" *Julie* or *Les Liaisons dangereuses*. The epistolary novel of observation remained what it always was (while being used less and less frequently); and an early, never popular epistolary novel of love – thirteen examples from 1668 to 1750! – was replaced, quite suddenly, by a different novel of love. I insist on this discontinuity because it is remarkable in the context of the present study. Again and again, we have observed slow growth of a nebula of artifacts, followed by a kind of "tipping point," when both the popularity and the homogeneity of the artifacts greatly increase. Although Figure 7.2 might suggest something similar, separating out observational epistolary novels makes it clear that

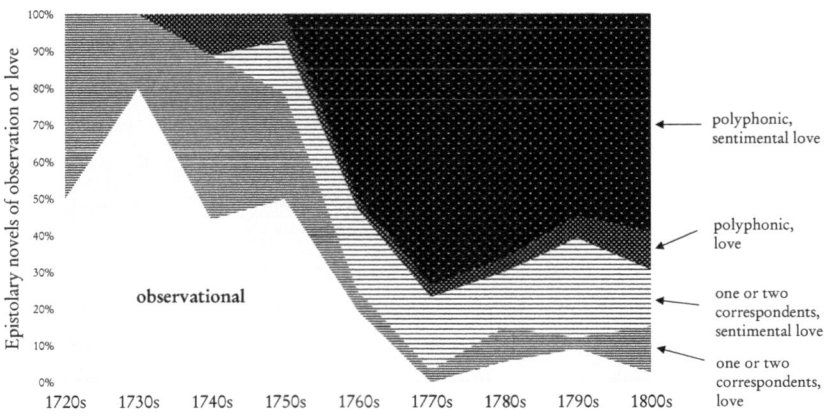

Figure 7.8 Epistolary novels by subject and correspondent type.

this case is different. Certainly, no one would expect all successful artifacts to take exactly the same time to meet with success. Yet the sudden ascent of a specific kind of epistolary novel, visible in Figure 7.5, stands apart. As does its descent, moreover: the market share of the epistolary novel as a whole exceeds 15 percent for only two decades.[17] Finally, though the ascent of the form is quick, it is also limited, never approaching the peak popularity of the memoir novel. Epistolary novels have a long pedigree in France, and this fact makes it tempting to see a "tradition," and a developing one at that. But it is important to remember that if one takes away the success of the sentimental variant, this particular document novel wouldn't amount to more than a trace presence on the literary scene, barely cracking the 10-percent barrier and only for two decades. Indeed, the history of this artifact looks much more like a "passing fashion" than anything observed until now: the polyphonic sentimental epistolary novel arrives quickly, then quickly disappears. Disappears *relatively* quickly, at any rate, since it is a four-decade fashion. (I will return to the problem of fashions and fads, and how they may relate to artifactual evolution, in Chapter 10.)

If the epistolary novel doesn't appear to evolve quite like the other literary artifacts studied, there may be a specific cause, not captured in my data. Its name is *Clarissa*. Richardson's 1748 sensation was translated into French (in abridged form) in 1751.[18] The rapid ascent of the polyphonic, sentimental French epistolary novel follows. Of course, this may be a coincidence. But aside from its truly exceptional heft, *Clarissa* looks much more like the epistolary novel that triumphs than anything that had come before in France, and in this case, a successful artifact probably has a single origin.[19] Instead of being "worked on" by many adopters, over many decades, the success of the epistolary novel results from an *invention* in the commonly understood sense of the term: a "light-bulb moment" when form (polyphony) and content (sentiment) are united in a way that strikes many as useful. Time is still required for the invention to spread: in this respect, the literary system continues to display inertia. But less time – as if the ground had been in effect prepared by previous, unfruitful experimentation.[20]

In Chapter 10, I will draw out further how the technological explanation relates to document novels in general and the epistolary novel specifically. For now, and to conclude, I want to raise the issue of the epistolary novel's "documenticity" – the association between the literary form and real-world documents – and compare it to that of memoirs. We've observed that the terms *mémoires* and *vie* tend to disappear from titles toward the end of the eighteenth century, in a way that correlates roughly with the retreat of memoir novels free of explicit signs of invention. (That retreat also corresponds to increasing numbers of nonmemoir uses of the first person, which I interpreted as an additional sign of the de-documentification of the form.) Something similar is observable with letter novels. Figure 7.9 shows that as in the case of memoir novels, once the form is pressed into substantial use – here, in the 1760s – documenticity declines, measured either in terms of truth claims or of titling.[21] The loss is more rapid for the epistolary novel than for memoirs, though this is not really surprising: epistolary novels have much less of a career before the arrival of a new kind of third-person novel in the 1780s and 1790s that displaces document novels almost entirely. By the end of the period represented here, the epistolary nature of the novel is rarely a feature advertised in titles.

Though the overall behavior of the two major types of document novels is similar, there is one key difference. The initial loss of documenticity occurs at the same point in the career of each form – the point when the form starts to achieve real popularity. But Figure 7.10, which uses truth pretense alone as a measure, illustrates that the point is *historically* quite different. Of course, the fact that the loss of documenticity is temporally shifted has implications with regard to the arguments made in Chapter 1 against understanding the "fictionalization" of the novel as a kind of conceptual process – as if people "tired" of the truth pretense or "came to understand" fictionality. For Figure 7.10 further reveals the artifactual dimension of the truth pretense. All one needs look at is the years 1731–1760. During these decades, writers hardly ever presented their epistolary novels as their own works, whereas writers of memoir novels were doing so nearly half the time. In theory, these might not be the same novelists: we could imagine two separate literary ecosystems, one

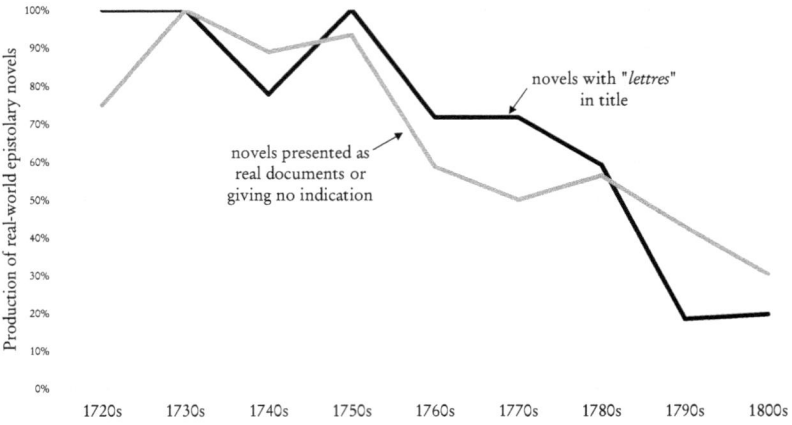

Figure 7.9 Documenticity of the epistolary novel.

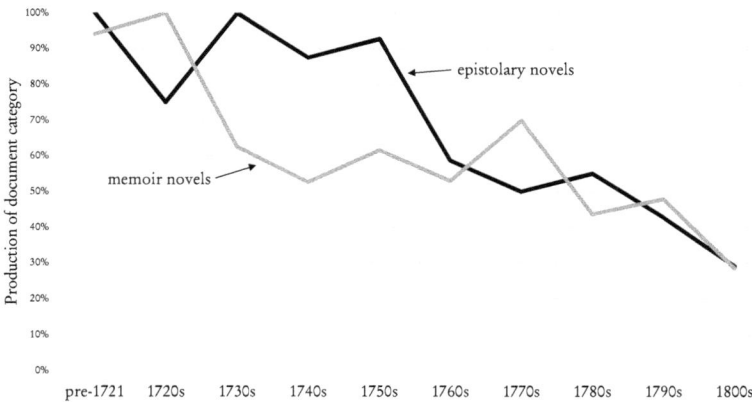

Figure 7.10 Documenticity of memoir and epistolary novels.

still beholden to literal truth the other on the way to understanding fictionality. But given that the stubborn plateau of documenticity displayed by memoir novels also undermines this narrative of unfolding understanding – from the 1730s to the 1790s they do not become significantly more likely to be advanced as inventions – it seems much more likely that when a given kind of document novel is scarce, its documenticity is much stronger than when it's common. If we replace a semantic understanding of truth pretense with a rhetorical one, this makes sense: it's not that readers and writers lose their naïveté, it's merely that the frequency of use interferes with the smooth functioning of the pseudofactual game. One might even hazard that the epistolary novel's (temporary) superiority was that its documenticity was fresh, and as such, was a better host for the pseudofactual play that the values of the time still encouraged. Epistolary novels retained the truth connotations of their real-world origins to the extent that they were not widely practiced, even though in the same years memoir novels had already lost – for some but certainly not for all – those same connotations.

At any rate, both types of document novel, as I've pointed out, retain a perhaps surprising amount of association with literal truth. Their documenticity is mitigated by frequent use, but it doesn't disappear. What disappears is the document novel itself.

8 | A "New" Third-person Novel

Types of novels – types, meaning formally similar narrative artifacts – appear to come and go with regularity: in the course of this part of the book, we've seen the rise and fall of Heliodorian novels, of *nouvelles*, of first-person document novels. And the question of the novel's fictionality, taken up in the first part, is to some extent bound up with this formal change. We can readily see, for example, that though broadly speaking the French novel is dominated by truth claims through the 1770s (Figure 1.6, page 29), those aren't quite the same claims since somebody novels and their reference to known heroes are edged out by nobody novels with their assertions of literal truth. What we may further suspect is that the serious erosion of those assertions around the turn of the eighteenth century is linked to the turn away from first-person document forms and toward a third-person novel. "Linked": but how? Is it that third-person novels, more readily avowed as invented, replace the first-person forms and their seemingly inherent documenticity? Is the correlation looser than that? And since third-person narration was certainly not the invention of the 1790s or 1800s, by what process might it possibly have *developed* an association with invented protagonists?

The correlation between these two marked modifications in the novel system, while not perfect, is detectible in Figure 8.1.[1] Starting in the 1780s, when the century's pseudofactual "plateau" starts to erode – with the erosion inverted in this graph – there commences as well a steady uptick in the production of third-person novels. One problem of course is the unexpected "return" of pseudofactuality in the last decade of the sample, which does not match at all the still more complete hegemony of the third person. Moreover, the third person had been quite popular before its late-century rise: just a little earlier, for its one-decade spike in the 1760s, and before that, during a different period of hegemony, this time *preceding* the dominance of the first-person document novel. Is there anything that separates the turn-of-the-nineteenth-century third-person novel from the one popular a hundred years earlier, and that may explain why the former has shed postures that were common in its earlier cousin?

8 A "New" Third-Person Novel

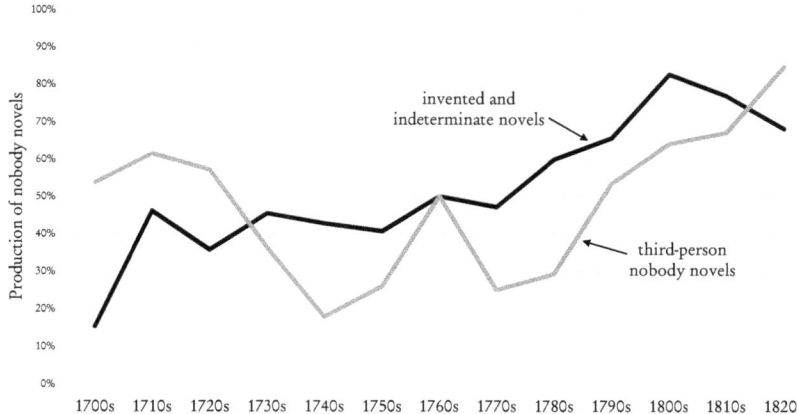

Figure 8.1 Truth posture and narrative person.

In order to tease apart third-person novels over the period, this chapter introduces three new variables. First, length: we'll see that the early third-person novel was short, whereas the later one was long. Then, chapters: though novels had long been segmented in various ways, the spread of chapterized novels specifically was another late-century phenomenon. Finally, incipits: the later third-person novel tends to begin in ways unfamiliar before. As we will see, none of these formal changes is in itself a mark of "fictionality"; plenty of chapterized novels, for instance, were still affirmed as true. But taken together, and proceeding along the lines of the "statistical" family portrait of *romans* and *nouvelles* developed in Chapter 5, they suggest that the turn-of-the-century third-person novel is for all intents and purposes a new beast.

Trends in length, while much less stark over this period than in the seventeenth century, are nonetheless discernable by a number of different measures. Overall, and despite obvious variation, novels lengthen noticeably in the 1770s (Figure 8.2). Prior to 1770, median novel length ranged between roughly 30,000 and 40,000 words, whereas in the 1770s, the figure is for the first time 50,000, with further lengthening occurring especially from the 1800s. The phenomenon, however, looks different if the data are disaggregated by narrative type, for generally speaking, first-person and epistolary novels are considerably longer than their third-person counterparts (Figure 8.3).[2] Prior to the 1780s, third-person novels tend to be shorter than epistolary and first-person works. Of course, the latter two categories do display considerable variation: from the 1730s to the 1760s, differences between narrative types are less pronounced than in other decades; and the sample from the 1750s registers an apparently anomalous

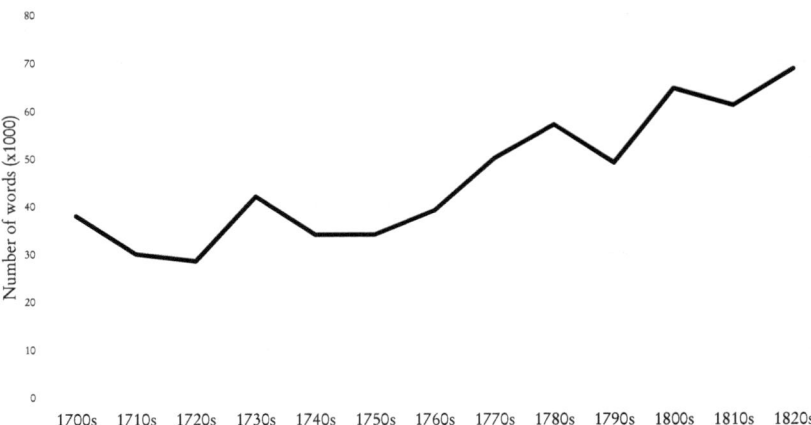

Figure 8.2 Median length of nobody novels.

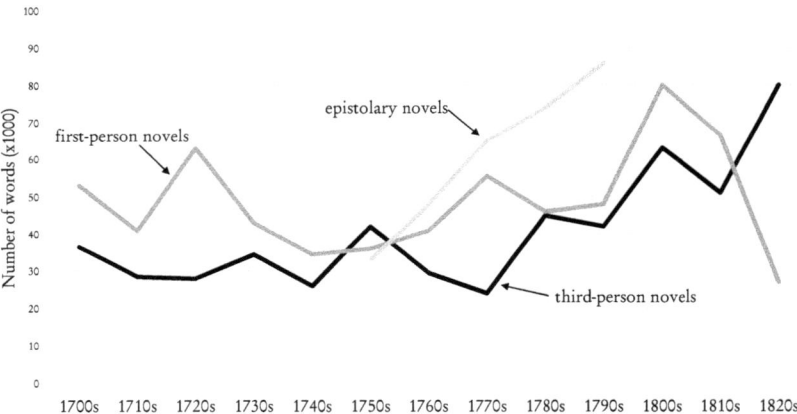

Figure 8.3 Median length of nobody novels by narrative type.

lengthening of third-person works. But surely the basic lesson is that third-person novels are a good bit shorter than the others until the 1780s, at which point they experience a steady lengthening, eventually catching up with first-person novels (if not epistolary novels, which remain the longest of all). Indeed, if we take 1780 as a kind of watershed, we can see that relative to their initial length, third-person novels increase much more than either first-person or epistolary novels: they lengthen by 71 percent, as opposed to 27 and 49 percent for the other varieties, respectively (Figure E8.1). (Taking 1770 would give roughly the same lesson.)

Some novels lengthen more than others; but one type of novel *resists* the lengthening more than any of the others. This is the pseudofactual third-person novel specifically. Overall, invented novels are the longest (53,000 words) and pseudofactual the shortest (38,000 words): this is not surprising since most invented novels come from the later decades, in which novels are longer. But prior to 1780 novels, novels of the same narrative type (i.e., first- or third-person) have roughly the same median length, regardless of their truth posture: third-person works have from 31 to 36,000 words and first-person works (including, here, epistolary novels) from 41 to 48,000 words. After 1780, first-person works lengthen, but across the board, with pseudofactual and indeterminate variants stretching by 22 percent and invented novels by 29 percent. But in the third-person novel, lengthening varies greatly according to truth posture. There, invented and indeterminate novels swell by 110 and 74 percent, respectively, while pseudofactual novels grow by a much more moderate 36 percent. So, while around the turn of the nineteenth century the third-person novel as a whole is undergoing drastic formal change in terms of length, pseudofactual third-person novels specifically change much less than those with other truth postures. This suggests that the new third-person invented novel may be formally distinguishable both from earlier third-person novels and from third-person novels published during the same years but advanced as true stories. By comparison, and at least in terms of this particular formal criterion, first-person and epistolary novels are much more uniform, both across the time span and from one truth posture to another.

A second formal criterion is segmentation. Needless to say, written narratives may display many different kinds of segmentation: epics were typically divided into books (the *Iliad*, the *Odyssey*, the *Aeneid*); Dante divides his *Divine Comedy* into three *canticas* (canticles) and then further into *cantos* (songs); Boccaccio's *Decameron* is of course made up of days. Chapters are another old division – Pliny the Elder's *Natural History* contain them – but they were not commonly used in Classical narrative literature: as Nicholas Dames points out, the Greek novel followed the epic's division into books.[3] Certainly, by the time of Rabelais and Cervantes, authors were breaking novels into chapters: both of these authors do. Yet excavating the deep history of narrative segmentation, or even just chapters, is probably not necessary for understanding developments in the eighteenth-century novel, which are obvious enough in Figure 8.4. Of the three major types of segmentation in first- and third-person works, books are broadly speaking a trace presence.[4] Parts are the major form of segmentation in the first half of the eighteenth century, at which point chapters start to take off. By the turn of the nineteenth century, chapters are, for all intents and purposes, the only kind of segmentation used in novels, and their popularity continues unabated in the last decades sampled.

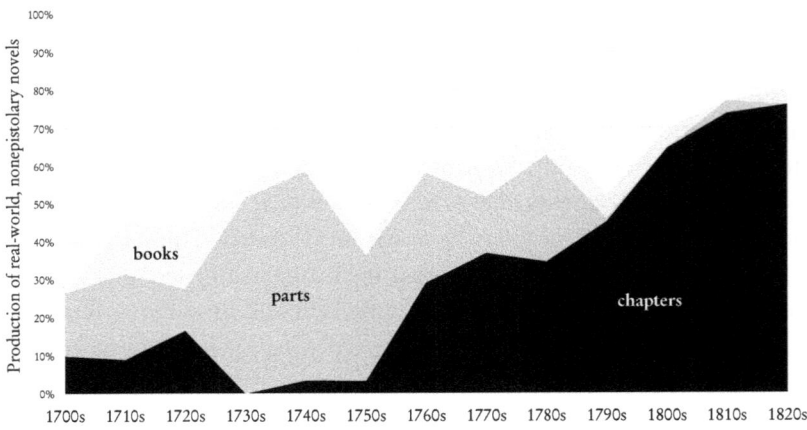

Figure 8.4 Major types of segmentation.

To what extent are these forms of segmentation simply different names for the same thing? Is a chapterized novel different from a novel divided into books or parts, or is it only the names of the segments that have changed? Judging by the length of the text contained by each category, these segmentations must have quite different functions: parts average 23,000 words per segment, books 9,000, and chapters 3,000. Using this measure, parts, books, and chapters cannot be confused. Unsurprisingly, no doubt, parts divide novels only in the most rudimentary way: the typical novel with parts has about three of them, a segmentation that often aligns, simply, with the number of physical volumes.[5] By contrast, books – the most pedigreed of segmentations, literarily speaking[6] – may be assumed to have more of a structural function: novels so divided contain an average of about eight of them. Chapters, too, have a structural function that parts do not, while imposing a rhythm more rapid than that of books – on average, chapterized novels are broken into thirty-three pieces.

Given that their sheer length makes parts hardly a segment at all – or a form of segmentation imposed by the physical medium – they are probably worth discounting entirely.[7] If so, then the only hegemonic form of segmentation over this period is the chapter, and its hegemony is quite bounded, temporally. Suddenly, in the 1760s, chapters can be found in roughly 30 percent of real-world novels, which maintain this level for another couple of decades; in the 1790s there commences a second increase, which soon brings the level to around 70 percent. The 1760s jump is surprising in the context of the present study, which generally hasn't documented many abrupt spreads.[8] In this case, the answer is probably close at hand: if relatively uncommon, chapters had nonetheless been a familiar feature of *alternate*-world novels specifically. Over this entire period, the latter feature chapters 49 percent of the time; the figure rises to 59 percent during the decades of the greatest popularity of alternate-world novels, from the 1740s through the 1760s. (This is the popular Enlightenment genre of the philosophical tale.) When the latter are admitted into the calculation, as in Figure 8.5, the rise is considerably more gradual. In this instance, it would seem that a feature has been successfully "imported" into the real-world novel from a different kind of novel.[9]

And as we've seen with many formal features, the broad evolution in segmentation is in fact made up of further, more precise evolutions. That is, it is not only that chapters become dramatically more popular but also that chapters themselves present evolving characteristics – specifically, with respect to their titles. Before 1760, most titles – 70 percent of them – are *descriptive* titles: these are titles, usually quite long, that detail the contents of the chapter. After 1760, less than 15 percent of chapters feature this type of title, with the percentage decreasing over time. The rest are taken up by previously uncommon variants. The first of these is chapters with titles I call "oblique" – titles bearing some relation, obviously, with the chapter contents but a relation that will become clear only after one has read the chapter. Thus, a chapter entitled "An Unexpected Meeting" will most likely contain an unexpected meeting, but the reader is in effect teased to read on so as to learn the nature of that meeting (between whom, why it is unexpected, and so on). These titles are typically much shorter than descriptive titles. And a second variant comprises chapters with no titles at all. These two are the varieties that increase spectacularly after 1760 (Figure 8.6).[10]

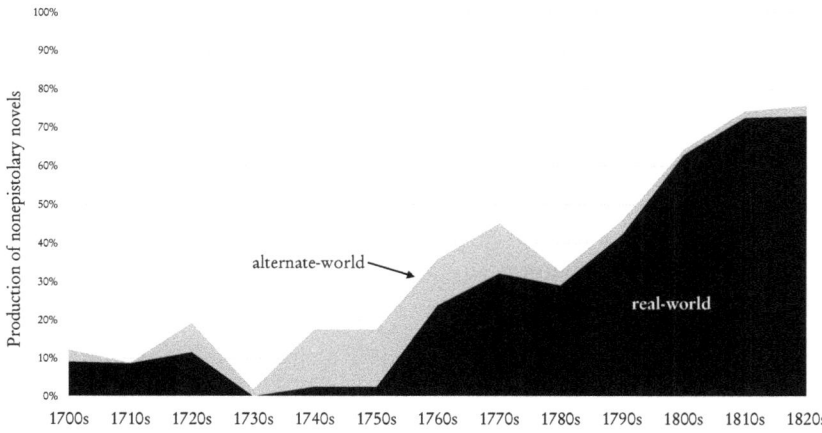

Figure 8.5 Chapterized novels by type.

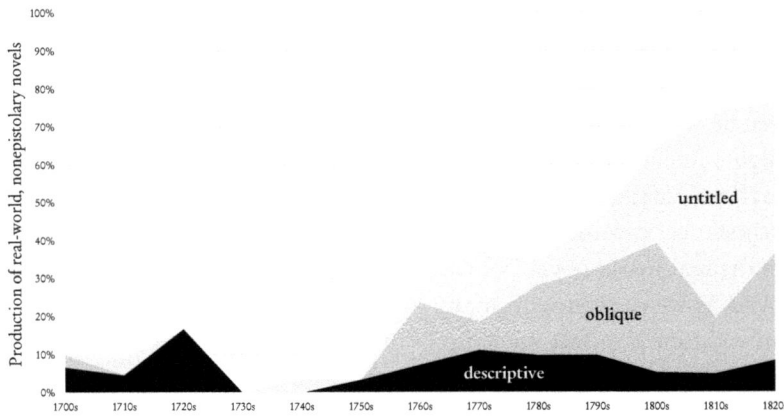

Figure 8.6 Chapter title types.

From 1760 to the end of the century, chapters predominantly feature oblique titles; untitled chapters, while much more common than before this period, are only marginally more popular than descriptive titles. From the 1800s on, the presence of descriptive titles diminishes, while untitled chapters become the go-to form of segmentation.

Returning the focus to third-person nobody novels – the category that makes such impressive gains around the turn of the nineteenth century – we find that just as length appears to be a function of truth posture, length also correlates with segmentation.[11] From 1701 to 1830, chapterized novels are well over twice as long as nonsegmented novels: the median figures are 69,500 words and 29,800 words, respectively. And this is very nearly a constant characteristic over the span (Figure 8.7).[12]

Figure 8.7 Median length of third-person nobody novels.

Aside from the figure for the 1770s – a decade for which there are only three chapterized third-person nobody novels in the sample – chapterized novels are markedly longer than their nonsegmented counterparts, with an especially wide gap (of over 500 percent) in the last decade of the period. Thus, the pronounced lengthening of the third-person novel from the 1780s on also reflects the growth of chapterized third-person novels specifically. Indeed, nonsegmented third-person novels show no obvious upward trend in length over this period. Is it chapterization that "permits" extended length, or do longer novels "develop" the segments that enable easier processing by writers and readers? From the data, it would seem that chapters start to spread first, as if techniques of segmentation must be in place before novelists write longer novels.[13] Being "in place" here does not exactly mean "invented" since chapters were hardly new to the eighteenth century, and indeed some very famous novels (e.g., *Don Quixote*) contained them. Rather, "in place" means something like "currently practiced in sufficient number by a broad swath of novelists." At any rate, the correlation between length and chapterization does suggest that on a purely practical level, the use of discrete substructures (chapters) makes it easier to construct large structures (long novels).[14]

If invented third-person novels are longer, and longer novels are more chapterized, we might expect chapterized novels to advertise their invention at greater rates than nonsegmented novels. In addition, chapterization may seem to scream "fiction" a way that an unsegmented text does not. Thus, Ugo Dionne has hypothesized that the spread of chapters was a direct result of the genre's newfound acceptance of its own fictionality: "If the chapter dominates the modern novel's structural system, it is because this novel is from this point on master of its own domain, freed from its masks, disguises, and camouflage, freed from the shame [i.e., of being a mere novel] that had for centuries suffocated it."[15] Yet, chapterized novels overall have the same truth profile as nonsegmented ones: chapterized novels after 1761 are presented as inventions as often as nonsegmented novels (at roughly 27 percent each); and they are presented as true stories only slightly less often as their nonsegmented counterparts (27 vs. 31 percent, respectively). Taking into account ironic and equivocal assertions of truth, which compose some 25 percent of all pseudofactual novels after 1780 and thus might make a difference, does not change this fact. Chapters and admissions of invention spread on roughly the same timetable, but the novels that contain them aren't the same novels.

The last variable to consider is the way third-person novels begin. Take, for example, the much parodied and much maligned incipit of Bulwer-Lytton's novel *Paul Clifford* (1830), "It was a dark and stormy night." One thing that stands out, obviously, is the ominous, pseudo-gothic weather. But on a more general level, whatever the weather described, the infamous phrase is a scene-setter: it posits a physical environment in which characters will appear and the action will start. Of course, clichés aren't born clichés, they have to be made over time; and scene-setting openings such as this have a circumscribed history. Popular by the time Bulwer-Lytton was writing, they had wrested their dominance from other formulas, above all the biographical portrait of the protagonist.

Figure 8.8 provides a breakdown of incipit types. From top to bottom, the categories represented are the following. The first contains incipits that feature sententious or authorial remarks – the former being of the "It is a truth universally acknowledged…" variety, the latter distinguished by an "I" that one might normally find in a preface. A second category opens with descriptions of the temporal or geographical setting in which the narrative will take place, while a third – this is the dominant technique – features character descriptions. These can be static – offering a moral portrait of a character, typically the protagonist or an ancestor of the protagonist; they can also take a biographical tack, presenting the character's familial background and life up to the time of the main narrative. Two further openings forego these preliminaries by getting right to the main action. "Action" openings simply start right in, typically with brief character introductions incorporated into the narrative: So-and-so, an upstanding resident of Whatever Place, went to inspect some land inherited from his uncle. "Scene" openings, by contrast, place this initial action within a

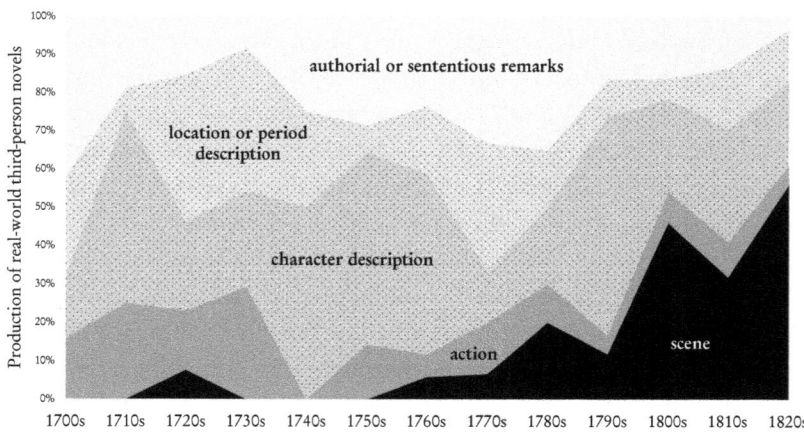

Figure 8.8 Incipits of third-person novels.

physical description; so, to reprise the hypothetical opening just used, the author might describe the carriage containing So-and-so or the appearance of the land where he will in due course arrive.[16]

Breaking openings down in this matter gives us some information, certainly. We can see the steady growth of scene openings, followed by their dramatic increase in the sample from the 1820s. We see as well that descriptive openings dominate for almost the entire span, with descriptions of characters being especially prevalent. But beyond this, the graph is "noisy": trends don't seem obvious. One is tempted to say that throughout the eighteenth century, novelists seem to choose at will from a limited array of possibilities.

Getting at other patterns may require more precision. Figure 8.8 measures incipits – the first sentences of a novel. I've also referred to these as "openings." We may do well, however, to distinguish between the two terms. After all, in many, if not most cases, reading on past the incipit brings us not to the main action of the novel but instead reveals further openings hiding behind the first one – concatenated preliminaries, then, preceding the narrative's main action. The most obvious case is that of authorial or sententious remarks, which in about 75 percent of cases are followed by descriptions of characters, places, or periods. But by the same token, authorial or sententious remarks occasionally *follow* descriptions; or a period description may precede a character description; or a novel can describe a character, and then set a scene. For the purposes of the present inquiry, therefore, let's agree that a novel has in effect two openings. The first is the incipit – the first sentences of the book. The second is the opening of the book's main action, which can coincide with the incipit – such works are labeled "action" or "scene" in Figure 8.8 – but they need not.[17] In most cases, a variable number and variety of preliminaries precede the action proper.[18]

Yet, if we look for trends in preliminaries in any combination – that is, acknowledging that novels may have more than one type, and in different orders – results are again noisy: there are no obvious trends in the use of descriptions (period, place, or character) or authorial and sententious remarks. (See Figure E8.3.) Perhaps there are trends in the length of preliminary remarks? Preliminary character descriptions, for example, may grow longer or shorter. Unfortunately, it turns out the lengths simply vary, again without any obvious pattern. (See Figure E8.4.)[19]

One could multiply calculations regarding different types of openings with similar results: the growth of scene openings specifically is the only significant trend in this data, and it therefore deserves deeper scrutiny. Figure 8.8 shows scenes only when the novels' first words drew them; it left out novels that may have opened with authorial remarks, or descriptions of places, periods, or characters, and then followed these with a scene. That is, the scene is a way of presenting action, and like any presentation of action, it can come right away or after the various types of deferrals I've just named. If we include all novels presenting their initial action by means of a scene, we see stronger numbers but no real change in the periodization (Figure 8.9). Overall, 77 percent of novels with scene openings use the latter as their incipit; the balance uses them only after some sort of preliminary. Indeed, if scene openings have a break-out decade, the latter would seem to be the 1800s, which is also the decade when the cumulative use of preliminaries – authorial and sententious remarks and descriptions – declines (Figure 8.10). For most of the eighteenth century, 80 percent or so of novels contain preliminaries that defer the presentation of the novel's main action; beginning in the 1800s, that percentage falls to about 50. As we see from Figure 8.8, the sea change is in scene openings rather than action openings: the latter's popularity is not enhanced by the abandonment of preliminaries, an abandonment which seems to be driven by the spread of scenes. One way of understanding the growth of scenes in novel openings is to say that although scenes *could* be used with other, older devices (these uses being visible in the "after preliminaries" category of Figure 8.9), in practice, they provided writers with a completely new way into the action that pushed out the more customary incipits. Once scenes gain traction, they are less likely to be combined with the types of novel openings that were popular over the eighteenth century.[20]

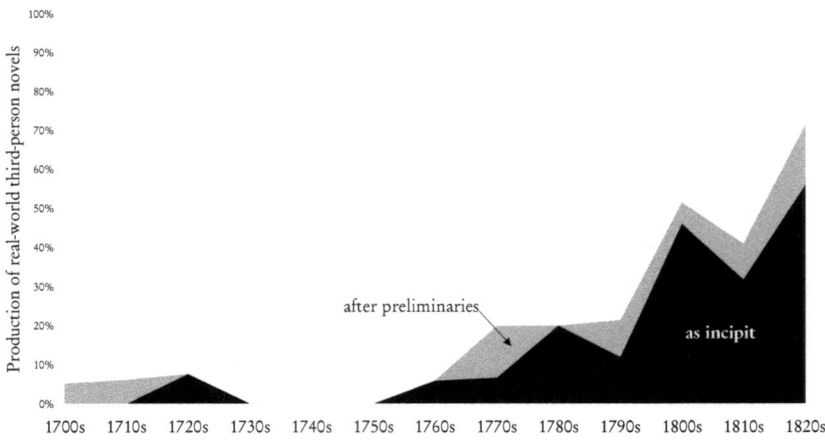

Figure 8.9 Scene use in presentation of main action.

Figure 8.10 Third-person novels containing preliminaries.

One major distinction is hiding in what I've considered to constitute a "scene." That category in fact amalgamates two artifacts. Most scenes provide a descriptive setting for the action – the weather, as in the famous Bulwer-Lytton example, but also the time of day (as measured by omnipresent church bells), and especially visual descriptions of the lay of the land or the disposition of a room. But I've also classified as scenes introductions of characters by their speech alone: some novels begin as a character is soliloquizing or in the middle of a dialogue. In Figure 8.11 we see that the chronological distribution of this variant roughly follows that of the main "setting" variety. Speech scenes seem to have done most of the work introducing scenes into the novel, for of novels that start without any preliminaries, speech scenes clearly constitute

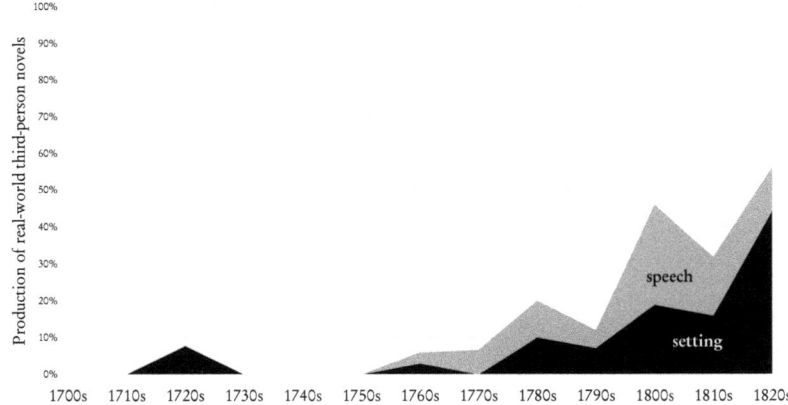

Figure 8.11 Scene types (incipit position only).

the earlier type of scene: novels opening with "setting"-type scenes remain for decades rarer than novels opening with speech scenes. And speech scenes themselves show an evolution. Through the 1780s, they consist of monologues; in the 1790s and 1800s, novelists experiment with opening on an ongoing dialogue, a technique that comes to dominate by the 1810s.

We've seen that length and chapters have a variable relation to truth posture: the lengthening of the novel correlates with its fictionalization, while chapterization – save perhaps at the end of the span – does not. Use of scenes follows the trend of longer novels: novels that open with them are more likely to contain admissions of invention, at least once scene novels gain real traction in the 1800s. From that point on, scene novels contain admissions of invention 43 percent of the time, whereas only 17 percent of nonscene novels contain them (see Figure E8.5). Conversely, novels with more traditional openings are more likely to be advanced as true (35 vs. 20 percent over the period, with a slight widening of the gap after 1801; see Figure E8.6). As with length, the presence of scenes is far from a *perfect* predictor of truth posture. But it too does appear to be a good one.

Is the third-person novel at the turn of the nineteenth century – the one that prospers following the heyday of first-person document forms – different from its earlier counterparts? Or does the third-person novel of the early eighteenth century merely return, after waiting out the upstart first person? The characteristics I've traced in this chapter are, individually, of some help: chapters and scenes are rare before the midpoint of the century; third-person novels lengthen somewhat. And as Figure 8.12 shows, the changes all take place on roughly the same calendar.

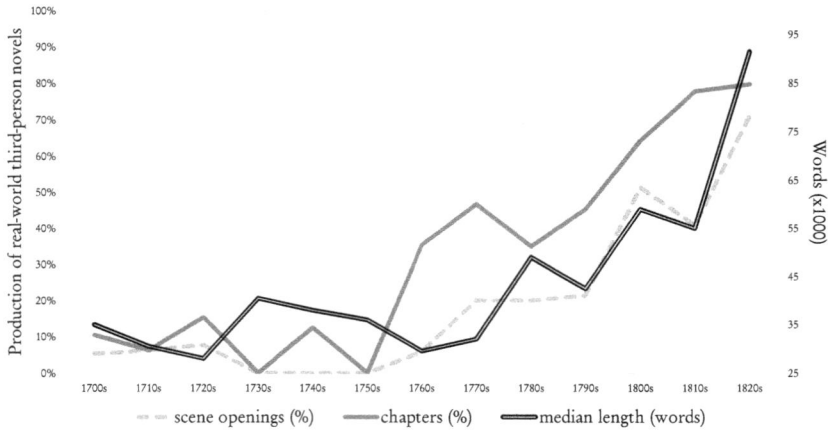

Figure 8.12 Three trends in third-person novels.

Taken together, therefore, these characteristics can give us a much rounder view of how the turn-of-the-century third-person novel is quite distinct from its earlier "ancestors." Certainly, the distinction between an early third-person novel and a later one is more fragile than one obtaining between, say, the memoir novel and the epistolary novel, artifacts that in the vast majority of cases are difficult to confuse.[21] And indeed, some novels with chapters are short, some novels with scene openings don't have chapters, and so on. Thus, any distinction will amount to a statistical portrait, akin to the one established in Chapter 5 between *romans* and *nouvelles*. In this understanding, the hypothesized turn-of-the-century novel is less one stable thing, presenting in all cases the same characteristics, than an assembly of parts, not all of which need to be present in order for it to be recognized – again, a Wittgensteinian family. The characteristics I've measured are relatively few but enough to separate out what I'll be calling simply the "new" third-person novel family. (I will retain the quotes around the term, so as to stress that it means simply "new to France at this time" and most certainly not "modern.")

Suppose we look for novels under the span's 50th percentile for length (47,000 words or less); we also want those novels to contain no chapters; and we further specify their openings: the latter must contain character portraits or else start directly on the action but cannot contain scenes. These we will call "old" third-person novels. A possible scenario for the "new" family might include novels whose length is in the 66th percentile (66,000 words or more), which have either scenes or chapters, contain no preliminary character portraits, and do not start immediately on action. These two scenarios are plotted on Figure 8.13.

Figure 8.13 "Old" and "new" third-person novels (one scenario each).

For the first seven decades of the span, novels responding to the criteria for the "old" family make up the majority of all third-person novels; but then they fall away, to become, by the eighteenth century, only a trace presence. The "new" novel family appears to take up at least some of the slack off the old one – though the graph certainly suggests the need for a longer view since we can see only the take-off of the form.

We can of course tweak and retweak the criteria used to measure the families. For the "old" variety, we can tighten down maximum length to the thirty-third percentile or open it up to the sixty-sixth or even the eightieth. We might furthermore insist that openings feature a character portrait (excluding, then, novels that start directly on the action) or allow back in novels featuring chapters with "descriptive" titles (which we've seen are the common type of chapter earlier in the span). "New" novel scenarios can likewise be made more permissive or stricter. On the permissive side, we can open the family to include novels with lengths greater than the thirty-third percentile and eliminate the exclusion of novels with preliminary character portraits. More restrictively, we can demand more exceptional length – say, above the 80th percentile (106,000 words) – while also insisting that novels feature *both* chapters and scenes. Figure 8.14 shows the distribution of ten scenarios for each of the novel families.[22]

As with the representations of *romans* and *nouvelles* in Chapter 4, the darker the shaded area, the stricter the criteria used. And there is quite a bit of variation in counts of "old" novels: stricter criteria capture only about 40 percent of novels over the first seven decades, whereas looser criteria capture more like 80 percent. But whichever criteria are used, the importance

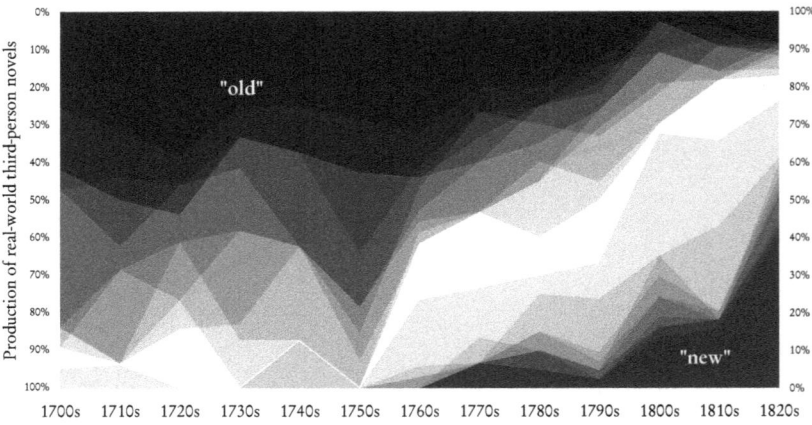

Figure 8.14 "Old" and "new" third-person novels (ten scenarios each).

of this family of "old" third-person novels declines steadily from the 1750s and then dramatically at the turn of the nineteenth century. Assuming no rebound occurs post-1830, the eclipse of this novel is definitive. For the "new" family, few scenarios show any before the 1760s and the ones that do return only three novels – one in the 1700s, one in the 1710s, and one in the 1740s. The family appears to grow slowly through the end of the century; the data from the 1800s and 1810s are in many scenarios somewhat inconclusive, in that an initial "breakout" moment is quickly followed by a retreat. (This effect is mostly due to a relatively restrained number of scene novels in the 1810s sample.) But surely the larger picture is unambiguous. The "new" third-person novel comes into its own precisely as the "old" variety is crumbling, and it doesn't come from nowhere: novelists had been modifying their practice – though only in small numbers – since the 1770s.

Figure 8.14 suggests a further remark, which is that these two novel families are not equally close-knit. That is, the "old" third-person novel was formally heterogeneous even in what appears to be its heyday (the first half of the century): most of the scenarios produce wide swings in the counts. By contrast, most of the scenarios for the "new" variant return roughly the same figures; only two permissive scenarios return substantially different counts (though even these respect the graph's general shape), and by the 1820s, nine out of ten scenarios return counts within 10 percent of the 50-percent mark. Such strong "family resemblance" tells us that the "new" third-person novel is artifactually much more consistent and identifiable than the old one. From this point of view, the latter's impressive dominance may well be enabled by its artifactual elasticity – that is, for a form to remain hegemonic over the span visible in Figure 8.14, its formal contours cannot be rigidly drawn.

Another factor behind the elasticity of the "old" third-person novel may well be that we are capturing less the heyday of an artifact than its disintegration. Chapter 6 describes the decline of *nouvelles* from their peak in the 1680s: during this decline, *nouvelles* became less and less like one another. Thus, a good supposition is that the upper portion of Figure 8.14 measures the formal dispersal of the *nouvelle*, this time with different criteria.

Unfortunately, I am unable to bring into focus the exact relation between *nouvelles* and what I'm now calling the "old" third-person novel because my data on novel openings and segmentation do not extend back before 1701. But I can better align the *nouvelles* calculations as previously performed with those of the "old" third-person novel and then compare the two. Figure 5.10 (page 103) considered *nouvelles* as a percentage of the entire production of real-world novels, whereas Figure 8.14 – like most of the graphs in this chapter – looks at the makeup of third-person real-world novels only. Viewing *nouvelles* in the same way, and averaging scenarios of the "old" third-person novel for legibility, we see in Figure 8.15 that for all intents and purposes, we seem to be measuring the same artifact. One guess might be that the family of "old" third-person novels is just a somewhat expanded version of the *nouvelle* family. This turns out to be true, but not uniformly over the whole span. For the six decades preceding the fall off of both forms, which seems to date to the 1760s, the novels I've classified as *nouvelles* almost always also answer the criteria used for selecting "old" third-person novels.[23] Starting in the 1760s, however, novels answering to the *nouvelle* scenario are "old" novels only half the time. The farther we get from the *nouvelle*'s historical home – the span from 1650s to the 1730s, during which the term was in use as a generic subtitle – the less coherence we find among the objects captured by a loose definition such as the one used here.

Still, the similarity between the two measurements, though probably somewhat more tenuous than Figure 8.15 suggests, is striking and, potentially, informative. Measurement of the "old" third-person novel is based on purely formal characteristics of the text – length, segmentation, opening type. Estimates for the *nouvelle* were produced from formal textual measures too – in addition to length, inset type – but also from a paratextual measure, that of truth posture. So to what extent is truth posture related to the form of third-person novels? We've already done some isolated calculations along these lines: the length of novels is a predictor of truth posture, as are openings; segmentation is not. Now we're in a position to ask whether novels that combine these features in the ways I've called "old"

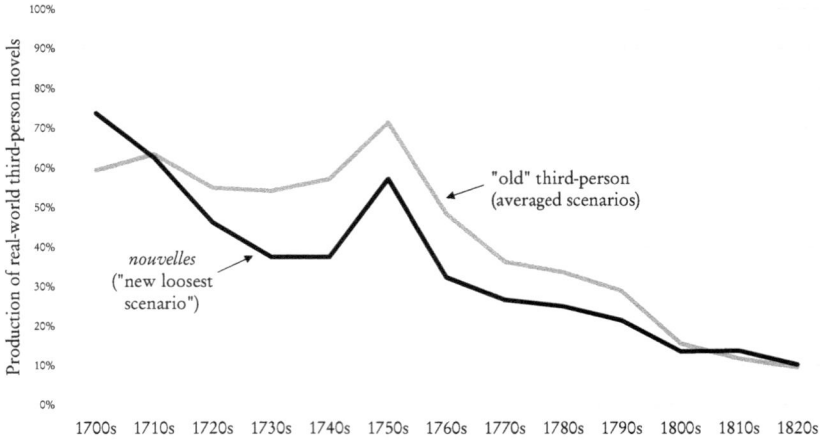

Figure 8.15 *Nouvelles* and "old" third-person novels.

and "new" are more or less likely to feature somebodies or to be advanced as true. Of course, since the "old" variety prospers during the part of the novel's history that is dominated by the truth pretense, one would expect the variety as a whole to be more heavily pseudofactual than the "new" variety, which is a player only during decades when pseudofactuality is on the wane. The question, however, is whether there are differences if we hold the decade constant. More specifically: Can the collapse of pseudofactuality be set at the door of the "new" third-person novel? A rough correlation between the fall of pseudofactuality and the rise of the "new" novel is clear enough since both are pronounced in the opening decades of the eighteenth century. But are "new" novels themselves more likely than others to be admitted as inventions?

The answer appears to be yes, but not necessarily from the start. During its heyday, the truth postures of the "old" novel were those of the novel overall. If we use the most moderate of the scenarios for the calculation,[24] prior to 1761 its pseudofactuality and invention rates (53 and 11 percent, respectively) are almost precisely those of third-person novels in general (57 and 10 percent). (There are too few examples of the "new" novel in those years to use as a comparison, even under the most expansive scenarios.) And as "old" novels decline in terms of percentage of the production, they continue to behave much as the third-person novel in general: their invention rate expands, and their pseduofactuality shrinks. By contrast, early "new" novels – of which there still are not many before 1801 – show decidedly different truth postures (Figure 8.16). Most obviously, they are much less likely than the "old" variety to contain truth claims.

Of course, since for these decades only seven nobody novels answer the criteria for the "new" novel scenario used, the figures are subject to caution. But they happen to match very well the distribution of "new" novels in the following century (Figure 8.17). In the early nineteenth century, "new" novels are consistently more likely to be presented as invented and less likely to be advanced as true than novels not corresponding to their parameters. Something odd, however, happens to "old" novels. The relatively few that are still around in these decades now have a different truth profile than the ones from the latter part of the previous century: they have become markedly more pseudofactual than the average. The "old" novel at first "fictionalizes"; but at a certain point – at the point at which pseudofactuality seriously retreats in the 1800s – it moves in the other direction, becoming associated with those residual postures that maintain literal truth.

Here, too, caution is warranted: subsets of the sample can be small and potentially misleading. Still, without overreaching, we can draw a few

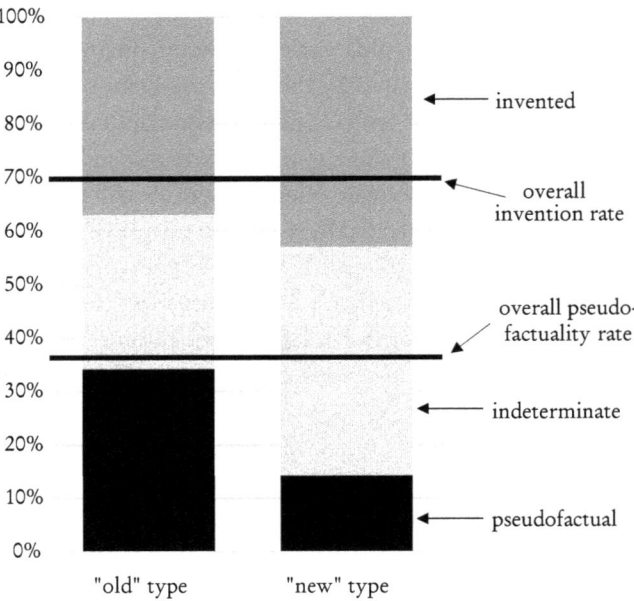

Figure 8.16 Truth postures of third-person nobody novels by novel type, 1761–1800.

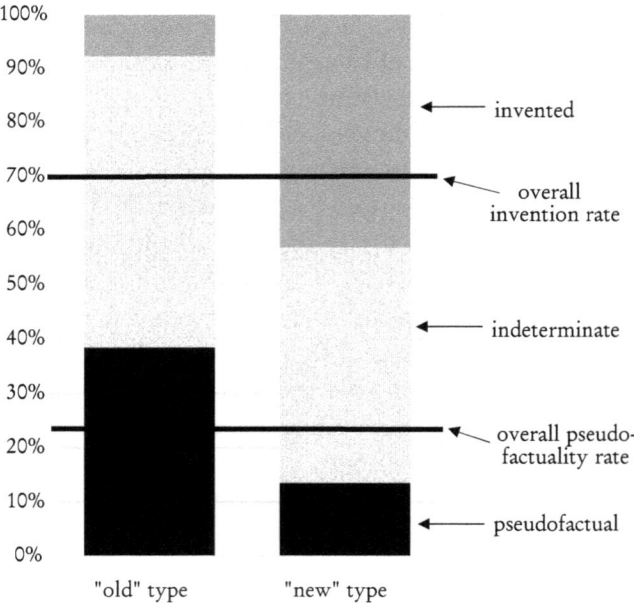

Figure 8.17 Truth postures of third-person nobody novels by novel type, 1801–1830.

conclusions. First, the "new" novel does seem especially resistant – though not immune – to pseudofactual affirmations. That said, the "new" novel is in no way the driver of "fictionalization." In other words, the French novel does not become less pseudofactual in proportion to the amount of "new" novels written. Pseudofactuality's retreat is evident well before there are anything more than trace amounts of "new" novels; and when admissions of invention swell in the last few decades of the eighteenth century, those admissions can readily be found in "old" novels. Thus, the "old" novel does "fictionalize" – it just doesn't "fictionalize" quite as well as the "new" novel. All of this means that "fiction" – and I'm keeping the term between quotes to emphasize my heuristic use of the term – does not inhere to any particular artifact. Against the hypothesis that the retreat of pseudofactuality was simply another name for the victory of a specific type of third-person novel – the "new" type – we see that paratexual postures are not yoked to any particular textual features.[25] Certain forms do seem, however, to be more *hospitable* to given postures: we saw in Chapter 1 that the first-person novel retains its pseudofactuality much longer than the third-person novel (see Figure 1.13, page 35), while now we see that the "new" third-person novel is particularly nonpseudofactual.[26] Therefore, rather than the spread of that type of novel explaining fictionalization, it may be more like the opposite. It is the declining value of literal truth that allows the form to commence its proliferation – with, however, a lag. New forms do not arise as if by sympathy with these new values. They must be invented over time.

9 | The Novel System in England, 1701–1810

The novel system in England over the entire eighteenth century is characterized by many of the same phenomena as the French system. English writers, too, start to privilege document forms such as memoir and epistolary novels, before abandoning these for a "new" third-person novel that looks substantially like the French one I've just described. And like its French counterpart, the English novel of the period is first characterized by pseudofactual postures it proceeds to lose. Most of this can be readily inferred from existing scholarship, and this chapter will bring much more precision to such inferences: it turns out, for example, that certain forms are markedly less or more popular on one side or the other of the Channel and that the timetable for any given change varies by country. Yet, I've suggested from the outset of this book that a more accurate description of such phenomena should not be thought of as the occupation of "positivist" (or simply nerdish) erudition: the precision afforded by quantitative study has the potential to upset the way we have long woven our standard literary–historical narratives. Both the similarities and the differences between France and England will prove critical for the technological model of literary evolution advanced in this study's last chapter.

Let's start where we started in the case the French novel – with truth pretense. In France, the eighteenth-century retreat of pseudofactuality is hesitant rather than progressive: while from the 1730s on, a significant number of writers start to present their novels as pure inventions, protestations of literal truth still characterize roughly half of the production of nobody novels through most of the century, falling off only from the 1780s on. In England, as Figure 9.1 shows, there is no such troublesome plateau: the switch from protestations of truth to admissions of invention is quick. Throughout the first half of the century, the decadal pseudofactual average is 76 percent, but in the space of two decades, the figure falls to under 25 percent and edges down from there. Viewing things from the side of admissions of invention, more discrepancies with respect to the French case emerge. In France, these admissions were commonplace – if certainly still in the minority – in the 1730s and especially the 1740s. Yet, if French writers start as early,

9 *The Novel System in England, 1701–1810* 159

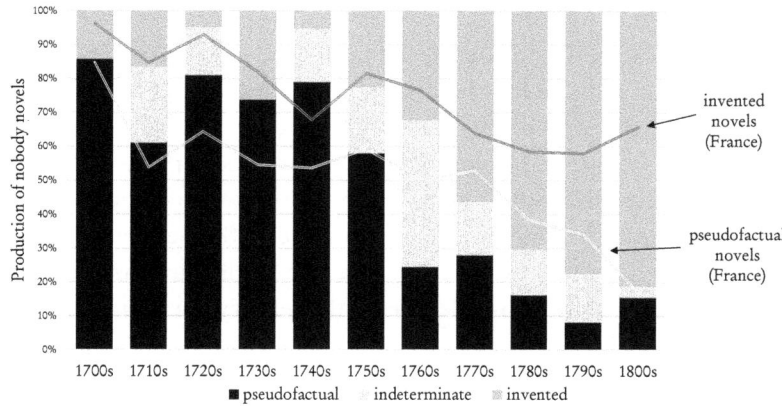

Figure 9.1 Truth status of nobody novels (England).

they never seem to warm up to "fictionality" like the English. Even when pseudofactuality is at its lowest ebb, in the sample from the 1800s, only a third of novels are accompanied by an admission of invention.[1]

What formal features accompany this quite different state of affairs? Perhaps the most obvious particularity of the English situation – and one that is directly responsible for the discrepancy between numbers of "indeterminate" novels around the turn of the nineteenth century – is the ready adoption in England of the generic subtitle "A Novel." In France, only starting in the 1800s is there any sustained use of the subtitle *roman*, and even in the 1820s – the high point of use in the period surveyed – only 15 percent of real-world novels feature it on their title pages. English novels, however, are routinely called out as such starting in the 1760s (Figure 9.2).

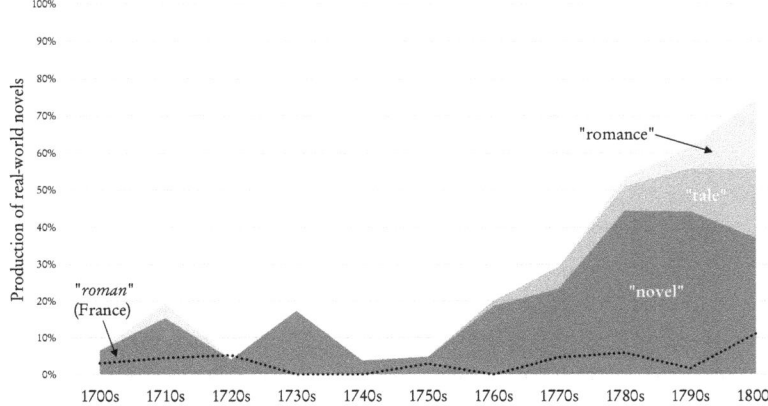

Figure 9.2 Major generic subtitles (England).

An explanation for France's comparative resistance to the subtitle can be found in some of the nomenclatural peculiarities discussed in Chapters 4 and 5: historically, *roman* had never been a popular subtitle, and its inappropriateness would only be compounded by the connotations of archaism circulating from around the time of the critic Du Plaisir. (*Nouvelle*, by contrast, prospered; yet we've seen that its run was over by the 1740s.) In England, however, "novel" came with none of the pejorative baggage of *roman*. It is a matter of debate just what the English understood by the subtitle "novel" in the opening decades of the century: for example, there is good reason to think that for some it was simply a translation of the French *nouvelle* and as such was a vehicle not for assertions of invention, but rather the opposite.[2] To generate Figure 9.2, I've ignored such complications and tagged as having admissions of invention any novels with the subtitles "novel," "tale," or "romance." (An alternate choice could make no substantial difference, given the rarity of the subtitle in the first part of the century.) The subtitle's fortune in the second half of the century is more interesting since it helps explain why turn-of-the-nineteenth-century English novels appear to be so much more forthright about their fictional status. If we try to mimic the fact that French novelists of this period use few subtitles by counting as indeterminate any English novel whose subtitle alone is responsible for its "invented" tag, the situation in these decades looks much the same in both countries: "invented" English novels shrink from around 80 percent of the production in the 1790s and 1800s to more like 35 percent, essentially the same figure as in France.[3] Part of the wholesale English embrace of "fictionality" is therefore due only to the artifactual particularity of its ready adoption of the subtitle "novel" (and its variants).

Part, but certainly far from all: there can be little question of the two-decade sea change in the English novel system accomplished by the 1760s. This is the decade of the dramatic retreat of pseudofactual affirmations, as well as the one that sees the first substantial change in the use of the subtitle "novel." What else is changing? Do the novels of the 1760s and 1770s look like the novels of the 1730s and 1740s, only minus their truth affirmations? Or do some artifactual changes accompany the mutation in truth postures?

An obvious place to look is in first-person forms, which in France make up about a third of all real-world novels already in the first decade of the new century. Yet, if England too sees a vogue for memoir and epistolary novels, the situation there is nonetheless quite different. Figure 9.3 takes nonepistolary first-person forms as a starting point. The difference between France and England does not lie so much in sheer numbers, at least for the first four decades of the century, but rather in the types of first person

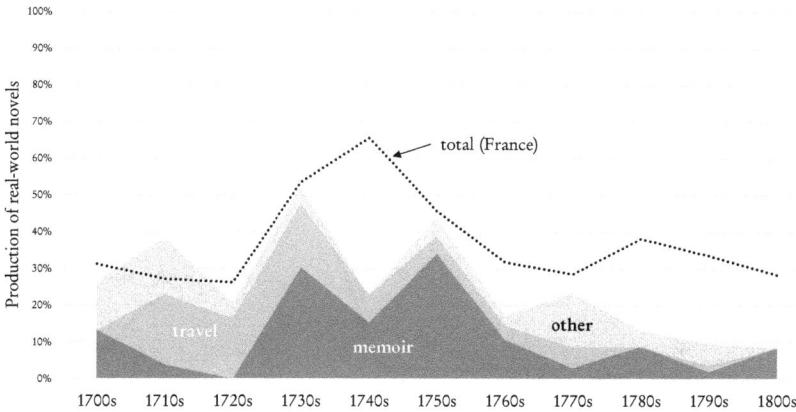

Figure 9.3 Nonepistolary first-person forms (England).

used. In France, we've seen the steady takeover of the memoir novel, which in the 1740s peaks at around 55 percent of the production (Figure 6.3, page 113). In England, the memoir novel also has its period of glory, but it is more subdued: only from the 1730s to the 1750s does it average more than a quarter of the novel market. And it's a late starter, in that the English first prefers a use of the first person that is rarely seen in France – travel narratives, which represent an average of about a quarter of the production between 1711 and 1740. (Included in this category are also military memoirs containing accounts of a campaign.) But like the English memoir novel, first-person travel narratives maintain their popularity only for a few decades. And interestingly, both have run their course by the 1760s – precisely the decade in England that pseudofactuality definitively becomes a minority posture. Previously, memoir and travel novels went hand in hand with pseudofactual affirmations: of 41 such works dating from before 1761, only 5 (4 memoirs and 1 travel narrative) are presented as fictional creations; after this point, the few such works left are still presented as true more than half the time – in rates, then, far above those of most other English novels at the time. (Figure E9.3 shows truth posture rates for all nonepistolary first persons.) Memoir and travel novels don't really "fictionalize" in England as the former largely do in France, where they continue moreover to remain popular throughout much of the century. Rather, they are abandoned at precisely the moment pseudofactual forms are on the out.[4]

And they are replaced by another "document" novel – the epistolary novel, whose sudden adoption in England is truly unprecedented in the context of the present study.

Figure 9.4 Epistolary novels (England and France).

Though not entirely obvious from the graph in Figure 9.4, the exploration of the epistolary form in England is markedly more hesitant than in France: notably, French "observational" epistolary novels (responsible for what I label in Chapter 7 the "first" rise of the form) have virtually no English counterparts. But while the basic periodization of the form's substantial popularity in the second half of the century doesn't differ much from one country to the other, the pace and amplitude of the market takeover in England is unparalleled. Still in the 1750s, when French writers were starting to explore the use of the form for sentimental plots and despite the runaway success of Richardson's *Clarissa* (1748), only 2 of the 41 real-world novels in the English sample are epistolary – one, a lovers' exchange, and the other, a rare English observational text. But in the sample from the next decade, 37 out of 75 real-world novels are epistolary, 70 percent of those are polyphonic, and epistolary hegemony lasts a good three decades before an abrupt falloff in the 1790s.[5]

At the end of this chapter and again in the next, I will advance an explanation for the epistolary novel's remarkable success in England – an explanation which, to be sure, will have nothing to do with the country's more bourgeois ideology, its system of postal delivery, or anything similar. For now, I would like to limit myself to the form's pseudofactuality – or really, lack thereof. After all, the epistolary novel explodes in the same decade that pseudofactuality retreats, which should make us suspect that for all intents and purposes the form never possessed the documenticity it did in France. It is true that the scarce early examples were proceeded by the standard pseudofactual declarations: all items from before 1761 were advanced as true documents. But the truth profile of works after this date is even less pseudofactual than that of the English novel in general (Figure 9.5).

9 *The Novel System in England, 1701–1810*

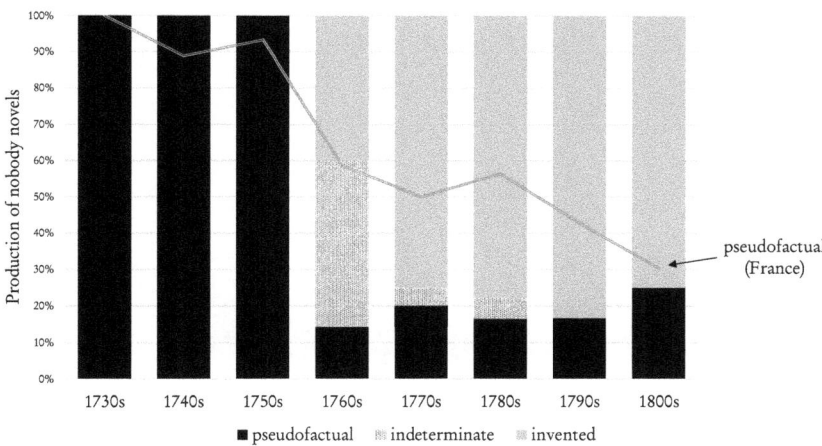

Figure 9.5 Truth postures of epistolary novels (England).

The large number of indeterminates in the 1760s may suggest some uncertainty as to whether to bother asserting the truth of the form. But surely the overall conclusion is clear: this artifact's popularity was never dependent on the potentially titillating promise of real secrets revealed. One could say that the epistolary novel in England was always very much a novel.[6]

In terms of first-person texts, then, the English novel starting in the 1760s is simply not the novel of the decades before. Are third-person texts cleaved in a similar way? Truth-wise, absolutely. Prior to 1751, third-person novels – when they are not (satirical) somebody novels, which prosper especially in the 1700s and 1710s during the tussles between Whigs and Tories[7] – are for the most part pseudofactual, and again by the 1760s, that pseudofactuality has permanently retreated. (See Figure E9.6.) But formally, can we observe changes similar to the distinction I've made in the previous chapter between "old" and "new" uses of the third person in France? And if so, will this help us understand the distinct path of pseudofactuality in the two countries?

Segmentation of the English novel is accomplished in many of the same ways in France, with only one discrepancy worth mentioning: if chapters are in both cases the dominant segment, the English rarely break novels into "parts," and when they do, those parts are much shorter than French parts (they behave, length-wise, much like English "books"). Remarkably, French and English chapters contain on average virtually the same number of words – 3,040 versus 2,994 in France. On one level, then, the novel segment in the two countries has the same shape. But as Figure 9.6 shows, chapterization occurs on a different timetable in England, where in addition the use of chapter titles patterns in a distinctive manner.

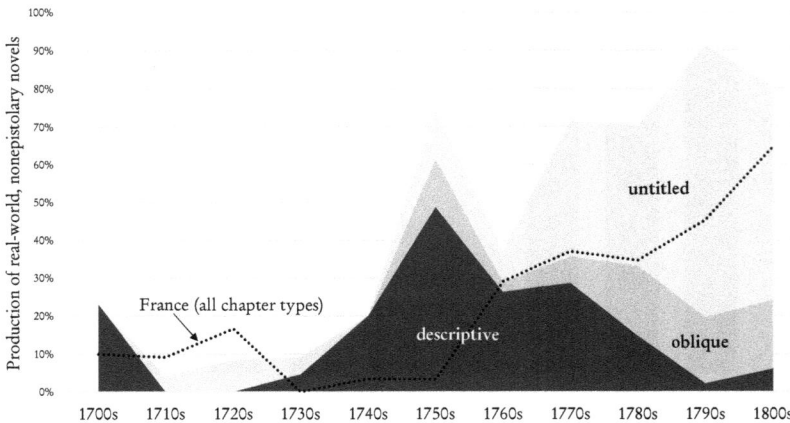

Figure 9.6 Chapterized novels (England).

The growth of chapterized novels in England is more sudden than in France and the use of chapters more pervasive – exactly and probably not accidentally the same phenomena we observed in the spread of epistolarity. Moreover, chapter titles tell their own story. In France, the growth of chapters in the second half of the century is essentially the growth of chapters with oblique titles or no titles at all: descriptive titles, which for a while are virtually the only labeling used, simply peter out. (See Figure 8.6, page 144.) In England, by contrast, there are essentially two chapter vogues, one coming on the heels of the other. Novels containing descriptive chapter titles spread quickly between the 1730s and 1750s before falling away over the next few decades. Untitled chapters prosper as descriptively titled chapters are waning, in the 1770s, and they maintain their strength for the duration of the observed period. (The English spread of obliquely titled chapters, which in France appear to have the historical function of transitioning between the descriptively titled chapter and the untitled chapter, is indistinguishable from that of untitled chapters.) Thus, the chapterized novel arrives in England in two waves, with the first cresting in 1750s – the same decade, then, that pseudofactuality commences its clear retreat.

The 1750s is also an important decade for another change, this time in third-person novels specifically. (As in France, third- and first-person novels in England acquire chapters simultaneously and at the same rates.) During most of the century, English novels are substantially longer than French novels: the latter start to average 60,000 words at the turn of the nineteenth century, whereas English novels hit (and maintain) this length much earlier, in the 1730s. But if we zero in on third-person novels specifically, another story emerges. As Figure 9.7 shows, for the first half of the eighteenth century,

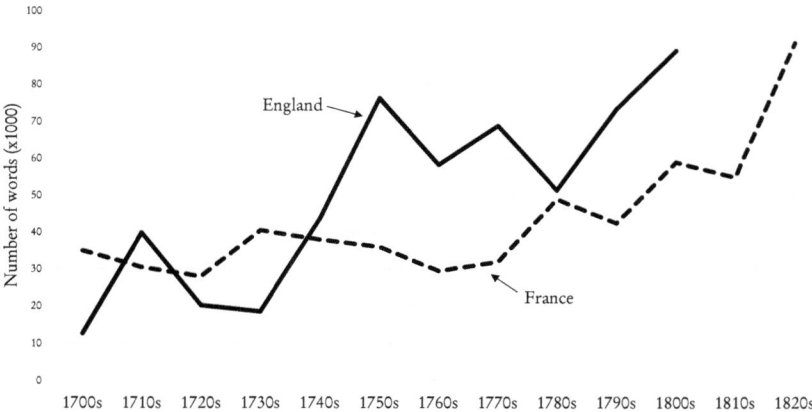

Figure 9.7 Median length of real-world third-person novels (England and France).

there is little systematic difference between the two countries; then, in the 1750s, the English third-person novel undergoes a remarkable lengthening.

It bears noting that this expansion occurs on the same timetable as that of chapterization, as if to suggest that the two phenomena were related. And indeed, they are, since the chapterized novel in England, whose median length is 65,000 words, is more than twice as long as the unsegmented novel, at 31,000 words. These figures, moreover, are comparable to those for France, where the median length of a chapterized novel is 56,000 words over the period covered by the English data and 76,000 words if we extend the period to 1830. (French unsegmented third-person novels are roughly 30,000 words, irrespective of the span – again, virtually identical to their English counterparts.) If the English third-person novel is longer than its French counterpart, this brute fact appears inseparable from this novel's earlier adoption of a technology that allows it to grow – segmentation into chapters. Thus, the phenomena are essentially the same on each side of the Channel, with the difference being only the lag of France with respect to England.

That same lag is visible, finally, in the use of scenes to open the novel's action. (Following the understanding developed in Chapter 8, scenes posit a describable, physical space in which characters start to do things.) My tagging of openings in the English novel is simplified with respect to the treatment given in French novels. I did not separate out other types of openings, such as the character portrait, which was surely as dominant in England as it was in France; I noted the presence of scenes alone and only when in incipit position (i.e., at the very start of the text). Judging by Figure 9.8, the use of scene setting might at first appear to be less of a specifically post-1751 phenomenon in England. In fact, the novels from before that date are

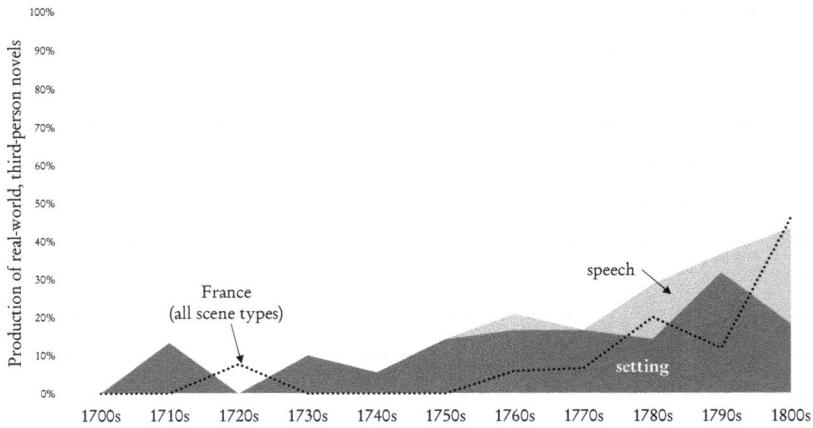

Figure 9.8 Scenes (incipit position only, England).

few (only four), and all have what we might want to call "rosy-fingered dawn" openings, that is, openings modeled on the classical genres of epic or pastoral. (*Exilius, or the Bannish'd Roman* [Barker, 1715]: "Night having withdrawn her sable curtains, discover'd the bright Aurora rising, whose beauty illustrated the whole hemisphere, and thereby excited Clelia, the fair niece of Publius Scipio, to her early devotions, in a grove….") Accordingly, all feature historical or unspecified settings. It is only in the 1750s that scene openings start to appear in English novels with contemporary settings. This is somewhat earlier than in France, and the practice spreads more quickly: here too, the morphological changes that in France are associated with the 1780s or after are more clearly in place in the 1750s and 1760s.

A cluster of formal changes occur in the English third-person novel and accompany the latter's "fictionalization": it lengthens; it chapterizes; and it experiments with scene setting. As in France, it may make sense to see these changes as characterizing a "new" third-person novel, by opposition to an "old" variety (shorter, nonsegmented, with no scenes). Because my tagging of English novel openings was summary, the test scenarios are less numerous than in the French case, but the same basic operation can be performed. We can generate six scenarios for each novel type by choosing three length limits and two configurations of chapters and scenes.[8] Heuristically shading the results in the manner used in previous chapters gives Figure 9.9. Save for the readings from the first decade of the century, the "old" third-person novel is not nearly as obvious presence on the English scene. This is perhaps not surprising if we recall that French "old" third-person novels were basically another name for the declining *nouvelle*, a form that in its late seventeenth-century

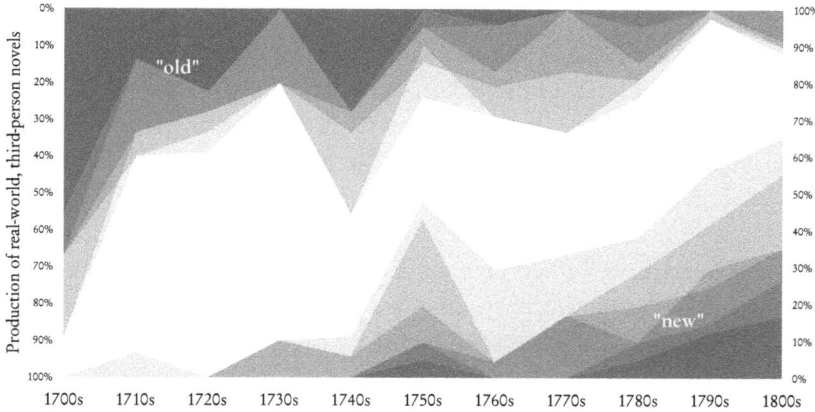

Figure 9.9 "Old" and "new" third-person novels (England).

heyday had no English counterpart. (I will address the question of England's seventeenth-century novelistic output in a moment.) But as in France, the two forms distribute in the same way, one virtually extinct by the end of the century and the other not yet practiced at the century's beginning.

The English "new" novel shows some presence from the 1750s (the sudden spike in that decade is caused by the quick spread of descriptively titled chapters) and by the 1790s is well established (if far from dominant) under most scenarios. Averaging the scenarios, we can see in Figure 9.10 some notable differences with respect to France. First, while in France "old" and "new" novels taken together make up a significant market share, in England they don't: English third-person novels are formally much more mixed.

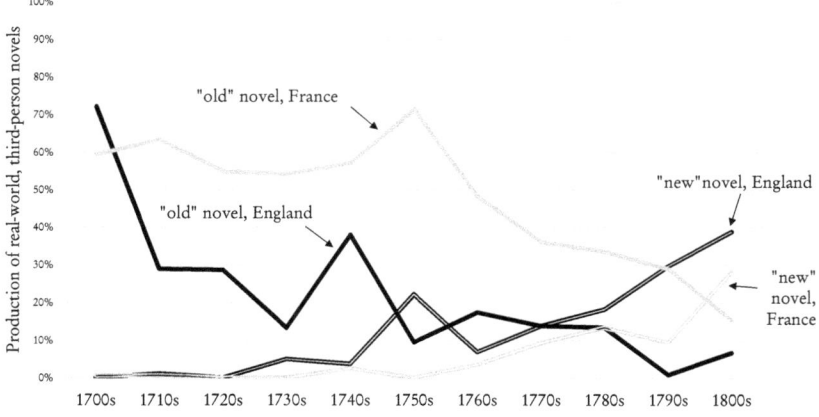

Figure 9.10 "Old" and "new" third-person novels (averaged scenarios, England and France).

Nonetheless, the "new" novel's appearance is clear in both countries, with England slightly ahead of France's curve. Even though there is only a one-decade differential in the moment each country's "new" novels arrive at the threshold of about 30 percent, the general impression is that the English novel is quicker to throw off the traits of the "old" novel – no doubt because they never really dominated the production at all.

If Figure 9.1 shows us that the English novel "fictionalizes" more quickly than the French novel, others demonstrate that this state of affairs is traceable to at least four interacting particularities. The first factor is minor, and I've already mentioned it: it stems simply from my tagging protocol, according to which the subtitles "novel," "tale," and "romance" are taken as admissions of invention. In England, the wide use of these subtitles is directly responsible for the much smaller number of novels classified as "indeterminate." That is, since French novelists don't much use these subtitles, the only way of indicating invention (at least for third-person texts) is by a preface, but in both countries, large numbers of novels are unprefaced. Second, and more decisively, the adoption of the epistolary novel in England is explosive, going from trace quantities in the 1750s and before to a roughly 50-percent market share in the next three decades; and the strikingly successful epistolary novel was rarely presented either as a true correspondence or, more minimally, as "based on" a true story. In France, by contrast, the form had a much deeper history as a document (going well back into the seventeenth century), and it lost that "documenticity" much more slowly. Third, English first-person novels other than epistolary (chiefly, the memoir novel) *did* possess such documenticity: even post-1761, they were more often presented as true than not. (See Figure E9.3.) But unlike in France, nonepistolary first-person novels became rare quickly, petering out in the 1760s and then all but disappearing by the 1780s.

Finally, the English third-person novel undergoes the morphological changes we saw first in the French novel but does so a bit earlier. As in the French case, it would be mistaken to see the "new" third-person novel as responsible for the decline of pseudofactuality. Certainly, "old" novels are much more likely to be presented as true than "new" novels, even in the same years. Thus, post-1750, the former have pseudofactual or Aristotelian ("somebody") stances over 50 percent of the time, compared to 20 percent of the latter; and conversely, "new" novels are given as inventions much more often than "old" novels (61 versus 38 percent of the time). But this is also to say that the two morphologies are merely decent predictors of truth posture: associations are far from ironclad. Moreover, it is really only the "old" morphology that is the predictor because *all* other third-person novels

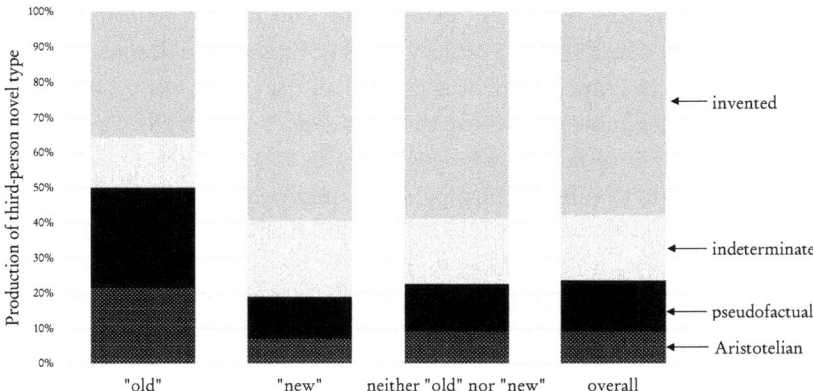

Figure 9.11 Truth postures of third-person novels by novel type, 1751–1810 (England).

after 1750 – the ones that I've described as "new" but also the novels that enter into neither scenario – have approximately the same truth profile (Figure 9.11). Thus, although "new" novels don't share the truth profile of "old" ones, they do share the profile of novels that are neither "new" nor "old," which are also admitted as inventions 60 percent of the time. This is why the "fictionalization" of the English novel hardly needs to wait for the adoption of the new morphology. On the contrary: as in France, the decline in interest in literal truth precedes the spread of "new" novels.

In her widely cited account of the rise of the fictional novel in England, Catherine Gallagher situated its "discovery" – her term – some time before 1742, while also positing that the French novel seems to have started fictionalizing at least a half-century earlier but taken much longer to complete the process – maybe sometime after 1800.[9] It is hardly a surprise that Gallagher's dates are not quite confirmed by the data in the present study: she derived them from only a handful of canonical coordinates. But her more basic suggestion that the change in novels was sudden in England but protracted in France does appear to be right. What could be behind this disparity? The obvious "historicist" solution is to imagine that sociocultural context is responsible, and indeed the gist of Gallagher's answer is that English modernity – perhaps on account of its proverbial "empiricism, capitalism, [and] materialism" – encouraged "disbelief, speculation, and credit," of which fiction is merely the literary manifestation.[10]

Leaving aside the all-purpose vagueness of such explanatory factors, surely the attraction of this type of explanation depends on our not knowing too much about the various movements in the novel system. That is, if what we think we know is that the shift to admittedly fictional novels is relatively quick in England as compared to France, then it is easy enough to point to some circumstances that might plausibly be said to be responsible for the difference. But why did the epistolary novel in England not know the "first" rise that it did in France? Why was its English rise in the second half of the century so much more impressive than in France? Why is the career of the French memoir novel so long, whereas in England the form falters definitively by the midcentury? Why do third-person novels in the two countries develop in roughly the same way (length, segmentation, scenes) and in both cases following the retreat of pseudofactuality? "Invented" novels are a steady if minority presence in France from the 1730s – how can the French be both "ahead" and "behind" with respect to the capitalist and empiricist English?

When we look at the behavior of the entire novel system in detail, we see a swirl of changes: each one cannot possibly have a specific sociocultural cause, still less the same infinitely elastic and infinitely forgiving ones (Capital, empiricism, and so on). Or, let's say that the difficulty may lie in the way literary historians think causality itself – usually along the lines of homology, as I've maintained at a number of points throughout this study. Thus, for Gallagher, fictionality is a kind of speculation and therefore must be caused by the credit economy or some phase thereof.[11] In the following chapter, I will turn in more detail to explaining the behavior of the literary system without recourse to such invisible hands. For the moment, I want to limit myself to one obvious "cause" of the discrepant behavior of the novel system in these two countries, which is simply production: arguably England didn't really have a novel "system" until the 1740s or 1750s, and this alone can help explain the quite sudden changes observed.

The English novel's "rise" has become proverbial since the publication of Ian Watt's use of the metaphor in his 1957 study, and for at least one good reason outside the brilliance of his book: even without serious quantitative study, basic scholarship has long made it clear that early in the eighteenth century few English novels are published, and that by the end lots are. By contrast, the simple fact that seventeenth-century France produced large quantities of novels – a fact that at no subsequent point has ever faded from scholarly memory – has inhibited the adoption of the metaphor by its specialists.[12] And indeed, Figure 9.12 helps us see why in one country the rise metaphor would find fortune and in the other it wouldn't.[13] Of course, from 1750s on, the similarities are striking: in both countries novels see a nearly fivefold increase in titles, and moreover production in each is nearly the same, save some slower growth in France during the 1780s and 1790s (partially explained by the Revolution's effect on novel production). But before the 1750s – and logarithmically plotted Figure E9.7 makes this more obvious – the respective situations are very different. English production

9 The Novel System in England, 1701–1810

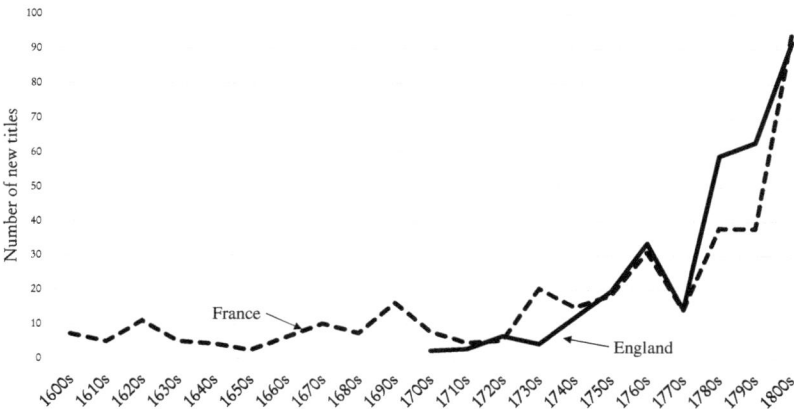

Figure 9.12 Yearly novel production (estimated, England and France).

is minimal: only in the 1740s does it hit an average of ten novels a year, whereas in France, there had been ten novels a year more than a century earlier and then again throughout most of the second half of the seventeenth century. It is true that the figures from the 1710s and 1720s are low in both countries, but whereas in France this is a trough, in England it appears to be representative of what was, in fact, a negligible market for homegrown novels before the takeoff in the 1740s and 1750s. (Homegrown, as opposed to translations, of which there were many.)

Does the appearance correspond to reality? Available quantitative information suggests that English figures for the 1690s are in all probability similar to those from the 1700s.[14] Meanwhile, the longstanding absence of scholarly monographs on the novel in England before 1690 is a good sign that its production is indeed negligible, and it's also true that scholars routinely remark that it's difficult to find older titles that correspond to what we might expect of a novel. "Any scholar adopting a teleological approach and searching for the forebears of *Moll Flanders*, *Pamela*, and *Joseph Andrews* will discover pickings thinner than slim," writes Robert D. Hume, who continues:

> To the reader of the 1660s, "fiction" might mean Francis Bacon's *New Atlantis* (in its 9th edition by 1660), or the *Gesta Romanorum* (14th edition, 1662), or Philip Sidney's *Arcadia* (15th edition, 1662). Alternatively, it could mean *The Noble Birth and Gallant Achievements of ... Robin Hood* (1662) or Richard Johnson's *The Most Pleasant History of Tom a Lincoln* (10th edition, 1668).[15]

Yet the conclusions that researchers draw from such observations is usually that what "we" think of as the novel simply didn't exist in the seventeenth century, and that to think that it might amounts to no more than an anachronistic projection. By this reckoning, the most one can responsibly do to recuperate this inchoate nebula of narrative flotsam is to cast it as the primordial soup from which our novel was to emerge.[16] Yet, French researchers don't register this problem, not because of their willy-nilly projections but for the simple reason that objects that contemporaries explicitly thought of as novels are plentiful in the French bibliographical record.[17] Certainly, those researchers are confronted with definitional problems, too: the outer boundaries of *any* category of artifacts will be hazy. But the bibliographic lesson is that in seventeenth-century France there is a good-sized consensual core of novels, whereas in England at that time there is not. This is not a matter of mindsets or anachronistic application of generic expectations. It is a matter of book history.

England's novel, then, sees a clear, steady, and soon vertiginous rise – from close to nothing in the early part of the century to near a hundred titles yearly at the turn of the nineteenth century. France, on the other hand, was not starting from virtually zero in 1700, far from it. In sheer number of titles, its production was substantial in the second half of the seventeenth century; and even before then, if we except the depression caused by the Fronde, production was low by 1750–1800 standards but nonetheless reliably constant. Moreover, for the 1630s and 1640s, we should remember that if titles were not particularly numerous, they were often long. Figure 9.13 counts the number of novel words produced yearly, revealing that these decades were in fact a high point not to be surpassed before the 1730s. (A method of counting taking into account the fact that long novels were often released in multiple installments would also give increased importance to those decades.)

Figure 9.13 Yearly novel production in words (estimated, logarithmic scale; England and France).

9 The Novel System in England, 1701–1810

A reasonable explanation for the very rapid midcentury changes observed in the English novel system, then, may lie simply in the system's youth. In France, changes were slow because novelists took their cue from the novelists preceding them: the system was characterized by inertia as well as change, since people kept doing what other people had been doing even as they constantly innovated. But in England, it is difficult to speak of a novel system before the 1740s or even 1750s. As such, the English epistolary novel doesn't need to displace another hegemonic form or modify a system with a history and the inertia that comes with it. The form's spectacularly sudden breakout in the 1760s – again, a breakout unmatched by anything observable in the French novel in the 230 years covered here – is thus inseparable from the immaturity of the English novel system itself. Similarly, a plausible explanation for why English writers were so quick to drop pseudofactual claims should appeal not to a conceptual advance, stemming perhaps from their capitalist experience of credit, but rather to the fact that those novelists were much less indebted than French ones to established habits and practices. The English novel rises so well simply because it has no history.

Naturally, I am well aware that such an explanation may not even seem like an explanation for many within the field of literary and cultural history: it does not offer the satisfying "snap" that comes from fitting a cultural symptom to the ideological or material cause we take as having produced it. It's an explanation, then, that demands a recalibration in what counts as an explanation. For some, the cost of the recalibration may be too high, since it excludes thinking in terms of necessity: no longer do the observed changes in the archive of artworks or cultural artifacts have specific causes; no longer do they register, through some opaque logic perceptible only to the critic, the profound coherence of their historical moment. By contrast, a zoomed out, quantitative view exposes us to a world of tendencies and recurring patterns. In Chapter 10, this study's last, I will try to make more sense of the various patterns of change within the novel archive by thinking of literary forms as technological artifacts, artifacts whose evolution is comparable to that of other technological artifacts – windmills, toilets, smartphones.

PART III

10 | The Evolution of Narrative Technologies

In this final chapter, I want to lay out a "technological" explanation for the changes traced in the preceding chapters. That is, I want to make the case that literary evolution should be understood as a kind of technological evolution. By this I don't mean that novels evolve exactly like airplanes; but at the same time I am proposing more than an analogy. Technological evolution has many different characteristics, and literature – like the airplane – displays some of them and not others. By contrast, the evolutionary record of the novel does not support the more common ways of explaining the form's fabled "rise."

The system of novels is in ceaseless but patterned flux. Which of the changes described in the previous chapters is the decisive change – the one that separates the "modern" novel, or The Novel *tout court*, from a qualitatively different predecessor? Obviously, none. And my point is certainly not that a clear separation is not possible because change is uneven or that the residual not-yet-modern "novel" persisted for a long time in the face of the (real) modern novel's gradually imposed dominance. Rather, both concepts are faulty – that of the modern novel and that of its rise.

Of course, the novel's rise can make sense in some meanings of the term. Maybe we want to refer to the fact that over the course of the eighteenth century there are always more and more novels published. But as Figure 9.12 (page 171) shows and Figure 9.13 (page 172) confirms, even this rise is hardly self-evident. While England does see a nearly uninterrupted growth in novel production, it owes it to the fact that as it started the century, it had no substantial production of novels at all: England was late to the novel game. But speaking of the novel's rise in France – where, of course, eighteenth-century growth trends were on balance identical to those in England – is much more problematic. Where is the rise of the French novel on Figure 9.12? The 1690s? But the numbers quickly retreat again. The 1730s, a decade sometimes dubbed the "golden age of the French novel"?[1] There, the numbers were barely higher than they were forty years earlier. For any sustained and dramatic increase, we have to look to the end of the eighteenth century. And if we quantify the production of novels not in terms of individual new titles but in terms of new words, as does Figure 9.13, the gains of the 1730s and after – as well as late-seventeenth-century activity – appear still more modest. Or maybe when we talk of the "rise of the novel" we really mean the process by which the novel moved to the prestigious center of the literary world, occupied previously by epic, or tragedy, or lyric poetry. I don't doubt that the novel did take over the market in such a way. But Figure 9.12 cannot really tell us at what point the novel increases its overall market share of printed literature generally – outpacing poems and plays. After all, increases in net production of new novels may simply reflect growth in the print market more broadly, which in turn may be linked to population or perhaps to literacy rates or income. Some rising tides do lift all boats.[2]

But all that is not what is usually meant by the rise of the novel, anyway. The rise of the novel, I've said more than once, is shorthand for something else – for the big change of modernity, the one that brings us from Then to Now. Some call it the empiricist or scientific revolution; or it may be cast as a subjective revolution, giving rise to the liberal, autonomous individual, or, more darkly, to a subject of ideological discipline and coercion. In the many cycles traced in the course of this book, however, there aren't any befores or afters; or rather, the after of any one thing is also the before of something else. Thus, the "new" third-person novel described in Chapter 8 is merely the endpoint of this study and not a telos of the novel itself: it is the last cycle I've been able, as a practical matter, to examine (no doubt too briefly). But with it nothing definitive has happened. It too shall pass – has already passed, long ago.

Perhaps, instead of a two-poled model of change, what we simply need is good old-fashioned periodization: roughly, the "seventeenth-century novel," or the "Enlightenment novel," and so on. More interestingly, we could go further by hitching the popularity of a given form to the particular ethos or mindset whose "logic" it would seem to share. I've already had multiple occasions to mention the frequent association of the *nouvelle* with the rectilinear aesthetics and politics of Louis XIV's court. From there, we might choose to view the enthusiasm for Heliodorian insetting as the narrative counterpart of a specifically "baroque" mentality – tolerant and indeed representative of a kind of preclassical fragmentation and recursiveness; or it could be cast as an extension of the type of not-yet-centralized aristocratic sociability predominating before the absolutist court pulled all social life into the orbit of the Sun King.[3] And of course, there is a longstanding association between the Enlightenment vogue for first-person forms and the advent of a certain type of interiorized bourgeois subjectivity.[4] Such explanations are underwritten largely by the trick of "motivating the device": presented with some formal property, the critic works back to its social origin, identified as such by dint of its resemblance to or homology with the artwork. Thus, the epiphenomena of culture are linked to the realm of true causes.

I will not belabor the suspiciously arbitrary, this-kind-of-reminds-me-of-that "method" used to generate such accounts, which some call symptomology.[5] The specific challenge posed by quantitative approaches is that they provide too much information to allow us to think in terms of coherent periods. Such thought is convincing only as long as we know just the right amount about the historical record – which is to say, not very much. If we want to argue that the first-person novel follows from the Individual's importance in the newly bourgeois eighteenth century, and maybe that the subsequent rise of the third-person novel is an effect of the State's importance in the now industrially capitalist nineteenth, it helps to know no more than that some important eighteenth-century novelists made a lot of use of the first person (witness A, B, and C), whereas their nineteenth-century counterparts preferred the third (as shown by X, Y, and Z). In such a case, the sketchiness of our knowledge enables the narrative, which doesn't demand that we really think about how one epoch (and its purportedly specific ideology) gave way to another. Once we know that the given forms appear to operate on a more artifactual timetable – the rises are gradual, the peaks are quickly past, the falls look like the rises – the mapping of practices onto the supposed "logic" of this or that period is much less tempting.

Indeed, are there even any periods? When we say "periods," we surely mean stretches of relative stability; these are separated from one another by "periods of transition" – buffer zones when things are up in the air. Over the span examined here, it is true that some decades do seem to possess little in the way of formal coherence. These are moments when no one form dominates – the 1650s and 1660s; or the 1710s and 1720s – and that do appear to be transitional. But the problem is that moments of formal dominance are as transitional as the moments of transition: literary forms – or at least the ones I have traced here – don't plateau. (Even the French memoir novel, probably the most enduring of the forms examined, clearly peaks and declines.) And when it comes, dominance is hardly hegemonic: the *nouvelle* can plausibly be said to represent over 40 percent of the French production for a half-century; at its peak, which is short-lived, it takes over something like three-quarters of the market; but this still means that a lot of novels over this half-century are not *nouvelles*. The same goes for the epistolary novel and the memoir novel. Thus, though we may well be able to identify a "typical" form for a given stretch of years, at any one moment, there are always many ways of writing novels – some quite untimely or idiosyncratic and some merely variations on the normal way of doing things. The archive of novels is unquestionably patterned; but those patterns look nothing like "periods."[6]

So how can we explain the patterns? Surely it can't be an accident that the career of the *nouvelle* – for example – corresponds so well to the personal reign of Louis XIV? Is my contention seriously that literature is unaffected by history, by "context"? Well, no; but we should be cautious. Most obviously, correlation is not causation. More important, we choose to see correlations that appear meaningful and ignore the complications. Some aspects of the *nouvelle*'s career do correlate well with Louis XIV's personal reign. It is first present in significant numbers in the 1660s; it peaks in the 1680s, as the "absolutist" court takes up permanent residence at Versailles. But looking closely at the form's falling off, we see that the numbers from the 1710s sample – which is moreover a sample containing years from *after* the death of the monarch in 1715 – are in fact comparable to those of the 1660s or 1670s. We thus retain the facts that fit our explanation – a takeoff after 1661, when Louis XIV decides to govern alone; a peak around the time of his definitive sedentarization at Versailles in 1682 – while leaving the ones that don't – the long "tail" of the form, which outlives the Sun King by a good deal. Or take memoirs, whose rise we could motivate by recourse to the *end* of absolutist court society. These novels hover at a bit under 10 percent of the production in the opening decades of the century, only to explode in popularity over the next three decades. We might reason that this can be no accident: the death of Louis XIV in 1715 signals the end of traditional courtly identity practices, thereby enabling the expansion of a new sort of "postabsolutist" subjectivity – something like an Individual, freed from the hierarchical pressure cooker of court life memorably described by Norbert Elias.[7] Yet, is it really likely that the Individual emerges so quickly, just where we want and need it – especially given that whenever a change is in need of motivation, scholars of European history and culture from the twelfth century on have, with almost comical compulsion, rushed to provide this very one? And what if the takeoff had come a bit earlier, in, say, the 1700s or 1710s? Wouldn't we still maintain, *mutatis mutandis*, the same explanation – arguing now that the senility of Absolutism, rather than the death of a monarch, was making the change possible? These are just-so stories. They will always make sense of the data, which is selected to bear out the stories whose contours are cut to fit it.

None of this means that literature's evolution has nothing to do with the values and preoccupations of the human beings who produce and consume it. But explaining changes in the literary record by reaching for the most proximate extraliterary event or for abstract historical developments – the "liberal subject," the "Enlightenment project," "market capitalism" – simply won't do. Literary forms are not produced by some sort of magical sympathy with the historical moment that might be seen as "resembling" them. They are fashioned and refashioned by people.

This, I believe, is where a technological understanding of literature comes in. Of course, technologies are typically thought of as physical things, and there is no physical difference between, say, an epistolary novel and a third-person novel with chapters: both are codexes, both are produced using the contemporaneously available technologies of papermaking, printing, and binding. I am certainly not proposing that the history of the novel – of the novel's many forms – is linked in anything more than a trivial or anecdotal manner to changes in the actual production of books. (That *some* novels engage thematically with the contemporary realities of book production, or that in the nineteenth century the novel in general was affected by the invention of cheap wood pulp paper, goes without saying.) Such a contention would answer to an intuitive sense of what technologies are; but it would also fail to explain any of the patterns we've observed in the novelistic record. It is preferable to explore a theory that does seem to describe that record, even if the theory rests on a nonintuitive sense of the word technology. My contention is that the various narrative forms I've identified are in fact technologies – or technological artifacts – even though the differences between them amount to nothing but the disposition of ink on paper.

It is probably obvious that speaking of formal change in this way departs from approaching it as a symptom of historico-ideological configurations; likewise, it has little to do with more typological accounts, as if writers chose – according to their taste, temperament, or epoch – from among a certain limited number of preexisting narrative stances.[8] But to step back for a moment from the technological proposition I've just broached, why not simply speak of formal change in another conventional way – that is, as a continual refinement of technique, a process by which the innovations of some writers are picked up by others, resulting in an ever more complex and complete art of the novel? In such an understanding, the forms of first-person narration in the eighteenth century become a stage in the novel's expanding ability to depict consciousness, thought, individuality: third-person omniscient narration and its attendant techniques of what Dorrit Cohn has famously called psychonarration (including free indirect discourse) will build on these earlier advances and in turn will be built on by modernist stream-of-consciousness.[9] A frequent corollary of this way of thinking posits that the advances are made by great writers. "*Madame Bovary*," writes a distinguished translator of Flaubert's famous novel, "permanently changed the way novels were written thereafter."[10] In between the disruptions visited by genius, there are moments of stasis – simian copying. Pierre Boulle's *Planet of the Apes*: "Of what is our literature made? Masterpieces? [N]o. But once an original book has been written – and no more than one or two appear in a century – men of letters *imitate* it, that's to say they copy it so that hundreds of thousands of books are published on exactly the same theme, with slightly different titles and modified phraseology. This should be able to be achieved by monkeys, who are essentially imitators, provided of course they are able to make use of language."[11]

Speaking of the evolution of the novel in this way is clearly teleological and inventor-centered: thanks to the efforts of a few visionaries, the novel is brought ever closer to realizing its full potential to being the form of expression that humans need. Such propositions no doubt have an old-fashioned ring, and indeed, the ring is in fact that of a traditional history of technology, the kind practiced before the constructivist variety associated with Science and Technology Studies (STS). Seeking to replace the commonplaces of an older history of science – the Great Inventor, the March of Progress – STS generally proceeds through finely grained case studies aimed at revealing the contingency of technological change. It is not the intrinsic superiority of a given technological artifact (often assumed to come from the insight of a single inventor) that explains its success; rather, an array of factors conjoin to produce an outcome – and typically an outcome *over time* – that is in no way inevitable. Yes, successful artifacts "work better" than the ones they displace; but "working" is actually something that is worked on and that in any case has only contextual meaning. Working for whom, exactly? To what end? "The 'working' and 'nonworking' of an artifact," writes one STS scholar, "are socially constructed assessments, rather than intrinsic properties of the artifact."[12] Calling literary forms *artifacts* compels, then, a shift in focus: invention is no longer an unpredictable, disruptive, and transformative event, imputable to individual writers, but rather a continuous, contingent, and heteronomous process, engaged in by multiple human agents whose independent actions nonetheless form a system.

How does such a view mesh with the data described in this book?

As I've emphasized, a basic pattern is that formal innovations take a good deal of time to spread and that their use peaks before falling away, usually slowly. This alone suggests that literature – at least at the formal level I have been focusing on – does not follow a pattern of transformative innovation. In other words, the system does not change suddenly; successful innovations require decades to take over, a time scale that doesn't support any simple idea of "imitation."[13] Indeed, we've also seen that artifacts homogenize over time. When the Aristotelian novel and the epistolary novel are new, the features each displays from example to example are quite varied; as the forms are widely adopted, the examples produced look more and more like one another. So "imitation" doesn't seem the right term: early adopters work the form, trying out different options, until some sort of stability is achieved. But once again, this takes considerable time.

That this takes time is one reason militating in favor of a technological explanation despite the fact that no physical inventions separate, say, the observational epistolary novel from the sentimental, polyphonic epistolary novel. If literary forms spread like Richard Dawkins's memes – easily repeatable elements – then we would expect to see much quicker adoption and abandonment; the phenomenon of homogenization would also be unnecessary since the repeatable elements would essentially be ready-made "plug-ins."[14] The record suggests, however, that novelistic forms possess a high coefficient of (metaphorical) inertia: the way people write novels seems deeply ingrained. This is counterintuitive: what prevents writers from distributing their ink on their pages in a new way? Granted, the writing of novels is measured in months or years: there's no reason to think the spread of the epistolary novel should be quite as rapid as that of the hula-hoop, which requires only the gearing up of factories to shape plastic into a new form. But for that novel to take decades to rise and decades to quit the scene? No doubt *some* literary features come and go on a more meme-like timetable – just not narrative forms.

If narrative forms show features we'd expect of bona fide technologies, this may be because technologies are best understood on a spectrum running from the physical (technology in a conventional sense) to the nonphysical. This broader understanding has been proposed by W. Brian Arthur in *The Nature of Technology* – probably the fullest theoretical account to date of technological innovation and evolution. Arthur argues that all technologies are organized, purposed systems, made up of component parts or rather – in all but the simplest technologies – assemblies of parts, or more commonly still, assemblies of subassemblies, and so on. In other words, technologies are recursive: they are made up of other technologies. But that recursiveness does not only extend "down" to the simplest elements; it also means that technologies that might appear autonomous or self-contained are also assemblies in a larger system. One of his examples is the F-35C Lightning II aircraft fighter – presumably an uncontroversial candidate for a technology. Arthur first decomposes the fighter into its many assemblies and subassemblies, showing how this one technology is made up of many other technologies – each a system functioning within the larger system that is the F-35C. Arthur's move is then to show that the F-35C is itself a system within a larger system – a carrier air wing – which in turn is an assembly within a carrier battle group, which is a subassembly of a theater-of-war grouping. All of these are technologies.[15] He stops there, while also making clear that organizations themselves are technologies; so presumably one could also speak of whole armies in the same way, as well as the governments that command them.

Arthur admits that all these technologies don't look exactly the same, don't share exactly the same features. And he addresses head-on the fact that many purposed systems devised by humans do not *feel* like technologies, seem to lack "'technology-ness'." These are technologies that are not based on physical phenomena but rather on "nonphysical 'effects' – organizational or behavioral effects or even logical or mathematical ones in the case of algorithms." *The Nature of Technology* does not deal in any detail with such nonphysical purposed systems: Arthur offers the example of monetary systems, which "mak[e] use of the 'phenomenon' [the quotes emphasizing that the latter is nonphysical] that we trust a medium has value as long as we believe that others trust it has value and we believe this trust will continue in the future"; a Mahler symphony is also a means to fulfill a purpose – "providing a sensual experience, say" – with component parts that also fulfill purposes. In general, he recognizes that people don't usually see such things as technologies and proposes that it may help to think of them as "first cousins to technologies, even if formally they qualify as technologies."[16]

So it is understandable that one would not normally think of the novel as a technology.[17] Yet diachronic, quantitative analysis hints that it may well be one – a purposed system composed of other technologies that come and go. But it's also clear from Arthur that systems are not all technologies in quite the same way and therefore that "the novel" isn't quite a technology in the same way "the epistolary novel" is. I said at the outset of this study that although it is common to think of the evolution of "the novel" as such, the novel isn't really one *thing* that is evolving. The novel is a system of other objects that have greater "thingishness" than the system of which they are part. This is a crucial point since the evolution of systems and the individual artifacts that compose them may not be the same evolution. More specifically, many of the artifacts that compose the system are *discontinuous*. "Recorded music" is a system of technologies that do (roughly) the same thing; but the vinyl record in no way "becomes" the cassette tape. (Yet, as I will point out in a moment, many artifacts *are* continuous with respect to others – say, the eight-track and the cassette.) Or, as Arthur puts it, again with reference to aircraft, "the jet engine is not a variation of the internal combustion engine or anything else that proceeded it, and it did not come into being by the steady accumulation of small changes in its predecessors."[18] This seems obvious enough; and yet the habit of thinking of all evolution along the lines characterizing biological (Darwinian) evolution – the "steady accumulation of small changes" – can hide it from view.

And indeed, how often is "the novel" spoken of as a single thing, changing from one period to the next? But just as the cassette tape cannot become the CD, the *nouvelle* does not become the memoir novel. These are two distinct artifacts. This does not mean that the memoir novel comes from nowhere: Arthur, like George Basalla before him, stresses that every technology evolves from a preceding technology: "to invent something is to find it in what previously exists."[19] How do we reconcile this imperative of continuity with the obvious discontinuity between the cassette or the CD, the *nouvelle* and the memoir novel? Well, the memoir novel does evolve from something – just not the *nouvelle*. Instead, it evolves from a technology that was – until the end of the seventeenth century – not part of the novel system. Unsurprisingly, this is the historical memoir – a seventeenth-century vogue in itself.[20] The same can obviously be said of the epistolary novel, derived from epistolary collections. Thus, the novel system is (partially) composed of discontinuous artifacts; those artifacts, themselves part of another sort of continuity, are pulled into the novel system, that is, made to serve as novels. Arthur calls this *redomaining*, defined as "the expressing of a given purpose in a different set of components, as when the provision of power changed from being expressed in waterwheel technology to being expressed in steam technology."[21] Redomaining is the source of the most radical technological changes, and it has no analogue in biological evolution. So while some technologies evolve by degrees, evolution by redomaining has an epochal dimension that sits well with casual catchphrases such as "the age of steam."[22]

The concept of redomaining is not necessary for explaining all the major artifacts in the history of the French novel examined here, just the two I've been calling document novels. In Chapters 6 and 7, we saw that the rise of memoir and epistolary novels was surprisingly protracted. These document novels, I pointed out, were introduced at approximately the same time as *nouvelles*; and yet the former were much slower than the latter to be adopted. But this makes sense if what is involved is a redomaining. For reasons I will explain presently, the *nouvelle* was simply a variation of an earlier Aristotelian novel, whereas the importation of the "real-world" forms of discourse that are the memoir and the letter – and the modifications necessary to make them function as novels – involved a much more radical change. For sure, there was an extensive practice of first-person narrative prior to the memoir novel, detailed in Chapter 6. It lay not so much in artifacts like frame narratives or observer narratives but *inside* the inset novel itself. Yet, the path between this first person and the dominant first person of the following century was not arrived at through incremental change. It would be if first-person inset narratives somehow "split off" from the larger narratives in which they were embedded and began circulating autonomously. But this isn't what happened, and it's obvious why: first-person narration was very popular, but it was bound to the *oral* exchange represented in the inset novel. What was needed was a *written* model for first-person narration. Hence, the document novel in general and the memoir novel in particular.

Making the model work, however, took a good deal of time. Again, this fact may be surprising if we conceive of literary change along the lines of innovation-followed-by-imitation, as if writers could at will adopt a new form once shown the way. But if what were involved were a technological redomaining, we would expect the process to be longer. In the case of the physical technologies described by Arthur, "building out" a new domain takes decades, not years; major innovations have to rewire the economy as a whole.[23] Granted, the book market probably possesses nothing like the inertia of the wider economy, composed of an interlocking network of manufacturing, organizational, and distribution technologies. Nonetheless, we have concrete evidence of the difficulties posed by redomaining: the scattershot profusion of document novels used before the nobody memoir novel rose to prominence took a long time to stabilize into a single artifact.

The epistolary novel presents a clearer example still. We saw in Chapter 7 that its rise was even more delayed than that of the memoir novel, and more complicated, too, despite the early success of two now-canonical masterpieces, *Lettres portugaises* (attrib. Guilleragues, 1669) and *Lettres persanes* (Montesquieu, 1721). Fifty years separate these works – fifty years during which there was some low-level experimentation with composing novels out of letters. The first significant vein exploited was the one used by the *Lettres portugaises*: that of amorous correspondence. There weren't many of these novels, and they were quite short, suggesting that this particular real-world model – epistolary exchange of the sort preserved in the letters of Heloise and Abelard – didn't offer much in terms of plotting possibilities. A second vein – which would eventually be responsible for the initial rise of the epistolary form – consisted of novels of social observation, in which the missives of one or more correspondents furnished a running cultural commentary. Like amorous epistolary novels, they had a nonnovelistic origin – the many collections of "letters on diverse subjects" such as *Lettres familières, galantes et autres sur toutes sortes de sujets* (Milleran, 1689) or the widely read *Relation du voyage d'Espagne* (D'Aulnoy, 1691), structured as a series of letters. And while observational epistolary novels were as weakly plotted as their amorous variant, they were often considerably longer since the subject matter offered much more variety than lovers' outpourings and recriminations. The conceit of exchanged letters provided a format that allowed discontinuous observations and narratives to be strung together. But this vein too had little uptake. If we judge by their numbers, both these models – amorous and observational – appear to have presented limited possibilities for novelists, even if they did underwrite two masterpieces.

Not so the "polyphonic" epistolary novel that rises to prominence a good deal later: the record shows that this was a powerful tool for novelists, allowing them a qualitatively different scope from what was furnished by the other real-world models. And I would argue that this new type of epistolary novel was an artifact arrived at through evolution. The redomaining of the document novel started with the modification of known, attested, nonnovelistic forms – memoirs and certain kinds of letter collections. But the polyphonic epistolary novel had no real-world counterpart. Of course, it is possible to *imagine* an entire correspondence between multiple senders and receivers being preserved – that indeed is what novelists asked their readers to imagine and even proposed that they credit as being literally true. But where were the real-world analogues of such published letter bundles? There were collections of model letters, such as the kind Richardson published in 1741, just as he was embarking on the early polyphonic *Clarissa* – *Letters Written to and for Particular Friends: On the Most Important Occasions*. Many scholars have pointed out that such collections can be seen as protofictional, in that some letters form series and thus show the lineaments of plotting.[24] But complete polyphonic correspondences were nowhere to be found in the real world of print. The epistolary novel writ large was the result of a redomaining; but the epistolary novel everyone thinks of when thinking of the epistolary novel was a kind of subsequent invention, a morphing that occurred within this new domain.[25] Given this, it probably *shouldn't* be surprising that the epistolary novel took so long to rise.[26]

But all significant moments in the evolution of the novel cannot be laid at the door of redomaining: many artifacts are indeed the result of incremental change. The first such moment – first in terms of this study's scope – lay not in the much-trumpeted, sometimes "epochal" arrival of the *nouvelle* but in the

Aristotelian form of which the *nouvelle* was merely a variant. The contention that the *nouvelle* was not radically new may seem odd, and not only with respect to traditional literary history: Chapters 3–5 measured by different means the break between *roman* and *nouvelle* long claimed by scholars, and Figure 5.10 (page 103) gave final visual form to the break. Yet the visualization is an effect of concomitant changes in a number of different variables, and *romans* and *nouvelles* should also be recognized as *usage patterns of similar and contiguous materials*. Chapter 2, for example, showed that across the divide of the 1650s, much change was in fact incremental: the novel on one side and the other was Aristotelian, though the later Aristotelian novel became *more* Aristotelian than the earlier one. And Chapters 3 and 4 showed that Heliodorian insetting specifically hung on much longer than the *roman* itself, again spanning the 1650s divide. Thus, the novel over the century preceding the document novel's rise in the 1720s can be seen as a cascade of small modifications that stabilized into identifiable artifacts – three of them, the Aristotelian *roman*, the Aristotelian *nouvelle*, and the nobody *nouvelle*.

We can see this by recalling some past calculations and making a few more. For starters, in previous chapters I've considered as candidates for *nouvelles* all novels with three distinct types of truth postures – Aristotelian novels with sufficiently proximate historical settings (frequently referred to by literary historians and some people of the time as the *nouvelle historique*), then novels about contemporary celebrities, and finally pseudofactual "true stories." But let's now break these out into two groups, speaking on the one hand of the Aristotelian *nouvelle* (including contemporary as well as the more numerous historical examples) and, on the other, of the contemporary *nouvelle* (comprising pseudofactual stances). This is simply to apply the division between somebody novels and nobody novels to the *nouvelle* (Figure 10.1). At least three things become clearer: nobody *nouvelles* are a good deal more enduring than their historical counterpart; those items from the beginning of the seventeenth century that fulfill the criteria for *nouvelles* are for all intents and purposes nobody novels; and, most important perhaps, the rise of the Aristotelian *nouvelle* is uncommonly abrupt.

The abruptness fades if we reunite the Aristotelian historical *nouvelle* with its older cousin, whose outsized length bears primary responsibility for the dramatic parting effectuated by Figure 5.10. In other words, that parting, datable to the 1660s and 1670s, is simply a result of choices about viewing the data. Those choices are most certainly motivated – they give us information relevant to the "rupture" felt by Du Plaisir and others – but they are not without appeal, since other choices can provide complementary information. Figure 10.2 provides a second look at the Aristotelian novel.

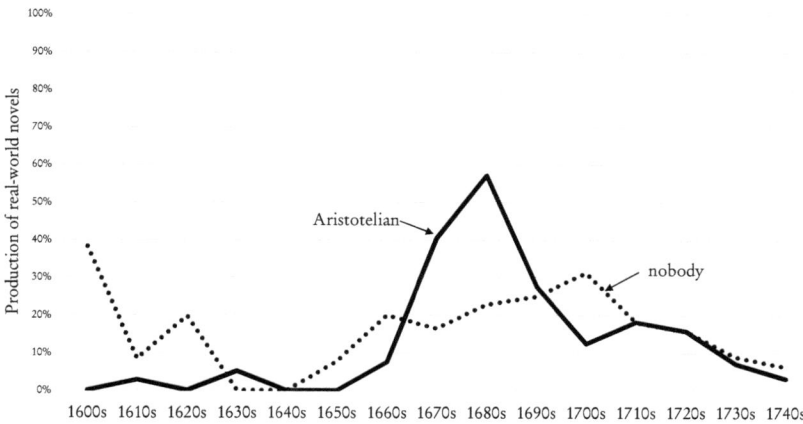

Figure 10.1 *Nouvelles*, Aristotelian versus nobody ("new loosest scenario").

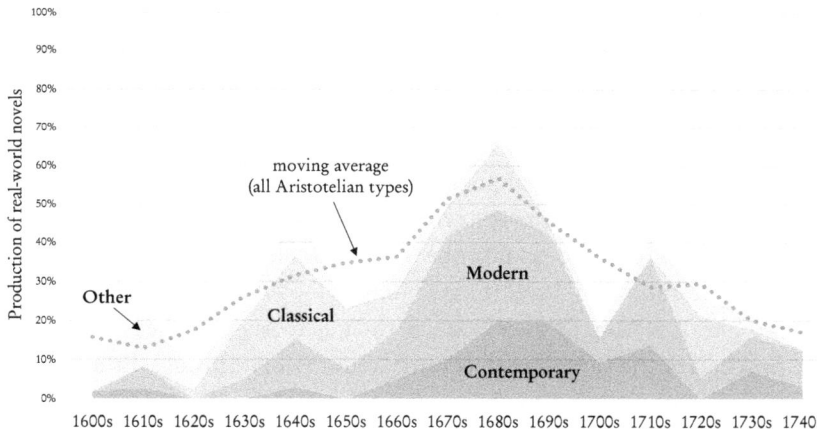

Figure 10.2 Aristotelian novels by period of subject matter.

Here, the degree of shading represents proximity to readers: the fainter the area, the more "excessive the antiquity" of protagonists (to use Du Plaisir's terms).[27] And while it's true that the classical and modern variants of Aristotelianism are more or less split by the 1650s and 1660s, the dip in those decades looks less significant: after all, had classical novels been a bit rarer in the 1640s and a bit more plentiful in the 1650s, we would most likely recognize that the Aristotelian novel rises and falls over the whole of the long seventeenth century. And indeed, this is what we see if we take a moving average of the totals. Moreover, the classical–modern "split" is really just a trend: classical settings don't disappear, and modern settings are already present in the 1640s and even before. Despite the fact that the *roman–nouvelle* distinction – which readers have long felt intuitively to be real – can indeed be measured (Figure 5.10), it's important to realize that the obvious shortening of the novel in the 1660s has caused scholars to overlook the profound commonality between novels on two sides of the so-called divide. When we separate the Aristotelian *nouvelle* from the nobody *nouvelle* and put it back with Aristotelian novels generally – ignoring, then, the famous shortening of the form that helps split it in two – it becomes obvious that the passage from one to the other is, technologically speaking, a small change. It results from a modification of existent parts, an artifactual evolution, not a redomaining.

If there is something approaching a redomaining in the seventeenth-century French novel, it lies in Aristotelianism itself – that is, in the aligning of novel writing with the poetological principles of epic. On the one hand, those principles involved subject matter: the novel was "dignified" via a new focus on somebodies from the Classical past. On the other, its prestige was enhanced by the importation – after many decades of sporadic use in non-Aristotelian settings, detailed in Chapter 3 – of Heliodorian insetting. The *Aethiopica* had long been promoted precisely because its dignified structure – "Aristotelian" not in the sense I've been using the term but because it had a clear architecture producing a sense of closure and totality – reminded people like Amyot not of the episodism of the medieval chivalric but rather of Homeric epic. Indeed, as it broke onto the scene, the Aristotelian novel was *also* a Heliodorian novel (Figure 10.3).

One interpretation of the evidence, then, is to say that the novel was in the first half of the seventeenth century redomained through its annexing

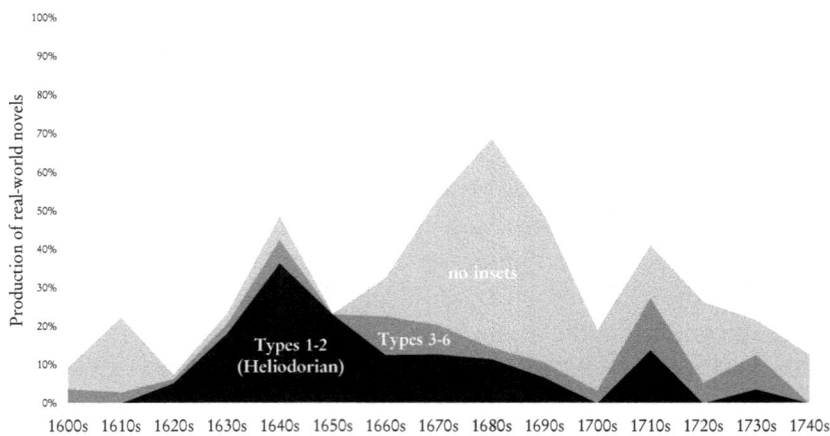

Figure 10.3 Aristotelian novels by inset type.

of epic subject matter and structure. To be sure, we can identify a group of artifacts that were (even at the time) called *nouvelles*, and we can moreover identify another group and call its members *romans*. But the important step is to remember that that many (but not all) of these artifacts share the profound similarity of their Aristotelianism. The big change of the century was not, as literary history has said since roughly 1682, the birth of the *nouvelle*. Rather, the big change was the invention of the *roman* itself.

But was this change truly a redomaining in Arthur's understanding of the word? After all, if Figure 10.3 shows that the Aristotelian novel was at the outset unambiguously and simultaneously Heliodorian, it's also true that many – indeed, most – Heliodorian novels were not Aristotelian. Similarly, over time, the Aristotelian novel shed its insets; and the nobody *nouvelle* might simply be seen as a further modification, again incremental, as the somebody *nouvelle* acquired a different set of protagonists. Unlike the document novel, unmistakably discontinuous with respect to other novels, the Aristotelian novel assembles in a particular way features that can and do come and go, and not always together. For sure, the Aristotelian novel embraces the epic's prestige by mimicking its construction and subject matter, and in that we may speak of a redomaining: a technology is pulled into the novel from elsewhere. More strictly speaking, however, the novel's Aristotelian turn is more like a particularly significant morphing within an extant technology – akin, perhaps, to the moment at which the invention of epistolary polyphony crystalized an interest in the epistolary novel that had been uneven at best.

What exactly the French novel was before this morphing is not particularly clear from my data collection, which simply starts too late. On the one hand, I have noted in Chapter 5 that a group of novels from the very start of the century answer to the criteria of later *nouvelles*; and Figure 10.1 shows that that the resemblance is with later nobody *nouvelles* specifically: these are novels advanced as true stories about unknown people. (They are also usually short and minimally inset.) To these we can add a quite different type of novel I alluded to in the course of Chapter 2: this is a novel, registering in Figure 2.10 (page 50), that features unspecified temporal settings. These are advanced as true stories only rarely – less than 8 percent of the time. Their "truth status" profile is an odd one: it doesn't resemble the novel at any other point in the 230 years studied in this book (Figure 10.4). In Chapter 5, all these novels save the "true" ones were lumped together with Aristotelian historical novels that featured "remote" subject matter: all these *romans* were united by their lax truth postures. But we can also pull out these "unspecified" novels, revealing in Figure 10.5 the diachronic contrast they offer with respect to Aristotelian novels.

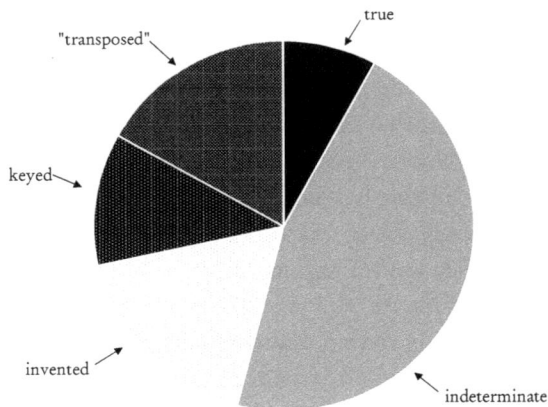

Figure 10.4 Truth status of "unspecified" novels.

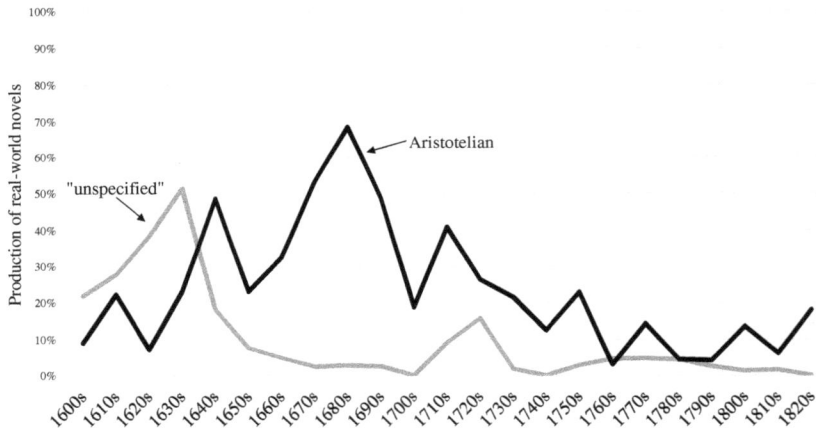

Figure 10.5 "Unspecified" and Aristotelian novels.

It's clear enough that the Aristotelian novel took over; but I can't tell from what. Was this "unspecified" novel itself a new development, as this graph suggests? Is it significant that its peak is so close to the first peak of Aristotelian novels? How does it relate to the early century texts answering to the criteria of the *nouvelle*? It is possible that French novels prior to the Aristotelian novel were simply much more heterogeneous: maybe it was a volatile new system, like England's a century later. Understanding the novel system as it existed at the end of the Renaissance, however, is beyond the scope of this study.

Armed with these further distinctions, we can now view in one glance all the major artifacts discussed in the course of this book. Screening out

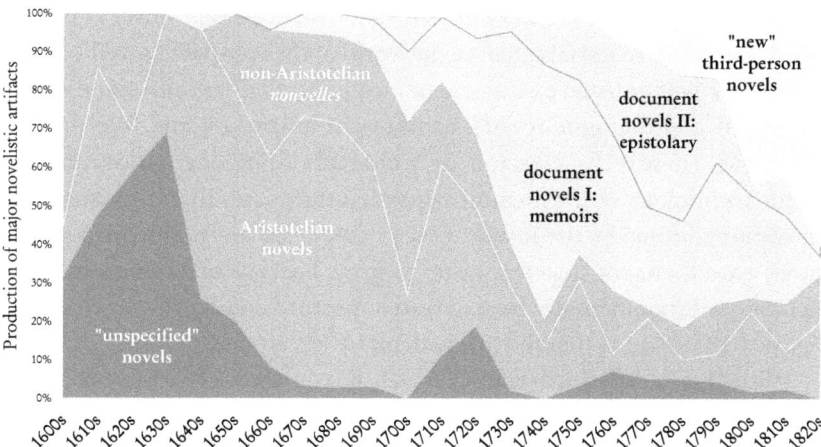

Figure 10.6 The major novelistic artifacts.

minor artifacts and formal idiosyncrasies (26 percent of the production over the span), clear waves become visible (Figure 10.6). The shades of gray indicate broad groupings of roughly related artifacts. In the case of document novels, these artifacts derive from redomainings: memoirs and letter collections are made to function within the novel system. (Note that the epistolary novel and the memoir novel are related only in the fact that both are redomainings since there is no artifactual continuity between them.) The Aristotelian novel, by contrast, is the result of a morphing within a narrative technology that is as old as literature itself, that of a third-person relation of past events. And finally – though of course this is not a teleological "finally" – there is the "new" third-person novel, the result of another morphing, one whose implications cannot be grasped due to the chronological bounds of the present study. As with the Aristotelian novel, this morphing is unusually significant, but it is indeed a morphing – the result of incremental change, as opposed to a discontinuous redomaining.

I have measured only a few banal characteristics – chapters, length, scene setting and used them to hypothesize the existence of an artifact whose contours are blurry but whose presence seems undeniable. None of these characteristics would appear epochal on its own, and indeed each had been seen before. Together, however – and together, surely, with features I have not measured and that may only be quantifiable through computational text analysis – they produce a very distinct kind of novelistic narration. The Aristotelian novel co-opted the stance of the traditional epic poet "singing" of the deeds of known heroes of the past; the document novel borrowed real-world discursive forms. But the "new" third-person novel is built of other materials, materials alien to the world of the epic poet as well as to the private *scriptor* enlisted by document novels. To chapters and scene setting we might add dialogue reporting, thought narration, and free indirect discourse. These techniques too no doubt had earlier incarnations, but just as the technology of the memoir expanded the possibilities of first-person narration, limited by the insets of the Heliodorian novel, the third-person novel gave them considerable room to grow because of its unproblematic fictivity: a fundamentally new narrative posture could grow and prosper because the value of literal truth had, bit by bit, eroded.

With the "new" third-person novel, narration was in the process of becoming *unnatural*, which is a good reason for recalling at long last the term fictional, which for rhetorical reasons I have banished for most of this study. By "unnatural," I mean that behind this novel's third person there was no longer any first person hiding – no one maintaining a contiguous link with the storyworld by dint of the fact that the storyworld was the real world. The features I have measured may scarcely seem antithetical to truth claims, and certainly chapters and scenes leave us well short of the kinds of narrative experimentation celebrated by the recent branch of narratology dealing with unnatural narration.[28] But narratology has long been riven precisely on this issue of the naturalness of literary narration. On the one hand lie those who, like Gérard Genette, view literary narration as homologous with respect to real-world, everyday narration; thus, for Genette, there are really no third-person novels since at any moment a narrator can always say "I."[29] On the other hand are scholars who have sought to argue that literary third-person narration is essentially narratorless – and indeed that "unspeakability" is precisely what defines literature.[30] What I am suggesting here is that this standoff can be resolved by considering the question historically: the morphing of the novel around the turn of the nineteenth century involves the invention of a technology that for once is not beholden to real-world forms of discourse.[31] The technology will take considerable time to build out but will ultimately allow the proliferation of all sorts of uncannily narrated – and indeed perhaps not even narrated – forms.[32] On this interpretation, the new domain of the novel was an uncanny one, one whose fundamental narrative oddity has been obscured by a long line of prestigious attacks on the purported transparency of the realist novel and its inartistic third person.[33] The "new" third-person novel is therefore not "fictional" merely in the sense that it admits the invention of its nobodies, since any memoir novel advanced as a creation of an author is fictional in that way too. More important, its narrative form is becoming "fictional," which is to say less and less like the discourse of a poet writing about heroes of renown or even like that of someone reporting a true story.[34]

"Fictional," "fictionalization": it is hard to keep the words from returning, but they do so accompanied by scare quotes to ward off the chauvinistic connotations that adhere to typical rise-of-fictionality narratives.[35] In the sense proposed here, fiction is something of a two-fold development. First, I've suggested that what's at issue is no more complicated than a change in values. At the same time, there is more here than simply one more chapter of the story that starts with Plato, that of the variable acceptance granted to literary inventions. For the value change, however simple, has big effects. All sorts of invented nobodies had inhabited literature previously but almost invariably in genres (or registers) coded as low. Those nobodies didn't and couldn't aspire to move and motivate readers with stories of exemplary somebodies doing important things. Only with the erosion of the value of literal truth, with the abandonment of classical commonplaces such as Horace's *incredulus odi*, could invented nobodies start doing work that previously they were not allowed to perform.[36] It was then that writers of ambition could build out novel technologies that were no longer yoked to the basic positions of the poet singing of memorable deeds or of the gossip trafficking in true stories. These technologies went beyond as well the first-person narrations made possible by the importing of memoirs and letters, and into the types of unnatural narrations that today are everywhere in our particularly promiscuous culture of fictionality.[37]

Technologies of the Novel was motivated by a desire to better understand the "pseudofactual" truth claims associated with the novel in the eighteenth century. From there, I was led to discriminate between a number of different artifacts, whose patterning suggested the technological explanation I have just sketched out. In light of that explanation, how should we understand the three major truth postures – the Aristotelian, the pseudofactual, and the invented? Are they technologies? Artifacts? Domains?

None of these, I think: the differences are merely the result of the interplay of technological artifacts and the values contributing to their invention. In the first half of the seventeenth century, for whatever reason, many writers sought to give the novel a new prestige.[38] For this, the novel had to be redomained in a loose sense – meaning made Aristotelian, like epic. The prestige was formal – linked to the insetting structure – but it also came from the novel's new subject matter. Yes, literature had always made space for a variety of invented subjects; and Aristotle duly noted that the latter could be made to work as well as attested subjects.[39] But the summit of the artistic food chain was always occupied by attested heroes engaged in important actions.[40] This was no mindset or episteme: it was just a valuation, though a stubborn one. And it didn't go away as the Aristotelian novel, focused on somebodies of the past, evolved a contemporary variant, featuring nobodies of the here and now. It is strange only in retrospect that novelists claimed that these protagonists no one had heard of were real people: the claim makes perfect sense in the context of this old and widespread value. Nor is it odd that the next major change in the novel – the redomaining that would import the real-world forms of the memoir and the letter and thereby facilitate the use of the first person – maintained the claim.

Yet the claim did, ultimately, recede. Values did change. Probably not values in general: many people today still prefer reading history to reading novels, for the good old Aristotelian reason that the real makes a greater claim on our attention than does the made up. But the values of novelists and their readers changed: it became OK to admit the invention of nobodies. In France, this was a slow development, and I've argued that the data does not support viewing the delay as a result of the time required for a population's conceptual rewiring or for the insights of a few to diffuse to the many. I prefer to explain the length of the process – and the apparent "plateau" of pseudofactuality described in Chapter 1 – as a result of various countervailing pressures. On the one side is the traditionally high valuation of real heroes and also the invention of the document novel form itself, which has such pretense "baked in," so to speak. On the other side, if maintaining the reality of novelistic nobodies is not surprising, at the same time the maintenance of that reality requires an *effort*, whereas the reality of somebodies is a given. In that, there is something impractical about pseudofactual pretense, even when intended rhetorically rather than as a literal, semantic statement. And in the case of the document novel in particular, truth pretense additionally interferes with admissions of authorship in a way that Aristotelian composition does not. So writing about "real" nobodies was a mixed bag, at least until the end of the eighteenth century, in a transformation that correlates, as we've seen, with the rise of a new third-person novel whose domain is not that of natural narration. My best guess is that there is some sort of feedback loop involved here: the invention of this new form, this pseudoredomaining, in fact accelerated the change in values, as writers and readers no longer "needed" real protagonists. The hypothesis is hardly far-fetched: new technologies constantly create new needs and values, while making old ones obsolete.[41] Of course, things look different across the Channel, where the novel system was much younger, and as such much more amenable to a quick rewiring.

While I think a technological explanation for the movements seen throughout this book has great appeal, it is clear that literary morphings and redomainings do not align perfectly with what happens with physical technologies. In the latter, redomainings – as well as the more incremental change that Arthur dubs "standard engineering" – are the result of a deliberate process: either a given need drives the uncovering of a physical phenomenon or effect (e.g., the jet engine) or a purpose is sought for a newly understood phenomenon or effect (the phonograph).[42] Literary invention is probably not deliberate in this way. Certainly, prefaces are full of statements of principle regarding formal matters – say, the proper selection of heroes, as in Scudéry's famous preface to *Ibrahim* (1641), mentioned in Chapter 2 in the context of Aristotelianism. Or, take the author of *Agathe et Isadore* (Benoist, 1768), who uses her preface to debate the pros and cons of the letter collection versus third-person narration:

> A novel in letters, as long as it is naturally written and conceived, is more conducive to illusion because one has the impression of talking to the character who is addressing to you everything he says: by virtue of the credence one accords to seemingly involuntary confessions, he makes you reflect with him, dive down into yourself, quiver with his weaknesses …; he beseeches you, he asks you questions and seeks your advice; by confiding to you his heart's troubles, he moves your own heart …; and at the same time he makes his despair your own, he also shares his joy, makes you identify with it [*il vous y intéresse*] as if it were your own. The highest art of the Historian will never take you so far.[43]

There is nothing particularly original about the remark: it echoes famous declarations on the virtues of the epistolary by Montesquieu and Richardson.[44] But while authors clearly think a good deal about the formal choices they make and devote public effort to justifying them, it is less sure that they search for technological "solutions" in the same way as do inventors in the physical realm. Was the author of the *Lettres portugaises* – assuming the text is indeed an invention – really trying to "redomain" the French novel? The same could be asked for the writers of all the early document novels or early Heliodorian novels. It is perhaps significant that the kinds of remarks I've cited are typically post hoc rationalizations: once people recognize a new form, they can theorize better what they think it does. But since recognizability comes about through a temporally dilated and decentralized process of stabilization, the form itself can hardly be said to be a "solution" arrived at via deliberate work on a "problem."

A related difference with respect to more traditional, physical technologies concerns not invention itself but the functioning of the invention. Is it logical to say that the document novel "works better" than the Aristotelian novel – even keeping in mind the familiar caveat of STS, according to which "working better" can only be contextually defined? To be sure, we can think of all manner of reasons an author might prefer nobodies to somebodies or vice-versa: somebodies have the prestige of tradition; nobodies are better for talking about today's Paris or London, and their proximity may make them better hosts for identification. Similarly, it does not seem to me unreasonable to suppose that the memoir novel presents practical advantages over first-person insets and thus that the career of the first person following its invention could be considerably more glorious than it was before. But the performance and efficiency of literary artifacts are clearly difficult if not impossible to measure, and we are probably dealing with what people *perceive* as a "working better." And this may help us make sense of the pattern that has emerged repeatedly in the course of the many decades analyzed here, for if new literary artifacts work better than the ones they replace, it is odd, to say the least, that the trajectory of their use is characterized by peaks. One would expect – maybe not in all cases but certainly in some – that the forms would work better more consistently. The regularly fluctuating popularity of those artifacts is a potential mystery: why are forms either coming or going?

An obvious answer is that maybe literary forms are not so much technological artifacts as mere *fashions*. Fashions unfold in various but predictable ways. At one extreme is the *fad* – an artifact whose success is meteoric but also highly fragile and which may be best explained through theories of informational cascades.[45] On the other end of the spectrum are fashions that march to a much slower drum, operating on a timetable that matches very well with the ups and downs of the artifacts of the novel. The career of these fashions is measured in many decades.[46] Thus, novels and (say) cars may well be similar artifacts – fashion artifacts rather than technological ones. But what does this rephrasing really amount to? First, given that now-standard constructivist accounts of technological innovation would surely allow *novelty* as one factor among the many that contribute to the adoption of a given artifact, it follows that the evolution of a technological artifact such as the bicycle is never separable from fashion.[47] Of the many reasons for selecting an artifact must be how many other people are selecting it; part of its "working better" involves the social messages of distinction and belonging it sends. Furthermore, it is entirely predictable that the types of non- or minimally physical arrangements Arthur helps us see as technologies should exhibit a different historical patterning from physical technologies. The distinctive patterns of nonphysical arrangements are probably not characterized by strong "lock-in" or "path dependence," for example – the kind of positive feedback which, to use a notorious example, makes the abandonment of the QWERTY keyboard unlikely.[48] Viewed thus, "fashion" is simply the word that we give to this particular type of technological patterning, especially where consumer goods are involved. In addition, consumer goods do not occupy a structurally "deep" domain of the economy: their change does not entail a rewiring of the latter. As such, these technologies are relatively easy to transform – though still quite distinct from transient fads.[49]

Since the object of the technological explanation proposed here is the patterns observed in the archive of French and English novels, and not any one particular transformation, I stop well short of the kind of case study typical in STS, where the researcher opens the "black box" of motivations in order to show the heteronomy of technology.[50] I am not sure how easy it would be to study the invention of literary forms in the way Steven Shapin and Simon Schaffer have studied the air pump or Bernard Carlson has studied General Electric.[51] To begin with, the production of nonphysical technologies is often decentered; compounding the difficulty, the creation of literary artifacts from two to four centuries ago has left relatively few traces outside the artifacts themselves. Still, even if we could reconstruct the full context of the rise of (for example) the polyphonic epistolary novel – and not simply describe it, as I have done – one can wonder how much would be gained. Perhaps some fascinating empirical detail, yes. But surely the larger conclusions would be familiar to anyone acquainted with STS – that the epistolary novel did not evolve inevitably, according to its own internal necessity, but rather was the contingent result of choices made by social actors.[52]

I think we can take this as a given; at the same time, it is surely worth emphasizing the point, which goes against the usual way historically minded literary critics think of form. For when Fredric Jameson delivered his famous injunction to "always historicize," he did not mean that literary scholars should seek the specific, local causes of this or that phenomenon.[53] Rather than open the black box of motivations, the historicizing scholar was ordered to find structural homologies between cultural products and the ideological system of which they were the effect. In a way, this is merely a darker, more suspicious version of the old view that explains forms as the expression of their "age." Yet the Aristotelian novel, the document novel, and the "new" third-person novel – or any of their individual variants – did not have to arise exactly when they did and quite possibly did not need to arise at all, even if in retrospect their arrival always makes perfect sense. I've shown, for example, that the polyphonic epistolary novel was also a sentimental novel, but my contention is not that there is some natural link between the form and the ideology. All we can say is that the form caught on among sentimental writers and that they found it useful. But in another otherwise similar world, it might not have caught on, and writers might have found something else useful. To say that the epistolary novel would be unimaginable in certain societies is surely right: you need the right "cultural soil." But nothing about the cultural soil of France in the 1760s and 1770s – as opposed to the 1720s or 1730s – dictated the explosion of interest in the form. The explosion could have come earlier or later; it could have been more modest or stronger still; and it might not have materialized at all.[54] What I do regard as inevitable is that whatever successful literary artifacts might have arisen in a different world, their use would still display the types of patterning (though not the exact patterns) visible in the artifacts that did arise.

But is patterning really *all* that is inevitable? Surely the narrative forms I have been talking about are bound up in some fashion with the passage from the oral to the written to the printed, and unless we are imagining a world so different as to be without that progression, aren't those forms a logical outcome? To a certain degree, yes, but only on a scale very different from the one typically used when linking form and material "cause." Here is Ian Watt, explaining the indebtedness of the novel to print:

> It is ... clear that all the major literary forms were originally oral, and that this continued to affect their aims and conventions long after the advent of print. In the Elizabethan period, for instance, not only poetry but even prose were still composed primarily with a view toward performance by the human voice. That literature was eventually to be printed was a minor matter, compared to pleasing patrons whose taste was formed on the old oral models. It was not until the rise of journalism that a new form of writing arose which was wholly dependent on printed performance, and the novel is perhaps the only literary genre which is essentially connected with the medium of print: it is therefore very appropriate that our first novelist [i.e., Richardson] should have been a printer himself.[55]

Watt's lead-up is sound and indeed vital: it is remarkable but nonetheless evident that something like a "culture of orality" continued to be a model for written and indeed printed literature for many, many centuries. Nor does it seem contestable that at some point literature (or most literature) lost this model. But when? Even if for the sake of argument we forget Heliodorus and suppose that the novel is *essentially* a print artifact – Watt's "perhaps" is a feint disguising the introduction of that "essentially" – why would this fact make the English eighteenth century very special? We're told that journalism marks the real arrival of print; but when do reports of current events – oral, manuscript, or printed – get to qualify as journalism? Presumably, when they are printed in the eighteenth or very late seventeenth century in England.[56] Watt thus poses but then completely elides the crucial problem of how literature lost (or at least relaxed) its link with the oral. Before we know it, journalism has risen and the novel too. The fact that the novelist Richardson was also a printer becomes, by our sheer belief in poetic justice (how "very appropriate"!), evidence that he was the first novelist.

Let us put to one side the inconvenient Greek novel and agree that the written and indeed printed status of novels is important and that at some point, the novel system reformulates itself to align more closely with its physical mode of production and circulation. It should be obvious that as much as literary forms that had unquestionably predated print continued to be deeply marked by orality, so was the novel. For one, it was doubtless read out loud;[57] but the actual oral uses of print may be less important than the oral "model" – symbolic representations of narrative situations that elided the mediation of writing and print. The many inset narratives proliferating in the novel from (at least) the start of the seventeenth century are a good indication of the extent to which oral narrative was quite at home in the world of print – not simply in the Renaissance or in the early seventeenth century but still in the eighteenth and no doubt beyond.[58] One of the virtues of the document novel was that it provided a new *written* model for first-person homodiegetic narrative. Yet *pace* Watt, nothing about the memoir or epistolary form acknowledged print; on the contrary, print was simply a conduit for writing that had originated elsewhere, that is, in the private, manuscript sphere. Thus, we might speak of printed narrative as *skeuomorphic* with respect to older narrative technologies: though printed, the text retains many features proper to its oral and written ancestors but no longer essential to the new mode of production.[59] And this, I think, is the significance of the third-person "fictional" novel at the end of the eighteenth century: it is a reengineering of the novel for the world of print – which by that point is already 300 years old.

The Aristotelian novel, still formulated along the lines of the old epic poet's voicing of the deeds and narrations of heroes; the document novel, making a place for anonymous writing subjects; the "new" third-person novel, divorced like never before from previous narrative modelled on the oral and the manuscript: none of these inventions was the result of any particular physical "stage" in the evolution of print; and there was no point at which stubborn orality finally tipped over into "print culture."[60] The invention of (nonphysical) narrative technologies capable of exploiting the characteristics of the (physical) technology of print took a long time, but it wasn't delayed any more than the invention of the light bulb was delayed: it happened when it happened. So, as I've said, this evolution could well have looked different. Yet, I do wonder if the history of the novel's technologies could have been *substantially* different – radically and emancipatorily other, as when Michel Foucault longed for another epistemic rupture that would eliminate "man" as a subject of knowledge, erasing him "like a face drawn in sand at the edge of the sea."[61] My belief is that the invention of narrative technologies commensurate with print was inevitable. Not inevitable in the details – this device in this year in this country – but inevitable in a larger, more elastic sense, like the wheel was inevitable, or electric lighting, or inventions we don't even suspect yet, or (to be pessimistic) the collapse of the planet under the weight of mankind's inexorable technological genius. At any rate, narrative technologies are still evolving, touched now by the digital world – which doesn't mean just those skeuomorphic e-books but also a media environment presenting unknown opportunities for new narrative technologies. If I had to, I'd wager that the latter won't be novelistic at all. Given how slowly our habits change, though, it's still a bit early to know how this is all going to turn out.

Annex

Premises and Protocols

This book is based on data gleaned from a primary corpus of French-language novels covering the years 1601–1830, and from a secondary corpus of English-language novels from 1701 to 1810. The data sets are available for public consultation and use, as explained later.

The 230-year French span was chosen for reasons relating to the main question I had regarding the novel's purported "fictionalization" over the course of the eighteenth century. The chronological stopping point was suggested by a general (though purely impressionistic) consensus that the fictional novel was in place by the early nineteenth century: examining roughly a third of that century, I reasoned, should be enough to verify if that were the case. My starting point was dictated by the conviction that the main opposition that scholars used to understand the fictionalization process was flawed. That opposition was, unsurprisingly, between a novel that was admitted as an invention and another, its foil and predecessor, one that was asserted as true. But I knew from my (still impressionistic) familiarity with the seventeenth-century French novel that many of these had historical subject matter, and that the fictionalization of the novel was probably inseparable from its dehistoricization; that is, its appropriation of a type of subject matter that had nothing to do with heroes from the past about whom readers had already heard. Covering the whole of the seventeenth century, then, would allow us to observe the eclipse – and indeed maybe the rise – of this neglected novel. In no way should either of these boundaries be taken to imply that I think of pre-1601 novels as the unchanging bedrock of tradition, or of post-1830 novels as having arrived, finally, at the end of history, the finish line of modernity, or for that matter any sort of stability at all. While these boundaries did end up capturing, I think, a couple of complete rises and falls, things keep on rising and falling and always have.

In selecting my corpus, I have used the available scholarly bibliographies of novels published over most of this period.[1] In the absence of any such works covering the first half of the nineteenth century in France, I relied on *La Bibliographie de la France*, an official weekly account of all books published in France, which was indexed annually, and included the generic rubric "*Romans et contes*" (novels and tales).[2] Obviously, the scholars who composed these bibliographies, and the people who kept track of the books published in early nineteenth-century France, made discriminations based on their ideas of what a novel was. However, as the titles of the bibliographies suggest – "prose fiction," the "novelistic genre" – the general goal was to err on the side of inclusiveness. Readers could decide for themselves whether or not the works included were bona fide novels; the job of the bibliographers was felt to lie in ferreting out works that had novelistic dimensions (some amount of narrative that wasn't patently empirico-historical).

But I wanted novels. Having looked at close to two thousand in the course of this study, I'm well placed to testify as to the haziness of categories; and even without such labor, it's obvious enough that generic partitions plow right over topographical complexities, that boundaries are always to some extent artificial, and that oppositions are "deconstructible." Still, I knew I didn't want and couldn't realistically hope to give a complete picture of every kind of "prose fiction" in French and English that was being produced and consumed over the period. "Prose fiction," at any rate, merely displaces the definitional problem. At a certain point, one has to make discriminations – subjective, surely, but not arbitrary, and hopefully ones that will seem logical and motivated to most people.[3] In this spirit, I excluded from consideration a certain number of works figuring in the above inventories.

First, I was interested only in books originally published in French or English, not translations. I don't doubt that tracking translations would be very interesting and perhaps even key: after all, we might see that this or that formal change in the French novel in fact derived from what was being done already in England or Germany, or that the French readily translated types of novels that in fact they didn't produce. On the other hand, one can't try to answer all questions at once, and 340 total years of nontranslated novels is already a lot. A complication, however, results from the fact that many French novels from 1750 on purport to be translations (most often from English) but are not. My policy was to exclude only translations of which bibliographers (or myself) had located the originals. It is probable that some of the pseudo-translations I've retained are really and truly translations of unidentified originals.

Second, I excluded collections of stories or anecdotes, as well as narratives appearing in periodicals: novels, for my purposes, are stand-alone narratives, recognized as such by their means of publication. This exclusion means that my data does not give proper weight to genres that appeared primarily in such venues: the fairy tale and the *conte moral* are two examples. (Texts in which multiple unrelated narratives are set inside a frame narrative, however thin, are retained.) I make an exception, however, in cases in which only two texts are published together: two do not strike me as constituting a collection, and at any rate very often the second of the narratives is obviously subordinate, filling out space. (By the same token, novels that are followed by other sorts of "filler" – verse, essays – are also retained, provided that the novel is clearly the core of the volume.) In such cases, relatively uncommon, I split the two into separate items and tag them (or exclude them) independently.

Third, I excluded a diverse range of nonnarrative items that bibliographers inventoried because they contained narrative sections – say, a treatise in which the author recounted a parable, or miscellanies that contained a tale. I excluded as well books that contained named "characters" but that I judged insufficiently narrative (such as allegorical tableaus, or conversations on one or more topics).

Fourth, I excluded items in verse.

Fifth, I excluded items under 10,000 words. This was an arbitrary cutoff, put into place because these extremely short novels are often formal oddities from a variety of perspectives besides just their length. This exclusion could be worrying if major novelistic innovations somehow tended to "incubate" in short, experimental texts before spreading throughout the system. I am convinced, however, that this is not the case; on the contrary, texts this short are far more likely to be idiosyncratic than longer works.

Sixth, I excluded republications and continuations. The interest of tracking republications is clear: all works do not have the same impact on the literary field. But such a survey presents many challenges as well, from the variable attention brought to reprints by bibliographers to questions of protocol (e.g., would the reprint count under the year of the initial publication, or of the reprinting?). As I stress in the Introduction, built into this study is an assumption of a sort of feedback loop: the formal influence of any given novel will be felt in the number of novelists who chose to imitate its formal characteristics. Continuations are not counted as separate titles, but their word counts are added to those of the original volumes (unless the continuation was clearly "unauthorized"). Radically posthumous publications (e.g., a novel written in 1630 but printed in 1710) were also excluded.

Seventh, for France, I decided to ignore many items that were functionally lost (i.e., that appear in no library catalogs indexed by WorldCat), or that were unavailable either in digital form (through platforms such as Google Books and Gale-Cengage's Eighteenth Century Collections Online) or in the collections of three libraries: the Bibliothèque Nationale de France (Tolbiac and Arsenal), the library of my home institution (UC Berkeley), and the Bibliothèque du Château d'Oron in Switzerland.[4] (This last holds a large number of titles from the late eighteenth and early nineteenth centuries that are unavailable elsewhere.) For the English novel, whose corpus is better represented digitally, I tagged only items with online availability. The decision not to attempt to track down titles held elsewhere was motivated by purely practical reasons: their number is so small that they could have no impact on my interpretations, and thus hardly justify the time and effort to tag them. For both countries, I did, however, retain lost or unavailable items for the purposes of estimating the total production of novels by decade, unless available bibliographical information indicated that they would have probably been excluded for a given reason (e.g., as part of a collection).

The last motive for exclusion is the most fraught. This was of narrative works that belonged to identifiable extra-novelistic genres – biography, travel narratives, and historical memoirs. The bibliographies I was working from already excluded most such items, but not all.[5] Of course, these exclusions are deeply paradoxical, since my entire inquiry is motivated by the interest in novelistic claims to truth over the period – in other words, by the fact that so many early novels claimed to be biographies, letter collections, travel narratives, and so on. What defines the novel in the first place if not its fictionality? In other words, if we can proceed with our inquiry without knowing what fiction "really is" – as I maintain – how do we even know what objects to study? How do we draw a line between novels, on the one hand, and histories and biographies and traveler's narratives on the other? My approach is first of all pragmatic and historical: I take as novels those books that generations of bibliographers have included in their bibliographies of novels. In other words, I'm working from an inherited, usually unspoken sense of what a novel is, not from a definition. But given the variable criteria used by bibliographers, I have also had to exclude items that to my eye are insufficiently *plotted*. Ultimately this comes down to accepting the oldest definition of literature we have, the one offered in Book 9 of Aristotle's *Poetics*.[6] Since novels – especially early novels – regularly take people from history as their subjects, the distinction between them and histories must lie in the way the subjects are treated: in the fact that novelists craft plots (no matter how episodic, dilated, or threadbare).[7] It goes without saying that on this question much more could be said.[8]

How many texts were excluded or ignored, and for what reason? Figure A.1 gives French figures for the years for which we have the best modern critical bibliographies (1601–1700 and 1751–1800); this will give a sense of the discrepancy between the number of entries included in these bibliographies

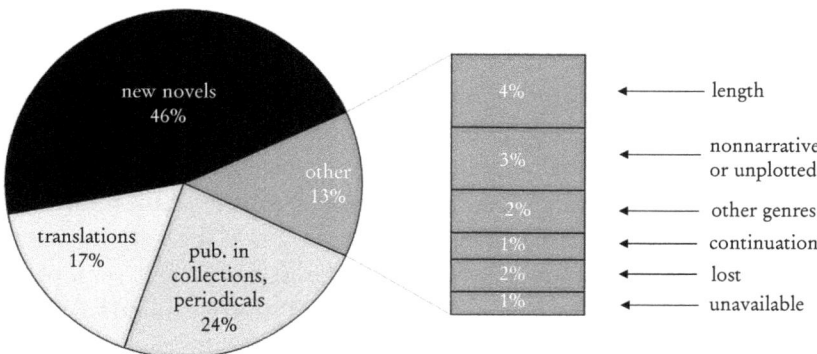

Figure A.1 Items retained and reasons for exclusions (1601–1700 and 1751–1800).

and my much lower production figures. (Note that except in some rare cases of errors, reprints did not receive separate entries in these source works, so in that sense they were already excluded and do not figure here.) Many items in the bibliographies are in fact translations, collections, parts of collections, or narratives appearing in periodicals.[9] It bears noting that a significant percentage of works excluded for length might also have been excluded for other reasons, notably for insufficient plottedness.

This study is not based on the examination of *all* French and English novels published over the spans indicated. That would be a phenomenally lengthy undertaking – and more important, a largely unnecessary one, because sampling can capture the information we need about historical trends. But just as a pollster mustn't ask only the voters she happens to know, or choose only those whom she has reason to believe will answer in a manner pleasing to her bosses, the literary historian needs to sample with method. The sampling procedure of *Technologies of the Novel* was designed to capture diachronic change: the growth (and senescence) of this or that artifact. As such, I obviously did not want to treat novels published in French over these 230 years as an aggregate, sampling – say – 20 percent of them. Dividing the period by decades – stratifying my corpus, in the parlance of sampling – was the logical choice. (Decades are arbitrary markers; I've chosen to start mine in year 01, so that here, 1830 is the last year of the 1820s.) Sampling of the decades was done by "clusters": all the available novels of a certain number of years in the decade were consulted. It would have been possible to have randomly selected a given percentage of all novels published in a decade, but this is more labor-intensive (it would have required having a clean list of all titles published in the decade, whereas with cluster sampling, one needs a clean list only of the sampled years).

The determination of proper cluster size – how many years of a decade should stand in for the decade as a whole – is dependent on the number of novels published. Basically, small populations must be sampled much more heavily than large populations. But because before starting I had no clear idea of what the "population" of any given decade was, my initial determinations were made on the basis of assumptions about the production of novels – notably, that the French production was at the start very small and grew steadily. This turned out not to be the case; as a result, some of the early decades might be considered "oversampled" (results would have been largely similar with somewhat smaller clusters), and I did have to increase my cluster size in some later decades. The final French clusters, along with the total numbers tagged and the expected margin of error, are found in Figure A.2.[10]

Decade	Cluster of years sampled	Number of novels in cluster	Margin of error[11]
1600s	1,2,3,4,5,7,8,9 (8 years)	57	5.0
1610s	1,2,3,4,5,7,8,9 (8 years)	39	5.9
1620s	1,2,3,4,5,7,8,9,0 (9 years)	95	2.6
1630s	1,2,3,4,5,7,8,9 (8 years)	38	5.0
1640s	1,2,3,4,5,7,8,9 (8 years)	33	6.3
1650s	1,2,3,4,5,7,8,9 (8 years)	18	9.1
1660s	1,2,3,4,5,7,8,9 (8 years)	46	5.0
1670s	1,2,3,4,5,7,8,9 (8 years)	81	4.1
1680s	6,7,8,9,0 (5 years)	33	9.7
1690s	6,7,8,9,0 (5 years)	78	6.5
1700s	6,7,8,9,0 (5 years)	25	9.6
1710s	6,7,8,9,0 (5 years)	22	12.0
1720s	6,7,8,9,0 (5 years)	27	11.0
1730s	7,8,9 (3 years)	60	8.8
1740s	7,8,9 (3 years)	43	10.3
1750s	6,7,8,9 (4 years)	42	9.3
1760s	8,9 (2 years)	78	8.2
1770s	7,8,9 (3 years)	46	10.0
1780s	8,9 (2 years)	77	8.3
1790s	8,9 (2 years)	125	6.5
1800s	8 (1 year)	83	8.4
1810s	8 (1 year)	66	8.8
1820s	8 (1 year)	75	9.0

Figure A.2 Composition of sample (France).

While for some decades the margin of error may appear large – and would be for a use such as political polling – it should be kept in mind that the conclusions of the present study are built on diachronic trends; specific values for any one decade are of minimal interest. Total number of French novels tagged is 1310.[12]

Samples of the secondary corpus of English novels, marginally less robust than that of the primary corpus, are indicated in Figure A.3. Total number of English novels tagged is 460.

Research on French epistolary novels was conducted in an alternate manner. Because for many years epistolary novels were few and far between, and because I wanted the sharpest possible picture of this long incubation, I undertook a census of all epistolary novels published up to and including 1810 (a point at which the form was moribund). The detailed bibliography of Yves Giraud and Anne-Marie Clin-Lalande made this possible; it provided the basis for the census, to which I added occasional items I had located by chance.[13] Assuming the result is a nearly complete list, I am obviously able to produce accurate figures for the various subcategories of epistolary novels. However, for many calculations, these figures are then reintegrated with the data obtained through sampling. Thus, if we want to know the proportion of, say, monophonic to polyphonic epistolary novels, the census produces results that are as accurate as the census itself. If, on the other hand, we want to know the production of epistolary novels relative to another form of novel or to the production of novels in general, the census can only produce estimates as good as the samples.

Decade	Cluster of years sampled	Number of novels in cluster	Margin of error
1700s	all (10 years)	20	6.8[14]
1710s	all (10 years)	28	n/a
1720s	6,7,8,9,0 (5 years)	27	12.3
1730s	3,4,5,6,7,8,9,0 (8 years)	24	11.5
1740s	6,7,8,9 (4 years)	28	13.0
1750s	7,8,9 (3 years)	46	10.6
1760s	7,8,9 (3 years)	80	8.0
1770s	7,8,9 (3 years)	34	12.4
1780s	8 (1 year)	49	11.3
1790s	8 (1 year)	52	10.9
1800s	8 (1 year)	72	9.3

Figure A.3 Composition of sample (England).

Specifically, this latter type of calculation relies on estimates of the total novel production per decade. (Such production figures are in fact unimportant for the bulk of this study, since in the vast majority of instances I am interested only in production *proportions* within the sample.) For most of the twenty-three decades surveyed, I simply assume that the production of the years not sampled is equivalent to that of the years sampled. This assumption is relatively untreacherous for decades in which I have sampled half or more years of the decade. However, smaller clusters are much more likely to fall in unrepresentative years. The quality of the information in the Martin, Mylne, and Frautschi bibliography was such that for the five decades it covers, I was able to estimate tallies of the novel production for the years not sampled.

How different are the results of the census and the results of the sample? Remarkably, hardly at all (Figure A.4). The sample produces a 3-percent higher peak, and what would seem to be an aberrant figure for the 1720s. But a margin of 3 percent is meaningless in the context of this study, as is a reading for any single decade. I would point out that the correspondence between the two counts does not come from reliance on the same data: the production figures for the sample are based only on the ratio of epistolary novels to nonepistolary novels within the sample; the census is set against production estimates generated by the total number of titles sampled (balanced as described earlier).

Word counts for novels were produced with the simplest of technologies: I counted the words on a page that seemed representative and multiplied that number by the number of pages in the work. In French, the protocol was to

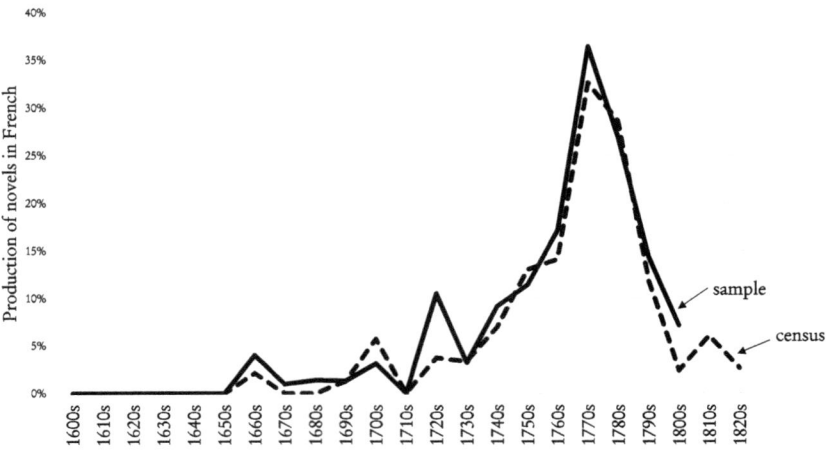

Figure A.4 Market penetration of French epistolary novels (two estimates).

count two elided words as one (e.g., "*j'aime*"). Thus, my word estimates will be lower than counts using a resource such as the ARTFL database, which splits elisions into component words.[15] For most purposes, the discrepancy is of no concern, since length has meaning only relatively. The method does, however, have the effect of shrinking French novels marginally when compared to their English counterparts, in which elision (specifically, contractions) is much rarer at the time.

A Glossary of Novel Types

Most of the novel types alluded to in this book have no accepted or consensual meaning: terms were invented for the purpose of describing the archive of French and English novels during the period studied. It is important to remember that these types are not discrete forms, since they allude to only *one* feature of novels that are tagged for *multiple* features. Thus, many of these tags can be combined: an inset novel, for example, may also be a somebody novel. Other combinations are logically impossible: a somebody novel cannot be pseudofactual.

Alternate-world novels – Novels with a variety of nonnatural content, from talking animals to imaginary voyages; many would have been termed "marvelous" by contemporaries. Their counterparts are real-world novels. Alternate-world novels are not tagged for somebody/nobody status, truth posture, or temporal setting; when they contain assertions of truth, these are categorized as parodic, rather than pseudofactual. Most calculations in this study ignore alternate-world novels.

Aristotelian novels – A class of real-world novels taking known people (from history, legend, or current events) as protagonists. The term alludes to Aristotle's contention that known heroes make for superior believability in a poem. These novels can further be divided into "weak" and "strong" variants: the former have an invented protagonist interacting with known historical characters, while the latter feature only people of renown as their main characters. Aristotelian novels can also be called somebody novels, and are therefore the counterparts of nobody novels.

Document novels – Novels presented as documents not originally intended for publication. Although some of these are third-person works (e.g., a manuscript found in a trunk), most are "private-sphere" documents such as letters and memoirs. While epistolary and first-person novels are document novels, it is also true that those without pseudofactual pretense might be said to have less "documenticity" than those with the pretense. Because of this, "document novel" is not a tag for an identifiable formal feature, but a term designed to highlight a key characteristic of many first-person narratives in this period.

Heliodorian novels – A subset of the class of inset novels, named after Heliodorus's *Aethiopica*, in which characters recount flashback narratives that elucidate enigmatic events in the main, typically third-person, narrative. It is this formal feature that corresponds to typical definitions of the seventeenth-century French *roman*, as opposed to the *nouvelle*.

Indeterminate novels – A class of nobody novels presenting no paratextual assertions of truth or invention. The indeterminate posture is one of three truth postures possible in nobody novels, the other two being pseudofactual and invented.

Inset novels – Novels featuring narrations inset into the main narrative; inset narratives are usually recounted orally by characters, although occasionally written texts are either read out loud or reproduced directly. I identify six types of insetting, depending on the relation of the inset narratives to the main narrative level. The most important are those relating to Heliodorian novels (inset types 1 and 2).

Invented novels – A class of nobody novels accompanied by paratextual assertions that the narrative did not actually transpire or that the documents (e.g., letters) that make it up are fabrications of the author. It may or may not be helpful to think of this kind of novel as "more fictional" than nobody novels with pseudofactual or indeterminate postures.

Keyed novels – Named after the French expression *roman à clef*, a class of novels in which paratextual cues invite readers to suspect that the actions recounted under assumed names are those of known public figures. In most cases, the assumed names are those of nobodies.

"New" third-person novels – A loose category or family of third-person novels appearing in the second half of the eighteenth century that display a cluster of morphological features (relative length, chapterization, and scene setting) that distinguish them from earlier third-person works. The quotes around "new" emphasize that the epithet should not be taken to mean modern.

Nobody novels – A class of real-world novels featuring protagonists unknown outside of the covers of the book. They are the counterpart of somebody (or Aristotelian) novels. Only nobody novels are tagged for truth posture (pseudofactual, indeterminate, invented).

Pseudofactual novels – A class of nobody novels accompanied by paratextual assertions of literal truth. These assertions range from elaborate to summary. No judgment of believability is implied, though some assertions are also tagged as ironic or equivocal. Along with indeterminacy and invention, pseudofactuality is one of the three truth postures possible in nobody novels.

Real-world novels – Novels whose setting is contiguous with the world of the reader and whose action is consistent with a widespread sense of the laws of nature. Since novels that pose the question of the miraculous or the supernatural (e.g., the gothic) are oriented by this sense, they are still considered real-world. The counterpart of the real-world novel is the alternate-world novel. Only real-world novels are tagged as somebody or nobody novels.

Somebody novels – Also called Aristotelian, a class of real-world novels whose characters are known people from history, legend, or the contemporary scene. Their counterparts are nobody novels.

"Unspecified" novels – A class of real-world novels common in the early seventeenth century whose settings are temporally unmarked. Many (but not all) pastoral and chivalric novels fall into this category, which could also be thought of as designating a specific chronotope, to use a familiar term of Mikhail Bakhtin's. The quotes around the term highlight the its inadequacy, which stems from the fact that they are a minor focus of this study.

Notes

Introduction

1 The following "composite portrait" of the history of the novel field is based on scholarship descending from what Michael McKeon calls the "Grand Theory" tradition initiated by György Lukács, José Ortega y Gasset, and Mikhail Bakhtin (*The Theory of the Novel: A Historical Approach* [Baltimore: Johns Hopkins University Press, 2000]). While I emphasize that my caricature targets a common *stance* rather than any specific scholar or title, deservedly well-known members of this lineage might include John B. Bender, *Imagining the Penitentiary: Fiction and the Architecture of Mind in Eighteenth-Century England* (Chicago: University of Chicago Press, 1987); Nancy Armstrong, *Desire and Domestic Fiction: A Political History of the Novel* (New York: Oxford University Press, 1987); and Deidre Shauna Lynch, *The Economy of Character: Novels, Market Culture, and the Business of Inner Meaning* (Chicago: University of Chicago Press, 1998).
2 For an appraisal of the resemblances between New Historicism and the New Critical formalism it would seem to belie, see Alan Liu, "The Power of Formalism: The New Historicism," *ELH* 56.4 (1989): 721–71, esp 740–44.
3 See Margaret Anne Doody, *The True Story of the Novel* (New Brunswick: Rutgers University Press, 1996) and Steven Moore, *The Novel: An Alternative History*, 2 vols. (New York: Bloomsbury Continuum, 2010–2013).
4 Fredric Jameson, *Postmodernism, or, the Cultural Logic of Late Capitalism* (Durham: Duke University Press, 1991).
5 Michel Foucault, *The Order of Things: An Archeology of the Human Sciences* (New York: Pantheon, 1971), 46.
6 Northrop Frye, *Anatomy of Criticism: Four Essays* (Princeton: Princeton University Press, 1957) and Franco Moretti, *Graphs, Maps, Trees: Abstract Models for a Literary History* (London: Verso, 2005), 17–30. Ted Underwood has cast doubt on Moretti's generational description; see *Distant Horizons: Digital Evidence and Literary Change* (Chicago: University of Chicago Press, 2019), 34–67.
7 Wiebe E. Bijker, *Of Bicycles, Bakelites, and Bulbs: Toward a Theory of Sociotechnical Change* (Cambridge: MIT Press, 1995), 75.
8 George Basalla, *The Evolution of Technology* (Cambridge: Cambridge University Press, 1988), 216.

9 Basalla, *Evolution of Technology*, 209. In ascribing to literary forms a "material" existence, I am not referring to the codex itself, but to features that from another point of view may seem not very material at all – say, the type of protagonist, or even whether a narrative is segmented into chapters. This elastic conception of materiality (and technology) will be defended in the book's final chapter.

10 The use of the word "evolution" to speak of nonbiological change can be controversial. Thus, in his technological work, Basalla cautions that he uses the word only analogically and metaphorically (2–3); and for the literary historian Matthew L. Jockers, "the metaphor ... breaks down quickly," because "books are not organisms; they do not breed" (*Macroanalysis: Digital Methods and Literary History* [Urbana: University of Illinois Press, 2013], 155). In my view, there is no reason genetics should have a monopoly on evolution "proper": constrained change is constrained by different factors in different domains, and just because natural selection is not operative in the cultural domain does not mean that the later can evolve only in a metaphorical sense. Natural selection is but one sort of evolution.

11 Franco Moretti, *Distant Reading* (London: Verso, 2013) and Jockers, *Macroanalysis* (Illinois: University of Illinois Press, 2013).

12 "It is possible," write James F. English and Ted Underwood in an introductory essay on macro-scale literary analysis, "that the empirical methods that matter most for literary scholars will continue to be the simpler forms of counting that have already proved themselves in book history and the sociology of reading..., perhaps assisted by computers but not unduly encumbered by them" ("Shifting Scales: Between Literature and Social Science," *MLQ* 77.3 [2016]: 287). This describes well the digital profile of the present study. For an argument that distant reading has a much longer history than the computational text analysis many associate with the digital humanities, see Ted Underwood, "A Genealogy of Distant Reading," *Digital Humanities Quarterly* 11.2 (2017), www.digitalhumanities.org/dhq/vol/11/2/000317/000317.html.

13 On the worry that conventional counting gives short shrift to the footprint of canonical novels, see David A. Brewer, "Counting, Resonance, and Form: A Speculative Manifesto (with Notes)," *Eighteenth-Century Fiction* 24.2 (2012): 161–70.

14 Catherine Gallagher, "The Rise of Fictionality," in *The Novel*, ed. Franco Moretti, vol. 1 (Princeton: Princeton University Press, 2006), 336–63; Nicholas Paige, *Before Fiction: The Ancien Régime of the Novel* (Philadelphia: University of Pennsylvania Press, 2011).

15 W. Brian Arthur, *The Nature of Technology: What It Is and How It Evolves* (London: Allen Lane/Penguin, 2009).

16 Nicholas Paige, "Datasets and Electronic Graphs for *Technologies of the Novel*," Zenodo, http://doi.org/10.5281/zenodo.3939066.

Chapter 1

1 The pioneering article is Arthur Jerrold Tieje, "A Peculiar Phase of the Theory of Realism in Pre-Richardsonian Fiction," *PMLA* 28.2 (1913): 213–52. A burst of interest in the pretense of literal truth in the context of a drive toward realism followed Ian Watt's *The Rise of the Novel: Studies in Defoe, Richardson, and Fielding* (Berkeley: University of California Press, 1957). For the French domain, see notably Philip Stewart, *Imitation and Illusion in the French Memoir Novel, 1700–1750* (New Haven: Yale University Press, 1969); Jacques Rustin, "Mensonge et vérité dans le roman français du XVIIIe siècle," *RHLF* 69 (1969): 13–38; and Vivienne Mylne, *The Eighteenth-Century French Novel: Techniques of Illusion*, 2nd ed. (Cambridge: Cambridge University Press, 1981). For the situation in England, see Geoffrey Day, *From Fiction to the Novel* (London: Routledge and Kegan Paul, 1987).

2 Key studies on the English context include Lennard J. Davis, *Factual Fictions: The Origins of the English Novel* (New York: Columbia University Press, 1983); Catherine Gallagher, *Nobody's Story: The Vanishing Acts of Women Writers in the Marketplace, 1670–1820* (Berkeley: University of California Press, 1994), and "The Rise of Fictionality," in *The Novel*, ed. Franco Moretti, vol. 1 (Princeton: Princeton University Press, 2006), 336–63; and Michael McKeon, *The Origins of the English Novel, 1600–1740* (Baltimore: Johns Hopkins University Press, 1987). For the French side, see Jan Herman, Mladen Kozul, and Nathalie Kremer, *Le Roman véritable: Stratégies préfacielles au XVIIIe siècle* (Oxford: Voltaire Foundation, 2008). Finally, Barbara Foley, who looks at the situation in both countries, insists on a more Foucauldian rupture between literalist (eighteenth century) and realist (nineteenth century) understandings of history; see *Telling the Truth: The Theory and Practice of Documentary Fiction* (Ithaca: Cornell University Press, 1986).

3 Kendall L. Walton, *Mimesis as Make-Believe: On the Foundations of the Representational Arts* (Cambridge: Harvard University Press, 1990).

4 *Poetics* 9 (1451b), in *Ancient Literary Criticism: The Principal Texts in New Translations*, ed. D. A. Russell and M. Winterbottom, (Oxford: Oxford University Press, 1972), 102.

5 Cicero, *Rhetorica ad Herennium*, trans. Henry Caplan (Cambridge: Harvard University Press, 1954), 25 (I,8). See also Quintilian, *Instituto oratoria* (II, iv, 2).

6 J. R. Morgan, "Make-Believe and Make Believe: The Fictionality of Greek Novels," in *Lies and Fiction in the Ancient World*, ed. Christopher Gill and T. P. Wiseman (Exeter: Exeter University Press, 1993), 175–229.

7 For recent critiques of efforts to locate the birth of something as apparently widespread as "fiction" only in the eighteenth century, see Françoise

Lavocat, *Fait et fiction: Pour une frontière* (Paris: Seuil, 2016); Monika Fludernik, "The Fiction of the Rise of Fictionality," *Poetics Today* 39.1 (2018): 67–92; and Julie Orlemanski, "Who Has Fiction? Modernity, Fictionality, and the Middle Ages," *New Literary History* 50.2 (2019): 145–70. Orlemanski offers an attentive genealogy of the chauvinism of such accounts, often predicated on Weberian narratives of disenchantment.

8 To be clear, I am concerned here with the presentation of texts as literally true or fictional, and not with the text-level distinctions that may or may not exist between fiction and nonfiction – an endlessly debated problem of philosophy and narratology that may be amenable to quantitative analysis as well. For the latter, see Andrew Piper, *Enumerations: Data and Literary Study* (Chicago: University of Chicago Press, 2018), 94–117.

9 Both of these authors in particular do not seem to be making a bid for their readers' actual belief, with Richardson's pretense being especially thin. I will return briefly below to the question of the relation of postures like these to the securing of actual belief.

10 For an overview of many of these questions, see Lavocat, *Fait et fiction*.

11 I am appropriating this distinction from Gallagher, *Nobody's Story*. However, in Gallagher's original coinage, the distinction is simply between characters claimed to be real people and characters acknowledged as invented. The use I develop later is different.

12 Guido Mazzoni has described the cultural interest of somebodies as follows: "The noble genres ... draw from a repertoire of events endowed with a meaning and a public value, backed by the great collective narratives that flowed through premodern and early modern European culture: mythology, ancient literature, sacred history, and epic communal stories. These are immediately readable events; they can be told again; they mean something to everyone; they are archetypes to which the narrative can always return" (*Theory of the Novel*, trans. Zakiya Hanafi [Cambridge: Harvard University Press, 2017], 110).

13 For me, this is one major obstacle to the frequent proposition that fictionality is a constant of literature; see Nicholas Paige, *Before Fiction: The Ancien Régime of the Novel* (Philadelphia: University of Pennsylvania Press, 2011), 1–9. But I repeat that for the purposes of this book, it doesn't matter what fictionality is or isn't: I will simply be inventorying distinct types of subject matter under a series of names (tags) that are ultimately arbitrary.

14 The term is that of Foley (*Telling the Truth*).

15 See Gérard Genette, *Narrative Discourse: An Essay in Method* (1972; repr., Ithaca: Cornell University Press, 1980). I bypass this terminology, which has the notable disadvantage of being designed without eighteenth-century "editorial" pretense in mind (see Jenny Mander, *Circles of Learning: Narratology and the Eighteenth-Century French Novel*, Studies on Voltaire and the Eighteenth Century 366 [Oxford: Voltaire Foundation, 1999]).

16 "To be sure, most readers didn't fall for claims of complete authenticity. But it is undeniable that the reading public of 1730 and still that of 1761 was monumentally gullible compared to our current 'age of suspicion' and its universal skepticism" (Georges May, *Le Dilemme du roman au XVIIIe siècle* [Paris: PUF, 1963], 144). Though most rise-of-fictionality accounts use language designed to tone down the blatant teleology of the argument, this – and especially the Coleridgian telos – is indeed their gist. "The modern, autonomous realm of the spirit enjoins a secularized sort of belief – not in an ineffably greater power that lies beyond us, but in the actuality of the fictive – in Coleridge's words, 'that willing suspension of disbelief for the moment, which constitutes poetic faith'" (McKeon, *Origins of the English Novel*, 128). See also Gallagher, "The Rise of Fictionality," 347–49.

17 I consider a number of cases – *Julie, The Castle of Otranto* (Walpole, 1764), *La Religieuse* (Diderot, pub. 1796) – in Paige, *Before Fiction*.

18 As I will clarify, I do have separate tags for novels with parodic, ironic, or equivocal truth pretense.

19 Elsewhere, I have called this distinction between real-world subject matter and the marvelous "the Great Divide" (Paige, *Before Fiction*, 174–79). Gothic ghosts inhabit the province of real-world novels, in my view, for whether explained away or not, ghosts insistently pose the question of what is real. (This, of course, is why Freud could find nothing "uncanny" about fairy tales; see Sigmund Freud, "The Uncanny," in *Collected Papers*, ed. Ernest Jones [New York: Basic Books, 1959], 4:368.) Finally, since the Great Divide dates only from around the mid-seventeenth century, some novels from before this time make circumscribed use of devices such as prophecy or – say – magic fountains. Such minor features do not tip these novels into the alternate-world category.

20 For some considerations on the difficulties inhering to the manual classification of cultural artifacts, see Peter M. Broadwell, David Mimno, and Timothy R. Tangherlini, "The Tell-Tale Hat: Surfacing the Uncertainty in Folklore Classification," *CA: Journal of Cultural Analytics*, February 8, 2017, http://culturalanalytics.org/2017/02/the-tell-tale-hat-surfacing-the-uncertainty-in-folklore-classification/. I would note that many of those difficulties are minimized by the fact that with one exception (in Chapter 7), I do not attempt to make fine-grained distinctions of content, but focus on larger, usually structural features of texts.

21 At certain periods, the distinction of text and paratext is not always obvious. In many early novels especially, an authorial, paratextual voice is sometimes clearly audible at the opening of the text proper. In many later novels, some paratexts are in fact part of the text: thus, an epistolary novel featuring an author's name on the title page – and thereby admitting invention – may at the same time include authenticating footnotes or other "mock" paratexts.

22 Relatedly, since I am not interested in the "real" referential status of the text – fiction or nonfiction – the fact that a later edition may dispense with the pretense maintained by the original edition means nothing for me. Categorization is based on the original edition.

23 The discontinuity visible here for the decades 1710–1730 deserves comment. Why do alternate-world novels expand so markedly in the 1720s, only to recede the following decade before regaining popularity again in the 1740s? It is important to recognize that although my samples generally display consistent trends, they don't always and shouldn't be expected to. (For a discussion, see the Annex.) In the case of Figure 1.3, the number that stands out as deserving of the most caution is the one from the 1720s, a decade whose low production contributes to volatility.

24 I am not swayed, then, by the objection that exclusive attention to the real-world "chronotope" skews our conception of the novel, a point made for the eighteenth century by Srinivas Aravamudan; see *Enlightenment Orientalism: Resisting the Rise of the Novel* (Chicago: University of Chicago Press, 2012).

25 Though fairy and oriental tales also make for coherent genres (and very popular ones), they usually do not appear in the samples because as a rule they are published in collections, which I do not tag.

26 Of course, the data presented here tells us something only about French-language novels; it is possible that English-language novels behave differently. As we will see in Chapter 9, this is indeed the case.

27 The sample from the 1700s gives the most unexpected results of any in my research: for reasons unknown – possibly just by chance – Aristotelian novels appear to retreat markedly but temporarily in the decade. Nonetheless, despite the anomaly, the correlation between nobody and contemporary novels holds.

28 The document novel is the subject of Chapters 6 and 7. There, I describe some other, quantitatively negligible, document novels that do not fit into the category of memoirs and epistolary collections; I also explain the double peak, which is caused by the asynchronous development of the two major types of document novels.

29 A second possibility, not tested here, is that people move from more vehement assertions to more lukewarm or perfunctory ones, with the distinction being one not of believability but sheer amplitude. Preliminary attempts to measure the latter convinced me that there would be no such decline over time, and I abandoned the effort.

30 Of course, by one reckoning all pseudofactual affirmations save true hoaxes could be considered ironic, in the sense that they are not intended as serious statements. Such a looser definition of irony would not, however, change anything, since we would still be able to distinguish such tacit irony from the explicit variety I am tagging as "ironic."

31 The epistolary novel's resistance may seem strange – if we consider the pretense of the found letter collection to be especially unlikely – but as we will see in Chapter 7, most of these novels are sentimental, and the sentimental text is probably not a hospitable place for irony.
32 Dorrit Cohn, *The Distinction of Fiction* (Baltimore: Johns Hopkins University Press, 1999), 3.
33 The remark is commonplace. The reading public becomes "less and less gullible" as "the assertion 'this is not a novel' starts to signify, by its very recurrence, 'this is a novel'"; the multiplication of so many found manuscripts thus leads to "increasingly delirious parodic extravagance" (Herman, Kozul, and Kremer, *Le Roman véritable*, 52 and 161). The exact date at which this "becoming" commences is always – for obvious reasons – left vague. (For Herman, Kozul, and Kremer, it appears to be quite early in the eighteenth century.) Thinking of pseudofactual pretense as rhetorical rather than semantic, as I've suggested above we should, frees us from the impossible determination of when serious use of the pretense gave way to an ironic one.
34 Samuel Richardson, *Selected Letters*, ed. John Carroll (Oxford: Clarendon, 1964), 85. For a reading of this letter, from 1748, see Paige, *Before Fiction*, 9–11.
35 Jean-Baptiste de Boyer, marquis d'Argens, *Lectures amusantes, ou les délassements de l'esprit, avec un discours sur les nouvelles*, 2 vols. (The Hague: Adrien Moetjens, 1739), 1:52–53.

Chapter 2

1 As in Chapter 1, and throughout much of this study, I will consider real-world novels alone. Alternate-world novels make up a negligible proportion of the pre-1681 corpus (less than 5 percent) and do not distribute in any historically meaningful way.
2 The dividing line between contemporary and historical is obviously arbitrary: how long gone does someone need to be before he or she is considered a historical figure? For the purposes of my categorization, "contemporary" refers to events of roughly fifty years prior to publication date. The line is obviously fuzzy, but the number of novels that fall on or around it is small: the great majority are easily classified.
3 The total for this category also includes a small number of texts that reprise established literary protagonists (those of Tasso's *Jerusalem Delivered* [1581], for example, are a favorite).
4 Such allusions would certainly understate the actual use of sources since only some Aristotelian novels contain prefaces at all.

5 To take a well-known example from the French dramatic canon – which operated according to Aristotelian logic as well – Corneille, in *Horace* (1640), creates the character of Sabine, necessary for the plot's symmetry.
6 See Nicholas Paige, *Before Fiction: The Ancien Régime of the Novel* (Philadelphia: University of Pennsylvania Press, 2011), 35–61.
7 The gendered aspect is not incidental: it allowed for women, given short shrift by classical historians, to become major players in the novel. This was vital both in feminocentric salon culture (see Joan DeJean, *Tender Geographies: Women and the Origins of the Novel in France* [New York: Columbia University Press, 1991]) and also for a genre whose backbone was the heterosexual love plot.
8 Note that I am not referring to more "accurate" or "empirical" uses of history but rather to easily identifiable categories of use or treatment. Accuracy would in all probability be difficult or impossible to quantify. I would also add that György Lukacs's assertion that prenineteenth-century historical novels are only "so-called historical novels" – "historical only as regards their purely external choice of theme and costume" – strikes me as justified, at least for the period before 1751 (*The Historical Novel*, trans. Hannah Mitchell and Stanley Mitchell [Lincoln: University of Nebraska Press, 1983], 19). In no sense am I proposing that the presentification of these novels reflects a growth in "historical consciousness."
9 For reasons I will develop, the dip in the 1650s and 1660s is in my view salient, whereas I have no explanation for the plunge in Aristotelian novels in the sample from the 1700s – a sample I flagged in the previous chapter also as being anomalous. Sampling may be to blame, or it may be a fluke in the production. Either way, figures on either side suggest that this data point is not meaningful.
10 What constitutes a historical marker? Clearly it would be too much to expect all novels with roughly contemporary settings to contain dates, references to the reigning monarch, or temporal deictics ("Two winters ago…"). However, references to an identifiable contemporary geography – that of the city or the nation state – are much more common and also help situate the novel as contemporary. In this way, temporal location is in fact inseparable from geographical location. The temporally "unspecified" novels I am referring to are thus unmoored from both place and time.
11 See, for example, Anna Arzoumanov, *Pour lire les clefs de l'Ancien Régime: Anatomie d'un protocole interprétatif* (Paris: Classiques Garnier, 2013). In England, satirical keyed novels were especially common in the very early part of the eighteenth century, during the heated rivalry between Whigs and Tories; see Chapter 9.
12 This invitation is for my purposes the defining characteristic of the keyed novel, whether or not there exist extant printed keys. However, the issue is delicate because some novels for which we possess contemporaneously

printed keys *do not* contain the invitation to read for a key. This means that keyed reading may have been more prominent than my figures capture: often the practice may have been triggered not by textual but by contextual clues, clues that are now lost (at least to this researcher). And of course, the invitation to read with a key may have been issued in the absence of a key itself. At any rate, my figures here amalgamate novels bound with actual printed keys and novels with invitations but no (extant) keys.

13 Other more formal traits tend to separate keyed novels from true stories. True stories usually had one main plot and a limited set of protagonists, whereas *romans à clef* were more sprawling affairs, with multiple inset narratives, each having its own set of characters. They also tended to be novels whose settings were not those of the modern nation state: instead, they were more geographically promiscuous, typically visiting various ports of call in the Mediterranean but on occasion ranging into the Near East and even as far as China. (As such, they are often tagged as featuring "unspecified" temporal settings.)

14 Tabulating keyed novels as a subcategory of nobody novels, as I do here, may seem a strange choice: after all, the implication is that the characters are known to readers. My reasoning is based on three characteristics of the French situation specifically: one, often only certain characters are identified in printed keys, and often these are not the protagonists; two, extant printed keys suggest the level of celebrity could be quite low (so only a small circle of readers would actually know the people involved); and three, the hint of a key was probably in many cases empty. At any rate, creating a special category for these novels – neither somebody nor nobody – would change only the presentation of the data, not the conclusions derived from it.

15 Over the years 1601–1730, the correlation coefficient is 0.91, where 0 indicates uncorrelated data and 1 perfectly correlated data.

16 For a genealogy of the literary-historical commonplace of a 1660s turning point, see Camille Esmein, "Le Tournant historique comme construction théorique: L'Exemple du 'tournant' de 1660 dans l'histoire du roman," *Fabula LHT* 0 (2005), www.fabula.org/lht/0/esmein.html

17 By incorporating additional measures not considered here, the following three chapters will further blur any sharp divide between the 1650s and 1660s by confirming that the change that is obvious by the 1660s is only a continuation of an earlier trend. I will return to what I believe is the "technological" importance of the rupture-or-no-rupture problem in Chapter 10.

18 "Many literary scholars feel a commitment to discontinuity that is almost moral in character, expressed as a celebration of fragments and rupture, or as a critique of master narratives" (Ted Underwood, *Why Literary Periods Mattered: Historical Contrast and the Prestige of English Studies* [Stanford: Stanford University Press, 2013], 159). To my mind rightly, Underwood

attributes to Michel Foucault much of the disciplinary prestige accruing to narratives of rupture.

19 Novel production in both France and England is represented more extensively in Figure 9.12 (page 195). On my production estimates, see the Annex.

20 This same effect may help explain the changes of the novel in the 1730s, mentioned in the previous chapter: a prolonged production trough, situated in the years bracketing the death of Louis XIV (the 1710s and 1720s), is followed by an explosion of interest in a heretofore unexploited form – the document novel.

21 *Ibrahim* is signed with his name. Modern critics usually attribute the novel proper to Georges's sister Madeleine (later the author of *Artamène* and *Clélie*) and the preface – written in any event in the masculine first-person singular – to Georges. I will follow this custom here, though for my purposes, authorship makes no difference.

22 "Préface," in Camille Esmein, ed., *Poétiques du roman: Scudéry, Huet, Du Plaisir et autres textes théoriques et critiques du XVIIe siècle sur le genre romanesque* (Paris: Champion, 2004), 139. All quotes used here are found on this and the following page.

23 *Poetics* 9 (1451b), in D. A. Russell and M. Winterbottom, eds., *Ancient Literary Criticism: The Principal Texts in New Translations* (Oxford: Oxford University Press, 1972), 102.

24 *Ibrahim* thus poses a dilemma for the tagger: is it *strongly* Aristotelian, on account of the historical nature of its titular hero, or is it *weakly* so, given that the loves of illustrious nobodies form its true subject? I've reasoned that the book's main protagonists are in fact the young lovers, not Ibrahim. As such, it is tabulated as a weak Aristotelian novel.

25 Scudéry explicitly defends the choice of nonroyal protagonists reasoning that they are of sufficiently illustrious condition to merit our interest ("Préface," in Esmein, *Poétiques du roman*, 144–45). Note that the logic is not exactly that such characters are fictional creations (and thus free from any referential constraints) but that they are inventions not contradicted by history: they could plausibly be historical.

26 Or, if the author of the novel and the author of the preface are indeed not the same person: the prefacer doesn't mind that his explanation doesn't quite fit the novel for which he is writing the preface.

Chapter 3

1 Ugo Dionne, *La Voie aux chapitres: Poétique de la disposition romanesque* (Paris: Seuil, 2008), 101. Remarks of the sort are commonplace in the scholarship. For a recent and nuanced treatment of the *roman – nouvelle*

problem along these lines, see Guido Mazzoni, *Theory of the Novel* (Cambridge: Harvard University Press, 2017); Mazzoni himself refers to the "symbolic threshold" of 1670 (79).

2 Du Plaisir, *Sentiments sur les lettres et sur l'histoire, avec des scrupules sur le style* (1683), in Camille Esmein, ed., *Poétiques du roman: Scudéry, Huet, Du Plaisir et autres textes théoriques et critiques du XVIIe siècle sur le genre romanesque* (Paris: Champion, 2004), 762.

3 On narrative order and novelistic economy in this period, see Camille Esmein-Sarrazin, *L'Essor du roman: Discours théorique et constitution d'un genre littéraire au XVIIe siècle* (Paris: Champion, 2008), 361–81.

4 Du Plaisir, *Sentiments*, in Esmein, *Poétiques du roman*, 763.

5 Heliodorus of Emesa, *L'Histoire aethiopique*, ed. Laurence Plazenet, trans. Jacques Amyot (Paris: Champion, 2008), 159.

6 Marc Fumaroli, "Jacques Amyot and the Clerical Polemic against the Chivalric Novel," *Renaissance Quarterly* 38.1 (1985): 22–40.

7 On the work's *ordo artificialis*, see Terence Cave, *Pré-Histoires: Textes troublés au seuil de la modernité* (Geneva: Droz, 1999), 129–41. I have addressed the importance of the *Aethiopica* and its interesting imbrication with the publication of the chivalric *Amadis* in *Before Fiction: The Ancien Régime of the Novel* (Philadelphia: University of Pennsylvania Press, 2011), 65–66 and 83–89. For more on the congruence between Amyot's 1547 preface and humanist poetics, as well as an account of the *Aethiopica*'s influence on subsequent French novels, see Gerald N. Sandy, "Classical Forerunners of the Theory and Practice of Prose Romance in France: Studies in the Narrative Form of Minor French Romances of the Sixteenth and Seventeenth Centuries," *Antike und Abendland* 28.2 (1982): 169–91. Humanist dissatisfaction with *Amadis*'s lack of closure is explored by Ullrich Langer, "Le Roman humaniste: Vers le plaisir du fini," in *Du roman courtois au roman baroque: Actes du colloque des 2-5 juillet 2002*, ed. Emmanuel Bury and Francine Mora (Paris: Belles Lettres, 2004), 437–48.

8 The only literary historian to take on such questions methodically is Laurence Plazenet, *L'Ébahissement et la délectation: Réception comparée et poétiques du roman grec en France et en Angleterre aux XVIe et XVIIe siècles* (Paris: Champion, 1997). Though capacious, Plazenet's study is not however a fundamentally quantifying one; as such, it can provide no estimation of how dominant Heliodorian novels might be with respect to others. Plazenet also defines her corpus in a manner that excludes many novels clearly deriving from and indeed sometimes explicitly referencing the *Aethiopica*. See also Marie-Gabrielle Lallemand, *Les Longs Romans du XVIIe siècle: Urfé, Desmarets, Gomberville, La Calprenède, Scudéry* (Paris: Classiques Garnier, 2013); Lallemand describes Heliodorian insetting in detail, but as her title indicates, her corpus is limited to a few well-known examples.

9 An inset, here, is any retrospective story told by a character to another character – a past-tense narrative, in either the first or third person. (I also include written narratives discovered by characters and then read, a more uncommon category.) How long do the narratives need to be? Very occasionally, in the course of an exchange such as a dialogue, characters offer brief information (a few pages) about themselves or others that do not (in my estimation) rise to the level of an inset. In the vast majority of cases, however, no judgment calls about length are necessary: the inset structure is so well understood, so conventionalized, that both the readers and the characters themselves know a narrative is coming. (Indeed, there exists an entire protocol for asking another for his or her story.)

Note that for simplicity, I did not look for insets in epistolary novels, which occasionally contain them; all epistolary novels, in other words, are considered noninset. The figures for inset novels shown in Figure 3.1 are thus lower than they would otherwise be, though only for the years in which epistolary novels are popular – roughly from the 1760s on.

10 It should perhaps be noted that the samples for this decade (taken from 1686 to 1690) post-date his affirmation (1683). Without additional sampling, we cannot know if his remark reflected his knowledge of what was already happening in the early 1680s or whether he merely had a good nose for a trend.

11 Nicolas Boileau, *Art poétique*, ed. Sylvain Menant (Paris: GF Flammarion, 1969), 91 (I, 153).

12 Daniel Riou, "Naissance du roman moderne au XVIIe siècle – idéologie, institution, réception," in *Histoire de la France littéraire*, ed. Jean-Charles Darmon and Michel Delon, vol. 2 (Paris: Quadrige/PUF, 2006), 673. "How can we avoid concluding that the cult of 'novelistic concentration' is celebrated in the name of the idea, indeed the ideology, of Classicism?" asks another critic (Nathalie Grande, "Du long au court: Réduction de la longueur et invention des formes narratives, l'exemple de Madeleine de Scudéry," *Dix-septième siècle* 215 [2002]: 265).

13 See Barthélemy Aneau, *Alector ou le coq, histoire fabuleuse*, ed. Marie-Madeleine Fontaine (Geneva: Droz, 1996), 1: lxxii–lxxvii. Aneau's modern editor notes that even Ronsard's epic *La Franciade* doesn't begin *in medias res*, even though the connection between the genre and the technique was an old one (lxxvi, n. 158).

14 The hoax seems to have been accepted until Huet's well-known treatise *De l'origine des romans* (1670); see Plazenet, *L'Ébahissement et la délectation*, 256–66. I am somewhat simplifying the genealogy here since one can also spot the Heliodorian influence in, say, the 1581 French translation of volume 20 of the *Amadis* serial – an installment patently modeled on the *Aethiopica* (Sandy, "Classical Forerunners," 175).

15 See Sandy, "Classical Forerunners," 176–79.

16 That the opening is a shipwreck makes particularly obvious the debt to the *Aethiopica*, which starts the same way. The insetting of this work is what I will be calling Type 2: it contains one major flashback rather than a number of interconnecting ones.
17 Here too I simplify since it is impossible to pull apart the influence of Heliodorus from that of Homer and Virgil. Thus, Tasso, who structures his epic *Gerusalemme liberata* with inset narratives, mentions in a letter both Heliodorius and Virgil as expert users of the device (Sandy, "Classical Forerunners," 173). On Tasso in this context, see Walter Stephens, "Tasso's Heliodorus and the World of Romance," in *Search for the Ancient Novel*, ed. James Tatum (Baltimore: Johns Hopkins University Press, 1994), 67–87.
18 The debt of the *New Arcadia* not just to Sannazaro but also to Heliodorus and Montemayor was noted at the time; in his *Directions for Speech and Style* (1599), John Hoskins comments specifically on Sidney's formal "web" and these sources (A. C. Hamilton, "Sidney's *Arcadia* as Prose Fiction: Its Relation to Its Sources," *English Literary Renaissance* 2.1 [1962]: 30). On Sidney and the Greek novels, see also Victor Skretkowicz, *European Erotic Romance: Philhellene Protestantism, Renaissance Translation, and English Literary Politics* (Manchester: Manchester University Press, 2010), 168–224. Although the precise filiation between Montemayor and Cervantes's pastorals and Heliodorus has not, to my knowledge, been traced, their debt to the Greek novel is commonly accepted.
19 Montreux's *Les Bergeries de Juliette* (1585–1598), a major French work of the genre, features shepherds who recount, *Decameron*-style, stories unrelated to the pastoral world.
20 "The years following its posthumous publication in 1617 witnessed ten editions, translations into French, Italian, and English, and imitations in prose fiction and drama. In the eighteenth century, new editions, imitations, and translations appeared, and in the early years of the nineteenth century, a scholar of the stature of Sismondi could still affirm that many readers considered it to be Cervantes' masterpiece" (Alban K. Forcione, *Cervantes' Christian Romance: A Study of* Persiles y Sigismunda [Princeton: Princeton University Press, 1972], 3). Naturally, this popularity *needs* to be forgotten because it cannot be made to square with our efforts to enshrine the *Quixote* as the first modern novel.
21 The only other titled inset from the 1600s sample occurs in the pastoral *Les amours d'Amynthio et de la belle Odylie* (Bazire, 1601), but there is only one such inset, and it has the particularity of being a verse narrative read by the protagonist. The pre-1601 inset novels I've consulted do not feature titled insets, which suggests that if they do exist, they are rare.
22 This graph extends only to 1700, the date at which I stopped collecting information on titled insets.

23 Given that the particular narrative arrangement of Type 3 novels is far from intricate, it is difficult to know how much these novels are actually indebted to Achilles Tatius: writers, especially the ones from the last half of the century, may have come to it independently. (At least one of the Type 3 novels from the opening decade of the century probably represents such a case – Thomas's regularly reprinted satirical travel narrative *L'Ile des hermaphrodites* [1605], whose subject matter would suggest that the formal resemblance with Achilles Tatius is fortuitous.)

24 Frank Greiner, *Fictions narratives en prose de l'âge baroque: Répertoire analytique I (1585–1610)* (Paris: Champion, 2007).

25 Despite the European pedigree of the framed narrative compendium, it is ultimately not autochthonous either: its European adoption simply antedates that of Heliodorian insetting. For a historical overview of the form, with special attention to its Arabic and Eastern roots, see Katharine S. Gittes, *Framing the Canterbury Tales: Chaucer and the Medieval Frame Narrative Tradition* (New York: Greenwood Press, 1991).

26 In some cases, there is a qualitative distinction between the diegetic levels: this happens when characters pause to tell, for example, a fairy tale. In others, the action of the insets takes place in the same world as that of the characters, but it does not intersect with the main narrative.

27 Plazenet declares French imitations and adaptations of the Greek novel "moribund" after 1661, but this is because the theme of the amorous voyage – and not a particular use of insetting – is the operative criterion for the selection of her corpus. See Plazenet, *L'Ébahissement et la délectation*, 166, 26.

28 That is, one could tag individual insets, in the hopes of seeing trends that are hidden by my limited categories. For example, many Type 1 novels contain, in addition to vital "backstory" insets, insets that are characteristic of Type 4 or Type 6 novels; plausibly, that proportion may change in significant ways.

29 Du Plaisir, *Sentiments*, in Esmein, *Poétiques du roman*, 761.

30 Protocol for establishing word counts can be found in the Annex.

31 With one exception, all sampled novels over 500,000 words fall within these decades: *L'Astrée* (d'Urfé, 1607, 1,015,000 words); *Le Polexandre* (Gomberville, 1637, 518,000 words); *Cassandre* (La Calprenède, 1642, 692,000 words); *Artamène* (Scudéry, 1649, 1,945,000 words); *Clélie* (Scudéry, 1654, 1,001,000 words); *Faramond* (La Calprenède, 1661, 1,060,000 words); and *Tarsis et Zélie* (Le Vayer de Boutigny, 1665, 520,000 words). The exception is *L'Alexis* (Camus, 1622, 625,000 words).

32 Figure 3.9 eliminates the calculations from the 1600s because the million words of the decade's one Type 1 novel would render the graph illegible. And no Type 1 novels figure in the sample from the 1740s.

Chapter 4

1. William Congreve, *Incognita, or Love and Duty Reconcil'd* (New York: Houghton Mifflin Company, 1922), 6–7. Congreve goes on to liken the opposition to that between tragedy and comedy.
2. On the confusing French terminology in the latter part of the seventeenth century, see English Showalter, *The Evolution of the French Novel, 1641–1782* (Princeton: Princeton University Press, 1972), 11–37, and Camille Esmein-Sarrazin, *L'Essor du roman: Discours théorique et constitution d'un genre littéraire au XVIIe siècle* (Paris: Champion, 2008), 36–43. In England, "seventeenth- and early eighteenth-century writers often use the terms 'romance,' 'history,' and 'novel' with an evident interchangeability that must bewilder and frustrate all modern expectations," writes Michael McKeon after reviewing booksellers catalogs (*The Origins of the English Novel, 1600–1740* [Baltimore: Johns Hopkins University Press, 1987], 25).
3. Notwithstanding the contribution of McKeon's *Origins of the English Novel* and many others, we still lack a thorough documentary account of this lexical shift. Some materials for such an examination are assembled in Ioan Williams, ed., *Novel and Romance, 1700–1800: A Documentary Record* (London: Routledge and Kegan Paul, 1970); see also Edith Kern, "The Romance of Novel/Novella," in *The Disciplines of Criticism: Essays in Literary Theory, Interpretation, and History*, ed. Peter Demetz, Thomas Greene, and Lowry Nelson, Jr. (New Haven: Yale University Press, 1968), 511–30.
4. See Jean Sgard, "Le Mot 'roman,'" *Eighteenth-Century Fiction* 13.2–3 (2001): 183–95. *Nouvelle* will eventually become the preferred French term for "short story."
5. For a sample of studies along these lines – studies that, to be sure, can also concede that things are "more complicated" – see Françoise Gevrey, *L'Illusion et ses procédés: De "La Princesse de Clèves" aux "Illustres Françaises"* (Paris: J. Corti, 1988); Alain Viala, "De Scudéry à Courtilz de Sandras: Les Nouvelles historiques et galantes," *Dix-septième siècle*, no. 215 (2002): 287–95; and Christian Zonza, *La Nouvelle historique en France à l'âge classique (1657–1703)* (Paris: Champion, 2007). Unsurprisingly, the canonical *Princesse de Clèves* – really the only *nouvelle* remembered by nonspecialists – synecdochally designates both the form and its supposed modernity; for a round-up of such treatments, see John Campbell, "La 'Modernité' de *La Princesse de Clèves*," *Seventeenth-Century French Studies* 29 (2007): 63–72. A few have sought to play down the notion of a rupture; see notably René Godenne, "L'Association 'nouvelle-petit roman' entre 1650 et 1750," *CAIEF* 18 (1966): 67–78, to which I will return. Finally, Thomas Pavel has suggested not diachronic shift from *roman* to *nouvelle* but a

harmonious coexistence of generically distinct forms; see Thomas Pavel, *La Pensée du roman* (Paris: Gallimard, 2003), esp. 133. (As we will see, such a hypothesis is not borne out by the evidence.)

6 Henri Coulet, *Le Roman jusqu'à la Révolution*, 9th ed. (Paris: Armand Colin, 2000), 221. I have substituted *roman* and *nouvelle* for the two terms of purely modern origin used by Coulet, *roman baroque* and *roman classique*.

7 "It is impossible to find one single definition that will work for all *nouvelles*" (Aron Kibédi-Varga, "Pour une définition de la nouvelle à l'époque classique," *CAIEF* 18 [1966]: 63); "the border between the *nouvelle* and the *roman* [is] sometimes hazy" (Raymond Picard and Jean Lafond, eds., *Nouvelles du XVIIe siècle* [Paris: Gallimard/Pléiade, 1997], liii).

8 See the remarks in the introduction to Picard and Lafond, *Nouvelles du XVIIe siècle*, esp. xiii.

9 Indeed, in French, the work had long been linked with the idea of news, information, or gossip. See Roger Dubuis, "Le mot 'nouvelle' au Moyen Age: De la nébuleuse au terme générique," in *La Nouvelle: Définitions, transformations*, ed. Bernard Alluin and François Suard (Lille: Presses Universitaires de Lille, 1990), 13–26.

10 Charles Sorel, *La Bibliothèque française*, 2nd ed. (Paris: Compagnie des libraires, 1667), 181.

11 In this and what follows, I'm taking "subtitle" to mean designations that follow a comma after the primary title. I do not count the second title of double-titled works (works with *ou* [or] separating two titles). Thus, *Clélie, histoire romaine* (Scudéry, 1654) has a subtitle, whereas *Faramond, ou l'histoire de France* (La Calprenède, 1661) does not. Subtitles typically figure on title pages, though I've also counted subtitles appearing only in the book's caption title (the title figuring directly above the text's incipit). (If the subtitle of the title page contradicts that of the caption title, only the former is tagged.) I do not count subtitles appearing only in the *privilège* (the document, printed with the novel, granting exclusive printing rights to the holder).

In order to harmonize this chapter's graphs with those from other chapters, I again restrict analysis to real-world novels. Inclusion of alternate-world novels – rare over this period – would have very minimal effect on the statistics and none at all on the conclusions I draw.

12 Witness for example Zonza, ending his study in 1703, convinced that the form "is born, lives out its life, and goes through its agony" in the second half of the seventeenth century (*La Nouvelle historique en France*, 13).

13 Sorel, *La Bibliothèque française*, 181.

14 Showalter wrote some time ago that "one may well conclude that the vogue was for the term *nouvelle*, not for any new quality in fiction" (*Evolution of the French Novel*, 21).

15 For clarity, the small number of *nouvelles* from the 1650s (two) have been omitted.
16 Probably: since I have no samples from before 1601, it is possible that the data from the opening decades of the seventeenth century is itself anomalous.
17 This graph too ignores the two *nouvelles* from the 1650s.
18 See Figures E4.1 and E4.2, which leave out the relatively few miscellaneous *nouvelle* and *histoire* subtitles that do not fit into the main categories tabulated.
19 See Figures E4.3 and E4.4.

Chapter 5

1 Ludwig Wittgenstein, *Philosophical Investigations*, trans. G. E. M. Anscombe (Oxford: Basil Blackwell, 1953), 31–32 (§66–67).
2 Columns represent all novels whose length is between the number of the column and the number of the next column. Novels under 10,000 words, which I have excluded for reasons set forth in the Annex, are less numerous than novels between 10,000 and 20,000 words; but this fact could obviously have no impact on the fundamental asymmetry of the distribution.
3 In a famous phrase occurring in Segrais's *Les Nouvelles françaises* (1657), a character opines that "*nouvelles* need to hew a little closer to history" (reproduced in Camille Esmein, ed., *Poétiques du roman: Scudéry, Huet, Du Plaisir et autres textes théoriques et critiques du XVIIe siècle sur le genre romanesque* [Paris: Champion, 2004], 549).
4 Du Plaisir, *Sentiments sur les lettres*, in *Poétiques du roman*, 762.
5 One should note, however, that about 10 percent of subtitled *nouvelles* are written in the first person (typically, with first-person frames or observer narrators). These will be treated in Chapter 6, where I dub them "report novels."
6 This gives partial confirmation to the heterodox theory advanced a half century ago by René Godenne, according to which the form resulted not from a complete break with respect to the *roman* but rather from a kind of concentration or condensing of the latter ("L'Association 'nouvelle-petit roman,'" *CAIEF* 18 [1966]: 67–78). Thus, for Godenne, the *nouvelle* has all of the *roman*'s traits – including multiple inset storylines – except for length. Given, however, the clear decline in Type 1 insetting, trends in historical setting, and other criteria still, Godenne's contention as a whole seems unjustified. It is nonetheless more robust than the theory Nathalie Grande has proposed replacing it with ("Du long au court: Réduction de la longueur et invention des formes narratives, l'exemple de Madeleine de Scudéry," *Dix-septième siècle* 215 [2002]: 263–71). According to Grande, the *nouvelle* is a detached inset narrative, set free upon the splintering of

the old *roman*. Other than the fact that insetting continues to characterize nearly half of subtitled *nouvelles*, an additional problem with the thesis is that the inset narratives of the *roman* are usually in the first person, whereas *nouvelles* are not. (See Chapter 6.)

7 Data from the RIAA. For simplicity I have excluded eight-track tapes.

8 Leaving aside the complication coming from the fact that superior technologies can in fact increase the total market. The CD provides a good example of this: it greatly expands per-capita music sales. See Michael De Gusta, "The Real Death of the Music Industry," *Business Insider*, February 18, 2011, www.businessinsider.com/these-charts-explain-the-real-death-of-the-music-industry-2011-2?IR=T.

9 Thus, opening his chapter on *nouvelles*, Coulet informs us that *romans* "rather quickly fell from fashion" (*Le Roman jusqu'à la Révolution*, 9th ed. [Paris: Armand Colin, 2000] 195). This is perfectly true, and their fall was much more precipitous than most of the other formal structures examined in this study. But such corroboration is in fact fortuitous, for Coulet is not making an empirical remark about formal decline in the first place. Rather, he is rhetorically distinguishing the embarrassing old form as a flash in the pan compared to *nouvelle* – a form whose legitimacy the critic refrains from tainting with the word "fashion." But if the *roman* is a fashion, so must be the *nouvelle*; and the latter's fall is simply a little more protracted than that of the former. I will return in Chapter 10 to the relevance of the term "fashion" to describe the ups and downs of the novel system.

10 "Becoming the novel of the soul," writes Christian Zonza, the *nouvelle* "displayed a new individual, that of modernity" (*La Nouvelle historique en France à l'âge classique [1657–1703]* [Paris: Champion, 2007], 572). In a slightly different version of the narrative, René Démoris sees the *nouvelle* as a step toward what will be perfected by the memoir novel, which finally marks "the arrival of an already bourgeois *individual* validating his own existence far from the political sphere that no longer makes him dream" ("Aux origines de l'homme historique: Le Croisement, au XVIIe siècle, du roman et de l'histoire (nouvelles et pseudo-mémoires)," in *Le Roman historique (XVIIe-XXe siècles): Actes de Marseille*, ed. Pierre Ronzeaud [Paris: Papers on French Seventeenth-Century Literature, 1983], 50, emphasis in original).

11 In lieu of such a book, which unfortunately does not exist, see James Grantham Turner, "'Romance' and the Novel in Restoration England," *The Review of English Studies* 63. 258 (2011): 58–85; Neil Kenny, "'Ce nom de Roman qui estoit particulier aux Livres de Chevalerie, estant demeuré à tous les Livres de fiction': La naissance antidatée d'un genre," in *Le Roman français au XVIe siècle, ou le renouveau d'un genre dans le contexte européen*, ed. Michèle Clément and Pascale Mounier (Strasbourg: Presses Universitaires de Strasbourg, 2005), 19–32; and especially Christine S.

Lee, "The Meanings of Romance: Rethinking Early Modern Fiction," *Modern Philology* 112.2 (2014): 287–311. Though Michael McKeon covers much of this territory, the information he provides is filtered through his preoccupation with a nascent empiricist spirit; see *The Origins of the English Novel, 1600–1740* (Baltimore: Johns Hopkins University Press, 1987).

12 Of course, Cervantes didn't call such texts *romances* but rather *libros de caballerías* [books of chivalry]: while the word romance exists in Spanish, it refers, like the French *romance*, to a kind of love song.

13 Clara Reeve, *The Progress of Romance through Times, Countries and Manners* (Colchester: W. Keymer, 1785), 59.

14 On this point, see also Nicholas Paige, *Before Fiction: The Ancien Régime of the Novel* (Philadephia: University of Pennsylvania Press, 2011), 83–86. I am certainly not the first to advance this argument: "Compared to *Amadis*, works written in the new manner – *The Trials of Persiles and Sigismunda*, *Polexandre* [Gomberville, 1619–1637], *Le Grand Cyrus* – must have had on their readers an effect of elegance and freshness similar to the one produced by the chateaus and churches of the Renaissance next to medieval citadels and gothic cathedrals" (Thomas Pavel, *La Pensée du roman*, [Paris: Gallimard, 2003] 135). The lesson, however, has not been widely absorbed by historiographers of the novel; see Scott Black, *Without the Novel: Romance and the History of Prose Fiction* (Charlottesville: University of Virginia Press, 2019), 25–41.

Chapter 6

1 Chrétien de Troyes, *Arthurian Romances*, trans. D. D. R. Owen (London: Dent, 1987), 91.

2 For some remarks on the subject, see Emmanuèle Baumgartner, *De l'histoire de Troie au livre du Graal: Le Temps, le récit (XIIe-XIIIe siècles)* (Orléans: Paradigme, 1994), 15–47.

3 It is no doubt important to distinguish this use of documents as novels from the hoaxes and forgeries that proliferated in Renaissance humanist circles; see Anthony Grafton, *Forgers and Critics: Creativity and Duplicity in Western Scholarship* (Princeton: Princeton University Press, 1990). Not only were these items not usually pressed into service as novels – one notable exception being Fumée's fake Greek novel, *Du vrai et parfait amour* (1598), mentioned in Chapter 3 – but more important, they were not noted vehicles for the first person.

4 Third-person found documents – French analogues of, say, *The Castle of Otranto* (Walpole, 1761) – certainly do exist over the period studied here

but will not figure in the present discussion, which focuses on technologies of first-person discourse. (Representing about 12 percent of all document novels, third-person texts are also a relatively rare presence on the novelistic scene.)

5 François Marchant, *Roman sans titre, histoire véritable ou peu s'en faut* (Paris: Maradan, 1788), 5.

6 My use of the untechnical term "first-person novel" refers in the main to what Gérard Genette terms homodiegetic narrations, that is, those written by characters active in the plot (*Narrative Discourse: An Essay in Method* [1972; repr., Ithaca: Cornell University Press, 1980]). Also included, however, are a small number of heterodiegetic narratives in which there is a relation of historico-spatial contiguity between narrator and characters, that is, the narrator offers a purportedly true "report" of contemporary actions in which he or she plays no role. (The first person in such cases is typically limited to the beginning and the end of the narrative.) This type of heterodiegetic narrator is inseparable from the pseudofactual truth claims examined in Chapter 1. By contrast, the I of "authorial" heterodiegetic narrators (e.g., of Homer, Fielding, or Balzac) is situated on a different plane with respect to the characters – either ontologically different (in the case of fiction) or temporally different (in the case of real-world historical subject matter). Such first persons do not figure in my tallies.

7 One complication is narrations organized around a courtship. These are theoretically single-action narrations (having the resolution that is marriage), but at the same time typically take up much biographical time. I have tagged these as memoirs.

8 Figures for brute population, as always, are estimates based on the number in the sample.

9 One additional observation about Figure 6.5: Prior to the 1660s and after the 1780s, there are of course completely distinct forms in the picture – the *roman* described in Chapter 4, and then a new type of third-person novel that is not a *nouvelle*, and that I will describe in Chapter 8.

10 Indeed, in many respects, this is a modest rise with respect to the situation in the late seventeenth century – hardly enough to indicate a qualitatively new interest in the novel. The latter hypothesis is further undermined if one takes the length of novels into account. For further graphs of the production, including remarks on the estimations involved, see Chapter 9.

11 On the novel as "bourgeois," see Nicholas Hudson, "Social Rank, 'The Rise of the Novel' and Whig Histories of Eighteenth-Century Fiction," *Eighteenth-Century Fiction* 17.4 (2005): 564–98. Though his specific object of study is England, Hudson's skepticism should hold for similar French narratives. Of course, the "rising bourgeoisie" has been deployed with almost comical compulsion to explain phenomena of vastly different historical moments. See J. H. Hexter, "The Myth of the Middle Class in Tudor England (1950)," in

Reappraisals in History: New Views on History and Society in Early Modern Europe (Chicago: University of Chicago Press, 1979), 71–117, cited by George Boulukos, "The Secret History of the Rise of the Novel: The Novel and the Middle Class in English Studies," *The Eighteenth Century* 52.3–4 (2011): 377.

12 Georges May, *Le Dilemme du roman au XVIIIe siècle* (Paris: PUF, 1963), 33 and 165.

13 A question, which I obviously cannot resolve here due to the chronological limits of my data, is whether later first-person novels can in any way be said to evolve from the memoir novel, from modifications to the episode and observer narrations that are expanding in the early nineteenth century, or from some other artifact entirely. At any rate, given some of the discontinuities emphasized here, it seems dubious to maintain that the first-person structure "demonstrates considerable stability and even an inability to undergo radical transformations" (Michał Głowiński, "On the First-Person Novel," *New Literary History* 9.1 [1977]: 110–11).

14 Blaise Pascal, *Les Pensées*, ed. Michel Le Guern (Paris: Gallimard, 1977), 351.

15 Thomas Pavel, *La Pensée du roman* (Paris: Gallimard, 2003), 112. See also Henri Coulet, who discounts first-person narration before the memoir novel: "the personal novel had no success in France during the baroque period; the classical period, by contrast, knew a number of different kinds of first-person novels: memoirs, letters, travel narratives" (*Le Roman jusqu'à la Révolution*, 9th ed. [Paris: Armand Colin, 2000], 200).

16 René Démoris, *Le Roman à la première personne: Du Classicisme aux Lumières* (Geneva: Droz, 2002), 6.

17 See Filippo D'Angelo, "« Je suis le héros véritable de mon roman » : L'Équivocité de la voix narrative dans les récits à la première personne au XVIIe siècle," *Les Cahiers du Centre de Recherches Historiques* 33 (2004), http://ccrh.revues.org/237.

18 Jean Rousset, *Narcisse romancier: Essai sur la première personne dans le roman* (Paris: Corti, 1973), 50. Laurence Plazenet has confirmed this "eviction" in her limited corpus (*L'Ébahissement et la délectation: Réception comparée et poétiques du roman grec en France et en Angleterre aux XVIe et XVIIe siècles* [Paris: Champion, 1997], 608–17).

19 I will lay aside the complication that many first-person frame narratives and observer narratives contain little sustained first-person narration; for the purposes of this heuristic, they will nonetheless count as "100 percent" first-person novels.

20 Antoine Prévost, *Lettres de Mentor à un jeune seigneur*, in *Oeuvres choisies*, vol. 34 (Paris, 1784), 54. Though one might easily suppose that the effusiveness associated with first-person confessions in the (sentimental) Enlightenment was absent from Heliodorian insets, in fact the exchange of personal stories was already marked by much sobbing and tears. In other words, over both centuries, the first person was considered a prime vehicle for affect.

Chapter 7

1. Bernard Bray and Isabelle Landy-Houillon, eds., *Lettres portugaises; Lettres d'une Péruvienne; et autres romans d'amour par lettres* (Paris: Flammarion, 1983).
2. The continuous history that Bray and Landy-Houillon imply is commonplace in accounts of the French epistolary novel and the novel more generally, where the letter novel's "appearance" in the second half of the seventeenth century is seen – often along with the memoir novel – as the sign of a literary sea change. See, for example, François Jost, "L'Évolution d'un genre: Le Roman épistolaire dans les lettres occidentales," in *Essais de littérature comparée II: Europaeana* (Urbana: University of Illinois Press, 1968), 89–179; Jean Rousset, *Narcisse romancier: Essai sur la première personne dans le roman* (Paris: Corti, 1973), 48–66; and Arnaldo Pizzorusso, *La Poetica del romanzo in Francia (1660-1685)* (Rome: Sciascia, 1962), 79–98. In his capacious study of European epistolarity, Thomas O. Beebee writes that "the publication of epistolary fiction in Europe, in both absolute numbers and relative literary and cultural importance, … peaks in the late seventeenth, the eighteenth, and late twentieth centuries" (*Epistolary Fiction in Europe, 1500-1850* [Cambridge: Cambridge University Press, 1999], 199). He offers no quantitative evidence of profusion before 1750, which does not in fact exist, as we will see – and as was acknowledged and graphed some time ago by Laurent Versini (*Laclos et la tradition: Essai sur les sources et la technique des* Liaisons dangereuses [Paris: Klincksieck, 1968], 251–52). English epistolary novels before this date were even scarcer (see Chapter 9).
3. Unlike in the rest of the chapters of this book, data on the epistolary novel is based not on samples but on a census of the production undertaken for all years up to and including 1810. (When graphs in this chapter include figures for the 1810s and 1820s, data for those decades is taken from the main sample.) The principal motivation for this choice is the very low production of epistolary works over many decades of the study – a production whose tracking would have been spotty using samples alone. Note that although the census of epistolary works is – I hope – close to exhaustive, the production percentages are still estimates since I do not have a corresponding census of *all* novels. As such, I have used the production estimates generated by the sample. For further information, see the Annex.
4. There is, however, a scholarly tradition of viewing letter manuals as incubators of the epistolary novel. The classic study is Bernard Bray, *L'Art de la lettre amoureuse, 1550-1700: Des manuels aux romans* (The Hague: Mouton, 1967); see also Yves Giraud, "La Dimension romanesque dans quelques ensembles épistolaires du XVIe siècle," in *Le Roman français*

au XVIe siècle, ou le renouveau d'un genre dans le contexte européen, ed. Michèle Clément and Pascale Mounier (Strasbourg: Presses Universitaires de Strasbourg, 2005), 81–92, and Magda Campanini, "Fragmentation et unité du récit: Autour de la genèse du roman par lettres," in *La Partie et le tout: La Composition du roman, de l'âge baroque au tournant des Lumières*, ed. Marc Escola et al. (Leuven: Peeters, 2011), 337–47. On the early modern culture of epistolarity writ large, see Beebee, *Epistolary Fiction in Europe, 1500–1850*; and Gary Schneider, *The Culture of Epistolarity: Vernacular Letters and Letter Writing in Early Modern England, 1500–1700* (Newark: University of Delaware Press, 2005).

5 I have also not inventoried here novels that take the form of *one* letter. This is the case for what I have called "report novels" in Chapter 6; a number of memoir novels are also addressed to the recipient who has purportedly requested them.

6 These are works that, in other words, I do not consider novels at all. I am not alone in this estimation: such books are typically excluded from the bibliographies I've used to establish the main data sample and appear only in Yves Giraud and Anne-Marie Clin-Lalande, *Nouvelle Bibliographie du roman épistolaire en France, des origines à 1842*, 2nd ed. (Freiburg: Editions Universitaires, 1995). (The latter includes many different sorts of works that contain letters and not just epistolary novels per se.) Their inclusion on the primary vertical axis of Figure 7.1, though motivated, is also logically flawed since these nonnovels are being tabulated as a subset of the population of novels.

7 This problem has been recognized by scholars working on the English domain where a "tradition" of the epistolary novel is harder to identify. Thus, Robert Adams Day remarks how difficult it is to make early works "add up" to what we recognize as the epistolary novel: "It would be pleasing to be able to suggest that the elements of the epistolary novel, scattered and waiting in various literary genres, gradually assembled themselves after the Restoration, and that once they had cohered in a recognizable form the form steadily developed and matured until it was ready, so to speak, for Richardson. This was not what happened. The examples of letter fiction discussed in the preceding pages form a very large and heterogeneous collection; a statement that neatly labels some few of them may be absurd when applied to the others. To look for development or evolution in this era of English fiction shows an ill-considered rage for order" (Robert Adams Day, *Told in Letters: Epistolary Fiction before Richardson* [Ann Arbor: University of Michigan Press, 1966], 192). This recognition, however, does not keep Day from titling his chapter "The Epistolary Novel Arrives."

8 Since epistolary novels are more reliably real-world than novels in general, its market share of this category is marginally greater than if all novels were taken into account.

9 Though it includes Type 2 observational novels, Figure 7.3 does not retain other novels from the permissive count (those having letters in an annex and those under 10,000 words). A very small number of novels – including the canonical *Lettres persanes* and *Lettres d'une Péruvienne* – mix an observational structure with a love plot. These are here tabulated with Type 1 observational novels since I consider that to be their structural principle.

10 The graphing of nonnovels (Type 2) along with novels (Type 1) explains why the cumulative bars can exceed the line for total epistolary novels. (See note 6.) As in Figure 7.1, though this choice is illustrative, it is also illogical.

11 In Chapter 10, I will say more about the proximity of these kinds of early epistolary novels to collections of published letters.

12 See David J. Denby, *Sentimental Narrative and the Social Order in France, 1760–1820* (Cambridge: Cambridge University Press, 1994), and Margaret Cohen, *The Sentimental Education of the Novel* (Princeton: Princeton University Press, 1999). I'd emphasize that sentimental novels can fulfill that promise or not: many end badly, usually due to the intransigence of parents (e.g., *Julie*) or the machinations of libertines (*Les Liaisons dangereuses*).

13 Erotic epistolary works – a very minor presence – are left out of both categories.

14 Perry Anderson, "*Persian Letters* (Montesquieu, 1721)," in *The Novel*, ed. Franco Moretti, vol. 2 (Princeton: Princeton University Press, 2006), 161–72, quotes at 162 and 163.

15 Novels of first two types do frequently contain the odd letter from another sender – often these occur at the opening or close of the book or are included as "attachments" by the main correspondent(s). This fact does not, however, make for much classificatory ambiguity: these two sorts of epistolary novels, even with admixtures of supplementary correspondents, do not have anything like a "polyphonic" structure.

16 We could, moreover, question how truly "polyphonic" these particular novels are: my qualitative impression is that Montesquieu is an outlier in the *types* of voices he orchestrates (eunuchs, harem women, Muslim clerics). Most others simply feature a number of men of similar status exchanging observations.

17 Although production estimates of epistolary novels are broadly and indeed strikingly similar whether derived from the sample or the census (see the Annex), the sample shows marginally higher levels in the 1780s (29 vs. 24 percent).

18 For an extensive analysis of the novel's international reception, see Thomas O. Beebee, *Clarissa on the Continent: Translation and Seduction* (University Park: Pennsylvania State University Press, 1990).

19 Indeed, Richardson was noted at the time for the variety of his correspondents. See Elie-Catherine Fréron, "Lettre I: Suite de l'Histoire de Grandisson [sic]," *L'Année littéraire* 5.4 (1758): 20; and especially Denis Diderot, "Eloge de Richardson" (1762), in *Contes et romans*, ed. Michel Delon (Paris: Gallimard, 2004), 899.

20 Understandably, scholars working on the English epistolary novel before Richardson have tried to portray him as merely building on a tradition (Jost, "L'Évolution d'un genre," 123; Day, *Told in Letters*). We will see in Chapter 9, however, that the history of the epistolary novel in England is every bit as discontinuous as it is in France.

21 For the purposes of Figure 7.9, letter novels admitted as fabrications but held to be "based on" real events are considered not to have documenticity, that is, do not figure in the gray line representing pseudofactual and indeterminate works.

Chapter 8

1 As always in the present study, when measuring truth posture, I limit the novel corpus to nobody novels: given the understandings laid out in Chapter 1, only nobody novels can be tagged for pseudofactuality or invention.

2 Figure 8.3 includes medians only for decades in which subsamples contain at least five works.

3 Nicholas Dames, "The Chapter in Western Literature," *The Oxford Research Encyclopedia of Literature*, 2016, http://literature.oxfordre.com/view/10.1093/acrefore/9780190201098.001.0001/acrefore-9780190201098-e-15.

4 Epistolary novels come with their own specific segmentation – letters, obviously – and thus are not included in Figure 8.4.

5 See Ugo Dionne, "Livres et chapitres: La Division du roman des Lumières," in *Le Second Triomphe du roman du XVIIIe siècle*, ed. Philip Stewart and Michel Delon (Oxford: Voltaire Foundation, 2009), 138. A novel is counted as having parts only when the text itself is headed by "Nth Part," as opposed to title–page indications of the volume number. Novels containing both parts and chapters are categorized here as chapter novels, so the use of the term part in the latter half of this span is more frequent than Figure 8.4 suggests.

6 On the prestige of segmentation into books, see Dionne, "Livres et chapitres," 142–43.

7 Indeed, in the rest of this chapter, the term nonsegmented novels will refer both to novels without any segmentation and to those segmented only by parts. (The category is not synonymous with that of nonchapterized novels on account of rarer forms of segmentation – books but also *chants*, *matinées*, *soirées*, and so on.)

8 That of the *nouvelle*, examined in Chapter 5, is the most obvious, and we'll see that the English novel's history contains some abrupt movements. Chapter 10 argues that these more sudden changes may not be especially surprising when seen through a "technological" lens.

9 Literary historians have noted a persistent association between chapters and comic novels, at least before the explosion of chapterized novels in the latter half of the eighteenth century. See Vivienne Mylne, "Chapters as a Structural Device in the *Conte* and the Novel," *Studies on Voltaire and the Eighteenth Century* 192 (1980): 1332–33, and Dionne, "Livres et chapitres." My tagging does not isolate comic novels per se, but to the extent that alternate-world novels are often facetious or satiric, and at the same time more consistently chapterized, the association between the comic novel and the chapter – at least before the 1760s – is supported by this data.

10 Occasionally, a novel presents a mixture of descriptive and oblique titles. In these (rare) cases, I make a judgment about which type seems dominant. Although my rudimentary distinctions between title categories are sufficient for present purposes, more elaborate typologies are certainly possible (see Ugo Dionne, *La Voie aux chapitres: Poétique de la disposition romanesque* [Paris: Seuil, 2008], 375–409).

11 As an aside, first-person novels chapterize on roughly the same timetable as third-person novels – a possible curiosity, if one reasons that the first-person novel's documenticity should be expected to eschew a presentation redolent of the world of print. See Figure E8.2.

12 The very small number of chapterized novels before 1760 – indeed, the samples show none for three decades – causes distracting variation in the decadal median figures from that span. Figure 8.7 suppresses those figures for clarity.

13 Along these lines, one might hypothesize that the impressive dimensions of the epistolary novel may in part derive from its built-in segmentation.

14 Eighteenth-century novelists essentially have to reengineer this substructure since they had long abandoned the segmentation that underwrote the long novels of the seventeenth century – the part-and-book structure familiar from novels such as *L'Astrée* (d'Urfé, 1607–1627) and *Artamène* (Scudéry, 1648–1653).

15 Dionne, "Livres et chapitres," 150. Conversely, "the nonsegmented text remains a mark of nonfictionality" (142).

16 Scene descriptions are sensory (typically visual, occasionally aural), whereas location descriptions are schematic, as in, "Paris is a large city; its most fashionable neighborhood can be found in the west and features wide streets and abundant parks." Though the distinction may appear impressionistic, in practice, tagging the two was unproblematic.

17 Scenes themselves can be variably dilated. Some get right to the action – "The church bell had just tolled two o'clock when a shabbily dressed man stepped into the path of an oncoming carriage" – while many first spend considerable time on physical description, typically using imperfect verbs.

18 A small subset of works offers no clear demarcation between biographical presentation (usually ancestry and birth) and the start of the action proper; these are classified as action openings (the action being quite simply birth). Much more typically, character "backstory" is marked as such by

signposting the transition to the main narrative: "It was around this time that…."

19 In Figure E8.4, the length of passages is estimated to the nearest quarter-page. Starting in the 1790s, the word length of character descriptions no longer tracks the percentage of the novel the latter occupy: thus, the absolute and relative lengths of the descriptions see different trends. This, however, is simply an effect of the lengthening of the third-person novel itself.

20 As an aside, scene setting is obviously not limited to openings: it is a technique that can be found throughout the text of novels – at the start of new chapters, for instance, though not exclusively. A good working assumption is that scene openings can furnish a proxy measurement for the spread of scene use tout court.

21 Limit cases certainly exist: for example, a novel consisting of a set of first-person retrospective, autobiographical letters to a confidant might be considered a memoir or an epistolary novel.

22 In no cases is there double counting: the "new"-novel scenarios are devised so as to exclude novels picked up by any of the "old"-novel scenarios.

23 Since for this particular calculation it is impossible to average the criteria of all the "old" scenarios, I have selected the most moderate one and (for consistency) substituted the same word-limit used for in the *nouvelle* scenario (56,000 words or less). In addition to this word limit, they contain portraits or start directly on the action and feature neither scenes nor chapters.

24 These are novels that comprise 49,000 words or less, that contain portraits or start directly on the action, and that do not feature scenes or chapters.

25 This was in fact my own hypothesis (Nicholas Paige, "Examples, Samples, Signs: An Artifactual View of Fictionality in the French Novel, 1681–1830," *New Literary History* 48.3 [2017]: 526).

26 It is possible that the scene-setting criterion, so important to the description of "new" novels, is part and parcel of what Andrew Piper has posited as the chief characteristic of (modern) fictionality: "The particular nature of fictional discourse since the nineteenth century has been its profound investment not simply with the world around us, but with our perceptual encounter with that world, the way 'making sense' is explicitly related with the physical senses" (*Enumerations: Data and Literary Study* [Chicago: University of Chicago Press, 2018], 99).

Chapter 9

1 In many other respects, the two countries do not present substantial differences for the purposes of this chapter. While France has a more important practice of alternate-world novels (Figure E9.1), the market percentages of somebody novels in the two countries are similar (Figure E9.2).

2 "In works from the 1720s, Eliza Haywood sometimes used both 'secret history' and 'novel' on the same title page – as in *The British Recluse: or, the Secret History of Cleomira, Suppos'd Dead. A Novel* (1722) – suggesting that what Haywood meant by 'novel' at this time was shaped by the French word *nouvelle*, meaning a piece of news or gossip, possibly about a real person" (Rachel Carnell, "Eliza Haywood and the Narratological Tropes of Secret History," *Journal for Early Modern Cultural Studies* 14.4 [2014]: 104).

3 Hence, the English situation would seem to support the hypothesis that the large proportion of "indeterminate" French novels in the early decades of the nineteenth century is not a sign that the French were at the time still hesitant to admit invention but rather a simple effect of the country's lack of a convenient generic subtitle – a lack imputable to the history of the term *roman*.

4 One might well wonder if the discrepancy in the production of such novels in England and France is not explained by the bibliographies used to generate the samples: perhaps the canonical importance of *Robinson Crusoe* incited bibliographers to include texts that French bibliographers would not have been tempted to think of as novels. My impression is that while France does have its share of travel narratives, they were almost uniformly produced by known travelers and that only in England is there a vogue for travel narratives featuring nobodies. (All of the travel narratives in the English sample before 1741 are nobody novels. Note that this does not mean that narratives by bona fide travelers were not published, only that I've excluded such texts because I judged them insufficiently plotted to qualify as novels.)

5 For the number of correspondents in English epistolary novels, see Figure E9.3. The use of the polyphonic form in England roughly follows that of France – though France sees more substantial polyphony before 1761 than England, where the only such example (in the sample) is *Clarissa*. (One work from the 1700s technically contains three correspondents but is in no way polyphonic.)

6 Accordingly, perhaps, the percentage of English epistolary novels featuring the word "letters" somewhere in their titles is considerably lower than in France: just over 40 percent in the 1760s, it declines to zero by the 1800s. Comparable figures for France are 72 and 20 percent; see Figure E9.5.

7 These are the satirical novels – often *à clef* novels, such as Manley's *Queen Zarah* (1705) – that Catherine Gallagher takes for representative of the (English) novel *tout court* before what she thinks is its subsequent takeover by nobodies; see *Nobody's Story: The Vanishing Acts of Women Writers in the Marketplace, 1670–1820* (Berkeley: University of California Press, 1994). In fact, they are quite identifiable and historically circumscribed artifacts, existing alongside these decades' (already) more numerous nobody novels.

8 Scenarios for the "old" novel (roughly from most restrictive to least): under the 20th percentile for length (29,550 words), no scenes, no chapters; under the 20th percentile, no scenes, no chapters, or chapters with descriptive titles only; under 33rd percentile (45,150 words), no scenes, no

chapters; under 33rd percentile, no scenes, no chapters, or chapters with descriptive titles only; under 66th percentile (85,600 words), no scenes, no chapters; under 50th percentile (63,620 words), no chapters or chapters with descriptive titles only. Scenarios for the "new" novel: over the 80th percentile for length (102,900 words), scenes and chapters having oblique titles or no titles; over the 66th percentile, scenes and chapters having oblique titles or no titles; over the 33rd percentile, scenes and chapters having oblique titles or no titles; over the 80th percentile, scenes or any chapters; over the 66th percentile, scenes or any chapters; and over the 50th percentile, scenes or any chapters.

9 Catherine Gallagher, "The Rise of Fictionality," in *The Novel*, ed. Franco Moretti, vol. 1 (Princeton: Princeton University Press, 2006), 344. Gallagher points to Defoe's *Robinson Crusoe* (1719) and Fielding's *Joseph Andrews* (1742) as bracketing the transformation in England while proposing that the already fictional *Princesse de Clèves* (Lafayette, 1678) and (for her) still pseudofactual *La Religieuse* (Diderot, pub. 1796) suggest a different unfolding in France. At other moments in her study, Gallagher speaks more vaguely of a "midcentury" phenomenon (336, 341, 343).

10 Gallagher, "Rise of Fictionality," 345.

11 For an extension of Gallagher's thesis, see Mary Poovey, *Genres of the Credit Economy: Mediating Value in Eighteenth- and Nineteenth-Century Britain* (Chicago: University of Chicago Press, 2008).

12 Some uptake of the metaphor among scholars of the French novel is detectable; see, for example, Camille Esmein-Sarrazin, *L'Essor du roman: Discours théorique et constitution d'un genre littéraire au XVIIe siècle* (Paris: Champion, 2008).

13 Estimates are based on the assumption that production in unsampled years is the same as in years sampled (see the Annex for one exception).

14 See Leah Orr, *Novel Ventures: Fiction and Print Culture in England, 1690–1730* (Charlottesville: University of Virginia Press, 2017), 185. Note that discrepancies in production numbers between the present study and Orr's are to be expected since Orr does not practice the exclusions that I do, notably for length and insufficient plot.

15 Robert D. Hume, "Authorship, Publication, Reception (2): 1660–1750," in *The Oxford History of the Novel in English*, ed. Thomas Keymer, vol. 1 (Oxford: Oxford University Press, 2017), 28.

16 "In the journalism of Ned Ward and Abel Boyer, the histories of John Oldmixon and Gilbert Burnet, the poems of Thomas Tickell and Ambrose Philips, the narratives of Charles Gildon and Delariviere Manley, and the jumbled mix of writings that come from everywhere and everyone, one can see which way the wind was blowing, but the time was not yet" (J. Paul Hunter, *Before Novels: The Cultural Contexts of Eighteenth-Century English Fiction* [New York: Norton, 1990], 16). For the argument that the

Defoe–Richardson–Fielding trinity is itself the prenovelistic magma out of which the novel proper condenses (but only around the time of Scott), see Homer Obed Brown, *Institutions of the Novel: From Defoe to Scott* (Philadelphia: University of Pennsylvania Press, 1997).

17 The consensus crystalized around the centrality of love: celebrated definitions include Pierre-Daniel Huet's "Fictions of Love-Adventures, writ in Prose with Art, for the Delight and Instruction of the Readers" (*A Treatise on Romances and Their Original* [London: R. Battersby, 1672], 3) and Samuel Johnson's "small tale, generally of love" ("Novel," in *A Dictionary of the English Language* [London: W. Strahan, 1755]). (I have not relied on that definition to assemble the corpus examined in this study, based instead on criteria elaborated in the Annex.) On the early years of the eighteenth century as being a low point for international novel production, see also J. A. Downie, "Mary Davys's 'Probable Feign'd Stories' and Critical Shibboleths about 'The Rise of the Novel,'" *Eighteenth-Century Fiction* 12.2–3 (2000): 309–26.

Chapter 10

1 The phrase is that of Georges May, who refers to the years 1728–1736 specifically (*Le Dilemme du roman au XVIIIe siècle* [Paris: PUF, 1963], 75). See also Anne Rivara, ed., *Le Roman des années trente: La Génération de Prévost et de Marivaux* (Saint-Étienne: Publications de l'Université de Saint-Étienne, 1998).

2 At least in France, the novel's takeover of literary production writ large may date only to the last quarter of the nineteenth century; see Alain Vaillant, *La Crise de la littérature: Romantisme et modernité* (Grenoble: ELLUG, 2005), 96. Meanwhile, in England, the novel's spectacular success in the second half of the eighteenth century may in good part simply track with rising population and literacy; see Michael F. Suarez, "Towards a Bibliometric Analysis of the Surviving Record, 1701–1800," in *The Cambridge History of the Book in Britain*, ed. Michael F. Suarez and Michael L. Turner, vol. 5 (Cambridge: Cambridge University Press, 2009), 44. In a slightly different measurement, attempts to assess the fortunes of nineteenth-century English literature (and not just the novel) within the print market as a whole suggest no progress (and even regression) over the years 1801–1870; see Simon Eliot, "*Patterns and Trends* and the *NSTC*: Some Initial Observations. Part 2," *Publishing History* 43 (1998): 77.

3 See Claire Goldstein, *Vaux and Versailles: The Appropriations, Erasures, and Accidents That Made Modern France* (Philadelphia: University of Pennsylvania Press, 2008), esp. 148. For an account of Heliodorian insetting

insisting on its aristocratic ideology, see Thomas DiPiero, *Dangerous Truths and Criminal Passions: The Evolution of the French Novel, 1569–1791* (Stanford: Stanford University Press, 1992), 113–21. A recent study that attempts to give ideological motivation to much later inset narratives highlights the just-so nature of such critical associations: "the preponderance of scenes of storytelling [in eighteenth-century sentimental novels] is a symptom of the historical tension between an emerging finance economy dependent upon the circulation of money as capital and a social morality that censures as avaricious the pure pursuit of profit…. Just as capitalism is built on the logic of infinite circulation …, sentimental fiction is grounded in an infinite accumulation of stories where … stories can generate more stories" (Katherine Binhammer, "The Story within the Story of Sentimental Fiction," *Narrative* 25.1 [2017]: 46 and 61). To be clear, my complaint is not that such devices *cannot* transmit ideological content but rather that such content – which at any rate is contingent – does not bring them into being.

4 "An exemplary bourgeois, the writer of the *I*-novel, under the guise of the narrator, offers up to the public his or her own experience" (René Démoris, *Le Roman à la première personne: Du Classicisme aux Lumières* [Geneva: Droz, 2002], 459); "The European novel started a new career with the rise of the *I* as a perceived vehicle for a fresh kind of truth, which was both ostensibly objective in its narrative apparatus and subjective in its access to the inner reaches of the soul" (Philip Stewart, "The Rise of *I*," *Eighteenth-Century Fiction* 13.2 [2001]: 181); "Interiority's enchantment is made immediately perceptible thanks to first-person narration" (Thomas Pavel, *La Pensée du roman* [Paris: Gallimard, 2003], 145); "Richardson's narrative mode … may also be regarded as a reflection of a much larger change in outlook – the transition from the objective, social, and public orientation of the classical world to the subjective, individualist, and private orientation of the life and literature of the last two hundred years" (Ian P. Watt, *The Rise of the Novel: Studies in Defoe, Richardson, and Fielding* [Berkeley: University of California Press, 1957], 176).

5 Stephen Best and Sharon Marcus, "Surface Reading: An Introduction," *Representations* 108.1 (2009): 1–21; Rita Felski, *The Limits of Critique* (Chicago: University of Chicago Press, 2015).

6 Thus, the violence done to traditional literary history by quantitative evidence lies not simply in its sidelining of close reading. Its revelation of change as continuous also disables the recourse to periodization and common critical investments in narratives of rupture; see Ted Underwood, *Why Literary Periods Mattered: Historical Contrast and the Prestige of English Studies* (Stanford: Stanford University Press, 2013), 157–75. This point should not be conflated with the familiar observation that periods are "constructs" that need to be deployed self-consciously or productively

re-constructed; see David Blackbourn, "'The Horologe of Time': Periodization in History," *PMLA* 127.2 (2012): 301–7.

7   Norbert Elias, *The Court Society* (New York: Pantheon, 1983).

8   The typological thrust of most narratology is well known. For Gérard Genette, the narratorial choices are largely arbitrary: "The writer, I imagine, one day wants to write this narrative in the first person and that narrative in the third, perhaps for no reason all, just for a change" (*Narrative Discourse Revisited,* trans. Jane E. Lewin [Ithaca: Cornell University Press, 1988], 113). Genette is contesting the critical gesture that links formal choices to specific artistic effect, as when Dorrit Cohn explains the narrative transformation of the initial first-person version of *The Castle* thus: "Kafka would surely not have bothered to make this laborious change in midstream, had he thought that it was of no consequence to his fiction. More or less consciously he must have known that there were advantages to the K. over the I…" (*Transparent Minds: Narrative Modes for Presenting Consciousness in Fiction* [Princeton: Princeton University Press, 1978], 171).

9   Cohn, *Transparent Minds.*

10 Gustave Flaubert, *Madame Bovary: Provincial Ways*, trans. Lydia Davis (New York: Viking Press, 2010), xi.

11 Pierre Boulle, *Planet of the Apes*, trans. Xan Fielding (London, 2001), 136–39. Thus, regarding turn-of-the-eighteenth-century novels in England, James Raven writes, "Much of this fiction slavishly followed model forms of lionized writers, predictably and with restrained ambition" ("Britain, 1750–1830," in *The Novel*, ed. Franco Moretti, vol. 1 [Princeton: Princeton University Press, 2006], 454).

12 Wiebe E. Bijker, *Of Bicycles, Bakelites, and Bulbs: Toward a Theory of Sociotechnical Change* (Cambridge: MIT Press, 1995), 75. This is something of a commonplace in revisionist scholarship on technology and innovation. Some other formulations: "Progress in technology must be determined within very restricted technological, temporal, and cultural boundaries and according to a narrowly specified goal" (George Basalla, *The Evolution of Technology* [Cambridge: Cambridge University Press, 1988], 216); "Studies of choice of technology show that alternatives often exist, and the fact that one technology supercedes another is not even evidence of superiority at all, since other factors are involved" (David Edgerton, "From Innovation to Use: Ten Eclectic Theses on the Historiography of Technology," *History and Technology* 16. 2 [1999]: 123).

13 One might instructively compare these patters to those observable in historical linguistics, which typically take the form of an S-curve – that is, slow increases in use, followed by a speedy takeover in the general population, followed by a slow conquest of remaining holdouts. See, for example, R. A. Blythe and William Croft, "S-curves and the Mechanisms of Propagation in Language Change," *Language*, 88.2 (2012): 269–304.

S-curves are broadly observed in the adoption of innovations; see Everett M. Rogers, *The Diffusion of Innovations*, 4th ed. (New York: The Free Press, 1995).

14 Richard Dawkins, *The Selfish Gene* (New York: Oxford University Press, 1989).
15 W. Brian Arthur, *The Nature of Technology: What It Is and How It Evolves* (London: Allen Lane/Penguin, 2009), 39–41.
16 Arthur, *Nature of Technology*, 54–56. Arthur also mentions "trading conventions, tort laws, and trade unions" (105). In a similar vein, Rogers distinguishes between "hardware" and "software" aspects of technologies: "We often think of technology mainly in hardware terms ... But in other cases, a technology may be almost entirely composed of information; examples are a political philosophy like Marxism, a religious idea, a news event, a rumor, assembly-line production, and quality circles" (*Diffusion of Innovations*, 13).
17 See, however, Tony E. Jackson, *The Novel as Technology: Writing and Narrative in British Fiction* (Baltimore: Johns Hopkins University Press, 2009). Jackson's sense of "technology" is derived from the work of Walter Ong and the single structuring opposition of speech and writing. As such, it has little to do with technological evolution in the sense used by Arthur, STS researchers, or myself.
18 Arthur, *Nature of Technology*, 17.
19 Arthur, *Nature of Technology*, 130. Basalla speaks of "the stream of made things" to express metaphorically the observation that artifacts are always modeled on preexisting artifacts (*Evolution of Technology*, 209).
20 Marc Fumaroli, "Les Mémoires du XVIIe siècle au carrefour des genres en prose" (1972), in *La Diplomatie de l'esprit: De Montaigne à La Fontaine* (Paris: Gallimard, 1998), 183–215; Marie-Thérèse Hipp, *Mythes et réalités: Enquête sur le roman et les mémoires, 1660–1700* (Paris: Klincksieck, 1976).
21 Arthur, *Nature of Technology*, 73.
22 "The history of technology is ... the chronicle of epochs – whole periods – that are defined by how their purposes are put together" (Arthur, *Nature of Technology*, 75). Lest this return us to the idea of coherent periods, however, it is important to remember that redomaining is inevitably a slow, continuous process, as I will point out later.
23 Arthur, *Nature of Technology*, 145 and 191–202. Similarly, on the disconnect between innovation and use, see David Edgerton, *The Shock of the Old: Technology and Global History since 1900* (Chicago: University of Chicago Press, 2007).
24 "In this rudimentary literature of manuals, thanks to the magic of the first and second person, a fictive sentimental reality appears, characters take form, the presence of time makes itself felt: all the essential points of a novel" (Bernard Bray, *L'Art de la lettre amoureuse, 1550–1700: Des manuels aux romans* [The Hague: Mouton, 1967], 22).

25 See Arthur, *Nature of Technology*, 150–51.

26 Although I am offering nothing more than interpretation of the evidence – and not, certainly, "proof" – compare this technological explanation of the form's belated development to a more traditional one, advanced by a pioneering authority on the epistolary novel. Laurent Versini reasons that the form does not develop before 1730 because "like the psychological novel [*le roman d'analyse*] in general, it is hurt by the retreat of sociability [*honnêteté*] and affectivity under the Regency, which discredits the heart in favor of the senses" (Laurent Versini, *Le Roman épistolaire* [Paris: PUF, 1979], 65). Less far from the technological hypothesis – though still distinct – is the cognitive explanation offered by Monika Fludernik, "Naturalizing the Unnatural: A View from Blending Theory," *Journal of Literary Semantics* 31.9 (2010): 17.

27 The representation of proximity is rough, since Gallic and Frankish subjects are included under "other," even though temporally they are closer to the present than Classical subjects.

28 See Brian Richardson, *Unnatural Voices: Extreme Narration in Modern and Contemporary Fiction* (Columbus: Ohio State University Press, 2006).

29 "The 'discourse of fiction' is in fact a patchwork … of heterogeneous elements borrowed for the most part from reality" (Gérard Genette, *Fiction and Diction* [Ithaca: Cornell University Press, 1993], 49). For Genette's defense of the idea that all narration must come from first-person narrators, see *Narrative Discourse Revisited*, 96–108.

30 A recent recap of the narrator debate can be found in Brian Boyd, "Does Austen Need Narrators? Does Anyone?," *New Literary History* 48.2 (2017): 285–308. Notable pioneers in no-narrator theory include Käte Hamburger, *The Logic of Literature* (Bloomington: Indiana University Press, 1973), and Ann Banfield, *Unspeakable Sentences: Narration and Representation in the Language of Fiction* (Boston: Routledge and Kegan and Paul, 1982). The idea can be arguably traced back to the calls of Henry James and his disciple Percy Lubbock to eliminate any detectable narratorial presence: "the art of fiction does not begin until the novelist thinks of his story as a matter to be shown, to be so exhibited that it will tell itself" (Percy Lubbock, *The Craft of Fiction* [New York: Scribner's, 1921], 62).

31 This proposal is congruent with Monika Fludernik's diachronic narratology; see especially "How Natural Is 'Unnatural Narratology'; Or, What Is Unnatural about Unnatural Narratology?," *Narrative* 20.3 (2012): 357–70.

32 Early third-person narrators are conspicuously voluble, along the lines of the traditional *histor*: "The commentary, often labeled 'intrusive,' is simply the *histor* going about his business.… The *histor* has an ancient and natural affinity with his narrative predecessor, the inspired bard of Homeric epic" (Robert Scholes, Robert Kellogg, and James Phelan, *The Nature*

of Narrative: Fortieth Anniversary Edition [1966; repr., Oxford: Oxford University Press, 2006], 266). In this respect, the "new" third-person novel retains – for a time – some features of earlier third-person forms.

33 "When one encounters a novel written according to all the rules of the past historical tense and third-person narration, one has not, of course, encountered 'literature'" (Maurice Blanchot, *Le Livre à venir* [Paris: Gallimard, 1959], 254, cited in Jonathan Culler, "Toward a Theory of Non-Genre Literature," in *Theory of the Novel: A Historical Approach*, ed. Michael McKeon (Baltimore: Johns Hopkins University Press, 2000), 56). But the point precisely would be that this narration and its "rules" are considerably odder than they are given credit for being. In addition to Fludernik, "How Natural Is 'Unnatural Narratology'?," see Elaine Freedgood, "Ghostly Reference," *Representations* 125.1 (2014): 40–53. On the history of investments in and against omniscience, see Rachel Sagner Buurma, "Critical Histories of Omniscience," in *New Directions in the History of the Novel*, ed. Patrick Parrinder, Andrew Nash, and Nicola Wilson (Basingstoke: Palgrave Macmillan, 2014), 121–33.

34 Vaillant, *La Crise de la littérature*, has made the argument that the nineteenth century, as the first real media age, fundamentally upended earlier models of literary communication, founded on the model of direct listening and discursive exchange. Such an interpretation fits well with an artifact such as the "new" third-person novel, though it must be remembered that this artifact's invention is clearly datable to decades Vaillant would presumably see as preceding the media age enabled by cheap print. This type of problem plagues accounts that seek to identify a given historical conjuncture as necessarily productive of given artifacts.

35 This is the chauvinism that implies the cognitive immaturity of periods and cultures said to be "without" fiction; see Julie Orlemanski, "Who Has Fiction? Modernity, Fictionality, and the Middle Ages," *New Literary History* 50.2 (2019): 145–70.

36 While the weight of classical heritage certainly loomed large in Europe, I suspect that the heritage itself was merely a variant on a tendency, visible at a more anthropological scale, to prize the truth over lies. On Horace's dictum and its relation to literary debates on the marvelous, see Paige, *Before Fiction: The Ancien Régime of the Novel* (Philadelphia: University of Pennsylvania Press, 2011), 174–79.

37 The profusion of fiction artifacts of the last two centuries is evident to Françoise Lavocat, for example, who at the same time holds fiction to be something close to a universal; Lavocat points to types of modern metalepsis (e.g., characters conscious of being characters in a novel) as an indication that while the desire to cross the border between fiction and reality "is not proper to our own time, it characterizes it in a particular fashion" (*Fait et fiction: Pour une frontière* [Paris: Seuil, 2016], 522).

38 The theoretical "legitimation" of the French novel is typically located later than these decades. For Camille Esmein-Sarrazin, for example, it essentially dates from the 1660s (*L'Essor du roman: Discours théorique et constitution d'un genre littéraire au XVIIe siècle* [Paris: Champion, 2008]). Despite the dearth of *theoretical* discourse on the novel in the 1630s and 1640s, the genre's new prestige is nonetheless evident in the material form of the novels themselves – often luxuriously produced octavos, proudly signed by their (usually noble) authors and dedicated to people of high nobility. The link between this new prestige and that of the contemporary theater remains to be explored; on the latter, see Déborah Blocker, *Instituer un "art": Politiques du théâtre dans la France du premier XVIIe siècle* (Paris: Champion, 2009).

39 "In Agathon's *Antheus*, for instance, the names as well as the events are made up, and yet it gives just as much pleasure [as tragedies that use real names]" (*Poetics* 9 [1451b], in D. A. Russell and M. Winterbottom, eds., *Ancient Literary Criticism: The Principal Texts in New Translations* (Oxford: Oxford University Press, 1972), 103).

40 "The fate of a prince or a hero counts for more than the fate of an ordinary person. This idea was a basic assumption of European literature at least until the second half of the eighteenth century: even those who opposed it still moved in its shadow" (Guido Mazzoni, *Theory of the Novel*, trans. Zakiya Hanafi [Cambridge, MA: Harvard University Press, 2017], 107). I owe the phrase "artistic food chain" to Lynn Festa, *Fiction without Humanity: Person, Animal, Thing in Early Enlightenment Literature and Culture* (Philadelphia: University of Pennsylvania Press, 2019), 49.

41 "Needs themselves derive more from technology itself than directly from human wants; they derive in the main from limitations encountered and problems engendered by technologies themselves. These must be solved by still further technologies, so that with technology need follows solution as much as solution follows need" (Arthur, *Nature of Technology*, 204).

42 Arthur, *Nature of Technology*, 110 and 132. Arthur covers the example of the jet engine specifically on 111–16. His account of standard engineering occurs on 90–95. The phonograph, for which Edison imagined many uses that turned out to be relatively useless, has often been invoked as giving the lie to the proverb "Necessity is the mother of invention"; see Basalla, *Evolution of Technology*, 139–42.

43 Françoise-Albine Benoist, "Préface," in *Agathe et Isidore* (Paris: Durand, 1768). The reference to the "historian," here, means simply a third-person narrator. Many contemporary references to "epic" in the context of the novel are also a way of designating third-person narration, as when Fanny Burney describes Camilla as being written in *"the prose Epic style"* (Fanny Burney, *Camilla, or A Picture of Youth*, ed. Edward A. Bloom and Lillian D. Bloom [Oxford: Oxford University Press, 1983], xiv).

44 "This sort of novel usually succeeds because the characters themselves give an account of their current state; this makes [the reader] better feel their passions than all the explanations someone else could offer" (Charles de Secondat, baron de Montesquieu, "Quelques réflexions sur les *Lettres persanes*," in *Oeuvres*, vol. 3 [London: Nourse, 1757], 3). "The nature of familiar letters, written, as it were, to the *moment*, while the heart is agitated by hopes and fears, on events undecided, must plead an excuse for the bulk of a collection of this kind. Mere facts and characters might be comprised in a much smaller compass: but would they be equally interesting?" (Samuel Richardson, *The History of Sir Charles Grandison in a Series of Letters*, 4th ed. [London: Rivington, 1762], 1:vi).

45 See, for example, Sushil Bikhchandani, David Hirshleifer, and Ivo Welch, "A Theory of Fads, Fashion, Custom, and Cultural Change as Informational Cascades," *Journal of Political Economy* 100.5 (1992): 992–1026.

46 The classic study of women's dress is Jane Richardson and A. L. Kroeber, "Three Centuries of Women's Dress Fashions: A Quantitative Analysis," *Anthropological Records* 5.2 (1940): 111–53. (Roland Barthes, whose interest in fashion systems culminated in *Système de la mode* [Paris: Seuil, 1967], cited Richardson and Kroeber at the outset of his early study, "Histoire et sociologie du vêtement," *Annales E.S.C.* 12.3 (1957): 433n1.) Other prominent literature on fashion cycles includes (on automobile design and men's facial hair specifically) William H. Reynolds, "Cars and Clothing: Understanding Fashion Trends," *Journal of Marketing* 32.3 (1968): 44–49; and Dwight E. Robinson, "Style Changes: Cyclical, Inexorable, and Foreseeable," *Harvard Business Review* 53.6 (1975): 121–31. See also George B. Sproles, "Analyzing Fashion Life Cycles: Principles and Perspectives," *Journal of Marketing* 45.4 (1981): 116–24.

47 "At least since the Renaissance, if not earlier, fads and fashions have served as one of the means by which selection is made from among competing novel technological possibilities" (Basalla, *Evolution of Technology*, 185). A "novelty imperative" in artistic creation has been postulated by Colin Martindale, *The Clockwork Muse: The Predictability of Artistic Change* (New York: Basic Books, 1990). Martindale makes use of the "Wundt curve" as it was applied to the cultural domain by D. E. Berlyne, *Aesthetics and Psychobiology* (New York: Appleton-Century-Crofts, 1971).

48 Stan J. Liebowitz and Stephen E. Margolis, *The Economics of Qwerty: Papers by Stan Liebowitz and Stephen Margolis*, ed. Peter Lewin (New York: MacMillan/NYU Press, 2002); Scott E. Page, "Path Dependence," *Quarterly Journal of Political Science* 1.1 (2006): 87–115.

49 Theories of fashion cycles and those of technological evolution have not been systematically brought together; but in this vein, see Eric Abrahamson, "The Iron Cage: Ugly, Uncool, and Unfashionable," *Organization Studies* 32.5 (2011): 615–29. One possible explanation for the

different behavior of fads and fashions may be the nature of the networks that propagate them; see Eric Abrahamson and Lori Rosenkopf, "Social Network Effects on the Extent of Innovation Diffusion: A Computer Simulation," *Organization Science* 8.3 (1997): 289–309.

50 The black box metaphor was much used by early STS, which very much wanted to open it. See Trevor J. Pinch and Wiebe E. Bijker, "The Social Construction of Facts and Artifacts: Or How the Sociology of Science and the Sociology of Technology Might Benefit Each Other," in *The Social Construction of Technological Systems: New Directions in the Sociology and History of Technology*, ed. Wiebe E. Bijker, Thomas P. Hughes, and Trevor J. Pinch (Cambridge, MA: MIT Press, 1987), 15.

51 Steven Shapin and Simon Schaffer, *Leviathan and the Air-Pump: Hobbes, Boyle, and the Experimental Life* (Princeton: Princeton University Press, 1985); W. Bernard Carlson, *Innovation as a Social Process: Elihu Thomson and the Rise of General Electric, 1870–1900* (Cambridge: Cambridge University Press, 1991). Rogers notes that "software" (nonphysical) technologies have proved resistant to researchers: "Such idea-only innovations have seldom been studied by diffusion scholars, perhaps because their spread is relatively difficulty to trace" (*Diffusion of Innovations*, 13).

52 On the poverty of STS explanations, see Langdon Winner, "Upon Opening the Black Box and Finding It Empty: Social Constructivism and the Philosophy of Technology," *Science, Technology, and Human Values* 18.3 (1993): 362–78. Winner's skepticism is explained by a firm commitment in his own work to technological determinism. Yet the STS pioneer Bruno Latour has also noted the predictability of the conclusions reached: "As she studies segments from Law, Science, The Economy or Religion, [the anthropologist of networks] begins to feel that she is saying almost the same thing about all of them: namely that they are 'composed in a heterogeneous fashion of unexpected elements revealed by the investigation'" (*An Inquiry into Modes of Existence: An Anthropology of the Moderns*, trans. Catherine Porter [Cambridge, MA: Harvard University Press, 2013], 35). Arthur, for his part, concedes the standard points of STS while maintaining that they still fail to explain how new technologies arise (*Nature of Technology*, 108).

53 Fredric Jameson, *The Political Unconscious: Narrative as a Socially Symbolic Act* (Ithaca: Cornell University Press, 1981), ix. Best and Marcus have called *The Political Unconscious* "the book that popularized symptomatic reading among U.S. literary critics" ("Surface Reading," 3). If Latour is to be believed, however, the divining of deep causes is hardly the province of literary critics alone: "When sociologists of the social pronounce the words 'society,' 'power,' 'structure,' and 'context,' they often jump straight ahead to connect vast arrays of life and history, to mobilize gigantic forces,

to detect dramatic patterns emerging out of confusing interactions, to see everywhere in the cases at hand yet more examples of well-known types, to reveal behind the scenes some dark powers pulling the strings" (Bruno Latour, *Reassembling the Social: An Introduction to Actor-Network-Theory* [Oxford: Oxford University Press, 2005], 22).

54 For a critique of the "widespread belief that the made world could not be otherwise than it is," see Basalla, *Evolution of Technology*, 189–206, quote at 190. See also Arthur, *Nature of Technology*: "If we were to 'replay' history a second time, we might end up with some similar collection of phenomena captured and therefore with roughly similar technologies. But the sequence and timing of their appearance would be different. And as a consequence, economic and social history would be different" (186).

55 Watt, *Rise of the Novel*, 196.

56 Watt's discussion of journalism can be found in *Rise of the Novel*, 50–52. For a more detailed account in the Wattian vein, with the standard yes-but-still commitment to English exceptionalism, see J. Paul Hunter, *Before Novels: The Cultural Contexts of Eighteenth-Century English Fiction* (New York: Norton, 1990), 167–94, esp. 172: "Journalism was beginning to 'rise' elsewhere too, but it became culturally significant more slowly and tentatively, and nowhere else does there seem to be, so early, the obsession with contemporaneity that characterizes English culture at the beginning of the eighteenth century." It goes without saying that I am not the first to complain that "Watt's attempt to pinpoint the rise of the novel depends on a loosely argued notion of causality and result" (DiPiero, *Dangerous Truths and Criminal Passions*, 9). J. A. Downie has written recently that "It should come as little surprise that, after begging the question so flagrantly, Watt proceeded to discover to his own satisfaction that social and cultural conditions were indeed propitious for the emergence of the novel in England in the early eighteenth century" ("Prologue," in *The Oxford Handbook of the Eighteenth-Century Novel*, ed. J. A. Downie [Oxford: Oxford University Press, 2016], xxi).

57 See Roger Chartier, "Leisure and Sociability: Reading Aloud in Early Modern Europe," in *Urban Life in the Renaissance*, ed. Susan Zimmerman and Ronald F. E. Weissman (Newark: University of Delaware Press, 1989), 103–20.

58 For some details on the French case, see Nicholas Paige, "The Storyteller and the Book: Scenes of Narrative Production in the Early French Novel," *MLQ* 67.2 (2006): 141–70.

59 Basalla defines a skeuomorph as "an element of design or structure that serves little or no purpose in the artifact fashioned from the new material but was essential to the object made from the original material" (*Evolution of Technology*, 107). The proposition that written and printed narratives are skeuomorphic with respect to their oral forebears shouldn't be taken to imply that one cannot detect subtle narrative changes as literature leaves

the oral mode; see Monika Fludernik, *Towards a "Natural" Narratology* (London: Routledge, 1996), esp. 92–128.
60 In my opinion, psychobiological constants probably make it unlikely that narrative technologies will *ever* become completely separated from the oral model of interpersonal communication.
61 Michel Foucault, *The Order of Things: An Archeology of the Human Sciences* (New York: Pantheon, 1971), 387.

Annex

1 For France, the bibliographies are: Frank Greiner, *Fictions narratives en prose de l'âge baroque: répertoire analytique I (1585–1610)* (Paris: Champion, 2007), and *Fictions narratives en prose de l'âge baroque: répertoire analytique II (1611–1623)* (Paris: Classiques Garnier, 2014); Maurice Lever, *La Fiction narrative en prose au dix-septième siècle* (Paris: CNRS, 1976); Silas Paul Jones, *A List of French Prose Fiction from 1700–1750, with a Brief Introduction* (New York: H.W. Wilson, 1939); Angus Martin, Vivienne Mylne, and Richard Frautschi, *Bibliographie du genre romanesque français, 1751–1800* (London: Mansell, 1977). Martin, Mylne, and Frautschi were working on a replacement for Jones's work but it has not appeared. Preliminary indications are that Jones may have missed up to 10 percent of titles, though many of these overlooked volumes are translations (and thus of no interest to the present study); see Richard Frautschi and Angus Martin, "French Prose Fiction Published between 1701 and 1750: A New Profile of Production," *Eighteenth-Century Fiction* 14.3–4 (2002): 737. I limited myself to correcting errors of date in Jones's listings where possible.

Bibliographies of the English novel used are: William H. McBurney, *A Check List of English Prose Fiction, 1700–1739* (Cambridge: Harvard University Press, 1960); Jerry C. Beasley, *A Check List of Prose Fiction Published in England, 1740–1749* (Charlottesville: University Press of Virginia, 1972); James Raven, *British Fiction, 1750–1770: A Chronological Check-List of Prose Fiction Printed in Britain and Ireland* (Newark: University of Delaware Press, 1987); and Peter Garside, James Raven, and Rainer Schöwerling, *The English Novel 1770–1829: A Bibliographical Survey of Prose Fiction Published in the British Isles*, 2 vols. (London: Oxford University Press, 2000).

2 *La Bibliographie de la France, ou journal général de l'imprimerie et de la librairie* (Paris: Pillet, 1814–1971). The *Bibliographie* started publication in 1814, and I have used it alone for the samples for the 1810s and 1820s. Its predecessor, the *Journal général de la littérature de France*, dates from 1798, but it is far from comprehensive. Thus, my corpus for the 1800s also

incorporates items listed in André Mongland, *La France révolutionnaire et impériale: Annales de bibliographie méthodique et description des livres imprimés*, 10 vols. (Paris: Imprimerie nationale, 1931). These sources have limitations. First, they normally incorporate novels published only within France. Second, their listings for a given year include some items with imprints from the previous year. To simplify sampling, I have inventoried the works listed in the needed years of these bibliographies, even if they bear an imprint from the year before.

3 Imagining the revision of available pre-1740 bibliographies of the English novel according to a "uniform editorial policy," Robert D. Hume writes that "the cloudiness of the boundaries and dizzying changes in the production of various types of fiction" would make the result "somewhat arbitrary": "what 'counts' is essentially what one chooses to classify as fiction," he concludes ("Authorship, Publication, Reception (2): 1660–1750," in *The Oxford History of the Novel in English*, ed. Thomas Keymer, vol. 1 (Oxford: Oxford University Press, 2017), 27). Such pessimism strikes me as unwarranted, though understandable coming from a scholar of the English tradition: as I've argued in Chapter 9, it's the paucity of early English novels that tempts bibliographers to include works that French researchers would not look at twice.

4 For the years 1601–1623, the detailed plot summaries in Greiner, *Fictions narratives en prose*, allowed me to tag novels that would otherwise have been recorded as unavailable.

5 Again, there is some discrepancy between French and English bibliographies, with the latter of necessity throwing an extremely wide net when it comes to pre-1740 material.

6 This is the passage where Aristotle distinguishes between the historian, who "tells us what did happen," and the poet, who tells us "the sort of thing that would happen, that is, what can happen in a strictly probably or necessary sequence" (*Poetics* 1451b, in D. A. Russell and M. Winterbottom, eds., *Ancient Literary Criticism: The Principal Texts in New Translations* [Oxford: Oxford University Press, 1972], 102.) Although this passage is often evoked as an ancestor of our fictional–nonfictional distinction, in fact Aristotle appears to be interested in plotting alone, not in the creation of something like a fictional world. For this argument, see Nicholas Paige, *Before Fiction: The Ancien Régime of the Novel* (Philadelphia: University of Pennsylvania Press, 2011), 5–9.

7 In my view, plotting (as opposed to mere sequencing) is probably inseparable from a presentation of character that Monika Fludernik calls "experiential" (*Towards a "Natural" Narratology* (London: Routledge, 1996), esp. 20–26). Readers wishing an illustration of the difference between sufficiently and insufficiently plotted works – works that on the surface of things might seem identical – could consult two travel narratives

from 1726, *The Voyages and Adventures of Captain Robert Boyle* (attrib. Chetwood) and *The Four Years Voyages* [sic] *of Captain George Roberts* (attrib. Defoe). Only the first of the pair is retained for the sample.

8 Notwithstanding the more philosophical issues involved, it bears pointing out that opening the bounds of the inquiry to more consensually historical narratives would in the end have little effect on my conclusions. This is because these now excluded narratives would chiefly fall under the rubric of Aristotelian contemporary novels, whereas the types of novels at the heart of this study are Aristotelian historical novels and nobody novels. In an enlarged population, the latter would represent a smaller slice of the pie, but their historical distribution would not change. At any rate, and whatever the inevitable inconsistencies in execution, the advantage of submitting a large span of two national traditions to the same criterion should be clear.

9 Notably, Lever, *La fiction narrative en prose*, itemizes as "novels" every story appearing in the periodical *Le Mercure galant*.

10 "Organic" factors relating to the way this study was built out over time explain observable asymmetries in the clusters.

11 Margin of error (confidence interval), corresponding to a confidence level of 90 percent, is calculated based on estimated population size (see below).

12 Data for all samples may be found in Nicholas Paige, "Datasets and electronic graphs for *Technologies of the Novel*," Zenodo, http://doi.org/10.5281/zenodo.3939066.

13 Yves Giraud and Anne-Marie Clin-Lalande, *Nouvelle Bibliographie du roman épistolaire en France, des origines à 1842*, 2nd ed. (Freiburg: Editions Universitaires, 1995). Though their title indicates a focus on epistolary novels per se, in fact they inventory a wide variety of books involving letters in any way (manuals, third-person novels that include letters, and so on). I would note that though Giraud and Clin-Lanlande proceed to break out this variety into categories (including that of the epistolary novel as traditionally understood), it appears that at least some titles may have been tagged without being inspected.

14 Although all available novels were sampled, unavailable items made the census incomplete.

15 See http://artfl-project.uchicago.edu/ARTFL.html. The ARTFL database includes only a small percentage of the novels sampled here.

Bibliography

Abrahamson, Eric. "The Iron Cage: Ugly, Uncool, and Unfashionable." *Organization Studies* 32.5 (2011): 615–29.

Abrahamson, Eric, and Lori Rosenkopf. "Social Network Effects on the Extent of Innovation Diffusion: A Computer Simulation." *Organization Science* 8.3 (1997): 289–309.

Anderson, Perry. "*Persian Letters* (Montesquieu, 1721)." In *The Novel*, edited by Franco Moretti, 2:161–72. Princeton: Princeton University Press, 2006.

Aneau, Barthélemy. *Alector ou le coq, histoire fabuleuse*. Edited by Marie-Madeleine Fontaine. 2 vols. Geneva: Droz, 1996.

Aravamudan, Srinivas. *Enlightenment Orientalism: Resisting the Rise of the Novel*. Chicago: University of Chicago Press, 2012.

Argens, Jean-Baptiste de Boyer, marquis d'. *Lectures amusantes, ou les délassements de l'esprit, avec un discours sur les nouvelles*, 2 vols. The Hague: Adrien Moetjens, 1739, 1:52–3.

Aristotle, *Poetics,* in Russell, D. A., and M. Winterbottom, eds. *Ancient Literary Criticism: The Principal Texts in New Translations*, 90–132. Oxford: Oxford University Press, 1972.

Armstrong, Nancy. *Desire and Domestic Fiction: A Political History of the Novel*. New York: Oxford University Press, 1987.

Arthur, W. Brian. *The Nature of Technology: What It Is and How It Evolves*. London: Allen Lane/Penguin, 2009.

Arzoumanov, Anna. *Pour lire les clefs de l'Ancien Régime: Anatomie d'un protocole interprétatif*. Paris: Classiques Garnier, 2013.

Banfield, Ann. *Unspeakable Sentences: Narration and Representation in the Language of Fiction*. Boston: Routledge and Kegan and Paul, 1982.

Barthes, Roland. "Histoire et sociologie du vêtement." *Annales E.S.C.* 12.3 (1957): 430–41.

  Système de la mode. Paris: Seuil, 1967.

Basalla, George. *The Evolution of Technology*. Cambridge: Cambridge University Press, 1988.

Baumgartner, Emmanuèle. *De l'histoire de Troie au livre du Graal: Le Temps, le récit (XIIe-XIIIe siècles)*. Orléans: Paradigme, 1994.

Beasley, Jerry C. *A Check List of Prose Fiction Published in England, 1740-1749*. Charlottesville: University Press of Virginia, 1972.

Beebee, Thomas O. *Clarissa on the Continent: Translation and Seduction*. University Park: Pennsylvania State University Press, 1990.

Epistolary Fiction in Europe, 1500–1850. Cambridge: Cambridge University Press, 1999.

Bender, John B. *Imagining the Penitentiary: Fiction and the Architecture of Mind in Eighteenth-Century England*. Chicago: University of Chicago Press, 1987.

Benoist, Françoise-Albine. *Agathe et Isidore*. Paris: Durand, 1768.

Berlyne, D. E. *Aesthetics and Psychobiology*. New York: Appleton-Century-Crofts, 1971.

Best, Stephen, and Sharon Marcus. "Surface Reading: An Introduction." *Representations* 108.1 (2009): 1–21.

Bibliographie de la France, ou journal général de l'imprimerie et de la librairie. Paris: Pillet, 1814–1971.

Bijker, Wiebe E. *Of Bicycles, Bakelites, and Bulbs: Toward a Theory of Sociotechnical Change*. Cambridge: MIT Press, 1995.

Bikhchandani, Sushil, David Hirshleifer, and Ivo Welch. "A Theory of Fads, Fashion, Custom, and Cultural Change as Informational Cascades." *Journal of Political Economy* 100.5 (1992): 992–1026.

Binhammer, Katherine. "The Story within the Story of Sentimental Fiction." *Narrative* 25.1 (2017): 45–64.

Black, Scott. *Without the Novel: Romance and the History of Prose Fiction* (Charlottesville: University of Virginia Press, 2019).

Blackbourn, David. "'The Horologe of Time': Periodization in History." *PMLA* 127.2 (2012): 301–7.

Blanchot, Maurice. *Le Livre à venir*. Paris: Gallimard, 1959.

Blocker, Déborah. *Instituer un "art": Politiques du théâtre dans la France du premier XVIIe siècle*. Paris: Champion, 2009.

Blythe, Richard A., and William Croft. "S-Curves and the Mechanisms of Propagation in Language Change." *Language* 88.2 (2012): 269–304.

Boileau, Nicolas. *Art poétique*. Edited by Sylvain Menant. Paris: GF Flammarion, 1969.

Boulle, Pierre. *Planet of the Apes*. Translated by Xan Fielding. London: Penguin, 2001.

Boulukos, George. "The Secret History of the Rise of the Novel: The Novel and the Middle Class in English Studies." *The Eighteenth Century* 52.3–4 (2011): 361–82.

Boyd, Brian. "Does Austen Need Narrators? Does Anyone?" *New Literary History* 48.2 (2017): 285–308.

Bray, Bernard. *L'Art de la lettre amoureuse, 1550–1700: Des manuels aux romans*. The Hague: Mouton, 1967.

Bray, Bernard, and Isabelle Landy-Houillon, eds. *Lettres portugaises; Lettres d'une Péruvienne; et autres romans d'amour par lettres*. Paris: Flammarion, 1983.

Brewer, David A. "Counting, Resonance, and Form: A Speculative Manifesto (with Notes)." *Eighteenth-Century Fiction* 24.2 (2012): 161–70.

Broadwell, Peter M., David Mimno, and Timothy R. Tangherlini. "The Tell-Tale Hat: Surfacing the Uncertainty in Folklore Classification." *CA: Journal of Cultural Analytics*, February 8, 2017. https://culturalanalytics.org/article/11069.

Brown, Homer Obed. *Institutions of the Novel: From Defoe to Scott*. Philadelphia: University of Pennsylvania Press, 1997.

Burney, Fanny. *Camilla, or a Picture of Youth*. Edited by Edward A. Bloom and Lillian D. Bloom. Oxford: Oxford University Press, 1983.

Buurma, Rachel Sagner. "Critical Histories of Omniscience." In *New Directions in the History of the Novel*, edited by Patrick Parrinder, Andrew Nash, and Nicola Wilson, 121–33. Basingstoke: Palgrave Macmillan, 2014.

Campanini, Magda. "Fragmentation et unité du récit: Autour de la genèse du roman par lettres." In *La Partie et le tout: La Composition du roman, de l'âge baroque au tournant des Lumières*, edited by Marc Escola, Jan Herman, Lucia Omacini, Paul Pelckmans, and Jean-Paul Sermain, 337–47. Leuven: Peeters, 2011.

Campbell, John. "La 'Modernité' de *La Princesse de Clèves*." *Seventeenth-Century French Studies* 29 (2007): 63–72.

Carlson, W. Bernard. *Innovation as a Social Process: Elihu Thomson and the Rise of General Electric, 1870–1900*. Cambridge: Cambridge University Press, 1991.

Carnell, Rachel. "Eliza Haywood and the Narratological Tropes of Secret History." *Journal for Early Modern Cultural Studies* 14.4 (2014): 101–21.

Cave, Terence. *Pré-Histoires: Textes troublés au seuil de la modernité*. Geneva: Droz, 1999.

Chartier, Roger. "Leisure and Sociability: Reading Aloud in Early Modern Europe." In *Urban Life in the Renaissance*, edited by Susan Zimmerman and Ronald F. E. Weissman, 103–20. Newark: University of Delaware Press, 1989.

Chrétien de Troyes. *Arthurian Romances*. Translated by D. D. R. Owen. London: Dent, 1987.

Cicero. *Rhetorica ad Herennium*. Translated by Henry Caplan. Cambridge: Harvard University Press, 1954.

Cohen, Margaret. *The Sentimental Education of the Novel*. Princeton: Princeton University Press, 1999.

Cohn, Dorrit. *Transparent Minds: Narrative Modes for Presenting Consciousness in Fiction*. Princeton: Princeton University Press, 1978.

The Distinction of Fiction. Baltimore: Johns Hopkins University Press, 1999.

Congreve, William. *Incognita, or Love and Duty Reconcil'd*. New York: Houghton Mifflin Company, 1922.

Coulet, Henri. *Le Roman jusqu'à la Révolution*. 9th ed. Paris: Armand Colin, 2000.

Culler, Jonathan. "Toward a Theory of Non-Genre Literature." In *Theory of the Novel: A Historical Approach*, edited by Michael McKeon, 51–6. Baltimore: Johns Hopkins University Press, 2000.

Dames, Nicholas. "The Chapter in Western Literature." In *The Oxford Research Encyclopedia of Literature*, 2016. http://literature.oxfordre.com/view/10.1093/acrefore/9780190201098.001.0001/acrefore-9780190201098-e-15.

D'Angelo, Filippo. "'Je suis le héros véritable de mon roman': L'Équivocité de la voix narrative dans les récits à la première personne au XVIIe siècle." *Les Cahiers du Centre de Recherches Historiques* 33 (2004). http://ccrh.revues.org/237.

Dawkins, Richard. *The Selfish Gene*. New York: Oxford University Press, 1989.

Day, Geoffrey. *From Fiction to the Novel*. London: Routledge and Kegan Paul, 1987.

Day, Robert Adams. *Told in Letters: Epistolary Fiction before Richardson*. Ann Arbor: University of Michigan Press, 1966.

De Gusta, Michael. "The Real Death of the Music Industry." *Business Insider*, February 18, 2011. www.businessinsider.com/these-charts-explain-the-real-death-of-the-music-industry-2011-2?IR=T.

DeJean, Joan. *Tender Geographies: Women and the Origins of the Novel in France*. New York: Columbia University Press, 1991.

Démoris, René. "Aux origines de l'homme historique: Le Croisement, au XVIIe siècle, du roman et de l'histoire (nouvelles et pseudo-mémoires)." In *Le Roman historique (XVIIe-XXe siècles): Actes de Marseille*, edited by Pierre Ronzeaud, 23–41. Paris: Papers on French Seventeenth-Century Literature, 1983.

Le Roman à la première personne: Du Classicisme aux Lumières. Geneva: Droz, 2002.

Denby, David J. *Sentimental Narrative and the Social Order in France, 1760–1820*. Cambridge: Cambridge University Press, 1994.

Diderot, Denis. *Contes et romans*. Edited by Michel Delon. Paris: Gallimard, 2004.

Dionne, Ugo. *La Voie aux chapitres: Poétique de la disposition romanesque*. Paris: Seuil, 2008.

"Livres et chapitres: La Division du roman des Lumières." In *Le Second Triomphe du roman du XVIIIe siècle*, edited by Philip Stewart and Michel Delon, 127–50. Oxford: Voltaire Foundation, 2009.

DiPiero, Thomas. *Dangerous Truths and Criminal Passions: The Evolution of the French Novel, 1569–1791*. Stanford: Stanford University Press, 1992.

Doody, Margaret Anne. *The True Story of the Novel*. New Brunswick: Rutgers University Press, 1996.

Downie, J. A. "Mary Davys's 'Probable Feign'd Stories' and Critical Shibboleths about 'The Rise of the Novel'." *Eighteenth-Century Fiction* 12.2–3 (2000): 309–26.

"Prologue." In *The Oxford Handbook of the Eighteenth-Century Novel*, edited by J. A. Downie, xvii–xxiv. Oxford: Oxford University Press, 2016.

Dubuis, Roger. "Le mot 'nouvelle' au Moyen Age: De la nébuleuse au terme générique." In *La Nouvelle: Définitions, transformations*, edited by Bernard Alluin and François Suard, 13–26. Lille: Presses Universitaires de Lille, 1990.

Du Plaisir. *Sentiments sur les lettres et sur l'histoire, avec des scrupules sur le style* [1683], in *Poétiques du roman: Scudéry, Huet, Du Plaisir et autres textes théoriques et critiques du XVIIe siècle sur le genre romanesque*, edited by Camille Esmein, 709–814. Paris: Champion, 2004.

Edgerton, David. "From Innovation to Use: Ten Eclectic Theses on the Historiography of Technology." *History and Technology* 16.2 (1999): 111–36.

The Shock of the Old: Technology and Global History since 1900. Chicago: University of Chicago Press, 2007.

Elias, Norbert. *The Court Society*. New York: Pantheon, 1983.
Eliot, Simon. "Patterns and Trends and the NSTC: Some Initial Observations. Part 2." *Publishing History* 43 (1998): 71–115.
English, James F., and Ted Underwood. "Shifting Scales: Between Literature and Social Science." *MLQ* 77.3 (2016): 277–95.
Esmein, Camille. "Le Tournant historique comme construction théorique: L'Exemple du 'tournant' de 1660 dans l'histoire du roman." *Fabula LHT* 0(2005). https://www.fabula.org/lht/0/esmein.html.
Esmein, Camille, ed. *Poétiques du roman: Scudéry, Huet, Du Plaisir et autres textes théoriques et critiques du XVIIe siècle sur le genre romanesque*. Paris: Champion, 2004.
Esmein-Sarrazin, Camille. *L'Essor du roman: Discours théorique et constitution d'un genre littéraire au XVIIe siècle*. Paris: Champion, 2008.
Felski, Rita. *The Limits of Critique*. Chicago: University of Chicago Press, 2015.
Festa, Lynn. *Fiction without Humanity: Person, Animal, Thing in Early Enlightenment Literature and Culture*. Philadelphia: University of Pennsylvania Press, 2019.
Flaubert, Gustave. *Madame Bovary: Provincial Ways*. Translated by Lydia Davis. New York: Viking Press, 2010.
Fludernik, Monika. *Towards a "Natural" Narratology*. London: Routledge, 1996.
   "Naturalizing the Unnatural: A View from Blending Theory." *Journal of Literary Semantics* 31.9 (2010): 1–21.
   "How Natural Is 'Unnatural Narratology'; Or, What Is Unnatural about Unnatural Narratology?" *Narrative* 20.3 (2012): 357–70.
   "The Fiction of the Rise of Fictionality." *Poetics Today* 39.1 (2018): 67–92.
Foley, Barbara. *Telling the Truth: The Theory and Practice of Documentary Fiction*. Ithaca: Cornell University Press, 1986.
Forcione, Alban K. *Cervantes' Christian Romance: A Study of Persiles y Sigismunda*. Princeton: Princeton University Press, 1972.
Foucault, Michel. *The Order of Things: An Archeology of the Human Sciences*. New York: Pantheon, 1971.
Frautschi, Richard, and Angus Martin. "French Prose Fiction Published between 1701 and 1750: A New Profile of Production." *Eighteenth-Century Fiction* 14.3–4 (2002): 735–56.
Freedgood, Elaine. "Ghostly Reference." *Representations* 125.1 (2014): 40–53.
Fréron, Elie-Catherine. "Lettre I: Suite de l'Histoire de Grandisson [sic]." *L'Année littéraire* 5.4 (1758): 3–20.
Freud, Sigmund. "The Uncanny." In *Collected Papers*, edited by Ernest Jones, 368–407. New York: Basic Books, 1959.
Frye, Northrop. *Anatomy of Criticism: Four Essays*. Princeton: Princeton University Press, 1957.
Fumaroli, Marc. "Jacques Amyot and the Clerical Polemic against the Chivalric Novel." *Renaissance Quarterly* 38.1 (1985): 22–40.

"Les Mémoires du XVIIe siècle au carrefour des genres en prose" (1972). In *La Diplomatie de l'esprit: De Montaigne à La Fontaine*, 183–215. Paris: Gallimard, 1998.

Gallagher, Catherine. *Nobody's Story: The Vanishing Acts of Women Writers in the Marketplace, 1670–1820*. Berkeley: University of California Press, 1994.

"The Rise of Fictionality." In *The Novel*, edited by Franco Moretti, 1:336–63. Princeton: Princeton University Press, 2006.

Garside, Peter, James Raven, and Rainer Schöwerling. *The English Novel 1770–1829: A Bibliographical Survey of Prose Fiction Published in the British Isles*. 2 vols. London: Oxford University Press, 2000.

Genette, Gérard. *Narrative Discourse: An Essay in Method. 1972*. Reprint, Ithaca: Cornell University Press, 1980.

Narrative Discourse Revisited. Translated by Jane E. Lewin. Ithaca: Cornell University Press, 1988.

Fiction and Diction. Ithaca: Cornell University Press, 1993.

Gevrey, Françoise. *L'Illusion et ses procédés: De "La Princesse de Clèves" aux "Illustres Françaises."* Paris: J. Corti, 1988.

Giraud, Yves. "La Dimension romanesque dans quelques ensembles épistolaires du XVIe siècle." In *Le Roman français au XVIe siècle, ou le renouveau d'un genre dans le contexte européen*, edited by Michèle Clément and Pascale Mounier, 81–92. Strasbourg: Presses Universitaires de Strasbourg, 2005.

Giraud, Yves, and Anne-Marie Clin-Lalande. *Nouvelle Bibliographie du roman épistolaire en France, des origines à 1842*. 2nd ed. Fribourg: Editions Universitaires, 1995.

Gittes, Katharine S. *Framing the Canterbury Tales: Chaucer and the Medieval Frame Narrative Tradition*. New York: Greenwood Press, 1991.

Głowiński, Michał. "On the First-Person Novel." *New Literary History* 9.1 (1977): 103–14.

Godenne, René. "L'Association 'nouvelle-petit roman' entre 1650 et 1750." *CAIEF* 18 (1966): 67–78.

Goldstein, Claire. *Vaux and Versailles: The Appropriations, Erasures, and Accidents that Made Modern France*. Philadelphia: University of Pennsylvania Press, 2008.

Grafton, Anthony. *Forgers and Critics: Creativity and Duplicity in Western Scholarship*. Princeton: Princeton University Press, 1990.

Grande, Nathalie. "Du long au court: Réduction de la longueur et invention des formes narratives, l'exemple de Madeleine de Scudéry." *Dix-septième siècle* 215 (2002): 263–71.

Greiner, Frank. *Fictions narratives en prose de l'âge baroque: Répertoire analytique I (1585–1610)*. Paris: Champion, 2007.

Fictions narratives en prose de l'âge baroque: Répertoire analytique II (1611–1623). Paris: Classiques Garnier, 2014.

Hamburger, Käte. *The Logic of Literature*. Bloomington: Indiana University Press, 1973.

Hamilton, A.C. "Sidney's Arcadia as Prose Fiction: Its Relation to Its Sources." *English Literary Renaissance* 2.1 (1962): 29–60.

Heliodorus of Emesa. *L'Histoire aethiopique*. Edited by Laurence Plazenet. Translated by Jacques Amyot. Paris: Champion, 2008.

Herman, Jan, Mladen Kozul, and Nathalie Kremer. *Le Roman véritable: Stratégies préfacielles au XVIIIe siècle*. Oxford: Voltaire Foundation, 2008.

Hexter, J. H. "The Myth of the Middle Class in Tudor England (1950)." In *Reappraisals in History: New Views on History and Society in Early Modern Europe*, 71–117. Chicago: University of Chicago Press, 1979.

Hipp, Marie-Thérèse. *Mythes et réalités: Enquête sur le roman et les mémoires, 1660–1700*. Paris: Klincksieck, 1976.

Hudson, Nicholas. "Social Rank, 'The Rise of the Novel' and Whig Histories of Eighteenth-Century Fiction." *Eighteenth-Century Fiction* 17.4 (2005): 564–98.

Huet, Pierre-Daniel. *A Treatise on Romances and Their Original*. London: R. Battersby, 1672.

Hume, Robert D. "Authorship, Publication, Reception (2): 1660–1750." In *The Oxford History of the Novel in English*, edited by Thomas Keymer, 1:26–46. Oxford: Oxford University Press, 2017.

Hunter, J. Paul. *Before Novels: The Cultural Contexts of Eighteenth-Century English Fiction*. New York: Norton, 1990.

Jackson, Tony E. *The Novel as Technology: Writing and Narrative in British Fiction*. Baltimore: Johns Hopkins University Press, 2009.

Jameson, Fredric. *The Political Unconscious: Narrative as a Socially Symbolic Act*. Ithaca: Cornell University Press, 1981.

Postmodernism, or, the Cultural Logic of Late Capitalism. Durham: Duke University Press, 1991.

Jockers, Matthew L. *Macroanalysis: Digital Methods and Literary History*. Urbana: University of Illinois Press, 2013.

Johnson, Samuel. "Novel." In *A Dictionary of the English Language*, 1374. London: W. Strahan, 1755.

Jones, Silas Paul. *A List of French Prose Fiction from 1700–1750, with a Brief Introduction*. New York: H.W. Wilson, 1939.

Jost, François. "L'Évolution d'un genre: Le Roman épistolaire dans les lettres occidentales." In *Essais de littérature comparée II: Europaeana*, 89–179. Urbana: University of Illinois Press, 1968.

Kenny, Neil. "'Ce nom de Roman qui estoit particulier aux Livres de Chevalerie, estant demeuré à tous les Livres de fiction': La Naissance antidatée d'un genre." In *Le Roman français au XVIe siècle, ou le renouveau d'un genre dans le contexte européen*, edited by Michèle Clément and Pascale Mounier, 19–32. Strasbourg: Presses Universitaires de Strasbourg, 2005.

Kern, Edith. "The Romance of Novel/Novella." In *The Disciplines of Criticism: Essays in Literary Theory, Interpretation, and History*, edited by Peter Demetz, Thomas Greene, and Lowry Nelson, Jr., 511–30. New Haven: Yale University Press, 1968.

Kibédi-Varga, Aron. "Pour une définition de la nouvelle à l'époque classique." *CAIEF* 18 (1966): 53–65.

Lallemand, Marie-Gabrielle. *Les Longs Romans du XVIIe siècle: Urfé, Desmarets, Gomberville, La Calprenède, Scudéry*. Paris: Classiques Garnier, 2013.

Langer, Ullrich. "Le Roman humaniste: Vers le plaisir du fini." In *Du roman courtois au roman baroque: Actes du colloque des 2–5 juillet 2002*, edited by Emmanuel Bury and Francine Mora, 437–48. Paris: Belles Lettres, 2004.

Latour, Bruno. *Reassembling the Social: An Introduction to Actor-Network-Theory*. Oxford: Oxford University Press, 2005.

— *An Inquiry into Modes of Existence: An Anthropology of the Moderns*. Translated by Catherine Porter. Cambridge: Harvard University Press, 2013.

Lavocat, Françoise. *Fait et fiction: Pour une frontière*. Paris: Seuil, 2016.

Lee, Christine S. "The Meanings of Romance: Rethinking Early Modern Fiction." *Modern Philology* 112.2 (2014): 287–311.

Lever, Maurice. *La Fiction narrative en prose au dix-septième siècle*. Paris: CNRS, 1976.

Liebowitz, Stan J., and Stephen E. Margolis. *The Economics of Qwerty: Papers by Stan Liebowitz and Stephen Margolis*. Edited by Peter Lewin. New York: MacMillan/NYU Press, 2002.

Liu, Alan. "The Power of Formalism: The New Historicism." *ELH* 56.4 (1989): 721–71.

Lubbock, Percy. *The Craft of Fiction*. New York: Scribner's, 1921.

Lukács, György. *The Historical Novel*. Translated by Hannah Mitchell and Stanley Mitchell. Lincoln: University of Nebraska Press, 1983.

Lynch, Deidre Shauna. *The Economy of Character: Novels, Market Culture, and the Business of Inner Meaning*. Chicago: University of Chicago Press, 1998.

Mander, Jenny. *Circles of Learning: Narratology and the Eighteenth-Century French Novel*. Oxford: Voltaire Foundation, 1999.

Marchant, François. *Roman sans titre, histoire véritable ou peu s'en faut*. Paris: Maradan, 1788.

Martin, Angus, Vivienne Mylne, and Richard Frautschi. *Bibliographie du genre romanesque français, 1751–1800*. London: Mansell, 1977.

Martindale, Colin. *The Clockwork Muse: The Predictability of Artistic Change*. New York: Basic Books, 1990.

May, Georges. *Le Dilemme du roman au XVIIIe siècle*. Paris: PUF, 1963.

Mazzoni, Guido. *Theory of the Novel*. Translated by Zakiya Hanafi. Cambridge: Harvard University Press, 2017.

McBurney, William H. *A Check List of English Prose Fiction, 1700–1739*. Cambridge: Harvard University Press, 1960.

McKeon, Michael. *The Origins of the English Novel, 1600–1740*. Baltimore: Johns Hopkins University Press, 1987.

McKeon, Michael, ed. *The Theory of the Novel: A Historical Approach*. Baltimore: Johns Hopkins University Press, 2000.

Mongland, André. *La France révolutionnaire et impériale: Annales de bibliographie méthodique et description des livres imprimés*. 10 vols. Paris: Imprimerie nationale, 1931.

Montesquieu, Charles de Secondat, baron de. "Quelques réflexions sur les *Lettres persanes*." In *Oeuvres*, Vol. 3. London: Nourse, 1757.

Moore, Steven. *The Novel: An Alternative History*. 2 vols. New York: Bloomsbury Continuum, 2010.

Moretti, Franco. *Graphs, Maps, Trees: Abstract Models for a Literary History*. London: Verso, 2005.

Distant Reading. London: Verso, 2013.

Morgan, J. R. "Make-Believe and Make Believe: The Fictionality of Greek Novels." In *Lies and Fiction in the Ancient World*, edited by Christopher Gill and T. P. Wiseman, 175–229. Exeter: Exeter University Press, 1993.

Mylne, Vivienne. "Chapters as a Structural Device in the *Conte* and the Novel." *Studies on Voltaire and the Eighteenth Century* 192 (1980): 1332–33.

The Eighteenth-Century French Novel: Techniques of Illusion. 2nd ed. Cambridge: Cambridge University Press, 1981.

Orlemanski, Julie. "Who Has Fiction? Modernity, Fictionality, and the Middle Ages." *New Literary History* 50.2 (2019): 145–70.

Orr, Leah. *Novel Ventures: Fiction and Print Culture in England, 1690–1730*. Charlottesville: University of Virginia Press, 2017.

Page, Scott E. "Path Dependence." *Quarterly Journal of Political Science* 1.1 (2006): 87–115.

Paige, Nicholas. "The Storyteller and the Book: Scenes of Narrative Production in the Early French Novel." *MLQ* 67.2 (2006): 141–70.

Before Fiction: The Ancien Régime of the Novel. Philadelphia: University of Pennsylvania Press, 2011.

"Examples, Samples, Signs: An Artifactual View of Fictionality in the French Novel, 1681–1830." *New Literary History* 48.3 (2017): 503–30.

Pascal, Blaise. *Les Pensées*. Edited by Michel Le Guern. Paris: Gallimard, 1977.

Pavel, Thomas. *La Pensée du roman*. Paris: Gallimard, 2003.

Picard, Raymond, and Jean Lafond, eds. *Nouvelles du XVIIe siècle*. Paris: Gallimard, 1997.

Pinch, Trevor J., and Wiebe E. Bijker. "The Social Construction of Facts and Artifacts: Or How the Sociology of Science and the Sociology of Technology Might Benefit Each Other." In *The Social Construction of Technological Systems: New Directions in the Sociology and History of Technology*, edited by Wiebe E. Bijker, Thomas P. Hughes, and Trevor J. Pinch, 11–44. Cambridge: MIT Press, 1987.

Piper, Andrew. *Enumerations: Data and Literary Study*. Chicago: University of Chicago Press, 2018.

Pizzorusso, Arnaldo. *La Poetica del romanzo in Francia (1660–1685)*. Rome: Sciascia, 1962.

Plazenet, Laurence. *L'Ébahissement et la délectation: Réception comparée et poétiques du roman grec en France et en Angleterre aux XVIe et XVIIe siècles*. Paris: Champion, 1997.

Poovey, Mary. *Genres of the Credit Economy: Mediating Value in Eighteenth- and Nineteenth-Century Britain*. Chicago: University of Chicago Press, 2008.

Prévost, Antoine. *Oeuvres choisies*. Vol. 34. Paris: Hôtel Serpente, 1784.

Raven, James. *British Fiction, 1750–1770: A Chronological Check-List of Prose Fiction Printed in Britain and Ireland*. Newark: University of Delaware Press, 1987.

— "Britain, 1750–1830." In *The Novel*, edited by Franco Moretti, 1:429–54. Princeton: Princeton University Press, 2006.

Reeve, Clara. *The Progress of Romance through Times, Countries and Manners*. Colchester: W. Keymer, 1785.

Reynolds, William H. "Cars and Clothing: Understanding Fashion Trends." *Journal of Marketing* 32.3 (1968): 44–9.

Richardson, Brian. *Unnatural Voices: Extreme Narration in Modern and Contemporary Fiction*. Columbus: Ohio State University Press, 2006.

Richardson, Jane, and A. L. Kroeber. "Three Centuries of Women's Dress Fashions: A Quantitative Analysis." *Anthropological Records* 5.2 (1940): 111–53.

Richardson, Samuel. *Selected Letters*. Edited by John Carroll. Oxford: Clarendon, 1964.

— *The History of Sir Charles Grandison in a Series of Letters*. 4th ed. 7 vols. London: Rivington, 1762.

Riou, Daniel. "Naissance du roman moderne au XVIIe siècle – idéologie, institution, réception." In *Histoire de la France littéraire*, edited by Jean-Charles Darmon and Michel Delon, 2:663–82. Paris: Quadrige/PUF, 2006.

Rivara, Anne, ed. *Le Roman des années trente: La Génération de Prévost et de Marivaux*. Saint-Étienne: Publications de l'Université de Saint-Étienne, 1998.

Robinson, Dwight E. "Style Changes: Cyclical, Inexorable, and Foreseeable." *Harvard Business Review* 53.6 (1975): 121–31.

Rogers, Everett M. *The Diffusion of Innovations*. 4th ed. New York: The Free Press, 1995.

Rousset, Jean. *Narcisse romancier: Essai sur la première personne dans le roman*. Paris: Corti, 1973.

Rustin, Jacques. "Mensonge et vérité dans le roman français du XVIIIe siècle." *RHLF* 69 (1969): 13–38.

Sandy, Gerald N. "Classical Forerunners of the Theory and Practice of Prose Romance in France: Studies in the Narrative Form of Minor French Romances of the Sixteenth and Seventeenth Centuries." *Antike und Abendland* 28.2 (1982): 169–91.

Schneider, Gary. *The Culture of Epistolarity: Vernacular Letters and Letter Writing in Early Modern England, 1500–1700*. Newark: University of Delaware Press, 2005.

Scholes, Robert, Robert Kellogg, and James Phelan. *The Nature of Narrative: Fortieth Anniversary Edition. 1966.* Reprint, Oxford: Oxford University Press, 2006.

Sgard, Jean. "Le Mot 'roman.'" *Eighteenth-Century Fiction* 13.2–3 (2001): 183–95.

Shapin, Steven, and Simon Schaffer. *Leviathan and the Air-Pump: Hobbes, Boyle, and the Experimental Life*. Princeton: Princeton University Press, 1985.

Showalter, English. *The Evolution of the French Novel, 1641–1782*. Princeton: Princeton University Press, 1972.

Skretkowicz, Victor. *European Erotic Romance: Philhellene Protestantism, Renaissance Translation, and English Literary Politics*. Manchester: Manchester University Press, 2010.

Sorel, Charles. *La Bibliothèque française*. 2nd ed. Paris: Compagnie des libraires, 1667.

Sproles, George B. "Analyzing Fashion Life Cycles: Principles and Perspectives." *Journal of Marketing* 45.4 (1981): 116–24.

Stephens, Walter. "Tasso's Heliodorus and the World of Romance." In *Search for the Ancient Novel*, edited by James Tatum, 67–87. Baltimore: Johns Hopkins University Press, 1994.

Stewart, Philip. *Imitation and Illusion in the French Memoir Novel, 1700–1750*. New Haven: Yale University Press, 1969.

"The Rise of I." *Eighteenth-Century Fiction* 13.2 (2001): 163–81.

Suarez, Michael F. "Towards a Bibliometric Analysis of the Surviving Record, 1701–1800." In *The Cambridge History of the Book in Britain*, edited by Michael F. Suarez and Michael L. Turner, 5:39–65. Cambridge: Cambridge University Press, 2009.

Tieje, Arthur Jerrold. "A Peculiar Phase of the Theory of Realism in Pre-Richardsonian Fiction." *PMLA* 28.2 (1913): 213–52.

Turner, James Grantham. "'Romance' and the Novel in Restoration England." *The Review of English Studies* 63.258 (2011): 58–85.

Underwood, Ted. *Why Literary Periods Mattered: Historical Contrast and the Prestige of English Studies*. Stanford: Stanford University Press, 2013.

Distant Horizons: Digital Evidence and Literary Change. University of Chicago Press, 2019

"A Genealogy of Distant Reading." *Digital Humanities Quarterly* 11.2 (2017). www.digitalhumanities.org/dhq/vol/11/2/000317/000317.html.

Vaillant, Alain. *La Crise de la littérature: Romantisme et modernité*. Grenoble: ELLUG, 2005.

Versini, Laurent. *Laclos et la tradition: Essai sur les sources et la technique des Liaisons dangereuses*. Paris: Klincksieck, 1968.

Le Roman épistolaire. Paris: PUF, 1979.

Viala, Alain. "De Scudéry à Courtilz de Sandras: Les Nouvelles historiques et galantes." *Dix-septième siècle* 215 (2002): 287–95.

Walton, Kendall L. *Mimesis as Make-Believe: On the Foundations of the Representational Arts*. Cambridge: Harvard University Press, 1990.

Watt, Ian P. *The Rise of the Novel: Studies in Defoe, Richardson, and Fielding*. Berkeley: University of California Press, 1957.

Williams, Ioan, ed. *Novel and Romance, 1700–1800: A Documentary Record*. London: Routledge and Kegan Paul, 1970.

Winner, Langdon. "Upon Opening the Black Box and Finding It Empty: Social Constructivism and the Philosophy of Technology." *Science, Technology, and Human Values* 18.3 (1993): 362–78.

Wittgenstein, Ludwig. *Philosophical Investigations*. Translated by G.E.M. Anscombe. Oxford: Basil Blackwell, 1953.

Zonza, Christian. *La Nouvelle historique en France à l'âge classique (1657–1703)*. Paris: Champion, 2007.

Index

Abrahamson, Eric, 251n49
Achilles Tatius, 72, 110
Amadis of Gaul, 65, 106
Amyot, Jacques, 65, 67, 75, 190
Anderson, Perry, 132
Aneau, Barthélémy, 68
Aravamudan, Srinivas, 220n24
Argens, Jean-Baptiste de Boyer, marquis d', 39
Aristotle, 9, 58, 195, 206
Armstrong, Nancy, 215n1
Arthur, W. Brian, 12, 183, 186, 197, 198, 248n25, 252n52, 253n54
Arzoumanov, Anna, 222n11

Banfield, Ann, 248n30
Barthes, Roland, 251n46
Basalla, George, 5, 6, 185, 216n10, 248n12, 250n42, 251n47, 253n54, 253n59
Baumgartner, Emmanuèle, 233n2
Beasley, Jerry C., 254n2
Bédacier, Catherine, 74
Beebee, Thomas O., 236n2, 237n4, 238n18
Bender, John, 215n1
Berlyne, D. E., 251n47
Best, Stephen, 245n5, 252n53
Bijker, Wiebe E., 5, 182, 252n50
Bikhchandani, Sushil, 251n45
Binhammer, Katherine, 245n3
Black, Scott, 233n14
Blackbourn, David, 246n6
Blanchot, Maurice, 249n33
Blocker, Déborah, 250n38
Blythe, R. A., 246n13
Boileau, Nicolas, 67
Boulle, Pierre, 182
Boyd, Brian, 248n30
Bray, Bernard, 125, 236n4, 247n24
Brewer, David A., 216n13
Broadwell, Peter M., 219n20
Brown, Homer Obed, 244n16
Bulwer-Lytton, Edward, 145, 149
Burney, Fanny, 250n43
Buurma, Rachel Sagner, 249n53

Campanini, Magda, 237n4
Campbell, John, 229n5
Carlson, Bernard, 199
Carnell, Rachel, 242n2
Cave, Terence, 225n7
Cervantes, Miguel de, 65, 69, 70, 81, 107, 141
Charrière, Isabelle de, 128
Chartier, Roger, 253n57
Chrétien de Troyes, 109
Cicero, 18
Clin-Lalande, Anne-Marie, 209, 237n6
Cohen, Margaret, 130
Cohn, Dorrit, 38, 246n8
Coleridge, Samuel Taylor, 22
Colonna, Francesco, 110
Congreve, William, 79, 106
Corneille, Pierre, 222n5
Cottin, Sophie, 128
Coulet, Henri, 80, 232n9, 235n15
Croft, William, 246n13
Cyrano de Bergerac, Savinien de, 120

D'Angelo, Filippo, 235n17
Dames, Nicholas, 141
Davis, Lennard J., 217n2
Davis, Lydia, 182
Dawkins, Richard, 183
Day, Geoffrey, 217n1
Day, Robert Adams, 237n7, 239n20
De Gusta, Michael, 232n8
Defoe, Daniel, 242n4, 243n9
DeJean, Joan, 222n7
Démoris, René, 232n10, 235n16, 245n4
Denby, David J., 130
Diderot, Denis, 238n19, 243n9
Dionne, Ugo, 63, 145, 239n6, 240n9, 240n10
DiPiero, Thomas, 245n3, 253n56
Doody, Margaret Anne, 215n3
Downie, J. A., 244n17, 253n56
Du Plaisir, 64–67, 74–76, 79–80, 87, 93, 95, 98, 100, 160, 188
Dubuis, Roger, 230n9

Edgerton, David, 246n12, 247n23
Elias, Norbert, 180
Eliot, Simon, 244n2
English, James F., 216n12
Esmein(-Sarrazin), Camille, 223n16, 225n3, 229n2, 243n12, 250n38

Felski, Rita, 245n5
Festa, Lynn, 250n40
Fielding, Henry, 243n9
Flaubert, Gustave, 182
Fludernik, Monika, 218n7, 248n26, 248n31, 249n33, 254n59, 255n7
Foley, Barbara, 217n2, 218n14
Forcione, Alban K., 227n20
Foucault, Michel, 2, 4, 6, 201, 224n18
Frautschi, Richard, 254n1
Freedgood, Elaine, 249n33
Freud, Sigmund, 219n19
Frye, Northrop, 5
Fumaroli, Marc, 225n6, 247n20
Fumée, Martin, 68

Gallagher, Catherine, 10, 170, 217n2, 218n11, 219n16, 242n7
Garside, Peter, 254n1
Genette, Gérard, 194, 218n15, 234n6, 246n8
Gevrey, Françoise, 229n5
Giraud, Yves, 209, 236n4, 237n6
Gittes, Katharine S., 228n25
Głowiński, Michał, 235n13
Godenne, René, 229n5, 231n6
Goldstein, Claire, 244n3
Graffigny, Françoise de, 125–26, 130, 238n9
Grafton, Anthony, 233n3
Grande, Nathalie, 226n12, 231n6
Greenblatt, Stephen, 2
Greiner, Frank, 73, 254n1, 255n4
Guilleragues, Gabriel-Joseph de Lavergne, comte de, 125, 130, 132, 134, 186, 197

Hamburger, Käte, 248n30
Hamilton, A. C., 227n18
Haywood, Elizabeth Fowler, 242n2
Heliodorus, 65, 68, 75, 190, 200
Herman, Jan, 217n2, 221n33
Hexter, J. H., 234n11
Hipp, Marie-Thérèse, 247n20
Hirshleifer, David, 251n45
Homer, 65, 227n17
Horace, 195
Hudson, Nicholas, 234n11

Huet, Pierre-Daniel, 226n14, 244n17
Hume, Robert D., 171, 255n3
Hunter, J. Paul, 243n16, 253n56

Jackson, Tony E., 247n17
Jameson, Fredric, 4, 199
Jockers, Matthew L., 7, 216
Johnson, Samuel, 244n17
Jones, Silas Paul, 254n1
Jost, François, 236n2, 239n20

Kellogg, Robert, 248n32
Kenny, Neil, 232n11
Kern, Edith, 229n3
Kibédi-Varga, Aron, 230n7
Kozul, Mladen, 217n2, 221n33
Kremer, Nathalie, 217n2, 221n33
Kroeber, A. L., 251n46

La Calprenède, Gautier de Coste, sieur de, 75, 80
Laclos, Pierre-Ambroise-François Choderlos de, 125, 128, 134
Lafayette, Marie-Madeleine Pioche de La Vergne, comtesse de, 46, 54, 66, 76, 79, 90, 92, 97, 99, 229n5, 243n9
Lafond, Jean, 230n7, 230n8
Lallemand, Marie-Gabrielle, 225n8
Landy-Houillon, Isabelle, 125
Langer, Ullrich, 225n7
Latour, Bruno, 252n52, 252–53n53
Lavocat, Françoise, 217–18n7, 218n10, 249n37
Lee, Christina S., 232–33n11
Lever, Maurice, 254n1, 256n9
Liebowitz, Stan J., 251n48
Liu, Alan, 215n2
Lubbock, Percy, 248n30
Lukacs, György, 222n8
Lynch, Deidre Shauna, 215n1

Mander, Jenny, 218n15
Manley, Mary de la Riviere, 242n7
Marcus, Sharon, 245n5, 252n53
Margolis, Stephen E., 251n48
Martin, Angus, 254n1
Martindale, Colin, 251n47
May, Georges, 219n16, 235n12, 244n1
Mazzoni, Guido, 218n12, 225n1, 250n40
McBurney, William H., 256
McKeon, Michael, 215n1, 217n2, 219n16, 229n2
Mimno, David, 219n20

Montaigne, Michel de, 119
Montemayor, Jorge de, 69
Montesquieu, Charles de Secondat, baron de, 125, 126, 130, 132–34, 186, 197, 251n44
Moore, Steven, 215n3
Moretti, Franco, 5, 7
Morgan, J. R., 217n6
Mylne, Vivienne, 217n1, 240n9, 254n1

Ong, Walter, 247n17
Orlemanski, Julie, 218n7, 249n35
Orr, Leah, 243n14

Page, Scott E., 251n48
Paige, Nicholas, 10, 218n13, 219n17, 219n19, 221n34, 222n6, 225n7, 233n14, 241n25, 249n36, 253n58, 255n6
Pascal, Blaise, 119
Pavel, Thomas, 119, 229n5, 233n14, 245n4
Petronius, 110
Phelan, James, 248n32
Picard, Raymond, 230n7, 230n8
Pinch, Trevor J., 252n50
Piper, Andrew, 218n8, 241n26
Pizzorusso, Arnaldo, 236n2
Plazenet, Laurence, 225n8, 226n14, 228n27, 235n18
Poovey, Mary, 243n11
Prévost, Antoine-François, 123

Quintilian, 217n5

Raven, James, 246n11, 254n1
Reeve, Clara, 107
Reynolds, William H., 251n46
Riccoboni, Marie-Jeanne, 128
Richardson, Brian, 248n28
Richardson, Jane, 251n46
Richardson, Samuel, 17–20, 22, 39, 125, 135, 162, 187, 197, 200–1, 237n7, 242n5, 245n4
Riou, Daniel, 226n12
Rivara, Anne, 244n1
Robinson, Dwight E., 251n46
Rogers, Everett M., 247n13, 247n16, 252n51
Rosenkopf, Lori, 252n49
Rousseau, Jean-Jacques, 17–20, 22, 125, 128, 134
Rousset, Jean, 120, 121, 123, 236n2
Rustin, Jacques, 217n1

Saint-Réal, César de, 80
Sandy, Gerald N., 225n7, 226n14–15, 227n17
Sannazaro, Jacopo, 69
Schaffer, Simon, 199
Schneider, Gary, 237n4
Scholes, Robert, 248n32
Schöwerling, Rainer, 254n1
Scott, Walter, 30, 47
Scudéry, Georges de, 58–59, 197
Scudéry, Madeleine de, 66, 86, 91, 106, 224n21, 240n14
Segrais, Jean Regnault de, 231n3
Sgard, Jean, 229n4
Shapin, Steven, 199
Showalter, English, 229n2, 230n14
Sidney, Philip, 69, 107
Skretkowicz, Victor, 227n18
Sorel, Charles, 81, 120
Sproles, George B., 251n46
Stephens, Walter, 227n17
Stewart, Philip, 217n1, 245n4
Suarez, Michael L., 244n2

Tangherlini, Timothy R., 219n20
Tasso, Torquato, 227n17
Tieje, Arthur Jerrold, 217n1
Turner, James Grantham, 232n11

Underwood, Ted, 215n6, 216n12, 223n18, 245n6
Urfé, Honoré d', 49, 69, 107, 240n14

Vaillant, Alain, 244n2, 249n34
Versini, Laurent, 236n2, 248n26
Viala, Alain, 229n5
Viau, Théophile de, 120
Virgil, 65, 227

Walpole, Horace, 233n4
Walton, Kendall L., 217n3
Watt, Ian P., 170, 200, 201, 217n1, 245n4
Welch, Ivo, 251n45
Williams, Ioan, 229n3
Winner, Langdon, 252n52
Wittgenstein, Ludwig, 91, 151

Zayas, María de, 81
Zonza, Christian, 229n5, 230n12, 232n10

For EU product safety concerns, contact us at Calle de José Abascal, 56–1°, 28003 Madrid, Spain or eugpsr@cambridge.org.